THE SCARECROW AUTHOR BIBLIOGRAPHIES

SEAN O'CASEY AND HIS CRITICS: an annotated bibliography, 1916-1982

by
E. H. MIKHAIL

Scarecrow Author Bibliographies, No. 67

The Scarecrow Press, Inc.
Metuchen, N.J., & London
1985

337673

cc

Library of Congress Cataloging in Publication Data

Mikhail, E. H.
    Sean O'Casey and his critics.

    (Scarecrow author bibliographies ; no. 67)
    Includes index.
    1. O'Casey, Sean, 1880-1964--Bibliography.
I. Title. II. Series.
Z8640.M55 1985 [PR6029.C33] 016.822'912   84-14166
ISBN 0-8108-1747-0

CONTENTS

(

ACKNOWLEDGMENTS

At various stages in the preparation of this work I received useful information, comments, support, or assistance from Ronald Ayling, Bernard Benstock, Patricia Cox, Emile J. Dumay, David Krause, Marianne Levander, Robert G. Lowery, James McAuley, Patrick O'Connell, S.J., John O'Riordan, Ronald Rollins, and Richard Wall.

Several publications have been of immense help to me, particularly Ronald Ayling and Michael J. Durkan's Sean O'Casey: A Bibliography (London: Macmillan, 1978); and David Krause's "Sean O'Casey" in Anglo-Irish Literature: A Review of Research, edited by Richard J. Finneran (New York: Modern Language Association, 1976).

I am grateful to Charlene Sawatsky and Bea Ramtej for their skillful preparation of the final typescript.

It is also a pleasant duty to record my appreciation to the staffs of the following libraries: the University of Lethbridge Library; the National Library of Ireland, Dublin; Trinity College Library, Dublin; the British Library, London; the Newspaper Library, Colindale; the National Library, Ottawa; and the New York Public Library.

E.H.M.

PREFACE

The importance of Sean O'Casey as a major playwright does not need
to be stressed. His works have been translated into 26 known languages. At least 135 dissertations, wholly or partially devoted to
him, have been submitted to universities around the world. His
plays appear in more than 50 anthologies. There have been some
2,000 performances of his plays, from The Shadow of a Gunman in
1923 to Red Roses for Me in 1980, at the Abbey Theatre alone. That
his prominence is still on the increase can be affirmed by the vast
volume of material that was published concerning him during 1980,
the 100th anniversary of his birth.

The first bibliography of O'Casey criticism, Otto Brandstädter's
"Eine O'Casey-Bibliographie," appeared in the Berlin periodical Zeitschrift für Anglistik und Amerikanistik in 1954. This was followed
ten years later by I. M. Levidova and B. M. Parchevskaya's full-
length Shon O'Keisi Biobibliograficheskii Ukazatel, published in Moscow. The first English-language bibliography, Charles A. Carpenter's "Sean O'Casey Studies Through 1964," appeared in the May
1967 issue of Modern Drama. In 1972, E. H. Mikhail's comprehensive
Sean O'Casey: A Bibliography of Criticism was published. However,
since this bibliography is now more than ten years old, there has
been need for a new work.

The present annotated bibliography, although based on the
author's earlier work, is not merely a second, updated edition; it
is in most respects an entirely new book. Some 4,500 entries have
now been included; new sections have been added; and a compreher.-
sive index has been appended. Furthermore, all entries have been
annotated unless the title is sufficiently self-explanatory. The

annotations, however, are not evaluative, but descriptive and indicative of the content of the material they describe. The general cut-off date is 1982, although several later studies have been included. This work will be updated by the running checklist "Sean O'Casey: An Annual Bibliography" in the O'Casey Annual (London: Macmillan).

In the BIBLIOGRAPHIES AND INDEXES section, I have excluded bibliographies and checklists appended to books wholly devoted to O'Casey for three reasons. First, these have been combed and entries incorporated into this book. Second, to include them would have unnecessarily contributed to the bulkiness of this book. Third, I assume that all users of this book know about these checklists.

Throughout the book, all entries have been arranged alphabetically, with the exception of those sections dealing with the productions of O'Casey's plays, which have been listed chronologically. Names beginning with the prefix Mc are arranged as if written Mac. Contributions to books wholly devoted to O'Casey are listed under the editor, not the author. In Part II: WORKS BY O'CASEY AND THEIR REVIEWS, the reader will notice some gaps in the citations' numbering system; these indicate the number of reviews listed with each book.

PART I:

BIBLIOGRAPHIES AND INDEXES

1 Adelman, Irving, and Rita Dworkin, "Sean O'Casey," in Modern
   Drama: A Checklist of Critical Literature on 20th Century
   Plays (Metuchen, N.J.: Scarecrow Press, 1967), pp. 206-10
   [Selected general criticism, and criticism on individual plays,
   in books and periodicals].

2 The American Humanities Index (Troy, N.Y.: The Whitston Publishing Company, 1975- [Material in periodicals not indexed
   elsewhere].

3 Ayling, Ronald, "Detailed Catalogue of Sean O'Casey's Papers at
   the Time of His Death," Sean O'Casey Review, 1 (Spring 1975),
   48-65; 2 (Fall 1975), 64-77; 3 (Fall 1976), 58-70 [The papers
   which are presently housed in the Berg Collection, New York
   Public Library].

4 _____, "Sean O'Casey," in The New Cambridge Bibliography of
   English Literature, Volume 4: 1900-1950, ed. I.R. Willison
   (Cambridge: Cambridge University Press, 1972), columns 879-
   85 [Primary books; selected material in books and periodicals].

5 _____ and Michael J. Durkan, "The Genesis of The Plough and
   the Stars: A Bibliographical Note," Sean O'Casey Review, 2
   (Spring 1976), 87-91 [Gives all information on the play, such
   as original title, first production, and reviews].

6 _____ and _____, "Sean O'Casey: A Bibliography," Sean
   O'Casey Review, 4 (Fall 1977), 49-50 [Describes the authors'
   Sean O'Casey: A Bibliography].

7 _____ and _____, Sean O'Casey: A Bibliography (London:
   Macmillan; Seattle: University of Washington Press, 1978).
   Reviewed by John O'Riordan in Library Association Record
   (London), 82 (Apr 1980), 185; by Fionn MacCool in Irish Post
   (London), (14 Oct 1978), p. 8; by Maurice Harmon in Irish
   University Review (Dublin), 8 (Autumn 1978), 271; by Kane
   Archer in Books Ireland (Dublin), no. 38 (Nov 1979), 194; by
   Robert G. Lowery in Daily World (N.Y.), (15 Nov 1978), p. 8;
   by Charles A. Carpenter in Modern Drama, 24 (Mar 1981), 119-
   20; by St. John Sweeney in Journal of Irish Literature, 7 (Sep
   1978), 172-3; by Robert G. Lowery in Sean O'Casey Review, 5
   (Fall 1978), 97-9; by E.H. Mikhail in Papers of the Bibliographical Society of America, 74, First Quarter (1980), 92-3; and by

Patrick Rafroidi in Etudes irlandaises (Lille), no. 3 (Dec 1978). 119-20 [Annotated primary bibliography].

8 _____ and _____, "Works by Sean O'Casey in Translation," Sean O'Casey Review, 1 (Spring 1975), 4-18; 2 (Fall 1975), 5-11 [Traces translations of O'Casey's works in twenty-five languages].

9 Bateson, F.W., and Harrison T. Meserole, "Sean O'Casey," in A Guide to English and American Literature, 3rd ed. (London and New York: Longman, 1976), pp. 203-4 [Selected criticism in books. For the beginning student].

10 Bell, Sam Hanna, "Lyric Players Theatre Productions (1951-71)," in The Theatre in Ulster: A Survey of the Dramatic Movement in Ulster from 1902 Until the Present Day (Dublin: Gill and Macmillan; Totowa, N.J.: Rowman and Littlefield, 1972), pp. 140-7 [Includes the productions of O'Casey's plays at the Lyric Players Theatre, Belfast].

11 Black, H[ester] M., "A Check-List of First Editions of Works by Lord Dunsany and Sean O'Casey," T.C.D. Annual Bulletin (Dublin), (1957), 4-9.

12 Bloomfield, B.C., "Sean O'Casey," in An Author Index to Selected British "Little Magazines" 1930-1939 (London: Mansell, 1976), p. 100 ["Greetings on May Day"].

13 Brandstädter, Otto, "Eine O'Casey-Bibliographie," Zeitschrift für Anglistik und Amerikanistik (Berlin), 2 (1954), 240-54 [Secondary material in books and periodicals].

14 Breed, Paul F., and Florence M. Sniderman, "Sean O'Casey," in Dramatic Criticism Index: A Bibliography of Commentaries on Playwrights from Ibsen to the Avant-Garde (Detroit: Gale Research Company, 1972), pp. 459-70 [Selected general criticism, and criticism on individual plays, in books and periodicals].

15 C., R.C.-, and W. P[artington], "Hints for Collectors and Marginalia: A Sean O'Casey First Edition Unveiled," Bookman's Journal (London), 15 (1927), 25-6 [Gives bibliographical information on The Irish Citizen Army].

16 Carpenter, Charles A., "Sean O'Casey Studies Through 1964," Modern Drama, 10 (May 1967), 17-23 [A selective list of biographical, critical, and other scholarly studies of O'Casey, including essays and letters by O'Casey about himself].

17 _____, "Sean O'Casey," in Modern British Drama. Goldentree Bibliographies in Language & Literature (Arlington Heights, Ill.: AHM Publishing Corporation, 1979), pp. 61-5 [Selected criticism in books and periodicals].

18 "Cast Lists from Some World Premiers of The Silver Tassie,"
    Sean O'Casey Review, 5 (Fall 1978), 12-13 [At the Abbey The-
    atre, Dublin; Apollo Theatre, London; Irish Theatre, New York;
    Theatre de l'Est Parisien, Paris; and Schauspielhaus, Switzer-
    land].

19 Chicorel, Marietta, ed., Chicorel Theater Index to Plays in An-
    thologies and Collections, 1970-1976 (New York: Chicorel Li-
    brary Publishing Corporation, 1977), pp. 251-2 [Bedtime Story,
    The End of the Beginning, Juno and the Paycock, The Plough
    and the Stars, Purple Dust, and The Shadow of a Gunman].

20 Coleman, Arthur, and Gary R. Tyler, "Sean O'Casey," in Drama
    Criticism, vol. I: A Checklist of Interpretation Since 1940 of
    English and American Plays (Denver: Alan Swallow, 1966), pp.
    154-6 [Selected criticism on individual plays in periodicals].

21 Connor, John M., and Billie M. Connor, "Sean O'Casey," in Ot-
    temiller's Index to Plays in Collections: An Author and Title
    Index to Plays Appearing in Collections Published Between 1900
    and Early 1975, 6th ed., rev. and enl. (Metuchen, N.J.: Scare-
    crow Press, 1976), pp. 140-1 [Bedtime Story, Cock-a-Doodle
    Dandy, The End of the Beginning, Hall of Healing, Juno and
    the Paycock, Nannie's Night Out, The Plough and the Stars,
    Purple Dust, Red Roses for Me, The Shadow of a Gunman, and
    The Silver Tassie].

22 Conolly, L.W., A Directory of British Theatre Research Resources
    in North America (London: British Theatre Institute, 1978),
    pp. 10, 11, 16, 19, 20 [O'Casey collections in libraries].

23 Cornyn, Stan, A Selective Index to "Theatre Magazine" (New
    York and London: Scarecrow Press, 1964) [Articles and re-
    views in Theatre Magazine from 1901-1931].

24 Daiches, David, "Sean O'Casey," in The Present Age After 1920
    (London: Cresset Press; Bloomington: Indiana University
    Press, 1958), pp. 325-6 [Primary bibliography for the begin-
    ning student].

25 Dumay, E.J., "A Comprehensive List of O'Casey Productions in
    France (1947-1975)," Sean O'Casey Review, 3 (Fall 1976), 37-8.

26 Eager, Alan R., "Drama," in A Guide to Irish Bibliographical Ma-
    terial: Being a Bibliography of Irish Bibliographies and Some
    Sources of Information, 2nd ed. (Westport, Conn.: Greenwood
    Press, 1980).

27 Fidell, Estelle A., ed., "Sean O'Casey," in Play Index 1968-1972:
    An Index to 3,848 Plays (New York: H.W. Wilson, 1973), p.
    217 [Individual plays and plays in collections].

28 "The Golden Jubilee of The Plough and the Stars: Performances
    by the Abbey Theatre 1976-1977," Sean O'Casey Review, 3
    (Spring 1977), 163-6 [Gives information on productions in Ire-
    land and the United States].

29 Havlice, Patricia Pate, "Sean O'Casey," in Index to Literary Bi-
    ography, vol. 2 (Metuchen, N.J.: Scarecrow Press, 1975),
    p. 885 [A quick reference tool for locating biographical infor-
    mation].

30 Hayes, Richard J., ed., "Sean O'Casey," in Sources for the His-
    tory of Irish Civilization, vol. 4 (Boston: G.K. Hall, 1970),
    pp. 111-13 [Selected criticism in Irish periodicals].

31 Heidenreich-Krawschak, Regina, "A Comprehensive List of O'Casey
    Productions in Berlin (1953-1977)," Sean O'Casey Review, 5
    (Fall 1978), 62-8 [Gives names of theatres, directors, dates of
    productions, and lists of reviews].

32 Hogan, Robert, "Bibliography: Sean O'Casey," in After the Irish
    Renaissance: A Critical History of the Irish Drama Since 'The
    Plough and the Stars' (Minneapolis: University of Minnesota
    Press, 1967; London: Macmillan, 1968), pp. 268-9 [Selected
    primary and secondary material].

33 Howard, Patsy C., ed., "Sean O'Casey," in Theses in English
    Literature 1894-1970 (Ann Arbor, Michigan: The Pierian Press,
    1973), pp. 204-5 [M.A. theses in American universities].

34 Jochum, K.P.S., "Sean O'Casey," in W.B. Yeats: A Classified
    Bibliography of Criticism (Urbana and London: University of
    Illinois Press, 1978), pp. 652-9 [Selected criticism in books and
    periodicals].

35 Keller, Dean H., "Sean O'Casey," in Index to Plays in Periodicals
    (Metuchen, N.J.: Scarecrow Press, 1971), p. 319; Supplement
    (Metuchen, N.J.: Scarecrow Press, 1973), p. 150.

36 Kersnowski, Frank L.; C.W. Spinks; and Laird Loomis, "Sean
    O'Casey," in A Bibliography of Modern Irish and Anglo-Irish
    Literature (San Antonio, Texas: Trinity University Press, 1976),
    pp. 87-91 [Works by O'Casey, and selected criticism in books].

37 Krause, David, "Sean O'Casey," in Anglo-Irish Literature: A
    Review of Research, ed. Richard J. Finneran (New York:
    Modern Language Association, 1976), pp. 470-517. Reviewed
    by E.H. Mikhail in Sean O'Casey Review, 3 (Spring 1977),
    172-4. [A representative survey and appraisal of the main
    critical literature on O'Casey. An updated edition is forthcoming].

38 Levidova, I.M., and B.M. Parchevskaya, Shon O'Keisi Biobiblio-
    graficheskii Ukazatel (Moscow: Izdatel' stvo 'Kniga,' 1964)

[Bibliographic guide to primary and secondary material. In Russian].

39 Lowery, Robert G., "Major English-Language Revivals [of The Silver Tassie]," Sean O'Casey Review, 5 (Fall 1978), 14 [Gives names of theatres, directors, and dates of productions in the United States, Ireland, and England].

40 _____, "Premieres and Casts of Sean O'Casey's Plays, " Sean O'Casey Review, 2 (Fall 1975), 22-37 [A checklist of the casts and dates of the premieres of O'Casey's plays].

41 _____, "Sean O'Casey Review: Five Year Index," Sean O'Casey Review, 6 (1980), 22-32 [Includes articles, book reviews, theatre reviews, playbills, recent productions, national premieres, photos, drawings, and miscellaneous].

42 _____, "Sean O'Casey at the Abbey Theatre," in Sean O'Casey Centenary Essays, ed. David Krause and Robert G. Lowery (Gerrards Cross, Buckinghamshire: Colin Smythe; Totowa, N.J.: Barnes and Noble, 1981), pp. 228-49 [A chronological record of the productions of O'Casey's plays at the Abbey Theatre, giving date, number of performances, and name of director].

43 MacNamara, Brinsley, ed., Abbey Plays 1899-1948, Including the Productions of The Irish Literary Theatre (Dublin: At the Sign of the Three Candles, [1949]) [Gives dates of productions of O'Casey's plays at the Abbey Theatre].

44 McNamee, Lawrence F., "Sean O'Casey," in Dissertations in English and American Literature: Theses Accepted by American, British and German Universities, 1865-1964. Supplement One, 1965-1968 (New York and London: R.R. Bowker, 1969), pp. 213-214; Supplement Two, 1969-1973 (New York and London: R.R. Bowker, 1974), p. 303.

45 McQuillan, Deirdre, comp., The Abbey Theatre Dublin 1966-1976: A Commemorative Record (Dublin: The Abbey Theatre, 1976) [Includes details of revivals of The Plough and the Stars, Red Roses for Me, The Shadow of a Gunman, Juno and the Paycock, The Silver Tassie, Purple Dust, The Hall of Healing, Bedtime Story, and The End of the Beginning].

46 Mellown, Elgin W., "Sean O'Casey," in A Descriptive Catalogue of the Bibliographies of Twentieth Century British Poets, Novelists, and Dramatists, 2nd rev. and enl. ed. (Troy, N.Y.: Whitston Publishing Company, 1978), pp. 266-8 [Annotated primary and secondary bibliographies].

47 Mersand, Joseph, "Sean O'Casey," in Guide to Play Selection: A Selective Bibliography for Production and Study of Modern Plays (Urbana, Ill.: National Council of Teachers of English; New

York: R.R. Bowker, 1975), p. 126 [Juno and the Paycock, The Plough and the Stars, Red Roses for Me, and The Shadow of a Gunman].

48 Mikhail, E.H., An Annotated Bibliography of Modern Anglo-Irish Drama (Troy, N.Y.: Whitston Publishing Company, 1981), passim.

49 _____, "Dissertations on Sean O'Casey," Sean O'Casey Review, 2 (Fall 1975), 47-51 [A checklist of dissertations wholly or partially devoted to O'Casey].

50 _____, Lady Gregory: An Annotated Bibliography of Criticism (Troy, N.Y.: Whitston Publishing Company, 1982), passim.

51 _____, "Sean O'Casey," in Dissertations on Anglo-Irish Drama (London: Macmillan; Totowa, N.J.: Rowman and Littlefield, 1973), pp. 21-5 [A checklist of dissertations wholly or partially devoted to O'Casey].

52 _____, "Sean O'Casey," in English Drama 1900-1950: A Guide to Information Sources (Detroit: Gale Research Company, 1977), pp. 263-5 [Annotated bibliography of bibliographies].

53 _____, "Sean O'Casey," in A Research Guide to Modern Irish Dramatists (Troy, N.Y.: Whitston Publishing Company, 1979), pp. 58-61 [Annotated bibliography of bibliographies].

54 _____, Sean O'Casey: A Bibliography of Criticism (London: Macmillan; Seattle: University of Washington Press, 1972). Reviewed in English (London), 21 (Summer 1972), 79; by John O'Riordan in Library Review (Glasgow), 23 (Summer 1972), 259-60; by Terry Kelleher in Hibernia (Dublin), (17 Mar 1972), p. 24; by Michael J. Sidnell in Modern Drama, 16 (June 1973), 108-9; by Stanley Weintraub in Books Abroad, 47 (1973), 370; by Bernard Benstock in American Committee for Irish Studies Newsletter, 4 (Apr 1974), 2; in Choice, 9 (Nov 1972), 1114-5; by Judith Rosenberg in American Reference Books Annual, 4th ed. (1973), pp. 513-14; by Thomas J. Galvin in Library Journal, 97 (Aug 1972), 2263; and by Heinz Kosok in Die Neueren Sprachen (Frankfurt), 5 (1973), 286-7. [Reviews of works by O'Casey; criticism in books and periodicals; reviews of play productions; and dissertations].

55 _____, "Sean O'Casey Studies: An Annual Bibliography," Sean O'Casey Review, 3 (1976) 6 (1980); continued in O'Casey Annual (London, 1982-) [A running checklist of criticism on O'Casey].

56 Millet, Fred B., "Sean O'Casey," in Contemporary British Literature: A Critical Survey and 232 Author-Bibliographies, 3rd

rev. and enl. edition, eds. John M. Manly and Edith Rickert
(New York: Harcourt, Brace, 1935), p. 399 [Selected criticism
in books and periodicals. For the beginning student].

57 New York Public Library, Dictionary Catalog of the Albert A.
and Henry W. Berg Collection of English and American Literature (Boston: G.K. Hall, 1969), vol. 3, pp. 394-5.

58 The New York Times Directory of the Theater (New York: Arno
Press, 1973), p. 686 [Material on O'Casey drama published in
The New York Times 1920-1970].

59 O hAodha, Micheál, "O'Casey Broadcasts on RTE (Radio and Television)," Irish University Review (Dublin), 10 (Spring 1980),
122-6.

60 O'Malley, Conor, "Sean O'Casey at the Lyric Theatre, Belfast,"
Sean O'Casey Review, 6 (1980), 41 [Checklist of productions,
giving dates].

61 Palmer, Helen H., and Anne Jane Dyson, "Sean O'Casey," in
European Drama Criticism (Hamden, Conn.: The Shoe String
Press, 1968), pp. 300-5; Supplement I (1970), pp. 130-2; Supplement II (1974), pp. 116-17 [Selected criticism on individual
plays in books and periodicals].

62 "Recent Productions of O'Casey's Plays," Sean O'Casey Review,
2 (Spring 1976)--5 (Fall 1978).

63 Roach, Helen, Spoken Records, 2nd ed. (New York and London:
Scarecrow Press, 1966), pp. 52, 98 [Juno and the Paycock];
3rd ed. (Metuchen, N.J.: Scarecrow Press, 1970), p. 66
[Sean O'Casey Reading from His Works].

64 Saddlemyer, Ann, "From William Butler Yeats to Sean O'Casey,"
in English Drama (excluding Shakespeare); Select Bibliographical Guides, ed. Stanley Wells (London: Oxford University
Press, 1975), p. 260 [Selected criticism in books].

65 Sader, Marion, ed., "Sean O'Casey," in Comprehensive Index to
English-Language Little Magazines, 1890-1970, vol. 6 (Millwood,
N.Y.: Kraus-Thomson, 1976), pp. 3369-70.

66 Salem, James M., "Sean O'Casey," in A Guide to Critical Reviews,
Part III: British and Continental Drama from Ibsen to Pinter
(Metuchen, N.J.: Scarecrow Press, 1968), pp. 174-8 [Selected
reviews of American performances].

67 Samples, Gordon, "Sean O'Casey," in The Drama Scholars' Index
to Plays and Filmscripts: A Guide to Plays and Filmscripts in
Selected Anthologies, Series and Periodicals (Metuchen, N.J.:

Scarecrow Press, 1974), p. 282 [Bedtime Story, Cock-a-Doodle Dandy, The Drums of Father Ned, Juno and the Paycock, Kathleen Listens In, Nannie's Night Out, The Plough and the Stars, A Pound on Demand, and Purple Dust].

68 "The Silver Tassie, " Sean O'Casey Review, 5 (Fall 1978), 29-32 [Gives cast lists of the Nottingham Playhouse revival, 1967; of the Interplayers' revival, 1949; and of the German premiere in Berlin, 1953].

69 Szladits, Lola L., "New in the Berg Collection, 1965-1969," Bulletin of the New York Public Library, 75 (Jan 1971), 9-29.

70 Temple, Ruth Z., and Martin Tucker, "Sean O'Casey," in Twentieth Century British Literature: A Reference Guide and Bibliography (New York: Frederick Ungar, 1968), p. 213 [Primary books].

PART II:

WORKS BY O'CASEY AND
THEIR REVIEWS

71 COLLECTED PLAYS, 4 vols. (London and New York: Macmillan, 1949-51):

Vol. 1: Juno and the Paycock. The Shadow of a Gunman. The Plough and the Stars. The End of the Beginning. A Pound on Demand (1949)

Vol. 2: The Silver Tassie. Within the Gates. The Star Turns Red (1949)

Vol. 3: Purple Dust. Red Roses for Me. Hall of Healing (1951)

Vol. 4: Oak Leaves and Lavender. Cock-a-Doodle Dandy. Bedtime Story. Time to Go (1951)

Reviewed in Times Literary Supplement (London), (9 Dec 1949), p. 806 and (21 Sep 1951), p. 596; by G[erard] F[ay] in Manchester Guardian (28 Dec 1949), p. 5 and (14 Aug 1951), p. 4; by John Garrett in Spectator (London), 184 (24 Feb 1950), 248; by Clifford Odets in New York Times Book Review (5 Feb 1950), p. 5; by Brooks Atkinson in New York Times (16 Sep 1951) section 2, p. 1; by Robert Friedman in Daily Worker (N.Y.), (3 Oct 1951), p. 7; by Francis Russell in Christian Science Monitor (Boston), (25 Feb 1950), p. 6; by W. R. W. in San Francisco Chronicle (9 Apr 1950), p. 15; and by Radu Lupan in Gazeta literară (Bucharest), 6-7 (14 Feb 1963), p. 2.

85 MIRROR IN MY HOUSE: THE AUTOBIOGRAPHIES OF SEAN O'CASEY, 2 vols. (New York: Macmillan, 1956). Reprinted as Autobiographies, 2 vols. (London: Macmillan, 1963; rpt. 1981); and as Autobiography, 6 vols. (London: Pan Books, 1971-3). Contains six volumes of autobiography:

Vol. 1: I Knock at the Door
Vol. 2: Pictures in the Hallway
Vol. 3: Drums Under the Windows
Vol. 4: Inishfallen, Fare Thee Well
Vol. 5: Rose and Crown
Vol. 6: Sunset and Evening Star

Reviewed by Granville Hicks in New Republic (N.Y.), 135 (22 Oct 1956), 17-18; in New York Herald Tribune Book Review

(28 Oct 1956), p. 17; by David H. Greene in Commonweal (N.Y.), 65 (25 Jan 1957), 440-3; by John O'Shaughnessy in Nation (N.Y.), 184 (16 Mar 1957), 237-9; by Marvin Magalaner in Sewanee Review, 65 (winter 1957), 170-4; by George Freedley in Library Journal, 81 (1 Dec 1956), 2869; in Theatre Arts (N.Y.), 41 (Apr 1957), 63; in Times (London), (3 Oct 1963), p. 15; in Times Literary Supplement (London), (6 Sep 1963), p. 674; by Robert Nye in Scotsman (Edinburgh), (7 Sep 1963), p. 2; by Valentin Iremonger in Spectator (London), 211 (27 Sep 1963), 391; by Florence O'Donoghue in Tablet (London), 217 (7 Sep 1963), 963; by John Wain in Observer (London), (11 Aug 1963), p. 16; by Philip Hengist in Punch (London), 245 (30 Oct 1963), 648; by Padraic Fallon in Irish Times (Dublin), (17 Aug 1963), p. 6; by Joachim Krehayn in Neues Deutschland (Berlin), (16 Nov 1963), p. 53; in Observer (London), (7 Mar 1971), p. 22; by Ian Aitken in Teachers World (London), (4 June 1971), 25; in Books and Bookmen (London), 18 (June 1973), 137; in Irish Times (Dublin), (26 Mar 1971), p. 10 [vols. 1-2]; in Irish Times (Dublin), (30 Mar 1972), p. 10 [vols. 3-4]; in Irish Times (Dublin), (29 Mar 1973), p. 10 [vols. 5-6]; by Sean McMahon in Irish Press (Dublin), (15 May 1971), p. 12; by Harold Hobson in Books and Bookmen (London), 25 (May 1980), 48-9; by John Jordan in Hibernia (Dublin), (27 Mar 1980), p. 27; by Leon Baya in Daily World (N.Y.), (14 May 1980), p. 13; by Ned Chaillet in Times (London), (21 May 1981), p. 15; by Richard Brown in Sunday Times (London), (10 May 1981), p. 42; by John Russell Brown in Times Literary Supplement (London), (14 Aug 1981), p. 935; by Cyril Cusak in Universe (London), (24 July 1981), p. 10; by John Stewart Collis in Spectator (London), (9 May 1981), p. 27 [See reply by John O'Riordan, (16 May 1981), p. 18; and counter-reply by Collis, (30 May 1981), p. 20]; by Joe Dowling in Irish Times (Dublin), (22 Aug 1981), p. 10; and by Robert G. Lowery in Irish Literary Supplement, 1 (Spring 1982), 9.

126 THE LETTERS OF SEAN O'CASEY, 3 vols., ed. David Krause:

Vol. 1: 1910-1941 (New York: Macmillan; London: Cassell, 1975)

Vol. 2: 1942-1954 (New York: Macmillan; London: Cassell, 1980)

Vol. 3: 1955-1964 (in preparation).

Reviewed by J. C. Trewin in Times (London), (29 Sep 1975), p. 9; by Jack Sutherland in Morning Star (London), (25 Sep 1975), p. 4 and (6 Oct 1975), p. 4; by Sean Day-Lewis in Daily Telegraph (London), (25 Sep 1975), p. 13; in Economist (London), (27 Sep 1975), 118; by Nigel Dennis in Sunday Telegraph (London), (5 Oct 1975), p. 14 [See reply by John

O'Riordan, (12 Oct 1975), p. 12]; by Julian Moynahan in Times Literary Supplement (London), (2 Jan 1976), p. 4 [See reply by John O'Riordan, (30 Jan 1976), p. 113]; by Bernard Levin in Observer (London), (28 Sep 1975), p. 23; by John Mortimer in Spectator (London), (4 Oct 1975), 441-2; in Sunday Times (London), (12 Oct 1975), p. 38; by Martin Esslin in Drama (London), no. 119 (Winter 1975), 27-8; by Ian Stewart in Country Life (London), (30 Oct 1975), 1133; by William A. Armstrong in Theatre Notebook (London), 31 (1977), 45-7; by Maurice Harmon in Review of English Studies, 28 (May 1977), 241-2; by J. C. Trewin in Birmingham Post, (4 Oct 1975), Saturday Magazine, p. 1; by W. T. in Oxford Times, (17 Oct 1975), p. 34; by John O'Riordan in Library Review (Glasgow), 25 (Autumn 1976), 280; by Denis Johnston in Irish Times (Dublin), (27 Sep 1975), p. 10; by Tomas MacAnna in Hibernia (Dublin), (3 Oct 1975), p. 12; by Gabriel Fallon in Irish Independent (Dublin), (29 Sep 1975), p. 6; by John O'Riordan in Irish Press (Dublin), (4 Oct 1975), p. 7; by Hugh Leonard in Sunday Independent (Dublin), (5 Oct 1975), p. 15; by Denis Johnston in Irish University Review, 5 (Autumn 1975), 336-8; by Richard Gilman in New York Times Book Review, (16 Mar 1975), p. 1; in New Yorker, 51 (5 May 1975), 143; in Newsweek, 85 (31 Mar 1975), 75; by Denis Donoghue in New Republic, 172 (26 Apr 1975), 19-21; by Robert G. Lowery in Sean O'Casey Review, 1 (Spring 1975), 66-7; in Booklist, 71 (15 June 1975), 1039; in Best Sellers, 35 (Sep 1975), 185; by Kevin Sullivan in Nation, (19 Jul 1975), 55; by Keith S. Fulton in Los Angeles Times (23 Mar 1975), pp. 1, 11; by Ernest Schier in Evening Bulletin (Philadelphia), (8 Apr 1975), p. 54; by Robert Cormie in Chicago Tribune Book World, (20 Apr 1975), section 7, p. 7; by Tom Nugent in Detroit Free Press, (14 Sep 1975), p. 2; by Robert Hogan in Journal of Irish Literature, 5 (May 1976), 139-40; by Malcolm Kelsall in Theatre Research International, 1 (May 1976), 229-31; by Maureen Murphy in College Literature, 4 (Spring 1977), 102-3; by Bernard Benstock in Sean O'Casey Review, 2 (Spring 1976), 220-8; in Library Journal, 99 (1 Nov 1974), 2840; in Publishers' Weekly, 206 (25 Nov 1974), 42; in Kirkus Reviews, 42 (1 Dec 1974), 1292; by Irma S. Lustig in South Atlantic Quarterly, 75 (Summer 1976), 389-90; by Gerald Weales in Sewanee Review, 84 (Winter 1976), 185-9; by Brenna Katz Clarke in Educational Theatre Journal, 29 (Mar 1977), 132-3; by Robert G. Lowery in Daily World (N.Y.), (12 Aug 1980), p. 13; and by Robert G. Lowery in Irish Literary Supplement, 1 (Spring 1982), p. 8.

180 THE GRAND OUL' DAME BRITANNIA (Dublin: Fergus O'Connor, 1916).

181 LAMENT FOR THOMAS ASHE (Dublin: Fergus O'Connor, 1917).

182 THOMAS ASHE (Dublin: Fergus O'Connor, 1917).

183 THE STORY OF THOMAS ASHE (Dublin: Fergus O'Connor, 1917?). Reprinted as THE SACRIFICE OF THOMAS ASHE (Dublin: Fergus O'Connor, 1918).

184 SONGS OF THE WREN NO. 1 (Dublin: Fergus O'Connor, 1918).

185 SONGS OF THE WREN NO. 2 (Dublin: Fergus O'Connor, 1918).

186 ENGLAND'S CONSCRIPTION APPEAL TO IRELAND'S DEAD (Dublin: Fergus O'Connor, 1918).

187 MORE WREN SONGS (Dublin: Fergus O'Connor, 1918).

188 THE STORY OF THE IRISH CITIZEN ARMY (Dublin and London: Maunsel, 1919; rpt. Dublin: Talbot Press, 1971).

Reviewed by E[imar] O'D[uffy] in Irish Statesman (Dublin), 13 (12 July 1919), 71.

190 TWO PLAYS (London and New York: Macmillan, 1925). [Contains Juno and the Paycock and The Shadow of a Gunman.]

Reviewed in Times Literary Supplement (London), (19 Feb 1925), p. 117; by Bonamy Dobrée in Nation and Anthenaeum

(London), 36 (Mar 1925), 891; by C. E. Lawrence in Bookman
(London), 68 (Apr 1925), 68-9; in Spectator (London), 134
(14 Mar 1925), 415-16; in New Statesman (London), 25 (18
Apr 1925), 20; by A. N. M. in Manchester Guardian, (10 Mar
1925), p. 7 and in Manchester Guardian Weekly, (13 Mar 1925),
p. 225; in Calendar of Modern Letters (London), 1 (Apr 1925),
174; in Catholic Times, (21 May 1926), p. 6; by L. St. S. in
Criterion (London), 5 (May 1927), 275; by Milton Waldman in
London Mercury, 13 (Feb 1926), 422-3; by A. E. [George
Russell] in Irish Statesman (Dublin), 3 (7 Mar 1925), 822-3;
in Irish Book Lover (Dublin), 15 (Jan 1925), 30; by W[illiam]
D[awson] in Studies (Dublin), 14 (Sep 1925), 493-5; by Y. S.
in Irish Truth (Dublin), (21 Feb 1925), 126; by M. MacC. in
Sunday Independent (Dublin), (22 Feb 1925), p. 6; by T. C.
M[urray] in Irish Independent (Dublin), (23 Feb 1925), p. 4;
by A. E. Malone in Dublin Magazine, 2 (Mar 1925), 535-8; in
Irish Sketch (Dublin), (Mar 1925), 39; in Irish Times (Dublin),
(6 Mar 1925), p. 3; by Stark Young in New York Times (14
June 1925), section 8, p. 1; by Padraic Colum in Theatre
Arts Monthly (N.Y.), 9 (June 1925), 397-404; by Joseph Campbell in Saturday Review of Literature (N.Y.), 2 (29 Aug 1925),
78-9; by Walter Prichard Eaton in New York Herald Tribune
Books (29 Mar 1925), p. 9; by F. W. B. in Boston Evening
Transcript, (14 Mar 1925), Book Section, p. 5; by J. Ranken
Towse in New York Evening Post Literary Review (21 Mar 1925),
p. 5; in New York Times Book Review, (8 Mar 1925), p. 5;
in Independent (Boston), 117 (18 Sep 1926), 332; by D.F.
in Christian Science Monitor, (24 Mar 1925), p. 10; by Shaemas O'Sheel in Commonweal (N.Y.), 2 (12 Aug 1925), 333;
and in Times of India, (8 Apr 1925), p. 13.

224　THE PLOUGH AND THE STARS (London and New York: Macmillan, 1926).

Reviewed in Times Literary Supplement (London), (15 Apr
1926), p. 280; by S. R. Littlewood in Bookman (London), 70
(May 1926), 128-30; by Ivor Brown in Saturday Review (London), 141 (10 Apr 1926), 473; in Contemporary Review (London), 130 (July 1926), 123-5; in Catholic Herald (London),
(17 Apr 1926), p. 11; by St. John Ervine in Observer (London), (16 May 1926), p. 4; in Catholic Times, (21 May 1926),
p. 6; by Horace Shipp in English Review (London), 42 (June
1926), 851-3; by L. St. S. in Criterion (London), 5 (May
1927), 275; in Dublin Magazine, 1 (July-Sep 1926), 64-5; by
Y.S. in Irish Truth (Dublin), (17 Apr 1926), 254; by Y.O.
[George Russell] in Irish Statesman, 6 (1 May 1926), 216-18;
by A.E. M[alone] in Irish Tribune (Cork), (7 May 1926),
p. 16; in Northern Whig (Belfast), (1 May 1926), p. 10; by

Walter Prichard Eaton in New York Herald Tribune Books (16 May 1926), pp. 9, 18; by Padraic Colum in Saturday Review of Literature (N.Y.), 2 (12 June 1926), 854; in Independent (Boston), 97 (18 Sep 1926), 332; in Living Age (Boston), 329 (22 May 1926), 432; by J. R. Towse in New York Evening Post Literary Review, (24 Apr 1926), p. 2; by Brooks Atkinson in New York Times, (16 May 1926), section 8, p. 1; by Oliver M. Sayler in Saturday Review (N.Y.), 4 (10 Dec 1927), 427; and by W. M. C[onacher] in Queen's Quarterly, 34 (Apr-June 1927), 420-9.

248   THE SILVER TASSIE (London and New York: Macmillan, 1928).

Reviewed in Times Literary Supplement (London), (5 July 1928), p. 501; by Paul Banks in New English Weekly (London), 3 (24 Aug 1933), 446-7 [see reply by O'Casey, (14 Sep 1933) 520-1; counter-reply by Paul Banks, (21 Sep 1933), 541-2; and counter-counter-reply by O'Casey, (12 Oct 1933), 622-3]; by I. B. in Manchester Guardian Weekly, 18 (22 June 1928), 493; by Ivor Brown in Saturday Review (London), 145 (23 June 1928), 801-2; by Sylvia Lynd in Daily News (London), (27 June 1928), p. 4; by W. A. Darlington in Daily Telegraph (London), (5 July 1928), p. 17; by St. John Ervine in Observer (London), (8 July 1928), p. 15; by A. Newsome in New Age (London), 43 (12 July 1928), 126; by F. S. Flint in Criterion (London), 8 (Apr 1929), 551; in Yorkshire Evening Post (Leeds), (7 July 1928), p. 5; by "Desmond" in Irish News (Belfast), (23 June 1928), p. 6; in An Poblacht (Dublin), (28 July 1928), 3; by Y. O. [George Russell] in Irish Statesman (Dublin), 10 (21 July 1928), 391-2 [see reply by O'Casey, (4 August 1928), 430-1; and counter-reply by Y. O., (4 Aug 1928) 431]; by A. E. M. in Irish Book Lover (Dublin), 14 (July-Dec 1928), 109-11; by M. S. P[rice] in Dublin Magazine, 3 (Oct-Dec 1928), 72; in Independent (Boston), 121 (18 Aug 1928), 165; by J. F. S. in Boston Evening Transcript (11 Aug 1928), Book Section, p. 2; by Jane Dransfield in Saturday Review of Literature (N.Y.), 5 (15 Dec 1928), 516; and by Vincent McHugh in New York Evening Post, (1 Sep 1928), p. 5.

273   WITHIN THE GATES (London: Macmillan, 1933; New York: Macmillan, 1934).

Reviewed in Times (London), (28 Nov 1933), p. 12; in Times Literary Supplement (London), (7 Dec 1933), p. 872 and (24 Jan 1935), p. 37; by Osbert Burdett in London Mercury, 30 (May 1934), 667-8; by A. G. Stock in Socialist Review (London), 5 (Jan 1934), 46-9; by Hugh MacDiarmid in Scots Observer (Edinburgh), 8 (17 Feb 1934), 7; by I[vor] B[rown]

in Manchester Guardian Weekly, 29 (22 Dec 1933), 495; by
John Shand in Sunday Referee (London), (3 Dec 1933), p. 13;
by St. John Ervine in Observer (London), (7 Jan 1934), p.
15; in Time and Tide (London), 15 (27 Jan 1934), 108-9; by
Richard Rees in Adelphi (London), 7 (Feb 1934), 385-7; in
Irish Times (Dublin), (16 Dec 1933), p. 4; by T. C. M[urray]
in Irish Press (Dublin), (19 Dec 1933), p. 6; in Dublin Maga-
zine, 9 (Apr-June 1934), 75-6; by J. J. H. in Irish Book
Lover, 22 (July-Aug 1934), 92-3; by Brooks Atkinson in
New York Times (31 Dec 1933), section 9, p. 1; by George
Jean Nathan in Vanity Fair (N.Y.), 41 (Jan 1934), 42, 56;
by Henry Ten Eyck Perry in Yale Review, 23 (Summer 1934),
842-4; by Walter Prichard Eaton in New York Herald Tribune
Books (28 Jan 1934), p. 17; by M[orton] D. Z[abel] in Poetry
(Chicago), 45 (Dec 1934), 152-8; by V. Geddes in New Masses
(N.Y.), no. 5 (30 Jan 1934), 25; by Elinor Hughes in Boston
Herald, (25 Mar 1934), section A, p. 9; by Florence Codman
in Nation (N.Y.), 138 (25 Apr 1934), 476-7; and by A. Brulé
in Revue Anglo-Américaine (Paris), 11 (June 1934), 463-5.

298 WINDFALLS (London and New York: Macmillan, 1934). [Con-
     tains early poems, short stories and two plays, The End of
     the Beginning and A Pound on Demand.]

     Reviewed in Times Literary Supplement (London), (8 Nov 1934),
     p. 770; by St. John Ervine in Observer (London), (11 Nov
     1934), p. 4; in Spectator (London), 153 (16 Nov 1934), 772;
     by Desmond MacCarthy in Sunday Times (London), (28 Oct
     1934), p. 8; by Samuel Beckett in Bookman (London), 86
     (Christmas 1934), 111; by W. H. in Time and Tide (London),
     15 (1 Dec 1934), 1543-4; by Ernest Boyd in American Specta-
     tor, 111 (Jan 1935), 10; by Peter Monro Jack in New York
     Times Book Review (11 Nov 1934), p. 8; by Horace Gregory
     in New York Herald Tribune Books (25 Nov 1934), p. 16; in
     Theatre Arts Monthly (N.Y.), 18 (Dec 1934), 962-3; and by
     Louis Cazamian in Revue Anglo-Américaine (Paris), 12 (June
     1935), 451-3.

310 FIVE IRISH PLAYS [Juno and the Paycock, The Shadow of a
     Gunman, The Plough and the Stars, The End of the Beginning,
     A Pound on Demand] (London: Macmillan, 1935).

     Reviewed by Edith Shackleton in Time and Tide (London), 16
     (23 Nov 1935), 1711-12; and by T. C. Murray in Irish Press
     (Dublin), (19 Nov 1935), p. 6.

313 THE FLYING WASP: A LAUGHING LOOK-OVER OF WHAT HAS

BEEN SAID ABOUT THE THINGS OF THE THEATRE BY THE
ENGLISH DRAMATIC CRITICS (London: Macmillan, 1937; rpt.
New York: Benjamin Blom, 1971).

Reviewed in Times Literary Supplement (London), (13 Mar
1937), p. 184; by D. Walker-Smith in English Review (London),
64 (May 1937), 625-6; by Derek Verschoyle in Spectator (London), 158 (26 Mar 1937), 591-2; by James Agate in Sunday
Times (London), (21 Mar 1937), p. 6 [see O'Casey's reply (28
Mar 1937), p. 5]; by J. S. Collis in London Mercury, 36 (May
1937), 93; by James Agate in John O'London's Weekly, 36 (19
Mar 1937), 1000, 1026 [see replies by Hugh Ross Williamson,
37 (2 Apr 1937), 25-6, and O'Casey (9 Apr 1937), 39]; in
Times (London), (19 Mar 1937), p. 11; by George Warrington
in Country Life (London), (20 Mar 1937), 313; by John Pud-
ney in Life and Letters Today (London), 16 (Summer 1937),
180; by Peter Neumark in Cambridge Review, 58 (4 June 1937)
459; by T. C. Murray in Irish Press (Dublin), (23 Mar 1937),
p. 6; by Gabriel Fallon in Irish Monthly (Dublin), 65 (May
1937), 336-43; by P. C. T. in Irish Book Lover (Dublin), 25
(May-June 1937), 70; in Dublin Magazine, 12 (July-Sep 1937),
86; by Brooks Atkinson in New York Times, (13 June 1937),
p. 6; by Peter Monro Jack in New York Times Book Review
(13 June 1937), p. 6; by H. H. in Christian Science Monitor
Weekly Magazine (Boston), 29 (30 June 1937), 11; by Walter
Prichard Eaton in New York Herald Tribune Books, (10 Oct
1937), p. 28; by B[arnard] H[ewitt] in Quarterly Journal of
Speech (Chicago), 23 (Dec 1937), 672; by L. A. MacKay in
Canadian Forum (Toronto), 17 (June 1937), 143; by Ch.-M.
Garnier in Etudes Anglaises (Paris), (1937), 343-4; by Karl
Arns in Englische Studien (Leipzig), 72 (1937), 428-9; and by
G. Alexander in International Literature (Moscow), no. 4 (1938),
123-5.

339 I KNOCK AT THE DOOR: SWIFT GLANCES BACK AT THINGS
THAT MADE ME (London and New York: Macmillan, 1939; rpt.
London: Pan Books, 1971).

Reviewed in Times (London), (3 Mar 1939), p. 21; in Times
Literary Supplement (London), (4 Mar 1939), p. 131; by Desmond MacCarthy in Sunday Times (London), (19 Mar 1939),
p. 6 [reprinted in Living Age (Boston), 356 (4 June 1939),
391-4]; by G. W. Stonier in New Statesman and Nation (London), 17 (11 Mar 1939), 396; by Howard Spring in Evening
Standard (London), (16 Mar 1939), p. 17; by D. H. V. in
Spectator (London), 162 (3 Mar 1939), 362; by Seán O'Faoláin
in London Mercury, 39 (Mar 1939), 561-2; by Max Wood in
Fortnightly (London), 145 n.s. (June 1939), 712-13; by Ivor
Brown in Manchester Guardian (7 Mar 1939), p. 7; in Listener

(London), 21 (16 Feb 1939), 380; by Montagu Slater in Daily Worker (London), (5 Apr 1939), p. 7; by A[ustin] C[larke] in Dublin Magazine, 14 (Apr-June 1939), 85-7; by P. C. T. in Irish Book Lover (Dublin), 26 (Jan-Feb 1939), 96; by Brooks Atkinson in New York Times (9 Apr 1939), section 10, p. 1; by Ralph Thompson in New York Times (18 July 1939), p. 17; by Horace Reynolds in New York Times Book Review (23 July 1939), pp. 4, 16; by V. S. Pritchett in Christian Science Monitor Weekly Magazine, 31 (15 Apr 1939), 10; by Ruth Page in Boston Evening Transcript, (29 July 1939), 4, p. 1; by Shaemas O'Sheel in New York Herald Tribune Books (23 July 1939), p. 5; in New Republic (N.Y.), 100 (16 Aug 1939), 56; in Time (Chicago), 34 (24 July 1939), 64; by Edith J. R. Isaacs in Theatre Arts Monthly (N.Y.), 23 (Aug 1939), 611; by Padraic Colum in Yale Review, 29 (Sep 1939), 182-5; by Katherine Bregy in Catholic World (N.Y.), 150 (Oct 1939), 114-15; by Ernest Boyd in Saturday Review of Literature (N.Y.), 20 (29 July 1939), 6; by J. Cambridge in Sunday Worker (N.Y.), (13 Aug 1939), p. 7; by Louis Kronenberger in New Yorker (N.Y.), 15 (22 July 1939), 65-7; by Shaemas O'Sheel in New Masses (N.Y.), (17 Oct 1939), pp. 26-7; by Jack Young in Daily People's World (San Francisco), (6 Sep 1939), p. 5; by Eleanor Godfrey in Canadian Forum (Toronto), 19 (July 1939), 127; by Ian Aitken in Teachers World (London), (4 June 1971), 25; in Observer (London), (7 Mar 1971), 22; by Sean McMahon in Irish Press (Dublin), (15 May 1971), p. 12; by Otto Brandstädter in Zeitschrift für Anglistik und Amerikanistik (Berlin), 3 (1955), 371-5; by Joachim Krehayn in Bibliothekar (Leipzig), 2 (1958), 163-4; and by Günther Cwojdrak in Die Weltbuhne (Berlin) (13 July 1960), 887-9.

375 THE STAR TURNS RED (London: Macmillan, 1940).

Reviewed in Times Literary Supplement (London), (13 Aug 1940), pp. 182, 186; by D[erek] V[erschoyle] in Spectator (London), 164 (15 Mar 1940), 388; by Benjamin Gilbert Brooks in Nineteenth Century and After (London), 128 (Aug 1940), 196-200; by Ivor Brown in Manchester Guardian (1 Mar 1940), p. 3; by Richard Prentis in John O'London's Weekly, (29 Mar 1940), p. 852; in Dublin Magazine, 15 (July-Sep 1940), 65-7; by J. J. H[ogan] in Studies (Dublin), 29 (Mar 1940), 156-8; and by W. A. Darlington in New York Times (24 Mar 1940), section 9, p. 2.

383 PURPLE DUST: A WAYWARD COMEDY IN THREE ACTS (London: Macmillan, 1940).

Reviewed in Times Literary Supplement (London), (23 Nov 1940),

p. 594; by A. S. W. in Manchester Guardian (31 Dec 1940),
p. 7; by Edward Farrer in Life and Letters Today (London),
28 (Jan 1941), 88-90; by L. A. G. Strong in Spectator (London), 166 (17 Jan 1941), 70; by Ivor Brown in Observer (London), (16 Mar 1941), p. 3; in Irish Times (Dublin), (14 Dec
1940), p. 5; by T. C. M[urray] in Irish Press (Dublin), (20
Dec 1940), p. 11; by J. J. H[ogan] in Irish Book Lover (Dublin), 28 (Sep 1941), 71; by Denis Johnston in Bell (Dublin),
1 (Jan 1941), 91-4; by J. J. H[ogan] in Studies (Dublin),
30 (Sep 1941), 463-4; in Dublin Magazine, 16 (Jan-Mar 1941),
67; and by Walter Prichard Eaton in New York Herald Tribune
Books (9 Feb 1941), p. 12.

398 PICTURES IN THE HALLWAY (New York and London: Macmillan,
1942; rpt. London: Pan Books, 1971).

Reviewed in Times Literary Supplement (London), (7 Mar 1942),
p. 118; by Stephen Gwynn in Time and Tide (London), 23 (28
Mar 1942), 272-3 [see reply by O'Casey, (11 Apr 1942), 306];
by Elizabeth Bowen in Spectator (London), 168 (1 May 1942),
423; by G. W. Stonier in New Statesman and Nation (London),
23 (28 Feb 1942), 147; by A. S. W. in Manchester Guardian
(13 Mar 1942), p. 3; by Ivor Brown in Observer (London),
(7 Mar 1942), p. 7; by John Brophy in John O'London's Weekly,
(10 Apr 1942), p. 5; in Listener (London), 28 (2 July 1942),
27; by Maurice James Craig in Life and Letters Today (London), 34 (July 1942), 74-6; by Patrick Kavanagh in Irish Times
(Dublin), (14 Mar 1942), p. 5; by Maurice Devane in Dublin
Magazine, 17 (July-Sep 1942), 44-5; by Robert Van Gelder in
New York Times (7 Mar 1942), p. 15; by Brooks Atkinson in
New York Times (5 Apr 1942), section 8, p. 1; by Padraic
Colum in New York Sun (16 Apr 1942), p. 30; by J. D. A.
in New York Times Book Review (22 Mar 1942), p. 2; by
Horace Reynolds in New York Times Book Review (22 Mar 1942),
p. 5; by Lewis Gannett in New York Herald Tribune, (19 Mar
1942), p. 19; by Jenny Ballou in New York Herald Tribune
Book Reviews, (22 Mar 1942), p. 4; in New Yorker (N.Y.),
18 (11 Apr 1942) 87-8; by Ernest Boyd in Saturday Review of
Literature (N.Y.), 25 (21 Mar 1942), 5; by Charles A. Brady
in America (N.Y.), 67 (11 Apr 1942), 20-21; by N. E[lizabeth]
M[onroe] in Catholic World (N.Y.), 155 (May 1942), 244-5; by
James Stern in New Republic (N.Y.), 106 (30 Mar 1942), 434;
by S. Sillen in New Masses (N.Y.), (21 Apr 1942), 24-5; by
Louis F. Budenz in Worker (N.Y.), (26 Apr 1942), p. 6; in
Observer (London), (7 Mar 1971), 22; by Ian Aitken in Teachers World (London), (4 June 1971), 25; by Sean McMahon in
Irish Press (Dublin), (15 May 1971), p. 12; and by Günther
Cwojdrak in Die Weltbuhne (Berlin), (13 July 1960), 887-9.

429 RED ROSES FOR ME (London: Macmillan, 1942; New York: Macmillan, 1943).

Reviewed in Times Literary Supplement (London), (9 Jan 1943), p. 22; in Spectator (London), 169 (25 Dec 1942), 606; by G. W. Stonier in New Statesman and Nation (London), 24 (14 Nov 1942), 324; by A. D. in Manchester Guardian (4 Dec 1942), p. 3; by M. R. K. in Irish Press (Dublin), (3 Dec 1942), p. 2; by Seán O'Faoláin in Bell (Dublin), 6 (May 1943), 112-21; by H. A. Milton in Reynolds News (London), (22 Nov 1942), p. 4; by Sylvia Townsend Warner in Our Time (London), 2 (Apr 1943), 21-22; by Sheila May in Dublin Magazine, 18 (Apr-June 1943), 73-4; by M. M. in Bell (Dublin), 5 (Feb 1943), 410-11; by Horace Reynolds in New York Times Book Review (30 Jan 1944), p. 10; by Walter Prichard Eaton in New York Herald Tribune Book Review (30 Apr 1944), p. 17; by Edmund Wilson in New Yorker (N.Y.), 19 (5 Feb 1944), 73-4; by Eric Bentley in Partisan Review (N.Y.), 12 (Spring 1945), 250; in Christian Century (Chicago), 61 (22 Mar 1944), 370; in Theatre Arts (N.Y.), 28 (Apr 1944), 256; by William P. Sears in Churchman (N.Y.), 158 (Mar 1944), 19; and by George Mayberry in New Republic (N.Y.), 110 (14 Feb 1944), 217-18.

448 DRUMS UNDER THE WINDOWS (London: Macmillan, 1945; New York: Macmillan, 1946; rpt. London: Pan Books, 1972).

Reviewed in Times Literary Supplement (London), (20 Oct 1945), p. 502 and (17 Nov 1945), p. 548; by G. W. Stonier in New Statesman and Nation (London), 30 (27 Oct 1945), 284; by George Orwell in Observer (London), (28 Oct 1945), p. 3; by E. M. Boyle in Irish Democrat (London), (Dec 1945), p. 7; by Allen Hutt in Daily Worker (London), (17 Oct 1945), p. 2; by John Betjeman in Daily Herald (London), (25 Oct 1945), p. 2; by St. John Ervine in Spectator (London), (2 Nov 1945), 416; by Desmond MacCarthy in Sunday Times (London), (4 Nov 1945), p. 3; by Louis MacNeice in Time and Tide (London), 26 (10 Nov 1945), 942; by John Edgell in Our Time (London), 5 (Dec 1945), 97-8; in Listener (London), 35 (31 Jan 1946), 154; by M. J. MacM[anus] in Irish Press (Dublin), (1 Nov 1945), p. 2; by W. J. W. in Irish Times (Dublin), (3 Nov 1945), p. 2; by Roibeárd ó Faracháin in An Iris (Dublin), (Dec 1945), 60-2; by Austin Clarke in Dublin Magazine, 21 (Jan-Mar 1946), 56-8; by N. N. in Irish Independent (Dublin), (12 Nov 1945), p. 4; in Sunday Independent (Dublin), (18 Nov 1945), p. 4; by Seán O'Faoláin in Bell (Dublin), 11 (Dec 1945), 815-21; by Orville Prescott in New York Times (8 May 1946), p. 23; by Brooks Atkinson in New York Times (22 Sep 1946), section 2, p. 1; by Richard Sullivan in New York Times Book Review, (12 May 1946), p. 8; in Time (N.Y.), 47 (13

May 1946), 46; by Horace Reynolds in New York Herald Tribune Weekly Book Review, (12 May 1946), p. 2; by Richard
Watts in New Republic (N.Y.), 114 (10 June 1946), 839-40;
by Kathleen O'Brennan in America (N.Y.), 74 (2 Feb 1946),
494; by Robert B. Heilman in Quarterly Review of Literature,
4 (1947), 105-13; by Rolfe Humphries in Nation (N.Y.), 162
(11 May 1946), 577-8; by William D'Arcy in Catholic Historical
Review, 32 (Jan 1947), 491-2; by Thomas Quinn Curtiss in
Theatre Arts (N.Y.), 30 (Aug 1946), 494; by Padraic Colum
in Yale Review, 36 (Autumn 1946), 154-6; by Gerald W. Johnson in New York Herald Tribune, (7 May 1946), p. 27; by
William McFee in New York Sun, (7 May 1946), p. 23; by
Patrick O'Donnell in Catholic World (N.Y.), 163 (July 1946),
375; in Newsweek (N.Y.), 27 (13 May 1946), 100-102; by
Frank Hynes in Saturday Review of Literature (N.Y.), 29 (11
May 1946), 7-8; by S. Finkelstein in New Masses (N.Y.), (11
June 1946), 21-2; in Story (N.Y.), no. 119 (May-June 1946),
8; and by Robert Friedman in Daily Worker (N.Y.), (13 Sep
1950), p. 11.

489 OAK LEAVES AND LAVENDER: OR, A WARLD ON WALLPAPER
(London: Macmillan, 1946; New York: Macmillan, 1947).

Reviewed in Times Literary Supplement (London), (4 May 1946),
p. 215 and (11 May 1946), p. 224; by G. W. Stonier in New
Statesman and Nation (London), 30 (25 May 1946), 380-1; by
A. Farjeon in Time and Tide (London), 27 (8 June 1946), 544;
by John Collier in New Theatre (London), 3 (July 1946), 22;
by J. C. Trewin in John O'London's Weekly, (3 May 1946),
p. 46; by J. B. Priestley in Our Time (London), 5 (June
1946), 238; by Ewart Milne in Irish Democrat (London), (Aug
1946), p. 7; by T. C. M[urray] in Irish Press (Dublin), (25
Apr 1946), p. 7; by Valentin Iremonger in Irish Times (Dublin),
(18 May 1946), p. 4; by A. J. Leventhal in Dublin Magazine,
21 (July-Sep 1946), 38-40; by Horace Reynolds in New York
Times Book Review (11 May 1947), p. 18; by Walter Prichard
Eaton in New York Herald Tribune Weekly Book Review (25
May 1947), p. 27; by P. S. in San Francisco Chronicle (11
May 1947), Magazine Section, p. 23; in Christian Century
(Chicago), 64 (14 May 1947), 626; and by George Freedley in
Library Journal (N.Y.), 72 (15 May 1947), 811.

506 "JUNO AND THE PAYCOCK" AND "THE PLOUGH AND THE
STARS" By SEAN O'CASEY. With Introduction and Notes by
Gus Boas (London: Macmillan, 1948).

507 INISHFALLEN FARE THEE WELL (London and New York: Mac-
     millan, 1949; rpt. London: Pan Books, 1972).

Reviewed in Times Literary Supplement (London), (19 Feb
1949), p. 115; by Desmond MacCarthy in Sunday Times (London), (30 Jan 1949), p. 3; by Louis MacNeice in New Statesman and Nation (London), 37 (19 Feb 1949), 184-5; by Seán
O'Faoláin in John O'London's Weekly (4 Feb 1949), 70-1; by
Una Pope-Hennessy in Spectator (London), 182 (4 Feb 1949),
160; by Bruce Bain [Richard Findlater] in Tribune (London),
no. 630 (4 Feb 1949), 16; by G[erard] F[ay] in Manchester
Guardian (1 Feb 1949), p. 3 [see O'Casey's reply (14 Feb
1949), p. 4]; by L. A. G. Strong in Observer (London), (30
Jan 1949), p. 3; by H. M. in Drama (London), no. 13 (Sum-
mer 1949), 36; by Hayter Preston in Cavalcade (London), 2
(26 Feb 1949), 10; by W. Gallacher in Labour Monthly (London),
31 (Apr 1949), 126-7; by Annabel Farjeon in Time and Tide
(London), 30 (5 Feb 1949), 130; by Harold Nicolson in Daily
Telegraph (London), (11 Feb 1949), p. 3; by Allen Hutt in
Daily Worker (London), (3 Feb 1949), p. 2; by Anne Kelly
in Irish Democrat (London), (Apr 1949), p. 7; by Henry Mc-
Crea in Life and Letters (London), 61 (Apr 1949), 92-4; by
Alec Digges in Irish Democrat (London), (Apr 1949), p. 7;
by Hugh MacDiarmid in New Theatre (London), 5 (Apr 1949),
22-23; by Fred Urquhart in Our Time (London), 8 (May 1949),
132; in Dublin Magazine, 24 (Apr-June 1949), 49-50; by M.
J. MacM[anus] in Irish Press (Dublin), (27 Jan 1949), p. 6;
by N. N. in Irish Independent (Dublin), (26 Feb 1949), p. 4;
by Gabriel Fallon in Irish Monthly (Dublin), 77 (Mar 1949),
119-23; by P. S. O'Hegarty in Irish Book Lover (Dublin), 31
(June 1949), 44; by Austin Clarke in Irish Times (Dublin),
(29 Jan 1949), p. 9 [see O'Casey's reply (5 Feb 1949), p. 8];
by Robert Greacen in Irish Writing (Cork), no. 8 (July 1949),
88-9; by Orville Prescott in New York Times (22 Feb 1949),
p. 21; by Brooks Atkinson in New York Times (27 Feb 1949),
section 2, p. 1; by Joseph Wood Krutch in New York Times
Book Review (27 Mar 1949), p. 30; by Richard Watts, Jr. in
New York Post (20 Mar 1949), p. M6; by Horace Gregory in
New York Herald Tribune Weekly Book Review (20 Feb 1949),
p. 3; in Catholic World (N.Y.), 196 (May 1949), 152; by C.
J. Rolo in Atlantic (Boston), 183 (Apr 1949), 83-4; in Time
(N.Y.), 53 (28 Feb 1949), 56; by Charles Humboldt in Masses
and Mainstream (N.Y.), 2 (Apr 1949), 71-5; in New Yorker,
25 (26 Feb 1949), 91; by Walter O'Hearn in America (N.Y.),
81 (11 June 1949), 342-3; in Coronet (Boulder, Colo.), 27
(Jan 1950), 14; by Horace Reynolds in Saturday Review of
Literature (N.Y.), 32 (5 Mar 1949), 18-19; by Horace Reynolds in Yale Review, 39 (Autumn 1949), 169-70; by William
Sears in Churchman (N.Y.), 163 (June 1949), 15; by Marshall

Wingfield in Christian Century (Chicago), 66 (4 May 1949),
563; in American Mercury, 68 (June 1949), 759; by R. M. H.
in Christian Science Monitor (Boston), (24 Mar 1949), p. 11;
by Margaret Eliason in Library Journal (N.Y.), 74 (15 Jan
1949), 125; by J. W. Bogan in Springfield Republican, (24
Apr 1949), section D, p. 5; and in Booklist, 45 (1 Apr 1949),
261.

558 COCK-A-DOODLE DANDY (London: Macmillan, 1949).

Reviewed in Times Literary Supplement (London), (27 May
1949), p. 340; by John Allen in Drama (London), no. 15
(Winter 1949), 36; by G[erald] F[ay] in Manchester Guardian
(13 May 1949), p. 4; by Alec Digges in Irish Democrat (London), (June 1949), p. 7; by E. C. in New Theatre (London),
5 (June 1949), iii; by Ivor Brown in Observer (London), (8
Jan 1950), p. 6; by Austin Clarke in Irish Times (Dublin),
(15 & 16 Apr 1949), p. 6; by A. J. Leventhal in Dublin Magazine, 24 (1949), 48-51; by Robert Greacen in Irish Writing
(Cork), no. 9 (Oct 1949), 69-70; by Horace Reynolds in New
York Times Book Review (19 Feb 1950), p. 12; by W. R. W.
in San Francisco Chronicle (9 Apr 1950), p. 15; by R. M. H.
in Christian Science Monitor Magazine (Boston), 42 (27 Feb
1950), 6; by Walter Prichard Eaton in New York Herald Tribune Book Review, (9 Apr 1950), p. 15; by Henry Hewes in
Saturday Review of Literature (N.Y.), 38 (1950), 9-10; in
Booklist, 46 (1 July 1950), 332; and in Chicago Sun-Times,
(16 Apr 1950), section 2, p. 9.

566 ROSE AND CROWN (London and New York: Macmillan, 1952;
rpt. London: Pan Books, 1973).

Reviewed in Times (London), (9 July 1952), p. 8; in Times
Literary Supplement (London), (1 Aug 1952), p. 502; in New
Statesman and Nation (London), 44 (26 July 1952), 114; by
Brian Inglis in Spectator (London), 189 (1 Aug 1952), 166;
by Richard Findlater in Theatre (London), 7 (27 Sep 1952),
19; by Gerard Fay in Manchester Guardian (15 July 1952),
p. 4; by Donagh MacDonagh in Drama (London), no. 27 (Winter 1952), 37-8; by Austin Clarke in John O'London's Weekly,
61 (18 July 1952), 692; by Louis MacNeice in Observer (London), (13 July 1952), p. 7; by Peter Quennell in Daily Mail
(London), (5 July 1952), p. 2; by T. A. Jackson in Daily
Worker (London), (10 July 1952), p. 2; by N[iall] C[arroll]
in Irish Press (Dublin), (23 Sep 1952), p. 6; by Robert Greacen in Irish Writing (Cork), nos. 20-21 (Nov 1952), 85-6; by
Gabriel Fallon in Irish Monthly (Dublin), 80 (Nov 1952), 354-
9; by Val Mulkerns in Bell (Dublin), 18 (Oct 1952), 290-3; by

R. M. Hammond in Christian Science Monitor, (6 Nov 1952),
p. 15; by Marie A. Updike White in South Atlantic Quarterly,
53 (Jan 1954), 156-7; by Walter Prichard Eaton in New York
Herald Tribune Book Review (2 Nov 1952), p. 3; by Horace
Reynolds in New York Times Book Review (2 Nov 1952), p. 5;
by Brooks Atkinson in New York Times (14 Sep 1952), section
2, p. 1; by Maurice Valency in Saturday Review of Literature
(N.Y.), 35 (15 Nov 1952), 25; by Harold Hobson in Christian
Science Monitor, (28 Aug 1952), p. 7; by Hugh Corbett in Books
Abroad, 27 (Spring 1953), 151-2; in Daily Worker (N.Y.),
(13 Nov 1952), p. 7; by Stephen P. Ryan in America (N.Y.),
88 (20 Dec 1952), 330-2; by Charles J. Rolo in Atlantic, (Bos-
ton), 190 (Dec 1952), 99; in New Yorker (N.Y.), 28 (8 Nov
1952), 172-3; in Time (N.Y.), 60 (10 Nov 1952), 86-7; by
Charles Humboldt in Masses and Mainstream (N.Y.), 6 (Jan
1953), 58-60; by Joseph Carroll in Theatre Arts (N.Y.), 36
(Dec 1952), 6-8; by Frederick E. Faverty in Chicago Sunday
Tribune (2 Nov 1952), pt 4, p. 4; by Eric Bentley in New
Republic (N.Y.), 127 (13 Oct 1952), 17-18; in Books and Bookmen (London), 18 (June 1973), 137; by A[nne] Elistratova in
Soviet Literature (Moscow), no. 11 (Nov 1952), 164-9; and
by André Müller in Die Tat (Frankfurt), (10 Aug 1963),
p. 10.

602 SUNSET AND EVENING STAR (London and New York: Macmillan, 1954; rpt. London: Pan Books, 1973).

Reviewed in Times (London), (30 Oct 1954), p. 8; in Times
Literary Supplement (London), (5 Nov 1954), p. 699; by T.
C. Worsley in New Statesman and Nation (London), 48 (30
Oct 1954), 544 [see O'Casey's reply (6 Nov 1954), 582]; by
J. C. Trewin in Drama (London), no. 35 (Winter 1954), 34-8;
by Austin Clarke in Time and Tide (London), 35 (13 Nov 1954),
1524; by Sean O'Herron in British Weekly (London), 135 (4
Nov 1954), 2; by E. D. O'Brien in Illustrated London News,
226 (26 Feb 1955), 376; by Ivor Brown in Observer (London),
(14 Nov 1954), p. 9; by Edith Shackleton in Lady (London),
140 (4 Nov 1954), 594; by Cicely Boas in English (London),
10 (Spring 1955), 151-2; by Eric Gillett in National and English Review (London), 143 (Dec 1954), 425; by Howard Spring
in Country Life (London), 116 (18 Nov 1954), 1787-89; by
Richard Findlater in Tribune (London), (28 Jan 1955), p. 7;
by Vernon Fane in Sphere (London), 219 (6 Nov 1954), 256
by Gerard Fay in Manchester Guardian (26 Nov 1954), p. 9;
by W. A. Darlington in Daily Telegraph (London), (26 Nov
1954), p. 8; by Frederick Laws in News Chronicle (London),
(5 Nov 1954), p. 2; by Philip Bolsover in Daily Worker (London), (4 Nov 1954), p. 2; by J. C. in Belfast News-Letter

(20 Nov 1954), p. 2; by Austin Clarke in Irish Times (Dublin), (6 Nov 1954), p. 6 in Sunday Independent (Dublin), (31 Oct 1954), p. 1; by W. L. in Irish Independent (Dublin), (30 Oct 1954), p. 6; by John Jordan in Irish Writing (Cork), no. 29 (Dec 1954), 57-63; in Standard (Dublin), 27 (18 Feb 1955), 1; by H. L. Morrow in Irish Press (Dublin), (13 Nov 1954), p. 4; by K. F. in Irish Book Lover (Dublin), 32 (July 1956), 118; by Marie A. Updike White in South Atlantic Quarterly, 55 (Apr 1956), 242-3; by Brooks Atkinson in New York Times Book Review (14 Nov 1954), pp. 1, 38; by V. S. Pritchett in New Yorker (N.Y.), 31 (16 Apr 1955), 147-56; by Charles J. Rolo in Atlantic (Boston), 195 (Jan 1955), 83; by Hugh Corbett in Books Abroad 29 (Summer 1955), 307; by Walter Prichard Eaton in New York Herald Tribune Book Review (14 Nov 1954), pt. 1, p. 5; by Horace Reynolds in Christian Science Monitor (Boston), (24 Nov 1954), p. 9; by George Freedley in Library Journal (N.Y.), 80 (1 Mar 1955), 577; in College English (Chicago), 16 (Mar 1955), 391; by Granville Hicks in New Leader (N.Y.), (29 Nov 1954), p. 22; by Philip Bolsover in Worker (N.Y.), (28 Nov 1954), p. 8; by Horace Gregory in Saturday Review of Literature (N.Y.), 37 (20 Nov 1954), 18-19; by Padraic Colum in New Republic (N.Y.), 131 (27 Dec 1954), 19; by Harold Clurman in Nation (N.Y.), 179 (27 Nov 1954), 468; in Time (N.Y.), 64 (15 Nov 1954), 102; by Donald A. Pitt in San Francisco Chronicle (5 Dec 1954), p. 22; by Gerald Weales in Commentary (N.Y.) 19 (Feb 1955), 201-2; by E. J. West in Educational Theatre Journal, 7 (Dec 1955), 354-6; by Milton Howard in Masses and Mainstream (N.Y.), 8 (Jan 1955), 20-6; by Philip Bolsover in Daily People's World (San Francisco), (3 Dec 1954), p. 7; by Robertson Davies in Saturday Night (Toronto), (5 Feb 1955), p. 12; and in Books and Bookmen (London), 18 (June 1973), 137.

651 SELECTED PLAYS OF SEAN O'CASEY. Selected with Foreword by the Author. Introduction by John Gassner (New York: George Braziller, 1954) [The Shadow of a Gunman, Juno and the Paycock, The Plough and the Stars, The Silver Tassie, Within the Gates, Purple Dust, Red Roses for Me, Bedtime Story, Time to Go].

Reviewed by George Freedley in Library Journal, 80 (1 Jan 1955), 83; and by E. J. West in Educational Theatre Journal, 7 (Dec 1955), 354-6.

655 THE BISHOP'S BONFIRE: A SAD PLAY WITHIN THE TUNE OF A POLKA (London and New York: Macmillan, 1955).

Reviewed in Times Literary Supplement (London), (8 July

1955), p. 378; by John Jordan in Irish Writing, no. 31 (Summer 1955), 59-60; by A. J. Leventhal in Dublin Magazine, 31 (1955), 51-4; by Brooks Atkinson in New York Times Book Review, (11 Sep 1955), p. 22; by P. L. Adams in Atlantic, 196 (Oct 1955), 96; and by George Freedley in Library Journal, 80 (1 Nov 1955), 2534.

662 THE GREEN CROW (New York: George Braziller, 1956; London: W. H. Allen, 1957). [Contains parts of The Flying Wasp, four stories from Windfalls, and some new essays.]

Reviewed in Times (London), (14 Feb 1957), p. 11; in Times Literary Supplement (London), (15 Feb 1957), p. 99; by J. P. Henderson in New Statesman and Nation (London), 53 (23 Feb 1957), 252-3; in Listener (London), 57 (9 May 1957), 761, 763; by J. W. Lambert in Sunday Times (London), (24 Feb 1957), p. 9; by John Wain in Observer (London), (10 Feb 1957), p. 13; by Peter Green in Time and Tide (London), 38 (6 Apr 1957), 424-5; by J. MacC. in Daily Worker (London), (21 Feb 1957), p. 2; by Alan Dent in News Chronicle (London), (14 Feb 1957), p. 8; by Joe MacColum in Irish Democrat (London), (Apr 1957), p. 7; by Walter Prichard Eaton in New York Herald Tribune Book Review (6 May 1956), p. 8; by Brooks Atkinson in New York Times Book Review (18 Mar 1956), pp. 3, 22; by Frederick E. Faverty in Chicago Sunday Tribune (8 Apr 1956), p. 12; by E. J. West in Educational Theatre Journal, 9 (May 1957), 157-9; by Henry Popkin in Kenyon Review, 18 (Autumn 1956), 663-8; by W[ilma] Cross in People's World Magazine (San Francisco), (22 June 1956), p. 7; by William Hogan in San Francisco Chronicle (22 Mar 1956), p. 22; by Max Cosman in Theatre Arts (N.Y.), 40 (July 1956), 8-9; in Time (N.Y.), 67 (26 Mar 1956), 97-8; by Wilma Cross in Daily Worker (N.Y.), (27 June 1956), p. 6; by R[aymond] Brugère in Etudes anglaises (Paris), 12 (Oct-Dec 1957), 366-7; by A[nne] Elistratova in Problems of Literature [Voprosy Literatury] (Moscow), no. 8 (Nov 1957), 238-41; and by Elena Kornilova in News (Moscow), 22 (Nov 1956), 25-6.

687 THREE PLAYS BY SEAN O'CASEY: JUNO AND THE PAYCOCK, THE SHADOW OF A GUNMAN, THE PLOUGH AND THE STARS (London: Macmillan, 1957).

688 FIVE ONE-ACT PLAYS BY SEAN O'CASEY: THE END OF THE BEGINNING, A POUND ON DEMAND, HALL OF HEALING, BEDTIME STORY, TIME TO GO (London: Macmillan, 1958).

689 THE DRUMS OF FATHER NED (London: Macmillan; New York: St. Martin's Press, 1960).

Reviewed by G. Wilson Knight in Stand (London), 4 (Summer 1960), 15-18; by Myke Myson in Daily Worker (London), (27 June 1960), p. 2; by Brett Duffield in John O'London's Weekly (30 June 1960), p. 795; by Gabriel Fallon in Evening Press (Dublin), (25 June 1960), p. 9; in Irish Times (Dublin), (27 Aug 1960), p. 6; by George Freedley in Library Journal, 85 (1 Nov 1960), 4003; by Vivian Mercier in Hudson Review, 13 (Winter 1960), 631-6; by Marketa Goetz in Canadian Forum, 40 (Jan 1961), 234; by Harold Clurman in Saturday Review of Literature (N.Y.), 43 (5 Nov 1960), 31, 48; and by René Fréchet in Etudes anglaises (Paris), 15 (July-Sep 1962), 511.

700 BEHIND THE GREEN CURTAINS (London: Macmillan; New York: St. Martin's Press, 1961). [Contains the title-play, Figuro in the Night, and The Moon Shines on Kylenamoe.]

Reviewed by Alan Simpson in Sunday Times (London), (23 July 1961), p. 26; by Myke Myson in Daily Worker (London), (19 June 1961), p. 2; in Twentieth Century (London), 170 (July 1961), 173; by Gabriel Fallon in Kilkenny Magazine, no. 5 (Autumn-Winter 1961), 34-41 [see reply by Robert Hogan (Spring 1962), 37-9; and counter-reply (Spring 1962), 40-1]; by Brooks Atkinson in New York Times (14 July 1961), p. 20; by George Freedley in Library Journal, 86 (15 Sep 1961), 2960; by Michael Newton in Kansas City Star, (23 Sep 1961), p. 7; by Alec Reid in Drama Survey, 3 (May 1963), 155-64; and by Renée Saurel in Temps modernes (Paris), 19 (Aug-Sep 1963), 571-2.

712 FEATHERS FROM THE GREEN CROW: SEAN O'CASEY, 1905-1925, ed. Robert Hogan (Columbia: University of Missouri Press, [1962]; London: Macmillan, 1963). [Contains two hitherto unpublished plays, Cathleen Listens In and Nannie's Night Out; some early newspaper articles; The Sacrifice of Thomas Ashe; and The Story of the Irish Citizen Army.]

Reviewed in Times (London), (3 Oct 1963), p. 15; in Times Literary Supplement (London), (6 Sep 1963), p. 674; by John Wain in Observer (London), (11 Aug 1963), p. 16; by Valentin Iremonger in Spectator (London), 211 (27 Sep 1963), 391; in Time and Tide (London), 44 (22-8 Aug 1963), 21; by Robert Nye in Scotsman (Edinburgh), (7 Sep 1963), p. 2; by Robert Greacen in Listener (London), 70 (8 Aug 1963), 212; by Philip Hengist in Punch (London), 245 (30 Oct 1963), 648; by Desmond Ryan in Irish Times (Dublin), (3 Aug 1963),

p. 8; by Augustine Martin in Studies (Dublin), 53 (Autumn
1964), 329-32; by Ronald Ayling in Dubliner 3 (Spring 1964),
54-67; by Gabriel Fallon in Kilkenny Magazine, no. 10 (Autumn-
Winter 1963), 65-73; in Christian Science Monitor, (29 Nov 1962),
p. 6B; by Wil Wharton in St. Louis Post-Dispatch, (25 Nov
1962), p. 4; by John R. Willingham in Kansas City Times,
(25 Jan 1963), p. 30; and by Jean Wells in St. Louis Review,
(8 Mar 1963), pp. 1, 4.

729 UNDER A COLORED CAP: ARTICLES MERRY AND MOURNFUL
WITH COMMENTS AND A SONG (London: Macmillan; New
York: St. Martin's Press, 1963).

Reviewed in Times (London), (11 Apr 1963), p. 15; in Times
Literary Supplement (London), (3 May 1963), p. 326; by Tim
Pat Coogan in Spectator (London), 210 (3 May 1963), 580;
by Louis MacNeice in New Statesman (London), 65 (3 May
1963), 678-9; by John Wain in Observer (London), (11 Aug
1963), p. 16; by Robert Robinson in Sunday Times (London),
(14 Apr 1963), p. 25; in Time and Tide (London), 44 (11-17
Apr 1963), 28; by Gerard Fay in Manchester Guardian (26
Apr 1963), p. 6; by Tim Enright in Daily Worker (London),
(11 Apr 1963), p. 2; by Eric Shorter in Daily Telegraph (London), (19 Apr 1963), p. 19; by Kenneth Allsop in Daily Mail
(London), (11 Apr 1963), p. 8 [see reply by Herbert Phillips
(16 Apr 1963), p. 8]; by Robert Greacen in Listener (London), 69 (18 Apr 1963), 685-7; by L. E. in Irish Times
(Dublin), (20 Apr 1963), p. 8; by Cahir Healy in Irish News
(Belfast), (11 May 1963), p. 2; by Augustine Martin in Studies
(Dublin), 53 (Autumn 1964), 329-32; by Gabriel Fallon in Kilkenny Magazine, no. 10 (Autumn-Winter 1963), 65-73; by
Frank O'Connor in Suday Independent (Dublin), (12 May 1963),
p. 12; by Anne O'Neill-Barna in New York Times Book Review
(23 June 1963), p. 7; by Sean Callery in Saturday Review of
Literature (N.Y.), (29 June 1963), 32; by Brooks Atkinson
in New York Times (17 May 1963), p. 30; by J. F. Moran in
Library Journal, 88 (1 June 1963), 2251; in New Yorker, 39
(3 Aug 1963), 70-1; and by Hilda Kirkwood in Canadian Forum,
43 (Sep 1963), 142.

753 THREE MORE PLAYS BY SEAN O'CASEY: THE SILVER TASSIE,
PURPLE DUST, RED ROSES FOR ME. With an introduction by
J. C. Trewin (London: Macmillan; New York: St. Martin's
Press, 1965).

754 BLASTS AND BENEDICTIONS: ARTICLES AND STORIES, ed.
Ronald Ayling (London: Macmillan; New York: St. Martin's
Press, 1967).

Reviewed in Times (London), (19 Jan 1967), p. 14; in Times
Literary Supplement (London), (26 Jan 1967), p. 65; in Sunday Times (London), (15 Jan 1967), p. 28; by Frederick Laws
in Daily Telegraph (London), (30 Mar 1967), p. 20; by Elizabeth Coxhead in Sunday Telegraph (London), (15 Jan 1967),
p. 14; by Irving Wardle in Observer (London), (22 Jan 1967),
p. 27; by John Arden in Machester Guardian (20 Jan 1967),
p. 7; by Gerald Colgan in Plays and Players (London), 14
(July 1967), 54; by Elizabeth Coxhead in Lady (London), 165
(16 Feb 1967), 308; by Katharine J. Worth in Shavian (London), 3 (17 July 1967), 25-7; by Michael Foot in Evening
Standard (London), (17 Jan 1967), p. 8; by Jack Sutherland
in Morning Star (London), (12 Jan 1967), p. 4; by Elizabeth
Jennings in Catholic Herald (London), (24 Feb 1967), p. 6;
by John O'Riordan in Tribune (London), 31 (2 June 1967),
11; by Piers Brendon in Books and Bookmen (London), 12
(Feb 1967), 54-5 [see reply by John O'Riordan (Apr 1967),
8-9]; by G. W. B. in New Theatre Magazine (Bristol), 8 (Summer 1967), 37-8; by C. S. in Glasgow Herald (14 Jan 1967),
p. 9; by J. C. Trewin in Birmingham Post, (14 Jan 1967),
p. 11; by John Midgley in News-Letter (Belfast), (28 Nov
1969), p. 4; by Mervyn Wall in Irish Times (Dublin),
(28 Jan 1967), p. 8; by John McCann in Sunday Press
(Dublin), (19 Feb 1967), p. 21; in Evening Herald (Dublin), (13 Jan 1967), p. 4; by David Krause in Modern Drama
11 (Dec 1968), 252-62; by Sam Wellbaum in Independent Shavian (N.Y.), 5 (Spring 1967), 46; in New York Times Book
Review (23 Apr 1967), p. 30; by Sean Cronin in Nation (N.Y.),
205 (2 Oct 1967), 315-16; in Choice, 4 (Dec 1967), 1118; by
Connolly Cole in Chicago Tribune Books Today, (16 Apr 1967),
section 9, p. 5; in Independent Press Telegram (Long Beach,
Calif.), (8 July 1967); in Booklist (Chicago), (11 Jan 1967);
in Huntington Herald-Advertiser (West Virginia), (5 May 1967),
Book Page; and by M. J. Sidnell in Canadian Forum (Toronto),
47 (Mar 1968), 288.

789 THE SEAN O'CASEY READER: PLAYS, AUTOBIOGRAPHIES,
OPINIONS, ed. with an Introduction by Brooks Atkinson (New
York: St. Martin's Press; London: Macmillan, 1968).

Reviewed in Times Literary Supplement (London), (17 July
1969), p. 771; in Times Educational Supplement (London), (16
May 1969), p. 1647; by John O'Riordan in Tribune (London),
(18 Sep 1970), p. 11; by Terence de Vere White in Irish Times
(Dublin), (10 May 1969), p. 8 [see correspondence by Gabriel
Fallon (14 May 1969); by L. Smith (15 May 1969); and by John
O'Riordan (20 May 1969)]; by William J. Clew in Hartford
Courant Magazine (19 Jan 1969), section J, p. 19; by Anne
O'Neill-Barna in New York Times Book Review, (15 Dec 1968),

p. 1; in Christian Science Monitor, (5 Dec 1968), p. 25; by
Marguerite McAneny in Library Journal, 94 (15 Jan 1969),
194; in Critic (Chicago), 27 (Feb 1969), 93; in Choice, 9
(May 1969), 368; by Robert Hogan in Modern Drama, 12 (May
1969), 107-8; and by John Chapman in San Francisco Chronicle, (15 Dec 1968), p. 10.

805 THE HARVEST FESTIVAL: A PLAY IN THREE ACTS, with a
Foreword by Eileen O'Casey and an Introduction by John
O'Riordan (New York: New York Public Library, 1979; Ger-
rards Cross, Buckinghamshire: Colin Smythe, 1980).

Reviewed by Katharine Worth in Times Literary Supplement
(London), (9 May 1980), p. 527 [passim]; by John Russell
Brown in British Book News (London), (Sep 1980), 562; by
John Kavanagh in Irish Post (London), (3 May 1980), p. 4;
by C. D[esmond] G[reaves] in Irish Democrat (London), (May
1980), p. 7; by Tony Poulton in Southgate Gazette (London),
(31 July 1980), p. 13; by Desmond Pratt in Yorkshire Post
(Leeds), (8 Apr 1980), p. 7; by Micheál O hAodha in Irish
Times (Dublin), (5 July 1980), p. 13; by Kane Archer in
Books Ireland (Dublin), no. 44 (June 1980), 112; in Daily
Worker (N.Y.), (18 Apr 1980), p. 12; in American Book Col-
lector, 1 (Mar 1980), 62; in Choice, 17 (July-Aug 1980), 674;
by David Bianco in Best Sellers, 40 (May 1980), 73; by Thomas
E. Luddy in Library Journal, 105 (1 Apr 1980), 874; by Bernard Benstock in O'Casey Annual (London), no. 1 (1982),
224-8; and by Gerald Weales in Georgia Review (Athens, Ga.),
34 (Fall 1980), 685.

PART III:

CRITICISM ON O'CASEY

A. REFERENCE WORKS

821 Anderson, Michael, et al., "Sean O'Casey," in Crowell's Handbook of Contemporary Drama (New York: Thomas Y. Crowell,
1971), pp. 332-3 [Biographical essay].

822 Armstrong, William A., "Sean O'Casey," in The Oxford Companion to the Theatre, ed. Phyllis Hartnoll (London: Oxford University Press, 1967), pp. 691-2 [Brief critical essay on the
later plays].

823 Ayling, Ronald, "Sean O'Casey," in Encyclopedia Americana,
vol. 20, International Edition (New York: American Corporation, 1969), pp. 606-7 [Biographical and critical essay].

824 _____, "Sean O'Casey," in Modern British Dramatists 1900-
1945, part 2, ed. Stanley Weintraub. Dictionary of Literary
Biography, vol. 10 (Detroit: Gale Research Company, 1982),
pp. 71-90 [Biographical and critical essay].

825 Benstock, Bernard, "Sean O'Casey," in Encyclopedia of World
Literature in the 20th Century, revised edition, ed. Leonard
S. Klein (New York: Frederick Unger, 1982), pp. 411-15
[Biographical and critical essay].

826 The Best Plays of 1919-1947, ed. Burns Mantle; The Best Plays
of 1947-1952, ed. John Chapman; The Best Plays of 1952-1961,
ed. Louis Kronenberger; The Best Plays of 1961-1964, ed.
Henry Hewes; The Best Plays of 1964- , ed. Otis Guernsey,
Jr. (New York: Dodd, Mead, 1920-) [Theatre yearbook
which gives details of the productions of the year].

827 Boylan, Henry, "Sean O'Casey," in A Dictionary of Irish Biography (Dublin: Gill and Macmillan, 1978), p. 248 [Biograph-
ical essay].

828 Cartmell, Van H., ed., Plot Outlines of 100 Famous Plays,
Dolphin Books (Garden City, N.Y.: Doubleday, 1962), pp.
243-7 [Synopsis of Juno and the Paycock].

829 Cleeve, Brian, "Sean O'Casey," in Dictionary of Irish Writers,
First Series (Cork: Mercier Press, 1966), pp. 100-1; Second

Series (Cork: Mercier Press, 1969), p. 82 [Biographical essays].

830 Cousin, John W., and D.C. Browning, comps., "Sean O'Casey," in Everyman's Dictionary of Literary Biography: English & American. Everyman's Reference Library (London: J.M. Dent; New York: E.P. Dutton, 1965), p. 511 [Introductory information].

831 Daiches, David, ed., "Sean O'Casey," in The Penguin Companion to English Literature (Harmondsworth: Penguin Books; New York: McGraw-Hill Book Company, 1971), p. 395 [Brief biographical essay].

832 de Baun, Vincent C., "Sean O'Casey," in Encyclopedia of World Literature in the 20th Century, ed. Wolfgang Bernard Fleischmann (New York: Frederick Ungar, 1969), vol. 3, pp. 4-7 [Biographical and critical essay].

833 Ellis-Fermor, Una, "Sean O'Casey," in The Oxford Companion to the Theatre, ed. Phyllis Hartnoll (London: Oxford University Press, 1967), p. 691 [Brief critical essay on the plays until Within the Gates].

834 Encyclopedia of Ireland (Dublin: Allen Figgis; New York: McGraw-Hill, 1968), p. 357 [Brief evaluation of O'Casey's role in Irish drama].

835 Esslin, Martin, ed., "Sean O'Casey," in Illustrated Encyclopaedia of World Theatre (London: Thames and Hudson, 1977), p. 204 [Biographical essay].

836 Freeman, William, Dictionary of Fictional Characters (London: J.M. Dent, 1967) [Identifies characters in Juno and the Paycock and The Plough and the Stars].

837 Gillie, Christopher, "Sean O'Casey," in Longman Companion to English Literature (London: Longman, 1972), p. 675 [Brief entry].

838 Grigson, Geoffrey, ed., "Sean O'Casey," in The Concise Encyclopaedia of Modern World Literature (London: Hutchinson; New York: Hawthorn pp. 261-2 [Biographical and critical essay].

839 Harvey, Sir Paul, ed., "Sean O'Casey," in The Oxford Companion to English Literature, 4th rev. ed. (Oxford: Clarendon Press, 1973), p. 587 [Introductory information].

840 Hogan, Robert, "Sean O'Casey," in Dictionary of Irish Literature

(Westport, Conn.: Greenwood Press; London: Macmillan, 1979), pp. 488-99 [Biographical and critical essay].

841 Hornstein, Lillian Herlands; Leon Edel; and Horst Frenz, eds., "Sean O'Casey," in A Reader's Companion to World Literature, 2nd ed. Mentor Books (New York: New American Library, 1973), pp. 374-5 [Brief biographical and critical essay].

842 Kennelly, Brendan, "Sean O'Casey," in Encyclopaedia Britannica, vol. 16 (London: William Benton, 1970), p. 835 [Biographical and critical essay].

843 Krause, David, "Sean O'Casey," in Colliers Encyclopedia (New York: Crowell-Colliers, 1963), vol. 18 [Biographical and critical essay].

844 _____, "Sean O'Casey," in The Reader's Encyclopaedia of World Drama, ed. John Gassner and Edward Quinn (New York: Crowell, 1969; London: Methuen, 1970), pp. 608-9 [Biographical and critical essay].

845 Kunitz, Stanley J., "Sean O'Casey," in Living Authors, ed. Dilly Tante (New York: H.W. Wilson, 1937), pp. 302-3 [Biographical sketch].

846 _____, and Howard Haycraft, eds., "Sean O'Casey," in Twentieth Century Authors (New York: H.W. Wilson, 1942), pp. 1039-40 [Biographical sketch and list of earlier works].

847 _____ and _____, eds., "Sean O'Casey," in Twentieth Century Authors, First Supplement (New York: H.W. Wilson, 1955), p. 729 [Biographical sketch and list of later works].

848 Langnas, I.A., and J.S. List, "Sean O'Casey," in Major Writers of the World (Paterson, N.J.: Littlefield, Adams, 1963), p. 345 [Introductory information].

849 Lennartz, Franz, ed., "Sean O'Casey," in Ausländische Dichter und Schriftsteller unserer Zeit, 4th rev. ed. (Stuttgart: Kröner, 1971), pp. 575-9 [Biographical and critical essay].

850 McGraw-Hill Encyclopedia of World Drama, vol. 3 (New York: McGraw-Hill, 1972), pp. 330-8 [Biographical and critical essay; and synopses of The Shadow of a Gunman, Juno and the Paycock, The Plough and the Stars, The Silver Tassie, Within the Gates, The Star Turns Red, Purple Dust, Red Roses for Me, Oak Leaves and Lavender, Cock-a-Doodle Dandy, The Bishop's Bonfire, and The Drums of Father Ned].

851 Magill, Frank N., ed., Cyclopedia of Literary Characters (New

York and London: Harper & Row, 1963) [Includes identification of characters in Juno and the Paycock, The Plough and the Stars, Purple Dust, and Within the Gates].

852   _____, ed., "Sean O'Casey," in Cyclopedia of World Authors (New York and London: Harper & Row, 1958), pp. 797-9 [Biographical and critical essay].

853   _____, ed., Masterpieces of World Literature in Digest Form (New York and London: Harper & Row, 1952) [Includes synopses of Juno and the Paycock, The Plough and the Stars, Purple Dust, and Within the Gates].

854   Matlaw, Myron, "Sean O'Casey," in Modern World Drama: An Encyclopedia (New York: E.P. Dutton; London: Secker & Warburg, 1972), pp. 560-2 [Biographical and critical essay].

855   May, Robin, A Companion to the Theatre: The Anglo-American Stage from 1920 (London: Lutterworth Press, 1973), pp. 15-16 [Juno and the Paycock]; pp. 54-5 [Brief biographical note].

856   Melchinger, Siegfried, "Sean O'Casey," in The Concise Encyclopedia of Modern Drama (London: Vision Press, 1970), p. 236 [Very brief entry, mainly listing O'Casey's plays].

857   Moritz, Charles, ed., "Sean O'Casey," in Current Biography Yearbook, 1962 (New York: H.W. Wilson, 1962), pp. 324-7.

858   _____, ed., "Sean O'Casey," in Current Biography Yearbook, 1964 (New York: H.W. Wilson, 1964), p. 326.

859   Myers, Robin, "Sean O'Casey," in A Dictionary of Literature in the English Language (Oxford: Pergamon Press, 1970), pp. 634-5 [Brief entry, mainly listing his works].

860   Nicoll, Allardyce, "Sean O'Casey," in Chambers's Encyclopaedia, new rev. ed. (Oxford: Pergamon Press, 1966), vol. 10, pp. 166-7 [Biographical and critical essay].

861   Obituaries from The Times 1961-1970 (Reading, England: Newspaper Archive Developments Limited, 1975), pp. 597-8. Reprinted from Times (London), (21 Sep 1964), p. 16.

862   O'Mahony, Mathew, Guide to Anglo-Irish Plays (Dublin: Progress House, 1960) [Gives synopses of, and production notes on, The Plough and the Stars, Red Roses for Me, The Silver Tassie, The Bishop's Bonfire, Purple Dust, Cock-a-Doodle Dandy, Juno and the Paycock, The Shadow of a Gunman, The End of the Beginning, Bedtime Story, A Pound on Demand, The Hall of Healing, and Time to Go].

863 R[obinson], E.H., "Sean O'Casey," in Webster's New World Companion to English and American Literature, ed. Arthur Pollard (Salisbury: Compton Russell, 1973), pp. 503-4 [Biographical and critical essay].

864 Seymour-Smith, Martin, "Sean O'Casey," in Guide to Modern World Literature (London: Wolfe Publishing, 1973), p. 259 [Brief biographical and critical essay].

865 _____, "Sean O'Casey," in Who's Who in Twentieth Century Literature (London: Weidenfeld and Nicolson, 1976), p. 262 [Brief biographical and critical essay].

866 Shank, Theodore J., ed., A Digest of 500 Plays: Plot Outlines and Production Notes (New York: Collier Books; London: Collier-Macmillan, 1963), pp. 412-16 [The Shadow of a Gunman, Juno and the Paycock, The Plough and the Stars, The Silver Tassie, Purple Dust, and Cock-a-Doodle Dandy].

867 Sharp, Harold S., and Marjorie Z. Sharp, comps., Index to Characters in the Performing Arts: An Alphabetical Listing of 30,000 Characters. Part I: Non-Musical Plays, 2 vols. (Metuchen, N.J.: Scarecrow Press, 1966) [Identifies characters in Juno and the Paycock, The Plough and the Stars, Within the Gates, and Purple Dust].

868 Shipley, Joseph T., Guide to Great Plays (Washington, D.C.: Public Affairs Press, 1956), pp. 461-5 [Gives synopses, history, significant aspects, and some reviews of Juno and the Paycock, The Plough and the Stars, and The Silver Tassie].

869 Sobel, Bernard, The New Theatre Handbook and Digest of Plays (New York: Crown Publishers, 1959) [Includes synopses of Juno and the Paycock, The Plough and the Stars, and Within the Gates].

870 Sprinchorn, Evert, "Sean O'Casey," in 20th Century Plays in Synopsis (New York: Thomas Y. Crowell, 1965), pp. 239-50 [Gives synopses of Cock-a-Doodle Dandy, Juno and the Paycock, The Plough and the Stars, and Purple Dust].

871 Swaffer, Hannen, "Sean O'Casey," in Hannen Swaffer's Who's Who (London: Hutchinson, [1929]), pp. 17-18 [Biographical essay].

872 Temple, Ruth Z., and Martin Tucker, eds., "Sean O'Casey," in A Library of Literary Criticism, vol. 2 (New York: Frederick Ungar, 1966), pp. 383-92 [Extracts from writings on O'Casey].

873- Theatre World, 1944- (New York: Crown Publishers, 1945-)
  4   [An annual which gives details of the productions of the year].

875   Ward, A.C., "Sean O'Casey," in Longman Companion to Twentieth Century Literature, 2nd ed. (London: Longman, 1975), p. 391 [Brief biographical and critical essay].

876   Webb, E.T., "Sean O'Casey," in Cassell's Encyclopaedia of World Literature, vol. 3, ed. J. Buchanan-Brown (London: Cassell, 1973), p. 251 [Brief biographical and critical essay].

877   Webster's Biographical Dictionary (Springfield, Mass.:   G. & C. Merriam, 1966), p. 1113 [Introductory information].

878   Who Was Who 1961-1970 (London: Adam & Charles Black, 1972), pp. 847-8 [Brief entry].

879   Who Was Who in the Theatre 1912-1976 (Detroit, Mich.:   Gale Research Company, 1978), vol. 3, pp. 1826-7 [Brief entry].

B. BOOKS WHOLLY DEVOTED TO O'CASEY

880 Achilles, Jochen, Drama als problematische Form: Der Wandel
zu nichtrealistischer Gestaltungsweise im Werk Sean O'Caseys.
SLRAAA, no. 16 (Frankfurt and Bern: Lang, 1979). Reviewed
by Heinz Kosok in Irish University Review, 10 (Spring 1980),
162-5. [Deals with the change from the predominantly "realistic" style of O'Casey's early plays to the predominantly "non-
realistic" form of the later ones.]

882 Armstrong, William A., Sean O'Casey. Writers and Their Work
(Harlow, Essex: Longman for the British Council, 1967; rpt.
1971). Reviewed by Johannes Hedberg in Moderna Språk
(Stockholm), 61 (1967), 394-6. [Biography and assessment
of O'Casey's work, relating the man to the period in which
he lived.]

884 Atkinson, Brooks, Sean O'Casey from Times Past, ed. Robert
G. Lowery (London: Macmillan, 1981; New York: Barnes
and Noble, 1982) [Anthology of Atkinson's writings on O'Casey].

885 _____, ed., "Introduction," in The Sean O'Casey Reader:
Plays, Autobiographies, Opinions (New York: St. Martin's
Press; London: Macmillan, 1968), pp. xi-xxiv ["O'Casey's
Communism had a flamboyant style"].

886 Ayling, Ronald, "Preface," in Blasts and Benedictions: Articles
and Stories by Sean O'Casey (London: Macmillan; New York:
St. Martin's Press, 1967), pp. ix-xix [Clarifies some of the
views held by O'Casey and shows the consistency and honesty
with which he maintained them. The Preface to the German
edition of the book is completely different from this one].

887 _____, Continuity and Innovation in Sean O'Casey's Drama:
A Critical Monograph. Salsburg Studies in English Literature,
no. 23 (Salsburg: Institut für Englische Sprache und Literatur; New York: Humanities Press, 1976). Reviewed by John
O'Riordan in Sean O'Casey Review, 3 (Fall 1976), 89-90; and
by R.W. Ingram in Canadian Journal of Irish Studies, 2 (Dec
1976), 77-8. [Contents: Chap. I: Recurrent Patterns in
O'Casey's Drama; Chap. II: Early Dramatic Experiments;
Chap. III: Expressionism, Epic Theatre, and O'Casey's Further Experiments; Appendix: A Note on O'Casey's Manuscripts
and His Working Methods.]

890 _____, ed., Sean O'Casey. Modern Judgements Series (London: Macmillan, 1969). Reviewed in Times Literary Supplement (London), (6 Mar 1969), p. 228; in Economist (London), (19 Apr 1969) pp. 79–80; by John O'Riordan in Tribune (London), 33 (26 Sep 1969) 14; by Seamus Treacy in Irish Democrat (London), (Sep 1969) p. 2; by Austin Clarke in Irish Times (Dublin), (12 July 1969) p. 8; by Brendan Kennelly in Hibernia (Dublin), 33 (25 Apr 1969), 18; by Saros Cowasjee in Dublin Magazine, 8 (Summer–Autumn 1970) 121–3; by Heinz Kosok in Die Neueren Sprachen, 8 (1969) 415–16; and by Bernard Benstock in Contemporary Literature, 13 (Winter 1972), 116–28. [Contents: Ronald Ayling, "Introduction"; Herbert Coston, "Prelude to Playwriting"; P.S. O'Hegarty, "A Dramatist of New-born Ireland"; A.E. Malone, "O'Casey's Photographic Realism"; James Agate, "Juno and the Paycock and The Plough and the Stars"; Denis Johnston, "Sean O'Casey: An Appreciation"; W.B. Yeats, "The Silver Tassie: A Letter"; Charles Morgan, "The Silver Tassie"; Bernard Shaw, "Letter to the Producer of The Silver Tassie"; Bonamy Dobrée, "Sean O'Casey and the Irish Drama"; Una Ellis-Fermor, "Poetry in Revolt"; John Gassner, "The Prodigality of Sean O'Casey"; Jacques Barzun, "O'Casey at Your Bedside"; A.G. Stock, "The Heroic Image: Red Roses for Me"; William A. Armstrong, "Sean O'Casey, W.B. Yeats and the Dance of Life"; John Jordan, "Illusion and Actuality in the Later O'Casey"; Robert Hogan, "In Sean O'Casey's Golden Days"; G. Wilson Knight, "Ever a Fighter: The Drums of Father Ned"; Katharine Worth, "O'Casey's Dramatic Symbolism"; Jack Lindsay, "Sean O'Casey as a Socialist Artist"; Hubert Nicholson, "O'Casey's Horn of Plenty"; Padraic Colum, "Sean O'Casey's Narratives"; Marvin Magalaner, "O'Casey's Autobiography"; David Krause, "A Self-Portrait of the Artist as a Man"; and Hugh MacDiarmid, "Slàinte Chùramach, Seán."]

911 Băleanu, Andrei, "Prefată," Sean O'Casey: Teatru (Bucureşti: Editura pentru Literatură Universală, 1967), pp. 5-14 [Introduction to O'Casey's Collected Plays].

912 Barnish, Valerie L., Notes on Sean O'Casey's "Juno and the Paycock." Study-Aid Series (London: Methuen Educational, 1971) [Introductory criticism].

913 Benstock, Bernard, Paycock and Others: Sean O'Casey's World (Dublin: Gill and Macmillan; New York: Barnes and Noble, 1976). Reviewed by Vivian Mercier in Times Literary Supplement (London), (13 Aug 1976), p. 1006; by Augustine Martin in Financial Times (London), (21 Jan 1977), p. 11; by Irene Haugh in Irish Times (Dublin), (23 Mar 1976), p. 8; by John O'Riordan in Irish Press (Dublin), (27 Mar 1976), p. 7; by Tomas MacAnna in Hibernia (Dublin), (22 Oct 1976), p. 20; by Gabriel Fallon in Sunday Independent (Dublin), (14 Mar

1976), p. 18; by Kane Archer in Books Ireland (Dublin), no. 7 (Oct 1976), 175; and John O'Riordan in Sean O'Casey Review, 3 (Fall 1976), 91-2. [A treatment of the O'Casey character types.]

922 _____, Sean O'Casey. Irish Writers Series (Lewisburg, Pa.: Bucknell University Press, 1970) [Critical assessment].

923 Besier, Werner, Der Junge Sean O'Casey: Eine Studie zum Verhältnis von Kunst und Gesellschaft (Bern: Lang, 1974) [Deals with the younger O'Casey and studies the relation between his art and society].

924 Boas, Guy, "Introduction," in "Juno and the Paycock" and "The Plough and the Stars" by Sean O'Casey (London: Macmillan, 1948; New York: St. Martin's Press, 1965), pp. vii-xii [Discusses the two plays and provides a "Biographical Note"].

925 Brandstädter, Otto, "Einleitung," in Sean O'Casey: Ausgewählte Dramen (Berlin and Weimar: Aufbau, 1966), pp. vii-xxxi [Introduction to O'Casey's plays].

926 Cowasjee, Saros, O'Casey (Edinburgh and London: Oliver & Boyd, 1966; New York: Barnes & Noble, 1967). Reviewed in Contemporary Review (London), 208 (June 1966) 335; in Sunday Statesman (Calcutta), (4 Sep 1966) p. 10; by Ronald Mason in The Shavian (London), 3 (Winter 1966-7) 31; in British Book News (London), (Sep 1966) p. 696; by P.F. Byrne in Evening Herald (Dublin), (4 June 1966) p. 8; in Times Literary Supplement (London), (23 June 1966) p. 561; and by Ronald Ayling in Dublin Magazine, 5 (Autumn-Winter 1966) 100. [Biography and critical study.]

934 _____, Sean O'Casey: The Man Behind the Plays (Edinburgh and London: Oliver & Boyd, 1963; New York: St. Martin's Press, 1964; rev. paperback ed., Oliver & Boyd, 1965) [Derived from a dissertation]. Reviewed in Times Literary Supplement (London), (21 Nov 1963) p. 943; by Denis Johnston in Modern Drama, 8 (Dec 1965) 344-5; by Carmela Moya in Etudes anglaises (Paris), 20 (Apr-June 1967) 160-4; by Mícheál O hAodha in Irish Press (Dublin), (23 Nov 1963) p. 12; by Ronald Ayling in Kilkenny Magazine, 2 (Spring-Summer 1964) 69-82; by Gabriel Fallon in Evening Press (Dublin), (26 Oct 1963) p. 9; in Plays and Players (London), 11 (Dec 1963) 22; in Current Literature (London), no. 657 (Jan 1964) 3; in Kirkus Reviews, 32 (15 Feb 1964) 194; by Brooks Atkinson in New York Times (14 Apr 1964) p. 34; and by Brendan Kennelly in Hermathena (Dublin), 98 (Spring 1964) 114-5. [A study of O'Casey's plays, relating them to his life.]

946 Da Rin, Doris, Sean O'Casey. World Dramatists Series (New

York: Frederick Ungar, 1976). Reviewed by Ronald Rollins in Sean O'Casey Review, 3 (Spring 1977), 169-70. [A study of the major 12 plays.]

948 Druzina, M.V., Shon O'Keĭsi--Dramaturg (Moscow: Znanie, 1963) [A critical study of O'Casey, concentrating on his political views].

949 Fallon, Gabriel, Sean O'Casey: The Man I Knew (London: Routledge & Kegan Paul; Boston: Little, Brown, 1965). Reviewed in Times (London), (5 Aug 1965) p. 13; in Times Literary Supplement (London), (8 July 1965) p. 576; by Nigel Dennis in Sunday Telegraph (London), (6 June 1965) p. 16 [see reply by John O'Riordan, "Could O'Casey Write" (13 June 1965) p. 7]; by Brendan Kennelly in Spectator (London), 215 (2 July 1965) 18; by Robert Greacen in Listener (London), 73 (17 June 1965) 906-9; by Desmond MacNamara in New Statesman (London), 70 (23 July 1965) 129; by Hilary Pyle in Review of English Studies, 17 (May 1966) 227-8; by Augustine Martin in Irish Times (Dublin), (19 June 1965) p. 8; by Francis Mac-Manus in Irish Press (Dublin), (10 June 1965) p. 13; by Ronald Ayling in Dublin Magazine, 4 (Autumn-Winter 1965) 69-82 [see Fallon's reply (Autumn-Winter) 82]; by Ulick O'Connor in Dublin Magazine, 4 (Autumn-Winter 1965) 83-9; by Brian O'Doherty in Book Week (19 Sep 1965) p. 27; by Ronald Ayling in Massachusetts Review, 7 (Summer 1966) 603-12; by Stephen P. Ryan in America (N.Y.), 113 (16 Oct 1965) 444; by Robert Warnock in Quarterly Journal of Speech, 52 (1965) 207-8; by Carmela Moya in Etudes anglaises (Paris), 20 (Apr-June 1967) 160-4; and by Walter Starkie in New York Times Book Review (24 Oct 1965) p. 10. [Recollections of O'Casey.]

969 Frayne, John P., Sean O'Casey. Columbia Essays on Modern Writers (New York: Columbia University Press, 1976). Reviewed by Barbara Brothers in Sean O'Casey Review, 3 (Spring 1977), 170-2; and by John Ditsky in University of Windsor Review, 13 (Fall-Winter 1977), 92.

972 Gassner, George, "Introduction: Genius Without Fetters," in Selected Plays of Sean O'Casey (New York: George Braziller, 1954), pp. v-xxi.

973 Gjorova, Sevelina, "Ubežište za presledvanata istina [Refuge for the persecuted truth]," Šon O'Kejsi: Červeni rozi za men [Red Roses for Me] (Sofia: Narodna kultura, 1972), pp. 128-36.

974 Goldstone, Herbert, In Search of Community: The Achievement of Sean O'Casey (Cork and Dublin: Mercier Press, 1972). Reviewed by Augustine Martin in Sean O'Casey Review, 1

(Fall 1974), 39-41; by C. D[esmond] G[reaves] in Irish Democrat (London), (Nov 1974), p. 2; and by Heinz Kosok in Literatur in Wissenschaft und Unterricht 9 (1976), 68-70. [A study of O'Casey's plays.]

978 Greaves, C. Desmond, Sean O'Casey: Politics and Art (London: Lawrence & Wishart; Atlantic Highlands, N.J.: Humanities Press, 1979). Reviewed by R[obert] H[ogan] in Journal of Irish Literature, 9 (Sep 1980), 104-6; by Heinz Kosok in Irish University Review (Dublin), 10 (Spring 1980), 162-5; by Robert G. Lowery in Sean O'Casey Review, 6 (1980), 87-9; by Kane Archer in Books Ireland (Dublin), no. 38 (Nov 1979), 194; by Jack Mitchell in O'Casey Annual (London), no. 1 (1982), 195-211; and by Robert G. Lowery in Clio, 9, no. 3 (1980), 486. [A study of the political and social aspects of O'Casey's life and work.]

985 Hayley, Barbara, Notes on "Juno and the Paycock" [by] Sean O'Casey. York Notes (London: Longman; Beirut: York Press, 1981) [A study guide].

986 Hogan, Robert, The Experiments of Sean O'Casey (New York: St. Martin's Press, 1960). Reviewed by Clayton Garrison in Quarterly Journal of Speech, 47 (1960), 312-13; by Kevin Sullivan in Nation (N.Y.), 192 (29 Apr 1961), 375-6; by Harold Clurman in Saturday Review (N.Y.), 43 (5 Nov 1960), 31, 48; by Denis Johnston in Modern Drama, 4 (Dec 1961), 324-8; by Vivian Mercier in Hudson Review, 13 (Winter 1960), 631-6; and by Alec Reid in Drama Survey, 3 (May 1963), 155-64. [Deals with O'Casey's theatrical technique.]

993 Hunt, Hugh, Sean O'Casey. Gill's Irish Lives (Dublin: Gill and Macmillan, 1980). Reviewed by Kane Archer in Books Ireland (Dublin), no. 49 (Dec 1980), 236; and by Robert G. Lowery in Sean O'Casey Review, 7 (1981), 26-9. [Biography.]

996 Kilroy, Thomas, ed., Sean O'Casey: A Collection of Critical Essays (Englewood Cliffs, N.J.: Prentice-Hall, 1975). Reviewed by John O'Riordan in Sean O'Casey Review, 2 (Fall 1975), 82-3 and in Irish Press (Dublin), (29 Mar 1975), p. 6; by Maureen Murphy in College Literature, 4 (Spring 1977), 102-4; by Milton Levin in Eire-Ireland, 10 (Winter 1975), 150-1; and by Keith S. Felton in Los Angeles Times, (23 Mar 1975), pp. 1, 11. [Contents: Thomas Kilroy, "Introduction"; Lady Gregory, "Journals"; Roger McHugh, "The Legacy of Sean O'Casey"; Raymond Williams, "Sean O'Casey"; John Arden, "Ecce Hobo Sapiens: O'Casey's Theatre"; Ronald Ayling, "Sean O'Casey's Dublin Trilogy"; David Krause, "The Antiheroic Vision"; Yeats, O'Casey, and Shaw, "The Silver Tassie: Letters"; Robert Hogan, "In Sean O'Casey's Golden

Days"; G. Wilson Knight, "Ever a Fighter: The Drums of Father Ned"; Bernard Benstock, "The O'Casey Touch"; Seamus Deane, "Irish Politics and O'Casey's Theatre"; John Jordan, "The Indignation of Sean O'Casey"; Samuel Beckett, "The Essential and the Incidental."]

1002 Kleiman, Carol, Sean O'Casey's Bridge of Vision: Four Essays on Structure and Perspective (Toronto: University of Toronto Press, 1982) [Concentrating on The Silver Tassie and Red Roses for Me, shows how O'Casey's plays bridge two radically innovative theatres: the Expressionist and the Absurd].

1003 Koslow, Jules, The Green and the Red: Sean O'Casey, the Man and His Plays (New York: Golden Griffin Books, 1950). Reprinted as Sean O'Casey: The Man and His Plays (New York: Citadel Press, 1966). Reviewed by Harold Clurman in New York Times Book Review, (10 Dec 1950), p. 5; by Herbert Goldstone in Wisconsin Studies in Contemporary Literature, 8 (Summer 1967), 468-72; and by Allys Dwyer Vergara in Renascence, 4 (Autumn 1951), 72-4. [A commentary on the social and political aspects of O'Casey's plays.]

1007 Kosok, Heinz, Sean O'Casey: Das dramatische Werk (Berlin: Erich Schmidt, 1972). Reviewed by Paul F. Botheroyd in Irish University Review (Dublin), 4 (Autumn 1974), 293-4; by H.M. Klein in Notes and Queries (Oxford), 21 (1974), 389-91; by K.P.S. Jochum in Journal of English and Germanic Philology (Urbana), 73 (1974), 144-6; by H.C.C. in Year's Work in English Studies, 1972 (London), 53 (1975), 406; in English and American Studies in German (Tübingen), (1974), 109-12; by Hermann Rasche in Erasmus (Darmstadt), 26 (1974), 867-9; by Uwe Multhaup in German Studies (Tübingen), 7, Section III, no. 2 (1974), 197-9; by Günter Ahrends in Archiv für das Studium der neueren Sprachen und Literaturen (Braunschweig), 211 (1974), 158-62; by Christiane Mans in Literatur in Wissenschaft und Unterricht (Kiel), 6 (1973), 204-6; by Joachim Krehayn in Deutsche Literaturzeitung (Berlin), 93 (Oct-Nov 1972), 846-9; by Gerd Rohmann in Anglia (Tübingen), 90 (1972), 553-5; in Neuer Bücherdienst (Vienna), no. 19 (Spring 1972), 18-19; by Erdmann Steinmetz in Buchanzeiger für Öffentliche Büchereien (Reutlingen), 25 (July 1972), 293; in Neue Zürcher Zeitung, no. 255 (4 June 1972), p. 54; by R. Krohn in Wissenschaftlicher Literaturanzeiger (Freiburg), 11 (Sep 1972), 125; in Deutsche Bibliographie: Das deutsche Buch (Frankfurt), no. 5 (1972), 728-9; by C. Tindemans in Streven (Antwerp), (1 Nov 1972), 208; by Martin Esslin in Die Welt (Hamburg), no. 87 (12 Apr 1973), 10; and by G. Seehans in Die Deutsche Bühne (Darmstadt), 44 (Jan 1973), 28. [A study of all O'Casey's plays.]

1027 Krause, David, Sean O'Casey and His World (London: Thames
      and Hudson; New York: Scribner's, 1976). Reviewed by
      Tony Butler in Evening Herald (Dublin), (4 Oct 1976), p. 9
      [See reply by Krause, (26 Nov 1976), p. 8; and counter-
      reply by Butler, (3 Dec 1976), p. 14]; by W.J. McCormack
      in Times (London), (30 Sep 1976), p. 8; by Augustine Martin
      in Financial Times (London), (21 Jan 1977), p. 11; by Denis
      Donoghue in Spectator (London), (21 Aug 1976), p. 21 [See
      letter by John O'Riordan, (28 Aug 1976), p. 12]; by Kane
      Archer in Books Ireland (Dublin), no. 7 (Oct 1976), 175;
      and by John O'Riordan in Library Review (Glasgow), 25 (Au-
      tumn 1976), 280-1. [A pictorial biography.]

1037 _____, Sean O'Casey: The Man and His Work (London:
      MacGibbon & Kee; New York: Macmillan, 1960; Collier Books,
      1962; London, rpt. 1967; enl. ed. New York: Macmillan;
      London: Collier Macmillan, 1975). Reviewed by V.S. Prit-
      chett in New Statesman (London), 59 (16 Apr 1960) 560; by
      Micheál MacLiammóir in Sunday Times (London) (27 Mar 1960)
      p. 26; by Louis MacNeice in Observer (London), (27 Mar
      1960) 23; by Charles Hamblett in Lilliput (London), 46 (June
      1960) 66; by Roy Walker in Listener (London), 63 (14 Apr
      1960), 672, 675; by Alan Brien in Spectator (London), 204
      (8 Apr 1960) 516-17; by Ewan Butler in Time and Tide (Lon-
      don), 41 (1960), 582-3; by Valentine Iremonger in Drama
      (London), no. 57 (Summer 1960), 43-4; in Times Literary
      Supplement (London), (8 Apr 1960) p. 220; in Times (Lon-
      don), (30 Mar 1960) p. 13; by Gerard Fay in Manchester
      Guardian (8 Apr 1960) p. 15; by Laurence Thompson in
      News Chronicle (London), (30 Mar 1960) p. 6; by W.A. Dar-
      lington in Daily Telegraph (London), (28 Mar 1960) p. 15; by
      H.A.L. Craig in Irish Times (Dublin), (30 Mar 1960) p. 8;
      by Robert W. Caswell in Studies (Dublin), 49 (Summer 1960)
      212-14; by Conor Sweeney in Comhar (Dublin), (Eanáir 1961),
      28-30; in Newsweek (N.Y.), 66 (8 Aug 1960) 77; by Alan
      Pryce-Jones in New York Herald Tribune Book Review (7
      Aug 1960) p. 3; by Brooks Atkinson in New York Times Book
      Review (7 Aug 1960) p. 1; by Vivian Mercier in Hudson Re-
      view 13 (Winter 1960) 631-6; by Kevin Sullivan in Nation
      (N.Y.), 192 (29 Apr 1961) 375-6; by Harold Clurman in Sat-
      urday Review of Literature (N.Y.), 43 (5 Nov 1960) 31, 48;
      by Denis Johnston in Modern Drama, 4 (Dec 1961) 324-8; by
      John O'Riordan in Books and Bookmen (London), 5 (May 1960)
      26; by John O'Riordan in Tribune (London), 31 (2 June 1967)
      11; by Ernst Schoen in Theater der Zeit, 15 (Mar 1960), 35-
      64; by Gerald Weales in Sewanee Review, 84 (Winter 1976),
      185-90; and by Alec Reid in Drama Survey, 3 (May 1963),
      155-64. [A critical study that concentrates on O'Casey's
      tragicomic and comic techniques.]

1065 _____, A Self-Portrait of the Artist as a Man: Sean O'Casey's
Letters (Dublin: Dolmen Press; London: Oxford University
Press, 1968). Reviewed in Times Literary Supplement (Lon-
don), (28 Nov 1968), p. 1333. See reply by Phiannon Good-
ing, ibid., (12 Dec 1968), p. 1409. [Uses quotations from
O'Casey's letters to illuminate O'Casey the man.]

1068 _____, and Robert G. Lowery, eds., Sean O'Casey: Centenary Essays (Gerrards Cross, England: Colin Smythe; New
York: Barnes and Noble, 1981). Reviewed by "Feioreanach"
in Irish Democrat (London), (May 1981), p. 7; by John Kav-
anagh in Irish Post (London), (14 Mar 1981), p. 4; by John
Kelly in British Book News, (Apr 1982), p. 255; by Micheál
O hAodha in Irish Times (Dublin), (11 Apr 1981), p. 12; by
Denis Johnston in Irish Press (Dublin), (19 Feb 1981), p.
10; by Kane Archer in Books Ireland (Dublin), no. 52 (Apr
1981), 62-3; by James J. McAuley in Studies (Dublin), 70
(Winter 1981), 360-2; by Tomás MacAnna in Sunday Tribune
(Dublin), (15 Feb 1981), p. 20; by Martin A. Drury in Irish
University Review (Dublin), 11 (Autumn 1981), 254-5; by
Renée Gibbons in Daily World (N.Y.), (25 Apr 1981), p. 9;
by Bricriu Dolan in Journal of Irish Literature, 10 (May 1981),
132; by Barbara Brothers in American Committee for Irish
Studies Newsletter, 12 (Apr 1982), 5; and by Bobby L.
Smith in Irish Literary Supplement, 1 (Spring 1982), p. 9.
[Contents: Robert G. Lowery, "Sean O'Casey: A Chronol-
ogy"; Ronald Ayling, "Sean O'Casey and the Abbey Theatre,
Dublin"; Bernard Benstock, "Sean O'Casey and/or James
Joyce"; Mary FitzGerald, "Sean O'Casey and Lady Gregory:
The Record of a Friendship"; David Krause, "The Druidic
Affinities of O'Casey and Yeats"; Robert G. Lowery, "Sean
O'Casey: Art and Politics"; William J. Maroldo, "Earliest
Youth: Pristine Catholicism and Green Patriotism in O'Casey's
Irish Books"; Alan Simpson, "The Unholy Trinity: A Simple
Guide to Holy Ireland c. 1880-1980"; Stanley Weintraub,
"Shaw's Other Keegan: O'Casey and G.B.S."; and Robert
G. Lowery, "Sean O'Casey at the Abbey Theatre."]

1082 Lowery, Robert G., ed., Essays on Sean O'Casey's Autobiographies (London: Macmillan; New York: Barnes and Noble,
1981). Reviewed by John Russell Brown in Times Literary
Supplement (London), (14 Aug 1981), p. 935; by Ned Chaillet in Times (London), (21 May 1981), p. 15; and by Bobby
L. Smith in Irish Literary Supplement, 1 (Spring 1982), p.
9. [Contents: Ronald F. Ayling, "The Origin and Evolution
of a Dublin Epic"; Deirdre Henchy, "Dublin in the Age of
O'Casey: 1880-1910"; Robert G. Lowery, "The Development
of Sean O'Casey's Weltanschauung"; Raymond J. Porter,
"O'Casey and Pearse"; Michael O'Maoláin, trans. by Maureen
Murphy, "That Raid and What Went With It"; E.H. Mikhail,

"Bernard Shaw and Sean O'Casey: An Unrecorded Friendship"; William J. Maroldo, "'A Kinda Trinitarian Soul': Sean O'Casey and the Art of Autobiography"; David Krause, "On Fabrications and Epiphanies in O'Casey's Autobiographies"; Carmela Moya, "The Autobiographies as Epic"; and Bernard Benstock, "Sean O'Casey as Wordsmith."]

1086 McCann, Sean, ed., The World of Sean O'Casey, Four Square Books (London: The New English Library, 1966). Reviewed by Hugh Leonard in Plays and Players (London), 14 (July 1967) 55-6; by Ronald Ayling in Tribune (London), 30 (23 Dec 1966) p. 16 [see Anthony Butler's reply (6 Jan 1967) p. 8, and Ayling's counter-reply (20 Jan 1967) p. 8; also letter to the Editor by John O'Riordan (20 Jan 1967) p. 8]; and by Mary Bergh in Irish Democrat (London), (Jan 1967) p. 7. [Contents: Sean McCann, "Introduction"; Anthony Butler, "The Early Background"; Sean McCann, "The Girl He Left Behind"; R.M. Fox, "Civil War and Peace"; Donal Dorcey, "The Great Occasions"; Beatrice Coogan, "Pink Icing"; Anthony Butler, "The Abbey Daze"; Tim Pat Coogan, "The Exile"; Niall Carroll, "The Bonfire"; David Krause, "Towards the End"; N.D. Emerson, "Notes on a Sermon"; Colm Cronin, ed. "The O'Casey I Knew"; John O'Donovan, "The Big Three"; Gabriel Fallon, "The Man in the Plays"; Kevin Casey, "The Excitements and the Disappointments"; Ulick O'Connor, "The Autobiographies of Sean O'Casey"; and Catherine Rynne, "O'Casey in His Letters."]

1093 Malone, Maureen, The Plays of Sean O'Casey, with a Preface by Harry T. Moore (Carbondale and Edwardsville: Southern Illinois University Press; London and Amsterdam: Feffer & Simons, 1969). Reviewed by David Krause in Modern Drama, 13 (Dec 1970), 336-40; and by C. Tindemans and Streven (Antwerp), (1 Nov 1972), 208. [Concentrates on "the political and sociological material from which he shaped his plays."]

1096 Margulies, Martin B., The Early Life of Sean O'Casey (Dublin: Dolmen Press, 1970). Reviewed by John O'Riordan in Tribune (London) 35 (9 Jul 1971), p. 11; by R.B. Marriott in Stage and Television Today (London), (12 Aug 1971), p. 8; by Sean McMahon in Irish Press (Dublin), (15 May 1971), p. 12; and by John O'Riordan in Library Review (Glasgow), 23 (Spring 1972), 211-13. [Reveals O'Casey's youth and early manhood in Dublin.]

1101 Metscher, Thomas, Sean O'Caseys dramatischer Stil (Braunschweig: Georg Westermann, 1968). Reviewed by Elisabeth Freundlich in Das Argument, 12 (9-10 Dec 1970), 755-7. [A comprehensive study.]

1103 Mikhail, E.H., and John O'Riordan, eds., The Sting and the Twinkle: Conversations with Sean O'Casey (London: Macmillan; New York: Barnes & Noble, 1974). Reviewed by Denis Donoghue in Times Higher Education Supplement (London), (16 Aug 1974), p. 12 [See reply by John O'Riordan, (23 Aug 1974), p. 8]; by Jack Sutherland in Morning Star (London), (23 Jul 1974), p. 4; in Guardian (London), (30 May 1974), p. 11; by Robert Eagle in Books and Bookmen (London), (Jul 1974), 104; in British Book News, (Sep 1974), 625; by B.A. Young in Financial Times (London), (25 June 1974), p. 3 [See reply by John O'Riordan, (10 Jul 1974), p. 2]; by Elizabeth Coxhead in Lady (London), (1 Aug 1974), 160; by R.B. M[ariott] in Stage and Television Today (London), (22 Aug 1974), 12; by Raymond Mortimer in Sunday Times (London), (4 Aug 1974), p. 35; in Tablet (London), (17 Aug 1974), 796; in Theatrefacts: International Theatre Reference (London), no. 4 (Nov 1974-Jan 1975), 18; by C[laire] N[ash] in Southgate Gazette (London), (11 Jul 1974), p. 13; by C. D[esmond] G[reaves] in Irish Democrat (London), (Nov 1974), p. 2; by J.C. Trewin in Birmingham Post, (8 June 1974); by Carol Coulter in Hibernia (Dublin), (9 Aug 1974), 18; by Adrian Vale in Irish Times (Dublin), (8 June 1974), p. 12; by John O'Donovan in Irish Press (Dublin), (27 Jul 1974), p. 6; by John McCann in Sunday Press (Dublin), (30 June 1974), p. 27 [See reply by John O'Riordan, (7 Jul 1974), p. 18]; by Mary MacGoris in Irish Independent (Dublin), (27 Jul 1974), p. 6; by Tony Butler in Evening Herald (Dublin), (10 June 1974), p. 5; in English, (Autumn 1975), 121; in Choice, 7 (Jan 1975), 1634; by Robert G. Lowery in Sean O'Casey Review, 1 (Fall 1974), 38-9; by Errol Durbach in Canadian Journal of Irish Studies, 1 (June 1975), 56-7; and by Gerald Weales in Sewanee Review, 84 (Winter 1976), 189-90. [Interviews and Recollections by R.M. Fox, Lady Gregory, Joseph Holloway, Constance Vaughan, Eileen Crowe, Beverley Nichols, Rupert Croft-Cooke, George Walter Bishop, Leslie Rees, J.L. Hodson, Bosley Crowther, Lillian Gish, Maurice Browne, Ria Mooney, Eileen O'Casey, Dom Wulstan Phillipson, Allan Chappelow, Laurence Thompson, Boris Izakov, Robert Emmett Ginna, Joseph Stein, Paul Shyre, Donal Foley, Don Ross, Barry Fitzgerald, Saros Cowasjee, W.J. Weatherby, David Phethean, Aidan Hennigan, Hugh Webster, Niall Carroll, Brooks Atkinson, John O'Riordan, Jack Levett, Angus Drummond, John Howard, Gjon Mili, David Krause, "Mandrake," Gerard Fay, Brooks Atkinson, and Harold Clurman.]

1132 Mitchell, Jack, The Essential O'Casey: A Study of the Twelve Major Plays of Sean O'Casey (New York: International Publishers; Berlin: Seven Seas Books, 1980). Reviewed by Ronald Ayling in Irish Literary Supplement, 1 (Fall 1982), p. 8;

by Robert G. Lowery in Daily World (N.Y.), (15 Jan 1982),
p. 9; and by Robert G. Lowery in Political Affairs (N.Y.),
(Apr 1982), pp. 20, 40 [see reply by C. Desmond Greaves
and rejoinder by Robert G. Lowery, ibid., Jul 1982, pp. 39-
40].

1138 Nathan, George Jean, "My Very Dear Sean": George Jean Na-
than on Sean O'Casey; Letters and Articles, ed. Patricia
Angelin and Robert G. Lowery (Cranbury, N.J.: Associated
University Presses, 1983).

1139 O'Casey, Eileen, "Clench Your Teeth," in The Harvest Festival:
A Play in Three Acts by Sean O'Casey (New York: New York
Public Library, 1979), pp. ix-x [Foreword to the play; pub-
lished for the first time].

1140 _____, Eileen (London: Macmillan, 1976). Reviewed by W.J.
McCormack in Times (London), (30 Sep 1976), p. 8; by Au-
gustine Martin in Financial Times (London), (21 Jan 1977),
p. 11; by John O'Riordan in Library Review (Glasgow), 25
(Autumn 1976), 280-1; by John Kelly in Sunday Press (Dub-
lin), (3 Oct 1976), p. 23; by Tomas MacAnna in Hibernia
(Dublin), (22 Oct 1976), p. 20; by Kane Archer in Books
Ireland (Dublin), no. 12 (Apr 1977), 65-6; and by John
O'Riordan in Sean O'Casey Review, 3 (Spring 1977), 168.
[A sequel to Eileen O'Casey's Sean, concentrating on her own
life.]

1148 _____, Sean. Edited with an Introduction by J.C. Trewin
(London: Macmillan; N.Y.: Coward-McCann, 1971; London:
Pan Books, 1973). Reviewed by H. Maxton in Listener (30
Dec 1971), 911; in Times Literary Supplement, (5 Nov 1971),
p. 1383; in Observer, (10 Oct 1971), p. 32; by Lorna Reyn-
olds in Hibernia, (22 Oct 1971), p. 16; by Miles Donald in
New Statesman, (15 Oct 1971), 513; by Christopher Murray
in Studies (Dublin), 62, (Summer 1973), 173-7; in Books and
Bookmen, (June 1973), 137; by John O'Riordan in Library Re-
view, (Spring 1972), 211; in Evening Standard, (30 Sep 1971),
p. 19; in Universe, (1 Oct 1971), 6; by Auberon Waugh in
Harpers' Queen, (Oct 1971), 62; by Mary Manning in Irish
Times, (18 Sep 1971), p. 8; by Peter Lennon in Sunday
Times, (3 Oct 1971), p. 42; by Sean Day-Lewis in Daily Telegraph, (30 Sep 1971), p. 12; by Honor Tracy in Sunday Telegraph, (3 Oct 1971), p. 23; by John D. Sheridan in Irish
Independent, (25 Sep 1971), p. 12; by John McCann in Sunday Press, (26 Sep 1971), p. 23; in Sunday Telegraph, (26
Sep 1971), p. 11; by R.B. Marriott in Stage and Television
Today, (30 Sep 1971), 8; in Daily Mirror, (30 Sep 1971), p.
21; by Barbara Lloyd Evans in Birmingham Post, (2 Oct 1971),
p. 11; in Birmingham Evening Mail, (1 Oct 1971), p. 14; by

Allen Wright in The Scotsman, (25 Sep 1971), p. 3; in York-
shire Post, (13 Oct 1971), p. 7; by John O'Riordan in Trib-
une, (22 Oct 1971), p. 14; by Gerald Colgan in Plays and
Players, 19 (Nov 1971), 26; by Don Chapman in Oxford Mail,
(4 Nov 1971), p. 6; by Elizabeth Coxhead in Lady, (23 Dec
1971), 976; by T.D. in Author, (Winter 1971), 177-8; in
Guardian, (6 Oct 1971), p. 8; by P. Adams in Atlantic
Monthly, 229 (Feb 1971), 109; by A. Alvarez in Saturday
Review, (29 Jan 1972), 57; by David H. Greene in Book
World, (6 Feb 1972), 5; by V.S. Pritchett in New York Times
Book Review, (12 Mar 1972), pp. 5, 10; by R.J. Thompson
in Library Journal, (Jan 1972), 66; in Kirkus Reviews, (15
Nov 1971), 1244; in Publishers' Weekly, (6 Dec 1971), 49; in
American Libraries, (Oct 1972), 1015; in Booklist, (15 Mar
1972), 585; in Best Sellers, (15 Jan 1972), 5; in Christian
Century, (2 Feb 1972), 150; by Roderick Nordell in Christian
Science Monitor, (27 Jan 1972), 10; in Choice, (May 1972),
370; by Brooks Atkinson in Critic, (May 1972), 74-6; in Wall
Street Journal, (24 Feb 1972), 16; in South Atlantic Quarterly,
(Winter 1973), 176; by Milton Levin in Eire-Ireland (Autumn
1972), 147-8; by Kathrun G. Boardman in St. Paul Sunday
Pioneer Press, (30 Jan 1972), p. 30; by Richard Watts in
New York Post, (11 Jan 1972), p. 73; by Julian Moynahan in
Washington Post, (1 Feb 1972), p. B1; by Will Wharton in St.
Louis Globe Democrat, (29 Jan 1972); by Barbara Zingman in
Louisville Times, (6 Jan 1972), p. A15; in St. Paul Sunday
Pioneer Press, (30 Jan 1972), p. 30; by Cody Hall in Annis-
ton Star, (30 Jan 1972), p. 4D; by Herbert A. Kenny in
Boston Sunday Globe, (2 Jan 1972), p. A81; by Robert Fa-
herty in Philadelphia Inquirer, (6 Feb 1972), p. 6-H; and
by Ernest Schier in Evening Bulletin, (27 Jan 1972), p. 8.
[O'Casey's widow tells her life with her husband.]

1207 O hAodha, Micheál, ed., The Sean O'Casey Enigma (Dublin and
Cork: Mercier Press, 1980). Reviewed by Martin A. Drury
in Irish University Review (Dublin), 11 (Autumn 1981), 254-
5; by Kane Archer in Books Ireland (Dublin), no. 52 (Apr
1981), 62-3; by Robert G. Lowery in Sean O'Casey Review,
7 (1981), 26-9; and by Michael Kenneally in Irish Literary
Supplement, 1 (Fall 1982), 9. [The Thomas Davis Lectures
by Tomás MacAnna, Denis Johnston, Cyril Cusack, James
Plunkett, C. Desmond Greaves, Hans-Georg Simmgen, Robert
Hogan, Brendan Kennelly, and Greaves, Hans-Georg Simmgen,
Robert Hogan, Brendan Kennelly, and Micheál O hAodha.]

1212 O'Riordan, John, "Introduction," in The Harvest Festival: A
Play in Three Acts by Sean O'Casey (New York: New York
Public Library, 1979), pp. xi-xv [Tells the story of, and
comments on, the play].

1213 Pauli, Manfred, Sean O'Casey: Drama, Poesie, Wirklichkeit
(Berlin: Henschelverlag Kunst und Gesellschaft, 1977). Reviewed by Heinz Zaslawski in Sean O'Casey Review, 4 (Fall
1977), 79-80.

1215 Remizov, B., "The Beginning of the Autobiographical Epic,"
in I Knock at the Door/Pictures in the Hallway (Kiev, 1975),
pp. 426-32 [In Ukrainian].

1216 Rollins, Ronald Gene, Sean O'Casey's Drama: Verisimilitude
and Vision (University: University of Alabama Press, 1979).
Reviewed by Errol Durbach in Modern Drama, 24 (June 1981),
234-6; and by Bobby L. Smith in Sean O'Casey Review, 6
(1980), 85-6. [Concentrates on The Plough and the Stars,
The Silver Tassie, Within the Gates, Cock-a-Doodle Dandy,
and The Drums of Father Ned.]

1219 Sarukhanian, Alla Pavlova, Tvorchestov Shona O'Keisi (Moskva:
Nauka, 1965) [Criticism on O'Casey's work].

1220 Scrimgeour, James R., Sean O'Casey. Twayne English Authors
Series (Boston: Twayne, 1978; London: George Prior, 1979).
Reviewed by Maureen Murphy in O'Casey Annual (London),
no. 1 (1982), 229-31; and by Errol Durbach in Canadian
Journal of Irish Studies, 7 (June 1981), 68-70.

1223 Smith, B.L., O'Casey's Satiric Vision (Kent, Ohio: Kent State
University Press, 1978). Reviewed by Declan Kiberd in Re-
view of English Studies (London), 32 (May 1981), 240-1; by
Martin A. Drury in Irish University Review (Dublin), 10
(Spring 1980), 168-70; by Errol Durbach in Modern Drama,
24 (June 1981), 234-6; and by Barbara Brothers in Sean
O'Casey Review, 6 (1980), 86-7. [Deals with all O'Casey's
plays.]

1228 Stapelberg, Peter, Sean O'Casey und das deutschsprachige Theater (1948-1974): Empirische Untersuchungen zu den Mechanismen der Rezeption eines angloirischen Dramatikers. NSAA,
no. 15 (Frankfurt and Bern: Lang, 1979) [Deals with the
reception of O'Casey's plays in Germany].

1229 Trewin, J.C., "Introduction," in Three More Plays by Sean
O'Casey (London: Macmillan; New York: St. Martin's Press,
1965), pp. vii-xvi [Discusses The Silver Tassie, Purple
Dust, and Red Roses for Me.]

1230 Völker, Klaus, Irisches Theater II: Sean O'Casey. Friedrichs
Dramatiker des Weltheaters, 55 (Velber: Friedrich Verlag,
1968) [Introductory study].

1231 Widmer, Urs, ed., Sean O'Casey: Eine Auswahl aus den Stücken, der Autobiographie und den Aufsätzen (Zürich: Diogenes, 1970), pp. 7-11 [Preface by Heinrich Böll]; pp. 319-27 [Epilogue by Klaus Völker]; pp. 331-46 [Editorial material by Urs Widmer].

1232 Wilson, Donald Douglas, Sean O'Casey's Tragi-Comic Vision (New York: Revisionist Press, 1976) [Concentrates on Nannie's Night Out, The Plough and the Stars, The Silver Tassie, Within the Gates, and Red Roses for Me].

1233 Winkler, Burchard, Wirkstrategische Verwendung populärliterarischer Elemente in Sean O'Caseys dramatischem Werk unter besonderer Berücksichtigung des Melodramas. Göppinger Akademische Beiträge, Nr. 104 (Göppingen: Alfred Kümmerle, 1977).

1234 Wittig, Kurt, Sean O'Casey als Dramatiker: Ein Beitrag zum Nachkriegsdrama Irlands (Leipzig: Fritz Scharf, 1937). Reviewed by A.B. in Archiv für d. Studium d. neueren Sprachen (Herrig), 173 (1937), 267; and by Karl Arns in Anglia Beiblatt, 49 (1937), 273-4. [Deals with O'Casey as a dramatist, and considers his contribution to the post-War drama in Ireland.]

1237 Yamaguchi, K., and F. Sakata, eds., Sean O'Casey: Toreador (Tokyo: Kôbunsha, 1967) [Introduction and notes to selections from Blasts and Benedictions, ed. Ronald Ayling].

1238 Zaslawski, Heinz, Die Werke Sean O'Caseys, unter Besonderer Berücksichtigung Seiner Zweiten Periode (Wien, 1949) [Concentrates on O'Casey's second period.]

1239   Achilles, Jochen, "Sean O'Casey's and Denis Johnston's National
        Plays: Two Dramatic Approaches to Irish Society," in Stud-
        ies in Anglo-Irish Literature, ed. Heinz Kosok (Bonn: Bou-
        vier, 1982), pp. 269-77 [Discusses O'Casey and Irish National-
        ism in the Dublin Trilogy].

1240   Adams, Michael, Censorship: The Irish Experience (University:
        University of Alabama Press, 1968), pp. 150-1 [Correspond-
        ence in the Irish Times in May 1957 on banning O'Casey's
        books in Ireland.]

1241   Agate, James, The Amazing Theatre (London: George G. Har-
        rap, 1939; rpt. New York: Benjamin Blom, 1969), p. 135
        [O'Casey's humor and trenchancy]; p. 181 [O'Casey on Lon-
        don sociology]; p. 194 [His Paycock]; p. 210 [His supremacy];
        p. 231 [On unintelligibility]; p. 275 [The Plough and the
        Stars].

1242   _____, The Contemporary Theatre, 1925. With an Introduc-
        tion by C. E. Montague (London: Leonard Parsons, 1926;
        rpt. New York: Benjamin Blom, 1969), pp. 114-18 [Juno and
        the Paycock at the Royalty Theatre, London].

1243   _____, The Contemporary Theatre, 1926. With an Introduc-
        tion by Arnold Bennett (London: Leonard Parsons, 1927;
        rpt. New York: Benjamin Blom, 1969), pp. 45-9 [The Plough
        and the Stars at the Fortune Theatre, London].

1244   _____, First Nights (London: Ivor Nicholson and Watson,
        1934; rpt. New York: Benjamin Blom, 1971), pp. 271-6
        [Within the Gates at the Royalty Theatre, London].

1245   _____, The Later Ego (New York: Crown Publishers, 1951),
        pp. 75, 89 [Comments on Juno and the Paycock and The
        Plough and the Stars]; p. 285 [Comments on Red Roses for
        Me]; pp. 309-10 [Replies to O'Casey's article "The People
        and the Theatre"]; p. 590 [Regards the whole of the later
        O'Casey as "pretentious twaddle"].

1246   _____, More First Nights (London: Victor Gollancz, 1937;
        rpt. New York: Benjamin Blom, 1969), p. 253 [The Silver

Tassie]; p. 352 [Arthur Sinclair "needs an O'Casey to stand up to him"].

1247 _____, My Theatre Talks (London: Arthur Barker, 1933; rpt. New York: Benjamin Blom, 1971), p. 90 [The rejection of O'Casey's plays]; p. 150 [The Plough and the Stars]; pp. 222-3 [The Silver Tassie].

1248 _____, Red Letter Nights (London: Jonathan Cape, 1944; rpt. New York: Benjamin Blom, 1969), pp. 230-3 [Juno and the Paycock at the Royalty Theatre, London]; pp. 233-6 [The Plough and the Stars at the Fortune Theatre, London].

1249 Allen, John, "Sean O'Casey," in Masters of British Drama (London: Dennis Dobson, 1957), pp. 154-69 [General criticism on O'Casey's plays and Autobiographies].

1250 Allison, Alexander W., et al., eds., Masterpieces of the Drama, 4th ed. (New York: Macmillan, 1979) [Anthology including the text of, and a commentary on, Juno and the Paycock].

1251 Anderson, Maxwell, Off Broadway: Essays About the Theater (New York: William Sloane Associates, 1947), pp. 49-50 [Poetry in O'Casey's plays].

1252 Arden, John, "Sean O'Casey," in To Present the Pretence; Essays on the Theatre and Its Public (London: Eyre Methuen, 1977), p. 24. Reprinted from Observer (London), (27 Sep 1964), p. 37 [O'Casey's later plays are by no means as "rancorous and rhetorically inflated" as Irving Wardle makes out].

1253 Armstrong, William A., "The Irish Point of View: The Plays of Sean O'Casey, Brendan Behan, and Thomas Murphy," in Experimental Drama (London: G. Bell, 1963), pp. 79-93 [Most of O'Casey's plays have been about Irish characters and Irish problems].

1254 _____, ed., Classic Irish Drama (Harmondsworth, Middlesex: Penguin Books, 1964) [Anthology including the text of, and a commentary on, Cock-a-Doodle Dandy. See also "Introduction: The Irish Dramatic Movement"].

1255 Arns, Karl, "Sean O'Casey," in Grundriss der Geschichte der Englischen Literatur von 1832 bis zur Gegenwart (Paderborn: Schoningh, 1941), pp. 217-18 [Brief study].

1256 _____, Literatur und Leben in heutigen England (Leipzig: Emil Rohmkopf, 1933), pp. 114-15 [Comments briefly on the Dublin Trilogy and The Silver Tassie].

1257 Atkinson, Brooks, Broadway (New York: Macmillan, 1974),
      p. 161 [O'Casey and George Jean Nathan]; p. 181 [Juno and
      the Paycock]; p. 183 [The Plough and the Stars]; p. 357
      [O'Casey on Broadway]; p. 362 [Within the Gates]; p. 463
      [Cock-a-Doodle Dandy]; pp. 485-6 [The Plough and the Stars];
      p. 487 [O'Casey on Off-Broadway]; p. 230 [Juno and the
      Paycock and The Plough and the Stars].

1258 _____, Broadway Scrapbook (New York: Theatre Arts, 1947),
      pp. 13-16 [Within the Gates]; pp. 147-51 [Juno and the Pay-
      cock].

1259 Ayling, Ronald, "Patterns of Language and Ritual in Sean
      O'Casey's Drama," in Literature and Folk Culture: Ireland
      and Newfoundland, ed. Alison Feder and Bernice Schrank
      (St. John: Memorial University of Newfoundland, 1977), pp.
      33-56 [O'Casey is above all a musical theatre and a theatre
      of exuberant physical movement and dance].

1260 _____, "Recurrent Patterns in O'Casey's Drama," in Myth
      and Reality in Irish Literature, ed. Joseph Ronsley (Water-
      loo, Ontario: Wilfrid Laurier University Press, 1977), pp.
      265-80 [Most important of O'Casey's recurrent interests is
      his desire to find order and harmony in a world rent by
      physical and spiritual chaos].

1261 _____, "Two Words for Women: A Reassessment of O'Casey's
      Heroines," in Women in Irish Life, Legend and Mythology, ed.
      S. F. Gallagher (Gerrards Cross, Buckinghamshire: Colin
      Smythe, 1982).

1262 Balashov, Peter S., "O'Keisi," in Istoriia angliiskoi literatury
      [The Soviet History of English Literature], Tom 3 (Moskva:
      Izdatel 'stvo Akademii Nauk SSSR, 1958), pp. 627-46 [Gen-
      eral criticism on O'Casey].

1263 Barnet, Sylvan; Morton Berman; and William Burto, eds., The
      Genius of the Irish Theatre. Mentor Books (New York: New
      American Library, 1960) [Anthology including the text of,
      and a commentary on, Purple Dust].

1264 Barrows, Herbert, et al., eds., An Introduction to Literature
      (Boston: Houghton Mifflin, 1959) [Anthology including the
      text of, and a commentary on, Juno and the Paycock].

1265 Beckerman, Bernard, Dynamics of Drama: Theory and Method
      of Analysis (New York: Alfred A. Knopf, 1970), pp. 126-8,
      235-6 [Red Roses for Me]; p. 238 [O'Casey abstracted re-
      gional qualities to produce a poetic prose].

1266 Beckett, J.C., The Anglo-Irish Tradition (Ithaca, N.Y.: Cornell University Press, 1976), pp. 119-20 [The notion of a Protestant superiority crops up in Autobiographies].

1267 Bennett, Benjamin, Modern Drama and German Classicism: Renaissance from Lessing to Brecht (Ithaca and London: Cornell University Press, 1979), pp. 309-14 [Discusses Juno and the Paycock and The Plough and the Stars].

1268 Benstock, Bernard, "Chronology and Narratology in Sean O'Casey's Beginnings," in The Genres of the Irish Literary Revival, ed. Ronald Schleifer (Norman, Okla.: Pilgrim Books; Dublin: Wolfhound Press, 1980), pp. 139-52. Reprinted from Genre, 12 (Winter 1979), 551-64 [What O'Casey sows in the first three pages of "A Child Is Born" are perennials that he nurtures and harvests throughout all six volumes of Autobiographies, but most closely in I Knock at the Door].

1269 Bentley, Eric, "The Case of O'Casey," in The Dramatic Event: An American Chronicle (Boston: Beacon Press, 1956), pp. 42-5. Reprinted from New Republic, 127 (13 Oct 1952) 17-18 [Rose and Crown].

1270 _____, In Search of Theater (New York: Vintage Books, 1953), pp. 315-21. Reprinted from Poetry (Chicago), 79 (Jan 1952), 216-32 [Realism in O'Casey's Abbey plays]; p. 99 [Juno and the Paycock]; pp. 219, 274 [O'Casey's dialogue]; pp. 244, 380 [O'Casey and Yeats].

1271 _____, The Life of the Drama (London: Methuen, 1965), pp. 82-3 [O'Casey's dialogue].

1272 _____, ed., The Modern Theatre, vol. 5 (Garden City, N.Y.: Doubleday Anchor Books, 1957) [An anthology including the text of, and a commentary on, Cock-a-Doodle Dandy].

1273 _____, The Playwright As Thinker (New York: Meridian Books, 1946). Reprinted as The Modern Theatre: A Study of Dramatists and the Drama (London: Robert Hale, 1948), passim [Naturalism in O'Casey].

1274 _____, The Theatre of Commitment (London: Methuen, 1958), pp. 4, 9 [O'Casey's plays are unpopular with the producers].

1275 _____, What Is Theatre? (New York: Athenaeum, 1968), pp. 25-8 [Rose and Crown]; pp. 265-8, 360-1 [Red Roses for Me]; pp. 26, 360 [The Star Turns Red]; pp. 26, 360 [Within the Gates]; p. 360 [Purple Dust]; p. 282 [Juno and the Paycock]; p. 210 [Odets compared to O'Casey]; p. 17 [O'Neill compared to O'Casey].

1276 Bergholz, Harry, Die Neugestaltung des Modernen Englischen
      Theaters 1870-1930 (Berlin: Karl Bergholz, 1933), pp. 158-
      9 [O'Casey and the Abbey Theatre].

1277 Bernard, Jean-Jacques, "Sean O'Casey," in Le Théâtre Anglais
      d'hier et d'aujourd'hui (Paris: Editions du Pavois, 1945),
      pp. 157-63 [Commentary on, and extract from, The Plough
      and the Stars].

1278 Bhatnagar, K.C., The Symbolic Tendency in Irish Renaissance
      (Chandigarh: University of the Panjab, 1962), pp. 14-17
      [Discusses Juno and the Paycock, The Silver Tassie, and
      Within the Gates].

1279 Bishop, George W., My Betters (London: William Heinemann,
      1957), p. 128 [Shaw on O'Casey]; p. 267 [O'Casey's blend
      of poetry and realism].

1280 Black, Hester M., The Theatre in Ireland: An Introductory
      Essay (Dublin: Trinity College, 1957), n.p. ["This realistic
      movement reached its highest point in the work of Sean
      O'Casey"].

1281 Blamires, Harry, Twentieth-Century English Literature (Lon-
      don: Macmillan, 1982), pp. 127-9 [General assessment].

1282 Blanshard, Paul, The Irish and Catholic Power (London: Derek
      Verschoyle, 1954), p. 87 [O'Casey and Father Walter McDon-
      ald]; p. 103 [O'Casey and censorship].

1283 Blau, Herbert, The Impossible Theater: A Manifesto (New York:
      Macmillan, 1964), pp. 205-10 [Cock-a-Doodle Dandy and The
      Plough and the Stars at the Actor's Workshop theatre, San
      Francisco].

1284 Block, Haskell M., and Robert G. Shedd, eds., Masters of
      Modern Drama (New York: Random House, 1962) [Anthology
      including the texts of, and commentaries on, Juno and the
      Paycock and Cock-a-Doodle Dandy.]

1285 Blum, Daniel, A Pictorial History of the American Theatre 1900-
      1956 (New York: Greenberg, 1956), pp. 175, 184 [Juno and
      The Paycock]; p. 184 [The Plough and the Stars]; p. 215
      [Within the Gates].

1286 Blunt, Jerry, Stage Dialects (San Francisco: Chandler, 1967),
      pp. 75-80 [Dialogue in O'Casey's plays].

1287 Blythe, Ernest, The Abbey Theatre (Dublin: The National
      Theatre Society, [1963]), n.p. ["As far as popularity in the

Abbey itself is concerned, first place is held by The Plough and the Stars by Sean O'Casey"].

1288 Böll, Heinrich, "The Poetry of Curses," in Missing Persons and Other Essays (London: Secker & Warburg; New York: McGraw-Hill, 1977), pp. 181-8 [Autobiographies have biblical dimensions and biblical greatness].

1289 Boulton, Marjorie, The Anatomy of Drama (London: Routledge & Kegan Paul, 1960), p. 56 [Juno and the Paycock]; p. 75 [A Pound on Demand]; p. 154 [The End of the Beginning].

1290 Boyd, Alice Katherine, The Interchange of Plays Between London and New York, 1910-1939: A Study in Relative Audience Response (New York: King's Crown Press, 1948), p. 93 [Juno and the Paycock and The Plough and the Stars are cited as "plays exchanged without success"].

1291 Bradbrook, M.C., English Dramatic Form: A History of Its Development (London: Chatto & Windus, 1965), p. 153 [The Silver Tassie borrows a scene from Toller].

1292 Bradby, David, and John McCormick, People's Theatre (London: Croom Helm; Totowa, N.J.: Rowman and Littlefield, 1978), p. 99 [O'Casey and the Unity Theatre]; p. 36 [The Silver Tassie]; pp. 100, 145 [The Star Turns Red].

1293 Brandt, G.W., "Realism and Parables: From Brecht to Arden," in Contemporary Theatre, ed. John Russell Brown and Bernard Harris. Stratford-upon-Avon Studies, 4 (London: Edward Arnold, 1962), pp. 36-40 [The Silver Tassie].

1294 Brockett, Oscar G., History of the Theatre (Boston: Allyn and Bacon, 1968), pp. 578, 630 [O'Casey as the most important Irish dramatist during the 1920's].

1295 _____, The Theatre: An Introduction, 3rd ed. (New York: Holt, Rinehart and Winston, 1974), p. 501 [Juno and the Paycock at the Tyrone Guthrie Theater, Minneapolis].

1296 _____, and Robert R. Findlay, Century of Innovation: A History of European and American Theatre and Drama Since 1870 (Englewood Cliffs, N.J.: Prentice-Hall, 1973), pp. 479-82 [Gives an assessment of O'Casey's drama, and concludes that "His early plays are clearly among the finest of the age, but the later works are somewhat disjointed"].

1297 Brook, Donald, The Romance of the English Theatre, rev. ed. (London: Rockcliff, 1952), pp. 168-70 [O'Casey's contribution to the English stage during the 1920s].

1298 Brown, Ivor, Theatre, 1954-5 (London: Max Reinhardt, 1955),
pp. 97-100 [The Bishop's Bonfire and Sunset and Evening
Star].

1299 _____, Theatre, 1955-6 (London: Max Reinhardt, 1956),
p. 13 [O'Casey compared with Osborne], p. 14 [O'Casey's
portrayal of the poor not appreciated by them]; p. 114
[O'Casey's exile].

1300 Brown, John Mason, Broadway in Review (New York: W.W.
Norton, 1940; rpt. Freeport, N.Y.: Books for Libraries
Press, 1969), p. 200 [O'Casey was one of the playwrights
"who commanded transatlantic audiences with new plays"].

1301 _____, Two on the Aisle (New York: W.W. Norton, 1938;
rpt. Port Washington, N.Y.: Kennikat Press, 1969), pp.
126-30 [Within the Gates]. Reprinted from New York Evening Post, (23 Oct 1934), p. 17.

1302 Brown, Malcolm, The Politics of Irish Literature, from Thomas
Davis to W.B. Yeats (London: Allen and Unwin; Seattle:
University of Washington Press, 1972), passim [Ireland in
the works of O'Casey].

1303 Browne, Terry W., Playwrights' Theatre: The English Stage
Company at the Royal Court Theatre (London: Pitman, 1975),
p. 2 [O'Casey at the Glasgow Unity Theatre]; pp. 105, 115
[Cock-a-Doodle Dandy].

1304 Brustein, Robert, The Culture Watch: Essays on Theatre and
Society, 1969-1974 (New York: Alfred A. Knopf, 1975), p.
92 [O'Casey's workingclass speech is idiomatically rich]; p.
155 ["It was seminal theatre that first took the risks on the
current staples of consumer theatre: Synge and O'Casey at
the Abbey Theatre"].

1305 _____, Seasons of Discontent: Dramatic Opinions 1959-1965
(London: Jonathan Cape, 1966), p. 43 [Many of the modern
masters, including O'Casey, have been "mauled, mangled,
and mishandled" by Off Broadway]; pp. 178-9 [O'Casey and
Behan compared]; p. 213 [O'Casey's roles and American ac-
tors]; p. 279 [The proscenium has proved hospitable to
O'Casey's plays].

1306 _____, The Theatre of Revolt: An Approach to the Modern
Drama (Boston: Little, Brown, 1964), pp. 22, 24 [O'Casey
and social revolt]; p. 271 [The Plough and the Stars].

1307 Burton, E.J., The Student's Guide to British Theatre and
Drama (London: Herbert Jenkins, 1963), pp. 151, 172 [Con-
siders Red Roses for Me O'Casey's best work].

1308 Busfield, Roger M., Jr., The Playwright's Art (Westport,
      Conn.: Greenwood Press, 1958), p. 142 [In O'Casey prose
      occasionally rises to poetic heights]; p. 168 [Language in
      Juno and the Paycock].

1309 Byrne, Dawson, "Sean O'Casey," in The Story of Ireland's
      National Theatre: The Abbey Theatre, Dublin (Dublin: Tal-
      bot Press, 1929; rpt. New York: Haskell House, 1971), pp.
      125-33 [Describes the productions of The Shadow of a Gun-
      man, Juno and the Paycock, and The Plough and the Stars
      at the Abbey Theatre].

1310 Cafan, Cevat, Irlanda Tiyatrosunda Gerçekçilik (Istanbul:
      Matbaasi, 1966), pp. 96-153 [Examines all O'Casey's plays and
      compares them with Synge's, concluding that "it was O'Casey
      who presented the full complexity of Ireland in his plays"].

1311 Cahill, Susan, and Thomas Cahill, A Literary Guide to Ireland
      (New York: Charles Scribner's, 1973), pp. 295-305 [De-
      scribes the houses in which O'Casey lived in Dublin, relating
      them to some of his works].

1312 Canfield, Curtis, ed., "Preface," in Plays of Changing Ireland
      (New York: Macmillan, 1936), pp. vii-viii [O'Casey is absent
      from the anthology because he is now "more concerned with
      the English than the Irish scene"].

1313 _____, ed., Plays of the Irish Renaissance, 1880-1930 (New
      York: Ives Washburn, 1929) [Anthology including the text
      of, and a commentary on, Juno and the Paycock].

1314 Carpenter, Bruce, The Way of the Drama: A Study of Drama-
      tic Forms and Moods (New York: Prentice-Hall, 1929), p. 65
      [O'Casey lacks Synge's technical perfection].

1315 Castein, Hanne, Die anglo-irische Strassenballade (München:
      Wilhelm Fink, 1971), pp. 103-6 [The influence of street bal-
      lads on O'Casey].

1316 Caute, David, The Fellow-Travellers: A Postscript to Enlight-
      enment (London: Weidenfeld & Nicolson, 1973), pp. 357-9
      [O'Casey and Irish nationalism].

1317 Chapman, John, ed., Theatre '54 (New York: Random House,
      1954), p. 18 [Bedtime Story at the Master Institute Theatre,
      New York].

1318 _____, ed., Theatre '56 (New York: Random House, 1956),
      pp. 6, 416-17 [Red Roses for Me]; p. 12 [Cock-a-Doodle
      Dandy]; pp. 13, 18, 19 [Autobiographies dramatized].

1319 Charques, R.D., ed., Footnotes to the Theatre (London: Peter Davies, 1938), p. 71 [O'Casey's individualistic strength]; p. 310 [O'Casey does not mean much "to the stage today"]; and passim.

1320 Chew, Samuel C., "The Irish Literary Renaissance," in The Nineteenth Century and After, 2nd ed. A Literary History of England, 4, ed. Albert C. Baugh (New York: Appleton-Century-Crofts, 1967), pp. 1514-15 [Deals with The Shadow of a Gunman, Juno and the Paycock, The Plough and the Stars, and The Silver Tassie].

1321 Chiari, J., Landmarks of Contemporary Drama (London: Herbert Jenkins, 1965; New York: Hillary House, 1966; rpt. New York: Gordian House, 1971), p. 36 [O'Casey is "one of the leading modern playwrights"]; p. 51 [O'Casey can "stab comedy with poignancy"]; p. 70 [O'Casey compared with Beckett]; p. 81 [O'Casey and poetic drama]; p. 108 [Juxtaposition of comedy and tragedy in O'Casey].

1322 Chisholm, Cecil, Repertory: An Outline of the Modern Theatre Movement (London: Peter Davies, 1934), p. 68-88 [Poetic symbolism in O'Casey]; pp. 91, 93 [Within the Gates and The Silver Tassie]; p. 95 [O'Casey as a naturalist]; p. 125 [O'Casey's symbolism and realism "may be too much for the British public"]; p. 214 [Within the Gates].

1323 Clark, William Smith, Chief Patterns of World Drama (New York: Houghton Mifflin, 1946), p. 889 ["The superb gusto of O'Casey's slum characters with their vivid, rhythmic dialect and naive humor gained fame for his plays abroad as well as at home"].

1324 Clayes, Stanley A., and David G. Spencer, eds., Contemporary Drama (New York: Charles Scribner's, 1962) [Anthology including the text of, and a commentary on, Juno and the Paycock].

1325 _____, and _____, eds., Contemporary Drama: Thirteen Plays, 2nd ed. (New York: Charles Scribner's, 1970) [Anthology including the text of, and a commentary on, Juno and the Paycock].

1326 Cleaver, James, "Sean O'Casey," in Theatre Through the Ages (New York: Hart Publishing Company, 1967), p. 310 [Introductory note].

1327 Clunes, Alec, The British Theatre (London: Cassell, 1964), pp. 166-7 [O'Casey used the joyful rhythms of Irish speech to show that dialect could reveal more than it obscured].

1328 Clurman, Harold, The Divine Pastime: Theatre Essays (New
York: Macmillan; London: Collier-Macmillan, 1974), p. 22
[Tennessee Williams compared to O'Casey]; p. 194 [Clifford
Odets compared to O'Casey].

1329 _____, Lies Like Truth (New York: Macmillan, 1958), pp.
122-4 [Review of Red Roses for Me, reprinted from Nation
(N.Y.), 182 (14 Jan 1956), 39-40].

1330 _____, The Naked Image: Observations on the Modern Theatre (New York: Macmillan; London: Collier-Macmillan, 1966),
p. 43 [Brendan Behan compared to O'Casey]; p. 202 [Arthur
Adamov praises O'Casey]; pp. 222-3 [O'Casey produced in
Warsaw]; p. 290 [Clifford Odets compared to O'Casey]; p.
301 [O'Casey without stars is impossible now on Broadway].

1331 Cochran, Charles B., I Had Almost Forgotten (London: Hutchinson, 1932), p. 197 [Eugene O'Neill compared to O'Casey];
pp. 263-5 [Recollections of the London production of The Silver Tassie].

1332 _____, Showman Looks On (London: J.M. Dent, 1945), p.
200 [Recollections of seeing Juno and the Paycock]; p. 226
[The finest symbolic scene on the London stage was that designed by Augustus John for The Silver Tassie].

1333 Coger, Leslie Irene, and Melvin R. White, Readers Theatre
Handbook (Glenview, Ill.: Scott, Foresman, 1967), pp. 12-
13, 18 [Paul Shyre's production of O'Casey's Autobiographies
in New York].

1334 Cole, David, The Theatrical Event: A Mythos, a Vocabulary,
a Perspective (Middletown, Conn.: Wesleyan University Press,
1975), pp. 120-1 [The language of The Plough and the Stars].

1335 Collins, A.S., English Literature of the Twentieth Century
(London: University Tutorial Press, 1954), pp. 300-2 [As-
sessment of O'Casey as a dramatist].

1336 Colum, Padraic, Arthur Griffith (Dublin: Browne & Nolan,
1959), p. 370 [The showdown between Republicans and Free-
Staters is recorded in Juno and the Paycock].

1337 _____, The Road Round Ireland (New York: Macmillan, 1926),
pp. 262-71 [Recollections of O'Casey and a discussion of
Juno and the Paycock].

1338 Connery, Donald S., The Irish (London: Eyre & Spottiswoode;
New York: Simon & Schuster, 1968), passim [Makes references to O'Casey's views on various aspects of Irish life].

1339 Coogan, Tim Pat, Ireland Since the Rising (New York and Lon-
      don: Frederick A. Praeger, 1966), p. 167 [The Shadow of
      a Gunman, Juno and the Paycock, and The Plough and the
      Stars were considered "both nationalistically and artistically
      unacceptable"].

1340 _____, The Irish: A Personal View (London: Phaidon Press,
      1975), pp. 62, 85, 143 [Attitude of religion toward O'Casey].

1341 Cookman, A.V., "The Prose Drama," in Theatre Programme,
      ed. J. C. Trewin (London: Frederick Muller, 1954), pp. 33-
      8 [Discusses The Silver Tassie, Within the Gates, The Star
      Turns Red, Red Roses for Me, Oak Leaves and Lavender,
      and Cock-a-Doodle Dandy].

1342 Cordell, Richard Albert, ed., Representative Modern Plays,
      British and American (New York: Nelson, 1929) [Anthology
      including the text of, and a commentary on, Juno and the
      Paycock].

1343 _____, and Lowell Matson, eds., The Off-Broadway Theatre:
      Seven Plays (New York: Random House, 1959) [Anthology
      including the text of, and a commentary on, Purple Dust].

1344 Corkery, Daniel, Synge and Anglo-Irish Literature (Cork:
      Cork University Press, 1955), passim [Rejects the works of
      O'Casey as a betrayal of holy Ireland].

1345 Corrigan, Robert W., ed., Masterpieces of the Modern Irish
      Theatre (New York: Collier Books, 1967) [Anthology includ-
      ing the texts of, and commentaries on, The Silver Tassie and
      Cock-a-Doodle Dandy].

1346 _____, ed., The Modern Theatre (New York: Macmillan,
      1964) [Anthology including the text of, and a commentary on,
      The Plough and the Stars].

1347 _____, The Theatre in Search of a Fix (New York: Dela-
      corte Press, 1973), p. 90 [It is clear from The Plough and
      the Stars and The Silver Tassie that the Abbey Theatre
      could not withstand for long the theatre's introspective ten-
      dencies].

1348 Corsani, Mary, Il Nuovo Teatro Inglese (Milan: U. Mursia,
      1970), pp. 141-4 [Critical study].

1349 Corvin, Michel, "Le Théâtre réaliste et politique: l'Irlande-
      O'Casey," in Le Théâtre nouveau à l'étranger (Paris:
      Presses Universitaires de France, 1964), pp. 71-5 [Considers
      O'Casey's political views in his plays].

1350 Costello, Peter, The Heart Grown Brutal: The Irish Revolution in Literature, from Parnell to the Death of Yeats, 1891-
1939 (Dublin: Gill and Macmillan; Totowa, N.J.: Rowman
and Littlefield, 1977), passim [Deals with nationalism in Juno
and the Paycock, The Plough and the Stars, The Shadow of
a Gunman, The Silver Tassie, and The Story of the Irish
Citizen Army].

1351 Cotes, Peter, No Star Nonsense (London: Theatre Book Club,
1949), p. 43 [The Star Turns Red and Purple Dust chosen
by the Rocket Theatre Players]; p. 94 [O'Casey's views on
production]; p. 104 [O'Casey "has to write, whatever happens"]; p. 117 [O'Casey is a great critic]; p. 158 [O'Casey
is a pioneer in the theatre of ideas]; p. 164 [The Plough and
the Stars at the Embassy Theatre, London]; p. 168 [O'Casey
"has been atrociously served recently"].

1352 Courtney, Richard, "Sean O'Casey," in Outline History of British Drama (Totowa, N.J.: Littlefield, Adams, 1982), pp.
239-44 [Surveys O'Casey's dramatic work, providing biographical information and some plot summaries].

1353 Cowell, John, "Sean O'Casey," in Where They Lived in Dublin
(Dublin: O'Brien Press, 1980), pp. 74-5 [Biographical es-
say].

1354 Cowell, Raymond, "O'Casey," in Twelve Modern Dramatists
(London and New York: Pergamon Press, 1967), pp. 66-75
[Introduction to, and extract from, Juno and the Paycock].

1355 Coxhead, Elizabeth, "Sean O'Casey," in Lady Gregory: A Literary Portrait (London: Macmillan, 1961; rev. ed., Secker
& Warburg, 1966; rpt. 1970), chap. 13 [Lady Gregory's association with O'Casey].

1356 Croft-Cooke, Rupert, The Numbers Came (London: Putnam,
1963), pp. 159-60. Reprinted from Theatre World (London),
5 (Oct 1926), 10 [Interview with O'Casey].

1357 Cubeta, Paul M., ed., Modern Drama for Analysis, rev. ed.
(New York: Dryden Press, 1955) [Anthology including the
text of, and a commentary on Juno and the Paycock].

1358 Cunliffe, John W., English Literature in the Twentieth Century
(New York: Macmillan, 1933; rpt. Freeport, N.Y.: Books
for Libraries Press, 1967), pp. 114-21 [Examines The Shadow
of a Gunman, Juno and the Paycock, The Plough and the
Stars, and The Silver Tassie].

1359 _____, Modern English Playwrights: A Short History of the

English Drama from 1825 (London and New York: Harper, 1927; rpt. Port Washington, N.Y.: Kennikat Press, 1969), pp. 231-50 [Assesses The Shadow of a Gunman, Juno and the Paycock, and The Plough and the Stars].

1360 Daiches, David, The Present Age after 1920 (London: Cresset Press, 1958), pp. 164-5, 325-6 [O'Casey transcended the local Irish situation as the Irish national playwrights cannot be said to have done].

1361 Dalgard, Olav, Theatret i det 20.Hundreåret (Oslo: Norske Samlaget, 1955), pp. 258-66 [Critical study].

1362 Darlington, W.A., I Do What I Like (London: MacDonald, 1947), pp. 319-22 [O'Casey broke away from the conventional methods when he wrote The Silver Tassie, and Within the Gates].

1363 _____, Six Thousand and One Nights: Forty Years a Critic (London: George G. Harrap, 1960), p. 168 [After The Silver Tassie, the gap between O'Casey and the London public widened steadily, and after Within the Gates, it became impossible].

1364 Daubeny, Peter, My World of Theatre, with a Foreword and Afterword by Ronald Bryden (London: Jonathan Cape, 1971), pp. 285-7 [Juno and the Paycock and The Plough and the Stars at the Aldwych Theatre, London]; and passim.

1365 Davis, Katie Brittain Adams, Federico García Lorca and Sean O'Casey: Powerful Voices in the Wilderness (Salzburg: Institut für Englische Sprache und Literatur, Universität Salzburg, 1978) [Examines the parallels between the dramaturgy of O'Casey and García Lorca].

1366 Davison, P.H., "Contemporary Drama and Popular Dramatic Forms," in Aspects of Drama and the Theatre (Sydney: Sydney University Press, 1965), pp. 148-9 [What Shaw did with melodrama in comedy, O'Casey did in Juno and the Paycock]; pp. 179-80 [The ending of Juno and the Paycock].

1367 de Blacam, Aodh, A First Book of Irish Literature (Dublin and Cork: Talbot Press, [1934]; rpt. Port Washington, N.Y. and London: Kennikat Press, 1970), p. 219 ["There is no gravity or sweetness" in O'Casey's work].

1368 de Blaghd, Earnán [Ernest Blythe], Trasna Na Bóinne [Across the Boyne] (Dublin: Sairséal Agus Dill, 1957) [Autobiography including references to O'Casey].

1369 De Burca, Seamus, The Soldier's Song: The Story of Peadar

Kearney, 2nd ed. (Dublin: P.J. Bourke, 1958), pp. 222-3
[O'Casey and Peadar Kearney].

1370 Dent, Alan, Nocturnes and Rhapsodies (London: Hamish Hamilton, 1950), pp. 100-1 [Review of Red Roses for Me at the
Embassy Theatre, London].

1371 _____, Preludes and Studies (London: Macmillan, 1942; rpt.
Port Washington, N.Y.: Kennikat Press, 1970), p. 155 [Lan-
guage of O'Casey's plays]; pp. 157-8 [The Plough and the
Stars revived in Dublin]; p. 160 [Paul Vincent Carroll compared to O'Casey].

1372 Dickinson, Thomas H., ed., Chief Contemporary Dramatists,
Third Series (Boston: Houghton Mifflin, 1958) [An anthology
including the text of, and a commentary on, Juno and the
Paycock].

1373 Dietrich, Margret, Das Moderne Drama: Strömungen-Gestalten-
Motive (Stuttgart: Alfred Kröner, 1961), pp. 479-80 [Crit-
ical introduction].

1374 Dolch, Martin, "Sean O'Casey: The Shadow of a Gunman," in
Insight II, ed. J.V. Hagopian and Martin Dolch (Frankfurt:
Hirschgraben, 1965), pp. 263-70 [An analysis of the play].

1375 Dooley, Roger B., Modern British and Irish Drama (New York:
Thor Publications, 1964), pp. 95-8 [Study guide to Juno and
the Paycock, The Plough and the Stars, The Silver Tassie,
Within the Gates, Red Roses for Me, Purple Dust, and Cock-
a-Doodle Dandy].

1376 Downer, Alan S., The British Drama: A Handbook and Brief
Chronicle (New York: Appleton-Century-Crofts, 1950), pp.
324-6 [O'Casey's plays are remarkable examples of the ability
of the realist to develop general and universal themes, as
can be seen in Juno and the Paycock and The Plough and
the Stars].

1377 Downs, Harold, The Critic in the Theatre (London: Isaac Pitman, 1953), pp. 11-12 [Richard Findlater on O'Casey]; p. 19
[Critics advised to study O'Casey]; p. 55 [O'Casey on the
drama of ideas]; p. 145 [O'Casey and the critics].

1378 Doyle, Paul A., Paul Vincent Carroll, Irish Writers Series
(Lewisburg, Pa.: Bucknell University Press, 1971), passim
[Carroll lacked O'Casey's lyrical control].

1379 Drescher, Horst W., "British Literature," in World Literature
Since 1945, ed. Ivar Ivask and Gero von Wilpert (New York:
Frederick Ungar, 1973), pp. 70-1 [Brief discussion].

1380 Drew, Elizabeth, Discovering Drama (New York: W.W. Norton;
      London: Jonathan Cape, 1937), p. 91 [O'Casey appeals to
      the theatregoer's intelligence and emotions]; p. 199 [The
      Plough and the Stars as an illustration of the challenge to
      the accepted conclusions of society]; p. 223-4 [Poetic lan-
      guage in The Plough and the Stars].

1381 Drinkwater, John, The Gentle Art of Theatre-Going (London:
      Robert Holden, 1927), pp. 146-50, 165, 167-70, 176-8, 180-1
      [Discusses Juno and the Paycock].

1382 Driver, Tom F., Romantic Quest and Modern Query: History
      of the Modern Theater (New York: Delta Book, 1970), p.
      341 [O'Casey is one of those playwrights who "tended to shy
      away from the fuller uses of irony and paid the price of fail-
      ing to come to grips with the complexities of modern exper-
      ience"]; p. 342 [O'Casey's plays have never quite escaped
      Irish provincialism].

1383 Dukes, Ashley, Drama, 2nd ed. (London: Oxford University
      Press, 1947), p. 98 [A passionate sincerity in the study of
      everyday life gives distinction to the plays of O'Casey].

1384 _____, The Scene Is Changed (London: Macmillan, 1942),
      p. 111 [The Plough and the Stars confirmed O'Casey the rank
      of the best Irish writer since Synge]; p. 148 [The Silver Tas-
      sie is an "outstanding work"]; p. 202 [O'Casey as a prose
      writer made his own original experiments in dramatic verse].

1385 Dukore, Bernard F., ed., Documents for Drama and Revolution
      (New York: Holt, Rinehart and Winston, 1971), pp. 71-108
      [Provides some original historical documents as a background
      for The Plough and the Stars].

1386 _____, ed., Drama and Revolution (New York: Holt, Rine-
      hart and Winston, 1971) [Anthology including the text of,
      and a commentary on, The Plough and the Stars].

1387 Durham, Willard Higley, and John W. Dodds, eds., British and
      American Plays 1830-1945 (New York: Oxford University
      Press, 1947) [Anthology including the text of, and a com-
      mentary on, Juno and the Paycock].

1388 Eaton, Walter Prichard, The Drama in English (New York:
      Charles Scribner's, 1930), pp. 290-1 [Juxtaposition of com-
      edy and tragedy in Juno and the Paycock and The Plough
      and the Stars].

1389 Edwards, Hilton, "The Irish Theatre," in George Freedley and
      John A. Reeves, A History of the Theatre, 3rd rev. ed.

(New York: Crown Publishers, 1968), pp. 738-9 [After the withdrawal of The Drums of Father Ned from the Dublin Theatre Festival in 1958, O'Casey refused permission for any of his plays to be produced professionally in Ireland]; and passim.

1390 Edwards, Philip, Threshold of a Nation: A Study in English and Irish Drama (Cambridge: Cambridge University Press, 1980), pp. 229-44 [The Shadow of a Gunman and The Plough and the Stars as a picture of Irish life].

1391 Egerton, George, A Leaf from The Yellow Book: The Correspondence of George Egerton, ed. Terence de Vere White (London: Richards Press, 1958), p. 108 [The Plough and the Stars "isn't as good as Juno and the Paycock"]; p. 131 [The defects of Juno and the Paycock "glare in a film"]; pp. 152-3 [Within the Gates "is not real"]; p. 166 [One of the volumes of Autobiographies is banned].

1392 Egri, Lajos, The Art of Dramatic Writing (New York: Simon & Schuster, 1946), p. 5 [The second act of Juno and the Paycock stands still because O'Casey "had only a nebulous idea to start his play with"].

1393 Elizarova, Maria Evgen 'Evna, and N.P. Mikhal 'Skaîa, "Shon O'Keĭsi," in Kurs lektsiĭ po istorii zarubezhnoĭ literatury xx veka (Moskva: Isdatel 'stvo Vysshaîa Shkola, 1965), pp. 321-35 [General criticism on O'Casey].

1394 Ellis-Fermor, Una, The Frontiers of Drama (London: Methuen, 1945; University Paperbacks, 1964), pp. 119-20 [The disintegration of society is one of the themes of The Plough and the Stars and The Silver Tassie]; pp. 122-5 [Different levels of consciousness interact through Within the Gates].

1395 _____ , The Irish Dramatic Movement (London: Methuen, 1954), pp. 196-200 [Assessment of O'Casey's dramatic work].

1396 Elsom, John, Post-War British Theatre Criticism (London and Boston: Routledge & Kegan Paul, 1981), p. 92 ["The true parallels to Wesker's achievement came from ... O'Casey"].

1397 Ervine, St. John, The Theatre in My Time (London: Rich & Cowan, 1933), p. 156 [O'Casey would have found no place for his plays and little inducement to write if W. B. Yeats, Lady Gregory, George Russell, and George Moore had not established the Irish Players].

1398 Evans, Gareth Lloyd, The Language of Modern Drama (London: Dent; Totowa, N.J.: Rowman and Littlefield, 1977), p. 25

[O'Casey's language is "as capable of communicating a fierce naturalism convincingly as it is able to take flight into the worlds of the imagination"].

1399 Evans, Sir Ifor, A Short History of English Drama, 2nd rev. ed. Riverside Studies in Literature (Boston: Houghton Mifflin, 1965), pp. 180-2 [At his best, O'Casey has a great command of the stage; and over language he exercises a compelling power].

1400 Fallis, Richard, The Irish Renaissance (Syracuse, N.Y.: Syracuse University Press, 1977; Dublin: Gill and Macmillan, 1978), pp. 182-94 [Assessment of O'Casey's works].

1401 Fallon, Gabriel, The Abbey and the Actor (Dublin: The National Theatre Society, 1969), pp. 22-3 [Comments on the production of Juno and the Paycock in Paris]; pp. 36-7 [Actors F. J. McCormick, Barry Fitzgerald, and Gabriel Fallon in Juno and the Paycock and The Shadow of a Gunman].

1402 Fast, Howard, Literature and Reality (New York: International Publishers, 1950), p. 124 [O'Casey is one of the communist writers "who stand out like giants"].

1403 Fay, Gerard, The Abbey Theatre, Cradle of Genius (Dublin: Clonmore & Reynolds; London: Hollis & Carter, 1958), pp. 142-52 [O'Casey is "one of the greatest writers Ireland has ever produced"].

1404 _____, "The Irish Theatre: A Decline and Perhaps, in the End, a Fall," in Theatre in Review, ed. Frederick Lumley (Edinburgh: Richard Paterson, 1956), pp. 80-9 [Discusses The Bishop's Bonfire].

1405 Fechter, Paul, Das Europäische Drama, vol. 3 (Mannheim: Bibliographisches Institut A.G., 1958), pp. 378-80 [Critical study, concentrating on The Bishop's Bonfire and Juno and the Paycock].

1406 Fehr, Bernhard, Die Englische Literatur der Gegenwart und die Kulturfragen Unserer Zeit, Hefte zur Englandkunde, 3 (Leipzig: Bernhard Tauchnitz, 1930), pp. 46-7 [Brief discussion on O'Casey as a dramatist].

1407 Findlater, Richard, At the Royal Court: 25 Years of the English Stage Company (Ambergate, Derbyshire: Amber Lane Press, 1981), p. 47 [George Devine's production of Cock-a-Doodle Dandy].

1408 _____, Banned! A Review of Theatrical Censorship in Britain

(London: MacGibbon & Kee, 1967), p. 127 [O'Casey and others experienced only minor interference from St. James' Palace and rarely took the field against the Chamberlain].

1409 _____, The Unholy Trade (London: Victor Gollancz, 1952), pp. 170-84 [Analyzes The Shadow of a Gunman, Juno and the Paycock, The Plough and the Stars, The Silver Tassie, Within the Gates, The Star Turns Red, Red Roses for Me, Purple Dust, Oak Leaves and Lavender, and Cock-a-Doodle Dandy; and concludes that O'Casey wrote for a people's theatre that lives only in his mind].

1410 Flanagan, Hallie, Shifting Scenes of the Modern European Theatre (New York: Coward-MacCann, 1928; rpt. Benjamin Blom, 1972), pp. 40-2 [Recollections of O'Casey by Lady Gregory].

1411 Fox, R.M., Green Banners: The Story of the Irish Struggle (London: Secker & Warburg, 1938), pp. 125, 164-5, 168, 177-8, 185 [O'Casey and the Irish Citizen Army]; pp. 334-6 [O'Casey's Abbey plays "gave the first sensitive reaction to the years of storm"].

1412 Fraser, G.S., The Modern Writer and His World, rev. ed. (Harmondsworth, Middlesex: Penguin Books, 1964), pp. 53-4 [Since, after The Silver Tassie, O'Casey jettisoned realism for a kind of German expressionism, his talent has become crippled]; pp. 206-11 [O'Casey is not a "lord of language" as Synge and Yeats are but is more of a dramatist of our own age than either of them].

1413 Fréchet, René, "Sean O'Casey: un épisode de la vie du théâtre irlandais," in Le Théâtre Moderne: Hommes et Tendances, ed. Jean Jacquot (Paris: Centre National de la Recherche Scientifique, 1958), pp. 309-20, 2nd ed. (Paris Centre National de la Recherche Scientifique, 1965), pp. 321-36 [Critical study].

1414 Freedley, George, "England and Ireland," in A History of Modern Drama, ed. Barrett H. Clark and George Freedley (New York: Appleton-Century-Crofts, 1947), pp. 226-9 [An assessment of O'Casey's work from the beginning to Red Roses for Me].

1415 Freedman, Morris, "The Moral Tragicomedy of Wilde and O'Casey," in The Moral Impulse: Modern Drama from Ibsen to the Present (Carbondale and Edwardsville: Southern Illinois University Press, 1967), pp. 63-73. Reprinted from College English, 25 (Apr 1964), 518-22, 527 [What connects Wilde and O'Casey most meaningfully is their tone of tragicomedy].

1416 Freier, Robert; Arnold Leslie Lazarus; and Herbert Potell, eds., Adventures in Modern Literature (New York: Harcourt, Brace, 1956) [Anthology including the text of, and a commentary on, The End of the Beginning].

1417 Fricker, Robert, Das Moderne Englische Drama (Göttingen: Vandenhoeck & Ruprecht, 1974), pp. 52-60 [Assesses O'Casey's dramatic achievement]; and passim.

1418 _____, "Sean O'Casey," in Das moderne englische Drama: Interpretationen. 3rd ed. rev., ed. Horst Oppel (Berlin: Erich Schmidt, 1976), pp. 188-207 [A brief assessment of O'Casey's achievement and an in-depth study of Juno and the Paycock].

1419 Frow, Gerald, ed., The Mermaid Theatre: The First Ten Years (London: The Mermaid Theatre, 1969), passim [Includes information on the productions of The Bishop's Bonfire, Purple Dust, Red Roses for Me, and The Plough and the Stars at the Mermaid Theatre, London].

1420 Galinsky, Hans, "Englische und anglo-irische Dichtung," in Die Gegenwartsdichtung der europäischen Völker (Berlin, 1939), pp. 159-60 [Assesses O'Casey's dramatic achievement to Within the Gates].

1421 Gascoigne, Bamber, Twentieth-Century Drama (London: Hutchinson University Library, 1962), pp. 23-4 [To O'Casey it is the characters least puffed-up with heroism who are the heroes]; and passim.

1422 Gassner, John, Directions in Modern Theatre and Drama (New York: Holt, Rinehart and Winston, 1967), pp. 178-9 [O'Casey on Yeats]; and passim.

1423 _____, Dramatic Soundings (New York: Crown Publishers, 1968), passim [Makes several references to O'Casey's plays].

1424 _____, Masters of the Drama, 3rd rev. and enl. ed. (New York: Dover Publications, 1954), pp. 566-71 [Assesses The Shadow of a Gunman, Juno and the Paycock, The Plough and the Stars, The Silver Tassie, and Within the Gates].

1425 _____, Producing the Play, rev. ed. (New York: Holt, Rinehart and Winston, 1953), p. 48 [Juxtaposition of comedy and tragedy in Juno and the Paycock]; pp. 448-9 [The effect of songs in Juno and the Paycock].

1426 _____, Theatre at the Crossroads (New York: Holt, Rinehart and Winston, 1960), pp. 284-6 [The dramatization of

Pictures in the Hallway]; pp. 286-8 [The dramatization of I Knock at the Door].

1427 _____, The Theatre in Our Times (New York: Crown Publishers, 1954), pp. 240-9 [An assessment of O'Casey's achievement]; and passim [References to O'Casey's plays].

1428 _____, and Ralph G. Allen, Theatre and Drama in the Making (Boston: Houghton Mifflin, 1964), passim [Makes some references to O'Casey's plays].

1429 _____, and Bernard F. Dukore, eds., A Treasury of the Theatre, from Henrik Ibsen to Robert Lowell, 4th ed. (New York: Simon and Schuster, 1970) [Anthology including the text of, and a commentary on, The Plough and the Stars].

1430 Geisinger, Marion, Plays, Players, & Playwrights (New York: Hart Publishing Company, 1971), p. 445 [Despite the grim realism of O'Casey's works, his dramas possess an essentially poetic quality].

1431 Gelb, Arthur, and Barbara Gelb, O'Neill (London: Jonathan Cape, 1962), pp. 787-90 [Describes O'Casey's meeting and friendship with O'Neill].

1432 Gilliatt, Penelope, Unholy Fools (London: Secker & Warburg, 1973), p. 242 [O'Casey on Joe Orton].

1433 Gillie, Christopher, "Drama 1900-1940," in Movements in English Literature 1900-1940 (Cambridge: Cambridge University Press, 1975), pp. 176-7 [Examines the Dublin Trilogy].

1434 Gish, Lillian, The Movies, Mr. Griffith, and Me (London: W.H. Allen; Englewood Cliffs, N.J.: Prentice-Hall, 1969), pp. 322-3 [Recollections of O'Casey's visit to New York to attend the American premiere of Within the Gates].

1435 Goetsch, Paul, "Das englische Drama seit Shaw," in Das Englische Drama, ed. Josefa Nünning (Dormstadt: Wissenschaftliche Buchgesellschaft, 1973), pp. 424-7 [A critical study].

1436 Gorelik, Mordecai, New Theatres for Old (New York: Samuel French, 1941; Dutton Paperbacks, 1962), p. 373 [The film version of The Plough and the Stars was a strange mixture of subjective and objective techniques].

1437 Gowda, H. H. Anniah, Dramatic Poetry from Mediaeval to Modern Times (Madras: Macmillan Company of India, 1972), pp. 279-86 [Discusses Juno and the Paycock, Oak Leaves and Lavender, The Plough and the Stars, Red Roses for Me, Within the Gates, and The Silver Tassie].

1438 Gozenpud, Abram H., "Shon O'Keĭsi," in Puti i pereput'ya. Angliiskaya i frantsuzskaya dramaturgiya xx v (Leningrad: Iskusstvo, 1967), pp. 139-53 [Critical study].

1439 Grandpierre, Emil Koboszvári, "Sean O'Casey," in Az angol irodalom a huszadik században, ed. László Báti and István Kristó-Nagy (Budapest: Gondolat, 1970), vol. 1, pp. 207-25; vol. 2, pp. 301-2 [General criticism].

1440 Granville-Barker, Harley, On Poetry in Drama (London: Sidgwick & Jackson, 1937), pp. 25-6 [Contrasts the second act of The Silver Tassie and Within the Gates with O'Casey's earlier plays].

1441 _____, The Study of Drama (Cambridge: Cambridge University Press, 1934), p. 73 [Recalls a "magnificent experiment" in the second act of The Silver Tassie].

1442 Graves, Charles, The Cochran Story: A Biography of Sir Charles Blake Cochran, Kt. (London: W. H. Allen, n.d.), pp. 163, 193 [The production of The Silver Tassie caused immense controversy].

1443 Grazhdanskaĭa, Zoĭa Tikhonovna, ed., "Irlandskaĭa literatura: Shon O'Keisi," in Istoriĭa zarubezhnoĭ literatury dvadtsogo veka (Moskva: Gosuchebnopedagog. izd-vo, 1963), pp. 540-7 [General criticism].

1444 Grebanier, Bernard, Playmaking (New York: Thomas Y. Crowell, 1961), passim [Cites illustrations from Juno and the Paycock and The Plough and the Stars].

1445 Greene, David H., ed., An Anthology of Irish Literature (New York: Modern Library, 1954; rpt. New York University Press, 1971) [Anthology including the text of, and a commentary on, "The Raid"].

1446 Greenwood, Ormerod, The Playwright (London: Isaac Pitman, 1950), passim [Cites illustrations from Juno and the Paycock, Red Roses for Me, The Star Turns Red, and Within the Gates].

1447 Gregory, Anne, Me and Nu: Childhood at Coole (Gerrards Cross, Buckinghamshire: Colin Smythe, 1970), pp. 83-6 [O'Casey's visits to Lady Gregory in Coole Park].

1448 Gregory, Lady, Lady Gregory's Journals, 1916-1930, ed. Lennox Robinson (London: Putnam, 1946; rpt. ed. Daniel J. Murphy. Gerrards Cross, Buckinghamshire: Colin Smythe, 1978), passim [O'Casey's relationship with the Abbey Theatre].

1449 _____, Seventy Years 1852-1922, ed. Colin Smythe (Gerrards

Cross, Buckinghamshire: Colin Smythe, 1974), passim
[O'Casey's relationship with the Abbey Theatre].

1450 Griffin, Gerald, "Sean O'Casey," in The Wild Geese: Pen Portraits of Famous Irish Exiles (London: Jarrolds, [1938]),
pp. 216-19 [Interview with O'Casey in London].

1451 Guerrero Zamora, Juan, "Entrana y sociedad en Sean O'Casey,"
in Historia del teatro contemporaneo, vol. 4 (Barcelona: Juan
Flors, 1967), pp. 45-57 [Society in the plays of O'Casey].

1452 Gunther, Margarete, Der englische Kriegsroman und das englische Kriegsdrama: 1919 bis 1930. Neue deutsche Forschun-
gen, 59 (Berlin, 1936), pp. 208-12 [Examines The Silver Tas-
sie].

1453 Guthrie, Tyrone, A Life in the Theatre (New York and London:
McGraw-Hill, 1959), pp. 297-9 [Recollections of the production of The Bishop's Bonfire in Dublin].

1454 Gwynn, Stephen, Irish Literature and Drama in the English
Language: A Short History (London: Thomas Nelson, 1936;
rpt. Folcroft, Pa.: Folcroft Press, 1969), pp. 209-12
[O'Casey "changed the quality of the Abbey's audiences"].

1455 Hampden, John, ed., Twenty-Four One-Act Plays. Everyman's
Library (London: Dent, 1954) [Anthology including the text
of, and a commentary on, A Pound on Demand].

1456 Hare, Arnold, "English Comedy," in Comic Drama: The European Heritage, ed. W. D. Howarth (London: Methuen, 1978),
p. 122 [Unlike O'Casey, the Irish dramatists Farquhar, Sheridan, Goldsmith, Wilde, and Shaw wrote consciously in an
English context].

1457 Hatcher, Harlan, ed., A Modern Repertory (New York: Harcourt, Brace, 1953) [Anthology including the text of, and a
commentary on, Juno and the Paycock].

1458 Hayman, Ronald, The Set-Up: An Anatomy of the English Theatre Today (London: Eyre Methuen, 1973), p. 107 [The Silver Tassie had been undeservedly neglected]; p. 157 [O'Casey
at the Royal Court Theatre]; p. 168 (O'Casey at the Mermaid
Theatre].

1459 Heffner, Hubert, ed., The Nature of Drama (Boston: Houghton
Mifflin, 1959) [Anthology including the text of, and a commentary on, Juno and the Paycock].

1460 Heilman, Robert Bechtold, The Iceman, the Arsonist and the

Troubled Agent: Tragedy and Melodrama on the Modern Stage (Seattle: University of Washington Press; London: Allen and Unwin, 1973), pp. 257-9 [Juno and the Paycock is a melodrama of disaster that gains a special character from a large infusion of Falstaffian and satiric comedy].

1461　　　　　, Tragedy and Melodrama (Seattle and London: University of Washington Press, 1968), pp. 287, 298 [Gabriel Fallon on Juno and the Paycock].

1462　　　　　, The Ways of the World: Comedy and Society (Seattle and London: University of Washington Press, 1978), pp. 23, 58 [The family world is joined with the world of politics in Juno and the Paycock and The Plough and the Stars].

1463　Heiney, Donald, and Lenthiel H. Downs, "Sean O'Casey," in Contemporary British Literature (Woodbury, N.Y.: Barron's Educational Series, 1974), pp. 134-6 [Introductory discussion].

1464　Henn, T. R., The Harvest of Tragedy (London: Methuen, 1956; University Paperbacks, 1966), pp. 212-14 [The work of O'Casey, as can be seen in Juno and the Paycock, The Silver Tassie, and The Plough and the Stars, includes the only examples of merit in the genre of realistic tragedy produced in the Irish Theatre].

1465　Heppner, Sam, "Cockie" (London: Leslie Frewin, 1969), pp. 156-8 [The production of The Silver Tassie by Charles B. Cochran]; p. 212 [O'Casey's communism was immaterial to Cochran]; p. 265 [Cochran commissioned Augustus John to design the second act of The Silver Tassie].

1466　Hickey, Des, and Gus Smith, "The Drums of Father Ned: O'Casey and the Archbishop," in A Paler Shade of Green (London: Leslie Frewin, 1972), pp. 134-51 [Brendan Smith recollects the withdrawal of the play from the Dublin Theatre Festival in 1958].

1467　Hobson, Harold, Theatre (London and New York: Longmans, Green, 1948), pp. 83-5 [The production of Oak Leaves and Lavender at the Lyric Theatre, Hammersmith]; p. 172 [Denis Johnston compared to O'Casey].

1468　　　　　, Verdict at Midnight: Sixty Years of Dramatic Criticism (London and New York: Longmans, Green, 1952), pp. 135-8 [The production of Juno and the Paycock at the Royalty Theatre, London].

1469　Hodgart, Matthew, James Joyce: A Student's Guide (London: Routledge & Kegan Paul, 1978), p. 12 [Unlike O'Casey who describes the lives of the working class in his plays and Autobiographies, Joyce describes the lives of the middle-class]; pp. 33-4 [O'Casey was "a master of language"].

1470 Hodson, James Lansdale, No Phantoms Here (London: Faber, 1932), pp. 147-56 [Interview with O'Casey].

1471 Hogan, Robert, After the Irish Renaissance: A Critical History of the Irish Drama Since "The Plough and the Stars" (Minneapolis: University of Minnesota Press, 1967; London: Macmillan, 1968), pp. 235-52 [Examines O'Casey's place in the pastoral tradition].

1472 _____, Dion Boucicault (New York: Twayne Publishers, 1969), pp. 10, 80, 86, 109-11 [O'Casey was influenced by Boucicault].

1473 _____, and Sven Eric Molin, eds., Drama: The Major Genres (New York: Dodd, Mead, 1967) [Anthology including the text of, and a commentary on, The Plough and the Stars].

1474 Holloway, Joseph, Joseph Holloway's Abbey Theatre: A Selection from His Unpublished Journal "Impressions of a Dublin Playgoer," ed. Robert Hogan and Michael J. O'Neill (Carbondale and Edwardsville: Southern Illinois University Press, 1967), passim [Records some impressions of the younger O'Casey].

1475 _____, Joseph Holloway's Irish Theatre, 3 vols., ed. Robert Hogan and Michael J. O'Neill (Dixon, Calif.: Proscenium Press, 1968-70), passim [Records some impressions of O'Casey].

1476 Hone, Joseph, W. B. Yeats, 1865-1939, 2nd ed. (London: Macmillan, 1962), pp. 387-9 [O'Casey's relationship with Yeats].

1477 Hope-Wallace, Philip, "Red Roses for Me," in Words and Music: A Selection from the Criticism and Occasional Pieces of Philip Hope-Wallace, made by Jacquiline Hope-Wallace (London: Collins, 1981), pp. 183-4 [Reprinted review of the production at the Embassy Theatre, London, 1941].

1478 Hortmann, Wilhelm, Englische Literatur im 20. Jahrhundert (Bern: A. Francke, 1965), pp. 92-6 [Critical study].

1479 Hoskins, Katharine Bail, Today the Struggle: Literature and Politics in England During the Spanish Civil War (Austin and London: University of Texas Press, 1969), pp. 152-6 [Discusses The Star Turns Red].

1480 Howarth, Herbert, The Irish Writers 1880-1940 (London: Rockcliff, 1958; New York: Hill & Wang, 1959), pp. 86-7 [Lady

Gregory helped to launch O'Casey's first plays]; p. 108
[O'Casey compliments Lady Gregory]; p. 303 [O'Casey had
to meet protests against his plays].

1481 Hudson, Lynton, The English Stage 1850-1950 (London: George
G. Harrap, 1951), p. 189 [O'Casey and the drama critics].

1482 _____, Life and the Theatre (London: George G. Harrap,
1949), p. 31 [O'Casey employed the chorus]; pp. 62-3 [The
Silver Tassie and Within the Gates show that Expressionism
is a live force in modern drama]; p. 178 [O'Casey turned his
back upon the theatre because "the beauty, fire and poetry
of drama have perished in the storm of fake realism"].

1483 _____, The Twentieth-Century Drama (London: George G.
Harrap, 1946), pp. 65-6 [Discusses Juno and the Paycock
and The Silver Tassie].

1484 Hughes, Catharine, Plays, Politics, and Polemics (New York:
Drama Book Specialists, 1973), pp. 69-76 [Discusses The Silver Tassie].

1485 Hughes, Glenn, A History of the American Theatre, 1700-1950
(New York and London: Samuel French, 1951), pp. 388-90
[Lists O'Casey's plays produced in the American theatre].

1486 Hunt, Hugh, The Abbey: Ireland's National Theatre, 1904-
1979 (Dublin: Gill and Macmillan; New York: Columbia University Press, 1979), passim [O'Casey's relationship with the
Abbey Theatre].

1487 _____, The Live Theatre (London and New York: Oxford
University Press, 1962), pp. 124, 137 [O'Casey, like many
of the naturalist playwrights, later turned to fantasy].

1488 _____, The Theatre and Nationalism in Ireland (Swansea,
Wales: University College of Swansea, 1974), pp. 18-19, 21
["O'Casey turned from political clichés to the human realities
of men and women caught in the vortex of national hatred"].

1489 _____; Kenneth Richards; and John Russell Taylor, The Rev-
els History of Drama in English, Vol. 7: 1880 to the Present
Day (London: Methuen; New York: Barnes & Noble, 1978),
pp. 205-7 [Assesses O'Casey's dramatic achievement].

1490 Huscher, Herbert, "Das Anglo-Irische und seine Bedeutung als
sprachkünstlerisches Ausdrucksmittel," in Festschrift für Max
Deutschbein (Leipzig: Quelle & Meyer, 1936), pp. 40-59
[Brief comments on the language of Juno and the Paycock
and The Silver Tassie].

1491 Hutchins, Patricia, "Sean O'Casey and James Joyce," in James Joyce's World (London: Methuen, 1957), pp. 235-6 [Within the Gates had been attributed to Joyce, and Finnegans Wake to O'Casey].

1492 Ivasheva, Valentina Vasil 'evna, Angliiskaĩa literatura xx vek (Moskva: Izdatel 'stvo "Prosvechnie," 1967), pp. 93-8, 114-17 [Critical assessment].

1493 Jacquot, Jean, Le Théâtre tragique (Paris: Editions du Centre National de la Recherche Scientifique, 1965), pp. 518-19 [Examines the tragic element in Red Roses for Me and The Plough and the Stars].

1494 Jeans, Ronald, Writing for the Theatre (London: Edward Arnold, 1949), pp. 65-6 [The opening scene of The Plough and the Stars is "a good example of preliminary establishing of off-stage characters"].

1495 Jeffares, A. Norman, Anglo-Irish Literature. Macmillan History of Literature, 3 (London: Macmillan, 1982), pp. 276-81 [O'Casey and the Twenties].

1496 _____, "Ireland," in Literatures of the World in English, ed. Bruce King (London and Boston: Routledge & Kegan Paul, 1974), pp. 112-13 [Though O'Casey experimented in new forms of more poetical drama he never matched the dramatic effectiveness of his early plays].

1497 Jochum, K. P. S., "Die spaten Dramen O'Casey," in Einführung in die zeitgenössische irische Literatur, ed. J. Kornelius, E. Otto, and G. Stratmann (Heidelberg: Carl Winter, 1980), pp. 79-91 [Discusses the later dramas of O'Casey].

1498 John, Augustus, "Sean O'Casey," in Finishing Touches (London: Jonathan Cape, 1964), pp. 49-50 [Recollections of O'Casey].

1499 Johnston, Denis, "Preface" and "Up the Rebels!" in Collected Plays, vol. 1 (London: Jonathan Cape, 1960) [Comments on The Silver Tassie and The Plough and the Stars].

1500 _____, "Sean O'Casey," in Living Writers, ed. Gilbert Phelps (London: Sylvan Press, 1947), pp. 28-38 [Critical study broadcast on the B.B.C.].

1501 Jones, Margo, Theatre-in-the-Round (New York: Rinehart, 1951), pp. 181-2 [Describes the first professional production of Cock-a-Doodle Dandy].

1502 Jordan, John, "The Irish Theatre: Retrospect and Premonition," in Contemporary Theatre, Stratford-upon-Avon Studies, 4, ed. John Russell Brown and Bernard Harris (London: Edward Arnold, 1962), pp. 165-78 [O'Casey, unlike most Irish dramatists before him, "wrote originally for a native Irish audience"].

1503 Kain, Richard M., Dublin in the Age of William Butler Yeats and James Joyce (Norman: University of Oklahoma Press, 1962), passim [Dublin as reflected in the writings of O'Casey].

1504 Kargova, A.M., "Stilisticheskoe ispol'zovanie glagol'nykh form v avtobiograficheskoi epopee Shona O'Keisi," in Nekotorye voprosy angliiskoi filologii. Chelyabinskii pedagogicheskii institut, Chelyabinsk (1971: vypusk 2), pp. 92-101 [The stylistic usage of verbal forms in the Autobiographies].

1505 Kavanagh, Patrick, Collected Pruse (London: MacGibbon & Kee, 1967), p. 239 [O'Casey "hasn't got a true poetic genius"]; p. 245 [O'Casey's anger is "worthless and even pitiful"]; p. 260 [Juno and the Paycock "couldn't exist if the Will hadn't been botched"].

1506 Kavanagh, Peter, "Sean O'Casey," in The Story of the Abbey Theatre from Its Origins in 1899 to the Present (New York: Devin-Adair, 1950), pp. 129-43 [O'Casey was "the first and only great playwright who wrote for the Abbey Theatre about the real Ireland"].

1507 Kearney, Colbert, The Writings of Brendan Behan (Dublin: Gill and Macmillan, 1977), pp. 62-5 [Behan and O'Casey compared].

1508 Kemp, Thomas C., The Birmingham Repertory Theatre (Birmingham: Cornish Brothers Ltd., 1943), p. 39 [John Davison compared to O'Casey]; p. 70 [O'Casey was one of the newcomers who "broke the apathetic spell woven by war"].

1509 Kenny, Herbert A., Literary Dublin: A History (New York: Taplinger; Dublin: Gill & Macmillan, 1974), pp. 244-50 [The reception of O'Casey's plays in Dublin].

1510 Kernodle, George R., Invitation to the Theatre (New York: Harcourt, Brace, 1967), pp. 229-31 [In both comic and tragic scenes, it is the Irish lilt and the vivid language that raise O'Casey's plays above the dead level of naturalism].

1511 Kerr, Walter, God on the Gymnasium and Other Theatrical Adventures (New York: Delta Books, 1971), p. 244 [O'Casey's association with Bernard Shaw].

1512 _____, How Not to Write a Play (Boston: The Writer, 1955),
p. 66 ["In his later plays, O'Casey's talent for language did
not desert him, but his love of the actual went down before
his prophetic apprehensions about the future"].

1513 Kiberd, Declan, "The Perils of Nostalgia: A Critique of the
Revival," in Literature and the Changing Ireland, ed. Peter
Connolly (Gerrards Cross, Buckinghamshire: Colin Smythe;
Totowa, N.J.: Barnes and Noble, 1982), pp. 1-24 [O'Casey
and other Irish writers' exile from Ireland].

1514 Kienzle, Siegfried, "Sean O'Casey," in Modern World Theater:
A Guide to Productions in Europe and the United States Since
1945 (New York: Frederick Ungar, 1970), pp. 340-1 [Gives
information on The Bishop's Bonfire].

1515 Kitchin, Laurence, Drama in the Sixties: Form and Interpretation (London: Faber and Faber, 1966), pp. 103-6 [Assesses
O'Casey's dramatic output]; p. 101 [O'Casey influenced Wes-
ker].

1516 _____, Mid-Century Drama, 2nd rev. ed. (London: Faber
and Faber, 1962), p. 76 [Few critics are satisfied with late
O'Casey]; pp. 107, 110, 114, 195 [O'Casey's influence on
Delaney, Behan, and Wesker]; p. 182 [Laestadius on O'Casey].

1516a Knight, G. Wilson, Christ and Nietzsche (London: Staples
Press, 1948; rpt. Folcroft, Pa.: Folcroft Press, 1970), passim [Within the Gates and The Silver Tassie].

1517 _____, The Christian Renaissance (London: Methuen, 1962),
pp. 341-7. Reprinted from Stand, 4 (Summer 1960), 15-18
[Discusses The Drums of Father Ned].

1518 _____, The Golden Labyrinth: A Study of British Drama
(London: Phoenix House, 1962; University Paperbacks, 1965),
pp. 373-80 [O'Casey is in the main a war dramatist; he uses
in turn every modern fight, social, civil, or international,
that comes within the range of his experience and on each
lavishes his art].

1519 Kornilova, E[lena], "Dramaturgiíã Shona O'Keisi," in Souremen-
naíã zarubezhnaíã drama, ed. Lev Zolmanovich Kopelev (Moskva:
Akademiíã Navk SSSR, 1962), pp. 63-131 [Critical assessment].

1520 Kosok, Heinz, "O'Casey: The Plough and the Stars," in Das
englische Drama: Vom Mittelalter bis zur Gegenwart, ed.
Dieter Mehl (Düsseldorf: Bagel, 1970), vol. 2, pp. 217-39,
375-7 [Critical study].

1521 Krause, David, "The Theatre of Dion Boucicault," in The Dolmen Boucicault (Dublin: Dolmen Press, 1964), pp. 9-47
[O'Casey owed a deep debt to Boucicault].

1522 _____, "Sean O'Casey: 1880-1964" in Irish Renaissance, ed.
Robin Skelton and David R. Clark (Dublin: Dolmen Press,
1965), pp. 139-57. Reprinted from Massachusetts Review,
6 (Winter-Spring 1965), 233-51 [Recollections of O'Casey].

1523 _____, The Profane Book of Irish Comedy (Ithaca and London: Cornell University Press, 1982) [Includes several discussions on O'Casey's works].

1524 _____, "Sean O'Casey and the Higher Nationalism: The
Desecration of Ireland's Household Gods," in Theatre and Nationalism in Twentieth-Century Ireland, ed. Robert O'Driscoll
(Toronto: University of Toronto Press; London: Oxford
University Press, 1971), pp. 114-33 [Argues that O'Casey
got involved through his works by questioning and even
desecrating the sanctity of the national idealism].

1525 Kronenberger, Louis, ed., Cavalcade of Comedy (New York:
Simon & Schuster, 1953) [Anthology including the text of, and
a commentary on, Juno and the Paycock].

1526 Krutch, Joseph Wood, "Modernism" in Modern Drama: A Defi-
nition and an Estimate (Ithaca, N.Y.: Cornell University
Press, 1953), pp. 97-101 [Discusses Juno and the Paycock
and The Plough and the Stars as a realistic picture of Irish
life].

1527 Larkin, Emmet, James Larkin: Irish Labour Leader 1876-1947
(London: Routledge & Kegan Paul, 1965), pp. xiii, xv, 303
[O'Casey's association with Larkin].

1528 Lawson, John Howard, Theory and Technique of Playwriting
(New York: G. P. Putnam's, 1936; Hill & Wang, 1960), pp.
xxiii-xxiv [The two modern playwrights who have done most
to restore the theatrical imagination are O'Casey and Brecht].

1529 Leal, Rine, ed., Teatro irlandès (Habana: Consejo Nacional
de Cultura, 1966) [Anthology including the text of, and a
commentary on, Juno and the Paycock].

1530 Leclerc, Guy, Les grandes aventures du Théâtre (Paris: Edi-
teurs Français Réunis, 1965), pp. 304-9 [Discusses The Shadow
of a Gunman, Juno and the Paycock, The Plough and the Stars,
and Red Roses for Me].

1531 Leech, Clifford, The Dramatist's Experience (London: Chatto

& Windus, 1970), p. 85 [Comedy in Juno and the Paycock];
p. 222 [In O'Casey "the words have a relish and the imagery
a fecundity that even the Irish cannot be expected to master
in their everyday talk]; p. 224 [O'Casey was privileged in
belonging to a country "where urban civilization had not worn
down the contours of words"].

1532 _____, Tragedy (London: Methuen, 1969), pp. 26, 37, 40
[The juxtaposition of comedy and tragedy in the plays of
O'Casey].

1533 Leroy, Bernard, "Two Committed Playwrights: Wesker and
O'Casey," in Aspects of the Irish Theatre, ed. Patrick Rafroidi, Raymonde Popot, and William Parker (Paris: Editions
Universitaires, Publications de l'Université de Lille, 1972),
pp. 107-17 [Both playwrights are similar, especially in a
number of common themes, techniques, aims, and attitudes].

1534 Levenson, Samuel, James Connolly: A Biography (London:
Martin Brian & O'Keeffe, 1973), pp. 249-51 [O'Casey and the
Irish Citizen Army].

1535 Lewis, Allan, American Plays and Playwrights of the Contemporary Theatre (New York: Crown Publishers, 1965), p.
43 [In investigating new techniques, Brecht, O'Casey, and
Sartre did not achieve perfection with their first new play
in a different form]; p. 124 [O'Casey and Odets added a
richness of common speech that outshines the mechanical im-
position of verse]; p. 130 [In his later plays, O'Casey produced feeble repetitions of his earlier work]; p. 223 [Juno
and the Paycock and Red Roses for Me as musicals].

1536 _____, "Irish Romantic Realism--Sean O'Casey," in The Con-
temporary Theatre: The Significant Playwrights of Our Time
(New York: Crown Publishers, 1962), pp. 169-91 [Assesses
O'Casey as a dramatist and gives detailed analysis of Red
Roses for Me].

1537 Lewis, Emory, Stages: The Fifty-Year Childhood of the American Theatre (Englewood Cliffs, N.J.: Prentice-Hall, 1969),
passim [Makes references to the productions of O'Casey's
plays on the American stage].

1538 Lezon, Jeanne, "The Easter Rising Seen from the Tenements,"
in Aspects of the Irish Theatre, ed. Patrick Rafroidi, Raymonde Popot, and William Parker (Paris: Editions Universitaires, Publications de l'Université de Lille, 1972), pp. 75-
95 [The Plough and the Stars and Irish nationalism].

1539 Lindsay, Jack, "Sean O'Casey as a Socialist Artist," in Decay

and Renewal: Critical Essays on Twentieth Century Writing
(London: Lawrence & Wishart, 1976), pp. 124-38. Reprinted
from Sean O'Casey, ed. Ronald Ayling (London: Macmillan,
1969), pp. 192-203 ["Although O'Casey's artistic vision natu-
rally grows deeper and richer as he goes on, he begins with
a central socialist focus, which remains with him throughout
his life and finds consistent expression"].

1540 Little, Stuart W., Off-Broadway: The Prophetic Theater. Delta
Books (New York: Dell, 1974), pp. 93-6 [Discusses Paul
Shyre's productions of Autobiographies, Purple Dust, and
Cock-a-Doodle Dandy].

1541 Loftus, Richard J., Nationalism in Modern Anglo-Irish Poetry
(Madison and Milwaukee: University of Wisconsin Press,
1964), pp. 247-8 [Examines the literary side of the controversy over The Plough and the Stars].

1542 Longaker, Mark, and Edwin C. Bolles, Contemporary English
Literature (New York: Appleton-Century-Crofts, 1953), pp.
64, 391 [O'Casey's plays show a concern with humanity which
gives them a universal interest].

1543 Lucas, F. L., The Drama of Chekhov, Synge, Yeats, and Pi-
randello, 2nd ed. (London: Cassell, 1965), p. 171 [O'Casey's
attempts to repeat Synge's music "seem to me much inferior"];
p. 325 [Yeats compared to O'Casey]; p. 345 [Yeats on The
Silver Tassie].

1544 Lucke, Helmut, "Sean O'Casey," in Zeitgenössische englische
Vichtung: Einführung in die englische Literaturbetrachtung
mit Interpretationen, Bd. 3: Drama, ed. Heinz Nyszkiewicz
(Frankfurt: Hirschgraben, 1968), pp. 134-47 [Discusses
Purple Dust].

1545 Lumley, Frederick, New Trends in 20th Century Drama: A
Survey Since Ibsen and Shaw (London: Barrie and Rockliff, 1967), pp. 294-6 [Discusses O'Casey's later plays and
finds them inferior to his Dublin Trilogy].

1546 Lunari, Gigi, ed., Teatro irlandese (Milano: Nuova Accademia,
1961) [Anthology including the text of, and a commentary on,
The Bishop's Bonfire].

1547 Lyons, F.S.L., "The Parnell Theme in Literature," in Place,
Personality and the Irish Writer (Gerrards Cross, Buckinghamshire: Colin Smythe, 1977), pp. 80, 88-9 [O'Casey's
Autobiographies draws attention to the "irrelevance of the
public drama of politics to the poor whose struggle for sur-
vival occupies them to the exclusion of all else"].

1548 Mabley, Edward, Dramatic Construction: An Outline of Basic
      Principles (Philadelphia: Chilton Book Company, 1972), pp.
      173-86 [Gives a synopsis and a detailed analysis of Juno and
      the Paycock].

1549 MacAnna, Tomás, "Nationalism from the Abbey Stage," in The-
      atre and Nationalism in Twentieth-Century Ireland, ed. Robert
      O'Driscoll (Toronto: University of Toronto Press, 1971),
      passim [Recognizes that O'Casey outraged the nationalists
      but believes that in the Dublin Trilogy he "takes no sides"].

1550 McCann, Sean, ed., The Story of the Abbey Theatre (London:
      New English Library, 1967), passim [O'Casey's relationship
      with the Abbey Theatre].

1551 MacCarthy, Desmond, Drama (London: Putnam, 1941; rpt. New
      York: Benjamin Blom, 1971), pp. 349-54. Reprinted from
      New Statesman and Nation (London), 7 (17 Feb 1934), 226-7
      [Review of the production of Within the Gates at the Royalty
      Theatre, London].

1552 McCollom, William G., Tragedy (New York: Macmillan, 1957),
      pp. 102-3 [Discusses the last act of Juno and the Paycock].

1553 MacDiarmid, Hugh [Christopher Murray Grieve], "Sean O'Casey,"
      in The Company I've Kept: Essays in Autobiography (Lon-
      don: Hutchinson, 1966), pp. 161-9 [Recollections]. Re-
      viewed, with adverse comments on O'Casey, by Bernard Ma-
      her in Irish Times (Dublin), (10 Nov 1966), p. 9. See re-
      ply by Ronald Ayling, ibid., (29 Nov 1966), p. 7.

1554 Macgowan, Kenneth, A Primer of Playwriting (New York: Ran-
      dom House, 1951), p. 6 [Like Shakespeare, O'Casey lacked
      formal education]; p. 96 [The movement of The Plough and
      the Stars is poorly plotted, but the play is unified by the
      superb handling of mood and character].

1555 _____, and William Melnitz. The Living Stage: A History
      of the World Theater (Englewood Cliffs, N.J.: Prentice-Hall,
      1955), pp. 413-4 [O'Casey on Strindberg]; p. 424 [O'Casey
      wrote realistic plays with outstanding distinction].

1556 McGrory, Kathleen, and John Unterecker, "Interview with Jack
      MacGowran," in Yeats, Joyce, and Beckett: New Light on
      Three Modern Irish Writers (Lewisburg, Pa.: Bucknell Uni-
      versity Press; London: Associated University Press, 1976),
      pp. 172-82 [Comments on O'Casey's communism, anti-
      clericalism, and his association with W. B. Yeats].

1557 McHugh, Roger, and Maurice Harmon, Short History of Anglo-

Irish Literature, from Its Origins to the Present Day (Dublin: Wolfhound Press, 1982), pp. 177-81 [The Dublin Trilogy]; pp. 287-9 [The later plays].

1558 MacLiammóir, Micheál, All for Hecuba: An Irish Theatrical Autobiography (London: Methuen, 1946), pp. 46, 53, 346 [O'Casey's relationship with the Abbey Theatre].

1559 _____, "Problem Plays," in The Irish Theatre, ed. Lennox Robinson (London: Macmillan, 1939), pp. 199-227 [Argues that the political problems of O'Casey's plays are already out of date].

1560 _____, Theatre in Ireland (Dublin: At the Sign of the Three Candles, 1950; rpt. with Sequel, 1964), passim [O'Casey's relationship with the Abbey Theatre].

1561 _____, and Edwin Smith, Ireland (London: Thames and Hudson, 1977), p. 45 [O'Casey is a "lesser figure" than Synge].

1562 MacLysaght, Edward, Changing Times: Ireland Since 1898 (Gerrards Cross, Buckinghamshire: Colin Smythe, 1978), pp. 61-2, 188-9 [Recollections of O'Casey].

1563 Macmillan, Harold, Winds of Change, 1914-1939 (London: Macmillan; New York: Harper & Row, 1966), p. 187 [O'Casey had "a truly Christian nature" and was "one of the kindest and most genuine men that I have known"].

1564 Malone, Andrew E., The Irish Drama, 1896-1928 (London: Constable, 1929; rpt. New York: Benjamin Blom, 1965), pp. 209-19 [Discusses The Shadow of a Gunman, Juno and the Paycock, and The Plough and the Stars].

1565 Marowitz, Charles, et al., The Encore Reader: A Chronicle of the New Drama (London: Methuen, 1965), p. 13 [O'Casey greets Beckett's Waiting for Godot with rejection].

1566 Marreco, Anne, The Rebel Countess: the Life and Times of Constance Markievicz (London: Weidenfeld and Nicolson; Philadelphia: Chilton Books, 1967), passim [O'Casey and Irish nationalism].

1567 Marriott, J.W., Modern Drama (London: Thomas Nelson, [1934]), pp. 200-2 [O'Casey is in many ways the most remarkable product of the Irish Dramatic Movement].

1568 _____, The Theatre (London: George G. Harrap, 1931), p. 35 [The reception of Juno and the Paycock]; pp. 147-9

[Discusses The Shadow of a Gunman, Juno and the Paycock, The Plough and the Stars, and The Silver Tassie]; p. 156 [The only truly original drama is inspired by life itself: O'Casey found it in the Dublin slums].

1569 Marx, Milton, The Enjoyment of Drama, 2nd ed. (New York: Appleton-Century-Crofts, 1961), p. 49 [In The Plough and the Stars O'Casey shows us that nationalism has become dominant over humanitarianism].

1570 Massey, Raymond, A Hundred Different Lives (London: Robson, 1979), chap. 10 [Recollections of the production of The Silver Tassie at the Apollo Theatre, London].

1571 Mathelin, Bernard, "From the Shadow of War to the Broken Tassie," in Aspects of the Irish Theatre, ed. Patrick Rafroidi, Raymonde Popot, and William Parker (Paris: Editions Universitaires, Publications de l'Université de Lille, 1972), pp. 97-105 [O'Casey presented his personal vision of war in The Shadow of a Gunman, Juno and the Paycock, The Plough and the Stars, The Silver Tassie, and Oak Leaves and Lavender].

1572 Maxwell, D.E.S., "The Shape-Changers," in Yeats, Sligo and Ireland: Essays to Mark the 21st Yeats International Summer School, ed. A. Norman Jeffares. Irish Literary Studies 6 (Gerrards Cross, Buckinghamshire: Colin Smythe, 1980), p. 165 [The Plough and the Stars].

1573 Melchinger, Siegfried, Theater der Gegenwart (Frankfurt: Fischer Bücherei, 1956), p. 140 [In O'Neill, there is pure love of humanity; but in O'Casey, it is mixed with politics].

1574 Merchant, Francis, A.E.: An Irish Promethean (Columbia, S.C.: Benedict College Press, 1954), pp. 205-7, 238-9 [O'Casey denounced George Russell].

1575 Mercier, Vivian, The Irish Comic Tradition (Oxford: Oxford University Press, 1962), passim [Comedy and satire in Cock-a-Doodle Dandy, Juno and the Paycock, The Plough and the Stars, Red Roses for Me, The Shadow of a Gunman, and Autobiographies].

1576 _____, and David H. Greene, eds., 1000 Years of Irish Prose: The Literary Revival (New York: Devin-Adair, 1952; rpt. Grosset & Dunlap, 1961) [Anthology including the text of, and a commentary of, The Shadow of a Gunman].

1577 Meserve, Walter J., An Outline History of American Drama (Totowa, N.J.: Littlefield, Adams, 1970), pp. 232, 284 [O'Casey on Eugene O'Neill].

1578 Metscher, Thomas, "Sean O'Casey," in Englische Dichter der
Moderne Ihr Leben und Werk, ed. Rudolf Sühnel and Dieter
Riesner (Berlin: Erich Schmidt, 1971), pp. 439-55 [Discusses
O'Casey as a socialist].

1579 Mikhail, E.H., ed., Lady Gregory: Interviews and Recollections
(London: Macmillan, 1977), passim [O'Casey's association with
Lady Gregory].

1580 _____, ed., W.B. Yeats: Interviews and Recollections (London: Macmillan, 1977), passim [O'Casey's association with
Yeats].

1581 Mili, Gjon, Photographs and Recollections (Boston: New York
Graphic Society, 1980), pp. 98-103 [Recollections of O'Casey].

1582 Miller, Anna Irene, The Independent Theatre in Europe, 1887
to the Present (New York: Ray Long & Richard R. Smith,
1931; rpt. Benjamin Blom, 1966), pp. 289-91 [Under the
humor of O'Casey's plays is understanding of Ireland, satire
of Irish weaknesses, as well as admiration for Irish strength
and sympathy for the humble worker everywhere]; pp. 309-
10 [Discusses The Silver Tassie].

1583 Mitchell, Jack, "The Role of Emotion in the Theatre of Sean
O'Casey," in Irland Gesellschaft und Kultur, II, ed. Dorothea
Siegmund-Schultze (Halle: Martin Luther Universität, 1979),
pp. 121-9 [O'Casey was able to become the national and people's dramatist of Ireland because he participated in the emo-
tionality of the labouring masses].

1584 Mittenzwei, Werner, Gestaltung und Gestalten im modernen Drama
(Berlin and Weimar, 1965), pp. 95-7 [Discusses Red Roses
for Me].

1585 Moon, Samuel, ed., One Act: Eleven Short Plays of the Modern
Theatre (New York: Grove Press, 1961) [Anthology including
the text of, and a commentary on, Bedtime Story].

1586 Morcos, Louis, and Ali Er-Rai, eds., Modern International
Plays (Cairo: Anglo-Egyptian Bookshop, 1957) [Anthology
including the text of, and a commentary on, A Pound on
Demand].

1587 Morgan, Charles, "On Sean O'Casey's The Silver Tassie," in
The English Dramatic Critics: An Anthology, 1660-1932, ed.
James Agate (London: Arthur Barker, 1932; rpt. New York:
Hill & Wang, [1958], pp. 347-9. Reprinted from Times (Lon-
don), (12 Oct 1929), p. 8 [Review of the production at the
Apollo Theatre, London].

1588 Morley, Sheridan, Review Copies: Plays and Players in London, 1970-74 (London: Robson Books, 1974), p. 164 [Bill Bryden compared to O'Casey]; p. 170 [Brian Friel compared to O'Casey].

1589 Muir, Kenneth, "Verse and Prose," in Contemporary Theatre, ed. John Russell Brown and Bernard Harris. Stratford-upon-Avon Studies, 4 (London: Edward Arnold, 1962), pp. 100-2 [In his early plays, O'Casey "invests all his characters with a wonderful gift of the gab," but in Within the Gates and The Star Turns Red, he turns away from this style].

1590 Natev, Atanas, Sovremenna Zapadna dramaturgiya [Contemporary Western Drama] (Sofia: Nauka i Jskustvo, 1965), pp. 252-3 [Critical assessment of O'Casey].

1591 Nathan, George Jean, "O'Casey," in Art of the Night (New York: Alfred A. Knopf, 1928), pp. 185-93. Reprinted in The Magic Mirror: Selected Writings on the Theatre, ed. Thomas Quinn Curtiss (New York: Alfred A. Knopf, 1960), pp. 180-5 [Discusses Juno and the Paycock and The Plough and the Stars].

1592 _____, "Sean O'Casey," in Encyclopaedia of the Theatre (New York: Alfred A. Knopf, 1940), pp. 286-8 [Points out that Communism has adversely affected O'Casey as a dramatic artist].

1593 _____, "The Contribution of the Irish," in The Entertainment of a Nation (New York: Alfred A. Knopf, 1942), pp. 68-75 [Argues that, except for O'Casey, "the quondam rich vein appears to have run dry"].

1594 _____, The Theatre Book of the Year 1946-1947 (New York: Alfred A. Knopf, 1947), pp. 231-9 [Discusses the production of A Pound on Demand].

1595 _____, The Theatre in the Fifties (New York: Alfred A. Knopf, 1953), p. 55 [O'Casey quoted]; p. 59 [Behrman compared with O'Casey]; p. 123 [American drama does not have "the poetic imagination and literary music" of O'Casey]; p. 156 [O'Casey is not popular on the English stage].

1596 _____, ed., Five Great Modern Irish Plays (New York: The Modern Library, 1941) [Anthology including the text of, and a commentary on, Juno and the Paycock].

1597 _____, ed., World's Great Plays (Cleveland, Ohio: World Publishing Company, 1944; New York: Grosset's Universal

Library, 1961) [Anthology including the text of, and a commentary on, The Plough and the Stars].

1598 _____, et al., eds., The American Spectator Year Book (New York: Frederick A. Stokes, 1934) [Anthology including the text of "Dramatis Personae Ibsenisenis"].

1599 Nelson, James, ed., "Sean O'Casey," in Wisdom: Conversations with the Elder Wise Men of Our Day (New York: W.W. Norton, 1958), pp. 25-33 [Interview by Robert Emmett Ginna, Jr.].

1600 Nevin, Donal, ed., 1913: Jim Larkin and the Dublin Lock-Out (Dublin: Workers' Union of Ireland, 1964), pp. 44-6, 61-4 [O'Casey and Irish nationalism].

1601 Newman, Evelyn, The International Note in Contemporary Drama (New York: Kingsland Press, 1931), pp. 36-43 [Discusses The Silver Tassie].

1602 Nichols, Beverley, "Sean O'Casey, or A Rough Diamond," in Are They the Same at Home? Being a Series of Bouquets Differently Distributed (New York: George H. Doran, 1927), pp. 235-8 [Interview with O'Casey].

1603 Nicholson, Hubert, "The O'Casey Horn of Plenty," in A Voyage to Wonderland and Other Essays (London: Heinemann, 1947), pp. 36-54 [Discusses O'Casey's Autobiographies].

1604 Nicoll, Allardyce, British Drama, 6th ed. rev. by J.C. Trewin (London: Harrap, 1978), pp. 232-4 [Discusses The Shadow of a Gunman, Juno and the Paycock, The Plough and the Stars, The Silver Tassie, and Within the Gates]; pp. 267-8 [Discusses the last plays briefly].

1605 _____, English Drama: A Modern Viewpoint (London: George G. Harrap, 1968), pp. 112-13 [O'Casey was virtually the only dramatist writing in English who succeeded in mastering the expressionist style].

1606 _____, The Theory of Drama (London: George G. Harrap; New York: Thomas Y. Crowell, 1931; rpt. New York: Benjamin Blom, 1966), passim [Includes illustrations from The Silver Tassie and Juno and the Paycock].

1607 _____, World Drama from Aeschylus to Anouilh, 2nd rev. and enl. ed. (London: George G. Harrap, 1976), pp. 686-8 [Expressionism and realism meet in the work of O'Casey].

1608 Noble, Peter, British Theatre (London: British Yearbooks, n.d.), pp. 188-9 [Describes the production of Red Roses for Me at the Embassy Theatre, London].

1609 Nowell-Smith, Simon, ed., "Sean O'Casey," in Letters to Macmillan (London: Macmillan; New York: St. Martin's Press, 1967), pp. 360-9 [Correspondence between O'Casey and Harold Macmillan, with commentary].

1610 O'Brien, Conor Cruse, ed., The Shaping of Modern Ireland (London: Routledge & Kegan Paul, 1960), pp. 6, 82 [O'Casey and Irish nationalism].

1611 O'Brien, John A., ed., The Vanishing Irish (New York and London: McGraw-Hill, 1953), pp. 6, 23-4 [O'Casey quoted on Irish emigration].

1612 O'Connor, Frank, "The Abbey Theatre," in My Father's Son (London: Macmillan, 1968; New York: Alfred A. Knopf, 1969), passim [O'Casey's relationship with the Abbey Theatre].

1613 _____, A Short History of Irish Literature: A Backward Look (London: Macmillan; New York: Capricorn Books, 1968), pp. 216-21 [Discusses The Shadow of a Gunman, Juno and the Paycock, and The Plough and the Stars].

1614 O'Connor, Ulick, Oliver St. John Gogarty: A Poet and His Times (London: Jonathan Cape, 1964), pp. 154-6 [Traces O'Casey's early plays back to Gogarty's Blight, a tragicomedy about Dublin tenement life].

1615 O'Faolain, Sean, "The Writers," in The Irish: A Character Study (New York: Devin-Adair, 1949), passim [Realism and nationalism in O'Casey].

1616 O hAodha, Micheál, "Sean O'Casey," in The Abbey--Then and Now (Dublin: The Abbey Theatre, 1969), pp. 60-1 [Extract from a broadcast tribute on the occasion of O'Casey's death].

1617 _____, "O'Casey and After," in Theatre in Ireland (Oxford: Basil Blackwell, 1974), pp. 105-18 [Assesses O'Casey's dramatic works].

1618 Olson, Elder, Tragedy and the Theory of Drama (Detroit: Wayne State University Press, 1966), p. 68 [In A Pound on Demand the plot explains itself as it unfolds].

1619 Olsson, Jan Olof, and Margareta Sjögren, Plogen och stjärnorna: Irländsk dramatik i verkligheten och på scenen (Stockholm: Sveriges Radios Förlag, 1968), pp. 148-77 [Introductory study of all O'Casey's works].

1620 Orr, John, Tragic Drama and Modern Society (London: Macmillan, 1981) [The chapter on O'Casey considers the Dublin
Trilogy].

1621 Orwell, George, "Drums Under the Windows by Sean O'Casey,"
in The Collected Essays, Journalism and Letters of George
Orwell. Volume 4, ed. Sonia Orwell and Ian Angus (London:
Secker & Warburg, 1968), pp. 13-15 [Reprinted from Observer
(London), (28 Oct 1945), p. 3].

1622 Ould, Herman, "Sean O'Casey," in The Art of the Play (London:
Isaac Pitman, 1938), pp. 99-100 [Discusses The Silver Tassie
and Within the Gates].

1623 Ovcharenko, A., Socialist Realism and the Modern Literary
Process (Moscow: Progress Publishers, 1978), pp. 61, 75,
118 [Socialist realism in the works of O'Casey, Maxim Gorky
and others].

1624 Pascal, Roy, Design and Truth in Autobiography (London:
Routledge & Kegan Paul; Cambridge, Mass.: Harvard University Press, 1960), pp. 151-5 [Examines the form and content of Autobiographies].

1625 Paul-Dubois, Louis, Le drame irlandais et l'Irlande nouvelle
(Paris: Perrin, 1927), pp. 208-9 [Political background to
O'Casey's Dublin Trilogy].

1626 Peacock, Ronald, The Poet in the Theatre (London: Routledge,
1946), p. 6; (London: Macgibbon & Kee; New York: Hill &
Wang, 1961), p. 9 [O'Casey's characters "are not as important as the larger political tragedy of which they are fortuitous
victims"].

1627 Pearson, Hesketh, Bernard Shaw: His Life and Personality
(London: Collins, 1942), p. 390; (London: Methuen, 1961),
pp. 282-3 [Shaw on O'Casey].

1628 Pellizzi, Camillo, English Drama: The Last Great Phase (London: Macmillan, 1935), pp. 236-40 [Discusses The Shadow
of a Gunman, Juno and the Paycock, The Plough and the
Stars, and The Silver Tassie].

1629 Pickering, Jerry V., Readers Theatre (Encino and Belmont,
Calif.: Dickenson Publishing Company, 1975), pp. 10-13
[Discusses Paul Shyre's adaptations of Autobiographies].

1630 Plunkett, Grace, Twelve Nights at the Abbey Theatre: A Book
of Drawings (Dublin: At the Sign of the Three Candles,
1929) [Includes drawings of Juno and the Paycock and The
Shadow of a Gunman].

1631 Power, Patrick C., A Literary History of Ireland (Cork: Mercier Press, 1969), pp. 174-6 [O'Casey was influenced by Boucicault].

1632 Prescott, Joseph, ed., "Sean O'Casey Concerning James Joyce," in Irish Renaissance: A Gathering of Essays, Memoirs and Letters from "The Massachusetts Review," ed. Robin Skelton and David R. Clark (Dublin: Dolmen Press, 1965), pp. 128-9. Reprinted from Massachusetts Review, 5 (Winter 1964), 335-6 [Three letters by O'Casey to Prescott on Joyce].

1633 Prior, Moody E., The Language of Tragedy (New York: Columbia University Press, 1947; Bloomington and London: Indiana University Press, 1966), passim [Makes few references to O'Casey].

1634 Pritchett, V.S., Dublin: A Portrait (London: The Bodley Head, 1967), pp. 10-11 [O'Casey "got closer than anyone to what Dublin felt"]; pp. 15-16 [In 1923 O'Casey was "the new master" of the Abbey Theatre].

1635 Rabkin, Gerald, Drama and Commitment: Politics in the American Theatre of the Thirties (Bloomington: Indiana University Press, 1964), p. 60 [The American thirties produced no playwright of the stature of O'Casey].

1636 Rafroidi, Patrick, "The Funny Irishman," in Aspects of the Irish Theatre, ed. Patrick Rafroidi, Raymonde Popot, and William Parker (Paris: Editions Universitaires; Lille: P.U.L., 1972), p. 19 [There is a touch of the Stage Irishman in the Captain Boyle of Juno and the Paycock].

1637 Reade, Arthur R., Main Currents in Modern Literature (London: Nicholson & Watson, 1935; rpt. Folcroft, Pa.: Folcroft Press, 1970), pp. 54-5 ["Of the post-war dramatists the most interesting figure is Sean O'Casey"].

1638 Reeve, Carl, and Ann Barton Reeve, James Connolly and the United States (Atlantic Highlands, N.J.: Humanities Press, 1978; Dublin: Academy Press, 1979, pp. 270-82 [Deals with O'Casey and Irish nationalism].

1639 Reiter, Seymour, World Theater: The Structure and Meaning of Drama (New York: Horizon Press, 1973), pp. 203-8 [Discusses the structural design of The Plough and the Stars].

1640 Reynolds, Ernest, Modern English Drama: A Survey of the Theatre from 1900 (London: George G. Harrap, 1949; Norman: University of Oklahoma Press, 1951), pp. 155-6 [Discusses The Silver Tassie and Within the Gates].

1641 Rice, Elmer, The Living Theatre (New York: Harper, 1959),
      p. 76 [In poetic beauty, imaginativeness, insight and the-
      atrical effectiveness it would be hard to match in any country
      the plays of O'Casey and other Irish dramatists]; p. 206
      [O'Neill compared to O'Casey]; p. 240 [O'Casey on off-
      Broadway].

1642 Richards, Stanley, ed., Best Short Plays of the World Theatre,
      1958-1967 (New York: Crown, 1968) [Anthology including
      the text of, and a commentary on, Nannie's Night Out].

1643 Rivoallan, A., L'Irlande (Paris: Librairie Armand Colin, 1934),
      p. 131 [O'Casey "did for the people of the city what Synge
      did for the peasants and fishermen"].

1644 _____, Littérature inlandaise contemporaine (Paris: Hachette
      1939), pp. 96-101 [Discusses The Shadow of a Gunman, Juno
      and the Paycock, The Plough and the Stars, and The Silver
      Tassie].

1645 Robbins, Frank, Under the Starry Plough: Recollections of the
      Irish Citizen Army (Dublin: Academy Press, 1977), passim
      [O'Casey as secretary of the Army; and his association with
      Jim Larkin, Madame Markievicz, and James Connolly].

1646 Roberts, Peter, Theatre in Britain: A Playgoer's Guide, 2nd
      ed. (London: Pitman, 1975), p. 8 [O'Casey "continues to
      be disgracefully neglected in the commercial theatre"].

1647 Roberts, Vera Mowry, The Nature of Theatre (New York and
      London: Harper & Row, 1971), p. 235 [Chekhov compared
      to O'Casey]; p. 237 [O'Casey counterpoints the foxtrot and
      the waltz in The Silver Tassie].

1648 Robinson, Lennox, Curtain Up: An Autobiography (London:
      Michael Joseph, 1942), pp. 138-41, 146 [Records some com-
      ments on the early rejected manuscripts O'Casey submitted to
      the Abbey Theatre in 1921-22; and includes recollections of
      O'Casey].

1649 _____, Ireland's Abbey Theatre: A History, 1899-1951
      (London: Sidgwick & Jackson, 1951; rpt. Port Washington,
      N.Y.: Kennikat Press, 1968), pp. 120-2 [The Shadow of a
      Gunman and Juno and the Paycock saved the Abbey Theatre
      from bankruptcy].

1650 _____, Pictures in a Theatre: A Conversation Piece (Dublin:
      The Abbey Theatre, [1947]), p. 12 [Sara Allgood created
      the part of Juno in Juno and the Paycock].

1651 _____, Towards an Appreciation of the Theatre (Dublin: Metropolitan Publishing Co., 1945), pp. 16-19 [Juno and the Paycock is an example of a carefully planned play].

1652 Rowe, Kenneth Thorpe, A Theater in Your Head (New York: Funk & Wagnalls, 1960), pp. 156, 157 [The juxtaposition of comedy and tragedy in the plays of O'Casey]; p. 260 [The Irish dialect in the plays of O'Casey contributes an inherent expressiveness and beauty to drama].

1653 Roy, Emil, "Sean O'Casey," in British Drama Since Shaw (Carbondale and Edwardsville: Southern Illinois University Press; London and Amsterdam: Feffer & Simons, 1972), pp. 68-82 [Discusses most of O'Casey's plays, and concludes that it is for his earlier plays that O'Casey will be remembered].

1654 Rubinstein, H.F., and J.C. Trewin, eds., The Drama Bedside Book (London: Victor Gollancz, 1966) [Anthology including part of, and a commentary on, The Plough and the Stars].

1655 Rudin, Seymour, "Playwright to Critic," in Irish Renaissance, ed. Robin Skelton and David R. Clark (Dublin: Dolmen Press, 1965), pp. 130-8. Reprinted from Massachusetts Review, 5 (Winter 1964), 326-34 [Describes O'Casey's letters to George Jean Nathan, with excerpts].

1656 Ruhle, Jurgen, Literatur und Revolution: Die Schriftsteller und der Kommunismus (Koln: Kiepenheuer & Witsch, 1960), pp. 417-21. Translated by Jean Steinberg as Literature and Revolution (New York: Praeger Publishers, 1969), pp. 386-9 [O'Casey and Irish nationalism].

1657 Russell, Caro Mae Green, "Sean O'Casey, Portrayer of Slum Life," in Modern Plays and Playwrights (Chapel Hill, N.C.: University of North Carolina Press, 1936), pp. 32-5 [Examines O'Casey as a dramatist and analyzes Juno and the Paycock and The Plough and the Stars].

1658 Russell, George W., Letters from AE, selected and edited by Alan Denson (London and New York: Abelard-Schuman, 1961), p. 167 [O'Casey's works are "pure literature"]; p. 171 [The Plough and the Stars is not as good as Juno and the Paycock].

1659 Ryan, Desmond, Remembering Sion: A Chronicle of Storm and Quiet (London: Arthur Barker, 1934), pp. 81-4 [Recollections of O'Casey].

1660 Sahal, N., "Sean O'Casey," in Sixty Years of Realistic Irish Drama (Bombay: Macmillan, 1971), pp. 90-119 [Discusses all

O'Casey's plays, and concludes that he is "the first modern dramatist to come out of brick and mortar and write about brick and mortar"].

1661 Salgãdo, Gãmini, English Drama: A Critical Introduction (London: Edward Arnold; New York: St. Martin's, 1980), pp. 184-6 [Discusses Cock-a-Doodle Dandy, Juno and the Paycock, The Plough and the Stars, Red Roses for Me, The Silver Tassie, and Within the Gates].

1662 Salter, Charles H., "Sean O'Casey: The Plough and the Stars," in Insight IV: Analyses of Modern British and American Drama, ed. Herman J. Weiand (Frankfurt: Hirschgraben, 1975), pp. 78-85 [Comprehensive study of the play].

1663 Samachson, Dorothy, and Joseph Samachson, The Dramatic Story of the Theatre (London and New York: Abelard-Schuman, 1955), pp. 131-2 [O'Casey's work is somewhat akin in spirit to Chekhov's]; p. 140 [In Within the Gates the symbolic characters have at the same time warm human qualities].

1664 Sarieva, L., "Shon O'Keĭsi," in Sŭvremenni angliĭski pisatelli (Sofiĭa: Nauka i izkustvo, 1965), pp. 218-44 [Critical study].

1665 Sarukhanĭan, Alla Pavlovna, Sovremennaĭa irlandskaĭa literatura [Contemporary Irish Literature] (Moskva: Izdatel 'stvo Nauka, 1973), passim.

1666 _____, "Tema natsional'no-osvoboditel 'nogo dvizheniĭa v irlandskoĭ literature 30-kh godov" [The Theme of the National and Liberation Movement in the Irish Literature of the Thirties]," in Zarubzhnaĭa literatura: 30-e gody xx veka, ed. Lidiĭa M. Ĭur'eva (Moskva: Izdatel 'stvo Nauka, 1969), pp. 269-92 [O'Casey and Irish nationalism].

1667 Schirmer, Walter F., Geschichte der Englischen und Amerikanischen Literatur (Tübingen: Max Niemeyer, 1968), pp. 723-5 [General assessment of O'Casey as a dramatist].

1668 Seehase, Georg, "Zum neuen Typ des künstlerischen Bewusstseins in Sean O'Casey Dramen," in Irland Gesellschaft und Kultur, II, ed. Dorothea Siegmund-Schultze (Halle: Martin Luther Universität, 1979), pp. 130-5 [Deals with "the new type of artistic consciousness" in the plays of O'Casey].

1669 Sheehy, Michael, Is Ireland Dying? Culture and the Church in Modern Ireland (London: Hollis & Carter, 1968), pp. 133-44 [O'Casey's plays show that he was conscious of both Irish puritanism and politics].

1670 Sherman, Joseph, ed., Contrasts in Drama: Twentieth-Century
     One-Act Plays (London: Edward Arnold, 1975) [Anthology
     including the text of, and annotations on, The End of the
     Beginning].

1671 Short, Ernest, Introducing the Theatre (London: Eyre & Spot-
     tiswoode, 1949), pp. 178-82 [Discusses The Silver Tassie,
     Within the Gates, The Star Turns Red, and Red Roses for Me].

1672 _____, Sixty Years of Theatre (London: Eyre & Spottiswoode,
     1951), pp. 376-8 [Discusses Juno and the Paycock, The Sil-
     ver Tassie, and Within the Gates].

1673 _____, Theatrical Cavalcade (London: Eyre & Spottiswoode,
     1942), pp. 208-10 [Discusses Juno and the Paycock, The Sil-
     ver Tassie, and Within the Gates].

1674 Simpson, Alan, Beckett and Behan and a Theatre in Dublin
     (London: Routledge and Kegan Paul, 1962), passim [Argues
     that O'Casey never overcame a Protestant bias, and makes
     several references to his plays].

1675 _____, "Introduction," in Brendan Behan: The Complete
     Plays (London: Eyre Methuen, 1978), pp. 22-23 [Includes
     an unpublished letter by O'Casey dated 17 July 1961].

1676 Snyder, Franklyn Bliss, and Robert Grant Martin, eds., A
     Book of English Literature, vol. 2 (New York: Macmillan,
     1943) [Anthology including the text of, and a commentary on,
     Juno and the Paycock].

1677 Sorell, Walter, Facets of Comedy (New York: Grosset & Dun-
     lap, 1972), pp. 122-5 [Discusses humour and eloquence in
     Within the Gates, Juno and the Paycock, and The Plough and
     the Stars].

1678 Southern, Richard, The Seven Ages of the Theatre (New York:
     Hill & Wang, 1963), p. 270 [Quotes O'Casey's views on the
     theatre].

1679 Speaight, Robert, Drama Since 1939 (London: Published for
     the British Council by Longmans, Green, 1947), pp. 25-7
     [O'Casey's later plays are "a sad record of true genius being
     contradicted by false judgement"].

1680 Spinner, Kaspar, Die Alte Dame Sagt: Nein! Drei Irische
     Dramatiker: Lennox Robinson, Sean O'Casey, Denis Johnston.
     Swiss Studies in English (Bern: Francke Verlag, 1961) [De-
     tailed study of O'Casey's plays].

1681 Stamm, Rudolf, Geschichte des Englischen Theaters (Bern: A. Francke, 1951), p. 408 [Brief assessment of the earlier plays up to Red Roses for Me].

1682 Starkie, Walter, "Sean O'Casey," in The Irish Theatre: Lectures Delivered During the Abbey Theatre Festival Held in Dublin in August 1938, ed. Lennox Robinson (London: Macmillan, 1939; rpt. New York: Haskell House, 1971), pp. 147-76 [Discusses The Shadow of a Gunman, Juno and the Paycock, The Plough and the Stars, The Silver Tassie, and Within the Gates].

1683 Stauffer, Ruth Matilda, et al., eds., Adventures in Modern Literature, 3rd ed. (New York: Harcourt, Brace, 1951) [Anthology including the text of, and a commentary on, The End of the Beginning].

1684 Stein, Walter, "Drama," in The Twentieth-Century Mind: History, Ideas, and Literature in Britain, ed. C. B. Cox and A. E. Dyson. Vol. 2: 1918-1945 (London and New York: Oxford University Press, 1972), pp. 417-56 [Includes discussion on O'Casey].

1685 Styan, J. L., The Dark Comedy: The Development of Modern Comic Tragedy, 2nd ed. (Cambridge: Cambridge University Press, 1968), pp. 130-6, 174-5, and passim [Discusses Cock-a-Doodle Dandy, Juno and the Paycock, The Plough and the Stars, Red Roses for Me, The Silver Tassie, and Within the Gates].

1686 _____, The Dramatic Experience: A Guide to the Reading of Plays (Cambridge: Cambridge University Press, 1965), passim [Discusses Juno and the Paycock and The Plough and the Stars].

1687 _____, The Elements of Drama (Cambridge: Cambridge University Press, 1960), pp. 189-95 [Discusses Juno and the Paycock and The Plough and the Stars].

1688 _____, Modern Drama in Theory and Practice, vol. 1: Realism and Naturalism (Cambridge: Cambridge University Press, 1981), pp. 104-8 [Discusses The Shadow of a Gunman, Juno and the Paycock, and The Plough and the Stars].

1689 _____, Modern Drama in Theory and Practice, vol. 2: Symbolism, Surrealism and the Absurd (Cambridge: Cambridge University Press, 1981), p. 69 [O'Casey on Yeats's Plays for Dancers].

1690 _____, Modern Drama in Theory and Practice, vol. 3:

Expressionism and Epic Theatre (Cambridge: Cambridge University Press, 1981), pp. 121-8 [Discusses the later O'Casey].

1691 Swortzell, Lowell, ed., All the World's a Stage: Modern Plays for Young People (New York: Delacorte Press, 1972) [Anthology including the text of, and a commentary on, The End of the Beginning].

1692 Taborski, Boleslaw, "A dla mnie bukiet czerwonych roz: O dramaturgii Seana O'Caseya," in Nowy teatr elzbietański (Kraków: Wydawnictwo literackie, 1967), pp. 55-98 [Discusses O'Casey's dramatic art].

1693 Taylor, John Russell, Anger and After: A Guide to the New British Drama, 2nd ed. (London: Methuen, 1969), p. 123 [Brendan Behan compared to O'Casey]; p. 146 [O'Casey at the Queens Theatre, Hornchurch].

1694 _____, Hitch: The Life and Work of Alfred Hitchcock (London: Faber and Faber, 1978), pp. 104-6 [Discusses the film version of Juno and the Paycock].

1695 Tetzeli von Rosador, Kurt, Das Englische Geschichtsdrama Seit Shaw (Heidelberg: Carl Winter, 1976), pp. 34, 202, 316 [Discusses The Plough and the Stars and The Silver Tassie].

1696 Thomas, Geoffrey, The Theatre Alive (London: Christopher Johnson, 1948), pp. 24-5 [O'Casey, in The Silver Tassie, brought poetry to the aid of his realism].

1697 Thompson, Alan Reynolds, The Anatomy of Drama, 2nd ed. (Berkeley and Los Angeles: University of California Press, 1946), p. 318 [O'Casey juxtaposes comedy and tragedy in Juno and the Paycock]; p. 383 [Maxwell Anderson quoted on O'Casey's language].

1698 Thompson, David, ed., Theatre Today. The Heritage of Literature Series (London: Longmans, 1965) [Anthology including the text of, and a commentary on, Hall of Healing].

1699 Thompson, William Irwin, "The Naturalistic Image: O'Casey," in The Imagination of an Insurrection. Dublin, Easter 1916: A Study of an Ideological Movement (New York: Oxford University Press, 1967), pp. 202-27 [O'Casey and Irish nationalism].

1700 Tindall, William York, Forces in Modern British Literature, 1885-1956 (New York: Vantage Books, 1956), pp. 51, 74 [O'Casey expresses his political views in The Star Turns Red and Oak Leaves and Lavender], pp. 70-2 ["Increasingly neither here nor there, O'Casey dissipated that realistic gift which had helped save the Abbey"].

1701 Torchiana, Donald T., W. B. Yeats and Georgian Ireland (Evanston, Ill.: Northwestern University Press; London: Oxford University Press, 1966), passim [O'Casey's association with Yeats].

1702 Trewin, J. C., The Birmingham Repertory Theatre, 1913-1963 (London: Barrie and Rockliff, 1963), pp. 134-5 [The production of Juno and the Paycock in Birmingham].

1703 _____, Drama 1945-1950 (London: Longmans, Green, 1951), pp. 24-5 [Discusses Red Roses for Me, Cock-a-Doodle Dandy, and Oak Leaves and Lavender].

1704 _____, Dramatists of Today (London and New York: Staples Press, 1953), pp. 56-66 [Assesses O'Casey's dramatic achievement from the beginning to Cock-a-Doodle Dandy].

1705 _____, The English Theatre (London: Paul Elek, 1948), pp. 65-9 [Assesses O'Casey's dramatic achievement from the beginning to Oak Leaves and Lavender].

1706 _____, A Play Tonight (London: Elek Books, 1952), p. 89 [The Silver Tassie quoted]; p. 122 [O'Casey "has been wantonly neglected in the West End theatre"]; p. 147 [O'Casey praises a schoolboys' performance].

1707 _____, The Theatre Since 1900 (London: Andrew Dakers, 1951), p. viii [O'Casey is neglected in the West End theatre]; p. 51 [Synge is compared to O'Casey]; pp. 175-6 [The best single war scene was the symbolic second act of The Silver Tassie]; pp. 187-91 [Discusses The Shadow of a Gunman, Juno and the Paycock, The Plough and the Stars, and The Silver Tassie]; pp. 217-18 [Discusses Within the Gates]; p. 276 [Christopher Fry compared to O'Casey]; pp. 288-90 [Discusses The Star Turns Red, Purple Dust, Cock-a-Doodle Dandy, Oak Leaves and Lavender, and Red Roses for Me].

1708 _____, The Turbulent Thirties: A Further Decade of the Theatre (London: Macdonald, 1960), p. 72 [Discusses Within the Gates].

1709 _____, We'll Hear a Play (London: Carroll & Nicholson, 1949), pp. 92-3 [Discusses O'Casey's dramatic speech]; pp. 102-3, 192 [Discusses Purple Dust]; pp. 239-41 [1946 was a good year for O'Casey]; pp. 243-4 [Walter Macken compared to O'Casey]; p. 247 [Discusses A Pound on Demand]; p. 253 [Discusses Oak Leaves and Lavender].

1710 Trouwborst, Rolf, "Sean O'Casey und sein Pflug und die Sterne," in Spectaculum 6: Sieben moderne Theaterstücke (Frankfurt/ M.: Suhrkamp, 1963), pp. 357-61 [Criticism on The Plough and the Stars].

1711 Truninger, Annelise, Paddy and the Paycock: A Study of the Stage Irishman from Shakespeare to O'Casey. The Cooper Monographs, vol. 24/Theatrical Physiognomy Series (Bern: Francke Verlag, 1976), pp. 103-12 [Juno and the Paycock].

1712 Tucker, S. Marion, and Alan S. Downer, eds., Twenty-Five Modern Plays (New York: Harper & Row, 1953) [Anthology including the text of, and a commentary on, The Plough and the Stars].

1713 Tynan, Kenneth, Curtains (London: Longmans; New York: Atheneum, 1961), pp. 83-5. Reprinted from Observer (London), (6 Mar 1955), p. 11 [The production of The Bishop's Bonfire at the Gaiety Theatre, Dublin]; pp. 285-8. Reprinted from New Yorker, 34 (6 Dec 1958), 112 [The production of The Shadow of a Gunman at the Bijou Theatre, New York].

1714 _____, Tynan Right & Left (London: Longmans, 1967), p. 4 [Writers like O'Casey "have ruined my taste for Synge"].

1715 _____, A View of the English Stage, 1944-63 (London: Davis-Poynter, 1975), pp. 141, 147, 148 [Synge and O'Casey stand beside Giraudoux in the great line]; p. 142 [Dylan Thomas compared to O'Casey]; p. 228 [Brendan Behan compared to O'Casey].

1716 Ulanov, Barry, ed., Makers of the Modern Theater (New York: McGraw-Hill, 1961) [Anthology including the text of, and a commentary on, Purple Dust].

1717 Van Doren, Carl, and Mark Van Doren, American and British Literature Since 1890, rev. and enl. ed. (New York: Appleton-Century-Crofts, 1953), pp. 338-40 [Discusses Juno and the Paycock, The Plough and the Stars, The Silver Tassie, and Within the Gates].

1718 Van Doren, Mark, "Considering the Source," in Private Reader (New York: Holt, 1942), pp. 351-2. Partially reprinted from Nation (N.Y.), 144 (13 Feb 1937), 194 [Discusses The Plough and the Stars].

1719 Van Druten, John, Playwright at Work (London: Hamish Hamilton, 1953), pp. 75-6 [Juxtaposition of comedy and tragedy in Juno and the Paycock and The Plough and the Stars].

1720 Van Laan, Thomas F., The Idiom of Drama (Ithaca and London: Cornell University Press, 1970), p. 169 [Parody in Juno and the Paycock]; p. 299 [The structure of O'Casey's plays].

1721 Vaughan, Stuart, A Possible Theatre (New York: McGraw-Hill, 1969), pp. 29-34, 43, 77 [On staging I Knock at the Door].

1722 Veitch, Norman, The People's: Being a History of The People's Theatre Newcastle upon Tyne 1911-1939 (Gateshead: Northumberland Press, 1950), pp. 177-8 [Juno and the Paycock]; p. 183 [The Plough and the Stars].

1723 Venneberg, Ute, "Problems in Translating Sean O'Casey's drama Juno and the Paycock," in The Languages of Theatre: Problems in the Translation and Transposition of Drama, ed. Ortrun Zuber (Oxford: Pergamon Press, 1980), pp. 121-31.

1724 Vigourous, Nicole, "La Nature dans l'oeuvre dramatique de Sean O'Casey," Actes du Congrès de Saint-Etienne, S.A.E.S. (Paris: Didier, 1977), pp. 125-36 [Discusses the role of nature in the plays of O'Casey].

1725 Wallechinsky, David, et al., The Book of Lists (New York: William Morrow, 1977), p. 246 [O'Casey nominated for the Nobel Prize in Literature].

1726 Ward, A. C., The Nineteen-Twenties: Literature and Ideas in the Post-War Decade (London: Methuen, 1930), pp. 73-5 [Discusses The Silver Tassie].

1727 _____, Twentieth-Century English Literature, 1901-1960 (London: Methuen, 1966), pp. 115-17 [Discusses Juno and the Paycock, The Plough and the Stars, The Silver Tassie, and Within the Gates].

1728 Wardle, Irving, The Theatres of George Devine (London: Cape, 1978), pp. 218-19 [The 1959 production of Cock-a-Doodle Dandy at the Royal Court Theatre, London].

1729 Warner, Alan, "Sean O'Casey," in A Guide to Anglo-Irish Literature (Dublin: Gill and Macmillan; New York: St. Martin's Press, 1981), pp. 132-42 [General assessment, with comments on I Knock at the Door, Cock-a-Doodle Dandy, Juno and the Paycock, The Plough and the Stars, Red Roses for Me, The Shadow of a Gunman, and The Silver Tassie].

1730 Warnock, Robert, ed., Representative Modern Plays: British (Chicago: Scott, Foresman, 1953) [Anthology including the text of, and a commentary on, Juno and the Paycock].

1731   , ed., Representative Modern Plays: Ibsen to Tennessee Williams (Chicago: Scott, Foresman, 1964) [Anthology including the text of, and a commentary on, Juno and the Paycock].

1732 Watson, E. Bradlee, and Benfield Pressey, eds., Contemporary Drama: European, English and Irish, American Plays (New York: Scribner's, 1931) [Anthology including the text of, and a commentary on, Juno and the Paycock].

1733   , and Benfield Pressey, eds., Contemporary Drama: Fifteen Plays, American, English and Irish, European (New York: Scribner's, 1959) [Anthology including the text of, and a commentary on, Purple Dust].

1734 Watson, G. J., Irish Identity and the Literary Revival: Synge, Yeats, Joyce and O'Casey (London: Croom Helm; New York: Barnes & Noble, 1979), pp. 245-87 [Discusses nationalism in The Shadow of a Gunman, Juno and the Paycock, and The Plough and the Stars].

1735 Weales, Gerald, A Play and Its Parts (New York: Basic Books, 1964), p. 33 [Comments on the comic characters in Juno and the Paycock].

1736   , Religion in Modern English Drama (Philadelphia: University of Pennsylvania Press, 1961), p. 75 [Shaw compared with O'Casey]; p. 204 [O'Casey quoted on T. S. Eliot].

1737 Wekwerth, Manfred, "Purpurstaub: Eine abwegige Komödie von Sean O'Casey," in Notate: Uber die Arbeit des Berliner Ensembles 1956 bis 1966 (Frankfurt/M.: Berlin & Weimar, 1967), pp. 168-82 [Examines Purple Dust].

1738   , Schriften: Arbeit mit Brecht (Berlin: Henschel, 1973), pp. 230-8 [Discusses the staging of Purple Dust].

1739 Wharton, John F., Life Among the Playwrights (New York: Quadrangle/The New York Times Book Company, 1974), pp. 315-16 [Gives complete information on the musical Juno].

1740 White, J. R., Misfit: An Autobiography (London: Jonathan Cape, 1930), pp. 247-51 [O'Casey and The Irish Citizen Army].

1741 White, Terence de Vere, The Anglo-Irish (London: Victor Gollancz, 1972), passim [Includes a discussion on O'Casey].

1742 Whiting, Frank M., An Introduction to the Theatre, 3rd ed. (New York and London: Harper & Row, 1969), p. 100 [Among

20th-century playwrights there are few who can match O'Casey's "power over language, his burning passion, or his deep sense of the tragic"]; pp. 124, 148 [Comments on O'Casey's language].

1743 Whitman, Charles Huntington, ed., Representative Modern Dramas (New York: Macmillan, 1936) [Anthology including the text of, and a commentary on, Juno and the Paycock].

1744 Wieczorek, Hubert, Irische Lebenshaltung im neuen irischen Drama (Breslau: Priebatsch's Buchhandlung, 1937), passim [Discusses The Shadow of a Gunman, Juno and the Paycock, The Plough and the Stars, and The Silver Tassie].

1745 Wild, Friedrich, Die englische Literatur der Gegenwart seit 1870, Bd. 1: Drama und Roman (Wiesbaden: Im Dioskuren, 1928), p. 104 [Includes brief discussion on the Dublin Trilogy].

1746 Williams, Raymond, "The Colour of Sean O'Casey," in Drama from Ibsen to Eliot, rev. ed. (London: Chatto & Windus, 1964), pp. 169-74 [Contains hostile criticism on O'Casey]. Considerably revised essay on O'Casey in Drama from Ibsen to Brecht (London: Chatto & Windus, 1968), pp. 147-53 ["It is to the Abbey plays that we still go back"].

1747 Williamson, Audrey, Contemporary Theatre, 1953-1956 (London: Rockliff, 1956), pp. 75-7 [Discusses The Bishop's Bonfire].

1748 _____, Theatre of Two Decades (London: Rockliff, 1951), pp. 186-9 [Discusses Juno and the Paycock, The Plough and the Stars, Within the Gates, and Red Roses for Me].

1749 Wilson, A. E., Post-War Theatre (London: Home and Van Thal, [1949]), p. 39 [The production of Red Roses for Me at the Embassy Theatre, London]; pp. 103-4 [The production of Oak Leaves and Lavender at the Lyric Theatre, Hammersmith].

1750 Wilson, Edwin, The Theater Experience (New York: McGraw-Hill, 1980), pp. 331, 338-9 [Comments on the characters in Juno and the Paycock].

1751 Winkler, Elizabeth Hale, "The Clown and Satire: Sean O'Casey," in The Clown in Modern Anglo-Irish Drama (Frankfurt: Peter Lang; Bern: Herbert Lang, 1977), pp. 132-204 [The relationship of clowning to satire undergoes a development in the course of O'Casey's work].

1752 Worth, Katharine, "O'Casey," in The Irish Drama of Europe, from Yeats to Beckett (London: Athlone Press, 1978), pp. 220-40 [Deals with O'Casey's experimental drama].

1753 _____, Revolutions in Modern English Drama (London: G. Bell, 1973), pp. 101-17 [Discusses Cock-a-Doodle Dandy and The Silver Tassie].

1754 Yeats, W. B., Pages from a Diary Written in Nineteen Hundred and Thirty (Dublin: Cuala Press, 1944), pp. 57-8.

1755 _____, The Letters of W. B. Yeats, ed. Allan Wade (London: Rupert Hart-Davis, 1954), passim [O'Casey's association with the Abbey Theatre].

1756 _____, Letters on Poetry from W. B. Yeats to Dorothy Wellesley, ed. Kathleen Raine (London: Oxford University Press, 1964), pp. 1, 22 [Makes references to The Silver Tassie].

1757 Young, Cecilia Mary, "The Irish Theatre," in Ring Up the Curtain (St. Paul, Minn.: Library Service Guild, 1941), pp. 134-52 [Argues that Protestant playwrights, including O'Casey, are unable to understand the Irish].

1758 Zeiss, Cecelia, "Sean O'Casey's Final Tragicomedies: A Comment on the Dramatic Modes Employed in Cock-a-Doodle Dandy and The Bishop's Bonfire," in Studies in Anglo-Irish Literature, ed. Heinz Kosok (Bonn: Bouvier, 1982), pp. 278-86 [Both plays employ a structure of incident in which comic fantasy and farce are counterpointed with scenes of intense violence].

1759 Zlobin, G., Za teatral'-nym zanavesom (Moscow: Progress, 1971) [Anthology including the text of, and a commentary on, Behind the Green Curtains].

D. PERIODICAL ARTICLES

1760 "The Abbey Directors and Mr. Sean O'Casey," Irish Statesman (Dublin), 10 (9 June 1928), 268-72 [The controversy over The Silver Tassie, including letters from O'Casey, Yeats, Lennox Robinson, and Walter Starkie].

1761 "Abbey Gets O'Casey Sculpture," Irish Press (Dublin), (25 Aug 1981), p. 3 [Bust of O'Casey is unveiled at the Abbey Theatre].

1762 Abirached, Robert, "Deux pièces de Sean O'Casey," Etudes (Paris), 309 (June 1961), 382-7 [Examines Juno and the Paycock and Red Roses for Me].

1763 Adamov, Arthur, "'La femme avenir de l'homme' dans l'oeuvre de Sean O'Casey," Les Lettres Françaises (Paris), no. 1028 (7-13 May 1964), pp. 1, 11 [Women in The Shadow of a Gunman, Juno and the Paycock, Red Roses for Me, The Star Turns Red, Behind the Green Curtains, and Purple Dust].

1764 _____, "Roses Rouges pour moi," L'Humanité (Paris), (5 Sep 1960), p. 2 [Interview by Mireille Boris with the French director of Red Roses for Me on his views on O'Casey and his works].

1765 _____, et al., "Wie stehen wir zu Brecht? [What Is Our Attitude Toward Brecht?]," Sinn und Form, 13 (1961), 938-47 [Includes references to O'Casey].

1766 Alcalay, Valeria M., "Concepţie şi creaţie artistică in teatrul lui O'Casey," Analele Universităţii Bucureşti. Literatură universală şi comparată, 1 (1970), 99-114 [Artistic conception in the plays of O'Casey].

1767 Alldridge, John, "What's Wrong with the Abbey?" Irish Digest (Dublin), 29 (Feb 1948), 17-19 [Includes references to acting in Juno and the Paycock and The Plough and the Stars].

1768 Allen, John, "Sean O'Casey: A Memoir," Drama (London), no. 136 (Apr 1980), 22-5.

1769 Allen, Ralph, "Pvt. Saroyan and the War," New York Times

Magazine, (4 June 1944), p. 46 [William Saroyan's greatest immediate ambition is to meet O'Casey, to whom he is carrying a letter of introduction from George Jean Nathan].

1770   Alsop, Joseph Jr., "Sean O'Casey, Irish Patriot," Vanity Fair (N.Y.), 43 (Dec 1934), 35, 76 [Biographical sketch].

1771   "American Committee for Sean O'Casey's Centenary," Sean O'Casey Review, 5 (Spring 1979), 128-9 [The Committee has been organized to celebrate O'Casey's 100th birthday in 1980].

1772   Anderson, Maxwell, "Prelude to Dramatic Poetry," New York Times, (6 Oct 1935), section 2, pp. 1, 3 ["Our modern dramatists, with the exception of O'Casey ..., are not poets"].

1773   Ankin, G.V., "Heroic Beginnings in Sean O'Casey's Novel, Drums Under the Windows," Voprosy Earubezhnoi Literatury i Iskusstva (Sverdlovsk), (1972), 16-29 [In Russian].

1774   Armstrong, William A., "History, Autobiography, and The Shadow of a Gunman," Modern Drama, 2 (Feb 1960), 417-24 [The personal element in the play is more important than the historical one].

1775   _____, "The Integrity of Juno and the Paycock," Modern Drama, 17 (Mar 1974), 1-9 [The tragic quality of Juno and the Paycock can be experienced in its fulness only if we know and appreciate the military and political background of this highly topical drama].

1776   _____, "The Sources and Themes of The Plough and the Stars," Modern Drama, 4 (Dec 1961), 234-42 [Drums Under the Windows and The Story of the Irish Citizen Army reveal some of the sources of O'Casey's play].

1777   Arnold, Sidney, "The Abbey Theatre," Arts and Philosophy (London), 1 (Summer 1950), 25-30 [O'Casey's "philosophic outlook upon life is ultra-modernistic"].

1778   "As It Happens," Times (London), (15 Mar 1967), p. 12 [Interview with O'Casey's daughter Shivaun, who has just begun rehearsing for her first professional role in The Shadow of a Gunman].

1779   Atkinson, Brooks, "Art and Dollars: Thousands for Rubbish But Not for O'Casey," New York Times, (11 Jan 1953), section 2, p. 1 [There have not been enough professional productions of O'Casey's plays].

1780   _____, "Critic Recalls the Dramatist as 'A Darlin' Man,'"

New York Times, (19 Sep 1964), pp. 1, 12. Reprinted as "The End of the O'Casey" in Theatre Programme on The Plough and the Stars. The Repertory Theater of Lincoln Center, 1 (Jan 1973), 5-7 [Tribute to O'Casey].

1781 _____, "In 84 Years of Unselfish Life, O'Casey Had His Heart Fail Him Only Once," New York Times, (22 Sep 1964), p. 36 [Recollections of O'Casey].

1782 _____, "O'Casey's Communism Is Really a Dream of a Better Life for Mankind," New York Times, (13 Sep 1960), p. 34 [In his writings, O'Casey's communism illustrates his private interpretation of that word: love for mankind].

1783 _____, "Paradox of O'Casey," New York Times, (2 Apr 1950), section 2, p. 1 [O'Casey is one of the great modern writers, but his plays are seldom offered].

1784 _____, "Sean O'Casey, Nearly Blind, Still Thunders But Always with Fondest Greetings," New York Times, (14 Apr 1964), p. 34 [Comments on O'Casey's life and views].

1785 _____. "Sean Sean Fare Thee Well," Idea and Image (N.Y.), 1 (1967), 11-13 [Tribute to O'Casey].

1786 _____, "Visit with Sean O'Casey: Despite Infirmities, The Green Crow Is Still in Good Form," New York Times, (31 Dec 1962), p. 5 [Interview with O'Casey by an American theatre critic and editor of The Sean O'Casey Reader].

1787 "Au Revoir to the Abbey Theatre," Sunday Times (London), (25 Jan 1959), p. 9 [To preserve a record of the Abbey Theatre before it is pulled down for rebuilding, some of its former illustrious members visited it to make a film, with references to O'Casey].

1788 "The Author of Juno: A Talk with Mr. O'Casey," Observer (London), (22 Nov 1925), p. 9 [Despite the anonymity of the interviewer, it is apparent from a subsequent interview that the interviewer is J.L. Hodson].

1789 Ayling, Ronald, "The Autobiographies of Sean O'Casey," Research Studies, 37 (June 1969), 122-9 [Although there is at present only a small body of good criticism on O'Casey's narrative writings, there are indications that the deficiencies will be remedied fairly soon].

1790 _____, "Character Control and 'Alienation' in The Plough and the Stars," James Joyce Quarterly, 8 (Fall 1970), 29-47 [One of the most significant dramatic devices in this play is the means by which characters are "distanced" when O'Casey wishes the audience to view the dramatic action with critical insight].

1791 _____, "Feathers Flying," Dubliner, 3 (Spring 1964), 54-67. Also as "Feathers Finely Aflutter," Modern Drama, 7 (Sep 1964), 135-47 [Deals with politics in the early life and thought of O'Casey].

1792 _____, "History and Artistry in Sean O'Casey's Dublin Trilogy," Theoria (Natal, S. Africa), no. 37 (1972), 2-13. Also as "Popular Tradition and Individual Talent in Sean O'Casey's Dublin Trilogy," Journal of Modern Literature, 2 (Nov 1972), 491-504 [The Shadow of a Gunman, Juno and the Paycock and The Plough and the Stars comprise a cycle of political and social drama given epic compass by the portrayal of the struggles of common citizens involved in revolution and social upheaval].

1793 _____, "History and Artistry in The Plough and the Stars," Ariel: A Review of International English Literature (Calgary, Alberta), 8 (Jan 1977), 73-85 [O'Casey's mastery of stagecraft is particularly well demonstrated in this play, which is also well documented without being overladen by historical and political details].

1794 _____, "Ideas and Ideology in The Plough and the Stars," Sean O'Casey Review, 2 (Spring 1976), 115-36 [Examines O'Casey's intentions in writing the play and the factors that determined its eventual shape].

1795 _____, "Juno and the Paycock: A Textual Study," Modernist Studies: Literature and Culture 1920-1940 (Edmonton, Alberta), 2, no. 1 (1976), 15-26 [Unlike the majority of O'Casey's plays, Juno and the Paycock was not revised after its publication].

1796 _____, "Nannie's Night Out," Modern Drama, 5 (Sep 1962), 154-63 [Examines the play in detail, showing it as a link between O'Casey's earlier and his later plays].

1797 _____, "A Note on Sean O'Casey's Manuscripts and His Working Methods," Bulletin of the New York Public Library, 73 (June 1969), 359-67 [An introduction to a list, prepared by Ayling, of O'Casey's papers, now in the Berg Collection, New York Public Library].

1798 _____, "O'Casey and the Old Vic," Times Literary Supplement (London), (26 June 1981), p. 729 [Letter to the Editor on O'Casey and Lilian Baylis].

1799 _____, "O'Casey's Poetic Symbolism," Research Studies, 42 (Mar 1974), 49-50 [O'Casey's use of ambivalent names for characters and places serves a variety of purposes, as is shown in The Plough and the Stars, Inishfallen, Fare Thee Well, Cock-a-Doodle Dandy, The Drums of Father Ned, and The Bishop's Bonfire].

1800 _____, "O'Casey's Words Live on," New World Review (N.Y.), 34 (Nov 1966), 52-9 [Examines inaccuracies in writings on O'Casey by Anthony Butler and Saros Cowasjee].

1801 _____, "Patterns of Language and Ritual in Sean O'Casey's Drama," Anglo-Irish Studies (Cambridge), 2 (1976), 25-44 [O'Casey is above all a musical theatre and a theatre of exuberant physical movement and dance].

1802 _____, "The Poetic Drama of T.S. Eliot," English Studies in Africa, 2 (Sep 1959), 247-50 [O'Casey possibly influenced Eliot's technique].

1803 _____, "Portrait of the Artist as a Slum Gutter-Snipe," O'Casey Annual (London), no. 1 (1982), 3-16 [Replies to the acrimonious controversy surrounding O'Casey's slum origins].

1804 _____, "Ritual Patterns in Sean O'Casey's Within the Gates," Theoria (Natal, South Africa), no. 43 (Dec 1974), 19-27 [Detailed textual analysis of an episode in the play illustrates O'Casey's experimentation in dramatic form, his use of liturgical and choric effects, and his success in heightening superficial idiomatic speech].

1805 _____, "Rowdelum Randy: A Postscript on O'Casey and His Critics," Enquiry (Nottingham), 1 (Mar 1958), 48-54; (June 1958), 36 [Examines inaccuracies in writings on O'Casey].

1806 _____, "Sean O'Casey: A Memoir," Canadian Journal of Irish Studies, 1 (Nov 1975), 5-10 [O'Casey drew many characters and incidents in his plays from real life].

1807 _____, "Sean O'Casey: A Personal View with Some Letters," Moderna Språk (Stockholm), 71 (May-June 1977), 109-19 [Recollections of O'Casey, with extracts from 7 letters, 1957-64].

1808 _____, "Sean O'Casey and His Critics," New Theatre Magazine (Bristol), 8 (Autumn 1968), 5-19 ["Reviewing O'Casey criticism up to the present, one is immediately struck by the irrelevance of much of it and by the number of false or misleading approaches to be encountered"].

1809   , "Sean O'Casey and Jim Larkin after 1923," <u>Sean O'Casey Review</u>, 3 (Spring 1977), 99–104 [Discusses O'Casey's views on the Irish Labour Movement and his relationship with Larkin].

1810   , "Sean O'Casey and the Abbey Theatre, Dublin," <u>Dalhousie Review</u>, 52 (Spring 1972), 21–33. Also in <u>English Studies in Africa</u>, 15 (Sep 1972), 71–80; and in <u>Irish University Review</u>, 3 (Spring 1973), 5–16 [Refutes the claim that much of O'Casey's success in Dublin can be attributed to the acting of the Abbey company and to the active collaboration of the theatre's directors in writing and revising his plays].

1811   , "Sean O'Casey, 1880–1964: A Retrospective Survey," <u>Research Studies,</u> 39 (Dec 1971), 259–270 [O'Casey was a prolific writer whose published work reveals a wide range of subject matter and style].

1812   , "Sean O'Casey: Fact and Fancy," <u>Dublin Magazine</u>, 4 (Autumn-Winter 1965), 69–82. Reprinted [revised] in <u>Massachusetts Review</u>, 7 (Summer 1966), 603–12 [Examines inaccuracies in Gabriel Fallon's <u>Sean O'Casey: The Man I Knew</u>]. See Fallon's reply and Ulick O'Connor's puff for Fallon, <u>ibid</u>.

1813   , "Seeds for Future Harvest: Propaganda and Art in O'Casey's Earliest Play," <u>Irish University Review</u> (Dublin), 10 (Spring 1980), 25–40 [A study of <u>The Harvest Festival</u>].

1814   , "Theatre Business: Six Letters by W.B. Yeats," <u>Threshold</u> (Belfast), no. 19 (Autumn 1965), 48–57 [Among the matters these unrecorded letters deal with are Abbey Theatre affairs and <u>The Silver Tassie</u>].

1815   , "'To Bring Harmony': Recurrent Patterns in O'Casey's Drama," <u>Eire-Irland</u>, 10 (Autumn 1975), 62–78 [In O'Casey's work, certain ideas and themes recur again and again, especially his desire to find order and harmony in a world rent by physical and spiritual chaos].

1816   , "W.B. Yeats on Plays and Players," <u>Modern Drama</u>, 9 (May 1966), 1–10 [Includes the controversy over <u>The Silver Tassie</u> and "I Wanna Woman"].

1817 Babenko, V.G., "About the Artistic Originality of Irish Comedy: Sean O'Casey and J.M. Synge," <u>Voprosy Earubezhnoi Literatury</u> (Sverdlovsk), 3 (1974), 27–48 [In Russian].

1818   , "Cock-a-Doodle Dandy--a Late Sean O'Casey Comedy," <u>Voprosy Earubezhnoi Literatury i Iskusstva</u> (Sverdlovsk), (1972), 30–44 [In Russian].

1819 _____ , "Socialist Author from Beginning to End," Voprosy
      Literatury, 1 (1973), 296-300 [Comments on several writings
      by O'Casey. In Russian].

1820 "Back to the Egyptians," Times (London), (13 Apr 1968), p.
      10 [Report on O'Casey's son Breon, the artist].

1821 Baggett, Patricia, "Sean O'Casey's Development of a Basic
      Theme," Dublin Magazine, 31 (Oct-Dec 1956), 25-34 [Attempts
      to find an answer to a basic question which O'Casey tries to
      answer in most of his plays: "What is the meaning of the
      struggle for existence?"].

1822 Bailie, Sister Ellen, O.P., "Bessie Burgess: Cathleen Ni Hou-
      lihan of the Tenements," Sean O'Casey Review, 2 (Spring
      1976), 208-13 [The Plough and the Stars is a classic example
      of O'Casey's effort to topple the comfortable deities which he
      believed had brought Ireland to its condition of fury and
      frustration].

1823 "Ban on Plays for Eire Radio: Mr. O'Casey's Decision," Times
      (London), (29 Jul 1958), p. 2 [O'Casey bans the professional
      production of his plays in Ireland following the withdrawal of
      The Drums of Father Ned from the Dublin Theatre Festival].

1824 B[annon], B.A., "Authors and Editors," Publishers' Weekly,
      200 (6 Dec 1971), 11-13 [Interview with Eileen O'Casey,
      O'Casey's widow].

1825 Barzun, Jacques, "O'Casey at Your Bedside," Griffin Magazine
      (London), 3 (Oct 1954), 4-9. Reprinted in Tulane Drama
      Review, 2 (Feb 1958), 57-61 [Where O'Casey proves himself
      a dramatist by instinct is in his violent mixing and effortless
      handling of passions and characters].

1826 "Bas-relief of O'Casey for Abbey," Irish Independent (Dublin),
      (25 Aug 1981), p. 7 [Bust of O'Casey is unveiled at the
      Abbey Theatre].

1827 Beckett, Samuel, "Gratitude and Homage," Irish Times (Dublin),
      (30 Mar 1960), p. 8 [Tribute to O'Casey on his 80th birth-
      day].

1828 Behan, Brendan, "O'Casey," Irish Times (Dublin), (29 Aug
      1961), p. 5 [Letter to the Editor defending O'Casey].

1829 Bellak, George, "Tea with Sean," Theatre Arts (N.Y.), 37
      (Sep 1953), 70-1, 91-2 [Interview with O'Casey].

1830 Benstock, Bernard, "Chronology and Narratology in Sean

O'Casey's Beginnings," Genre, 12 (Winter 1979), 551-64 [What O'Casey sows in the first three pages of "A Child Is Born" are perennials that he nurtures and harvests throughout all six volumes of Autobiographies, but most closely in I Knock at the Door].

1831 _____, "A Covey of Clerics in Joyce and O'Casey," James Joyce Quarterly, 2 (Fall 1964), 18-32 [Compares Joyce's religion with that of O'Casey as seen in their works]. See Phillip Marcus, "Addendum on Joyce and O'Casey," ibid, 3 (Fall 1965), 62-3.

1832 _____, "Kelly, Burke and Shea," James Joyce Quarterly, 8 (Fall 1970), 124-6 ["There is ample evidence that Sean O'Casey delighted in being able to épater les irlandais, a sport he undertook with full seriousness"].

1833 _____, "The Mother-Madonna-Matriarch in Sean O'Casey," Southern Review, 6 (Summer 1970), 603-23 [Except for a handfull of heroic women, a surprising number of O'Casey's mother-figures are unprepossessing and even disappointing].

1834 _____, "The O'Casey Tapes," Sean O'Casey Review, 2 (Spring 1976), 220-8 [Examines O'Casey's letters].

1835 _____, "The Plough Behind, the Stars Ahead," Sean O'Casey Review, 3 (Spring 1977), 149-56 [Discusses O'Casey's view of the world formulated in The Plough and the Stars].

1836 _____, "Sean O'Casey's Little Cloud," O'Casey Annual (London), no. 1 (1982), 64-72 [Discusses the poet manqué in The Shadow of a Gunman and Red Roses for Me].

1837 _____, "The Three Faces of Brian Nolan," Eire-Ireland, 3 (Autumn 1968), 51-65 [O'Nolan is ranked below Joyce, Yeats, and O'Casey because of his failure to commit himself in regard to the Church, or Ireland, or the social conditions of his characters].

1838 Bentley, Eric, "The Case of O'Casey," New Republic (N.Y.), 127 (13 Oct 1952), 17-18. Reprinted in The Dramatic Event: An American Chronicle (Boston: Beacon Press, 1956), pp. 42-5 [Examines Rose and Crown].

1839 _____, "Discovering a Play," Theatre Arts (N.Y.), 34 (Oct 1950), 40-3, 94-5 ["I observed for myself that Dublin still speaks the language the world knows from O'Casey's Juno and Plough"].

1840 _____, "The Drama: An Extinct Species?" Partisan Review

(N.Y.), 21 (Jul-Aug 1954), 411-17 [London producers ignore O'Casey's plays].

1841   , "The Drama at Ebb," Kenyon Review, 7 (Spring 1945), 169-84 ["There seem to be only two dramatists in Britain: O'Casey, who does not seem to grow, and Shaw, who is 88"].

1842   , "Irish Theatre: Splendeurs et Misères," Poetry (Chicago), 79 (Jan 1952), 216-32. Reprinted in In Search of Theater (New York: Vintage Books, 1953), pp. 315-21 [Realism in O'Casey's Dublin Trilogy].

1843   , "World Theatre: 1900-1950," Theatre Arts (N.Y.), 33 (Dec 1949), 22-7 ["There could be no greater contrast than between the theories of W.B. Yeats and the practice of Sean O'Casey"].

1844 Bergholz, Harry, "Sean O'Casey," Englische Studien (Leipzig), 65 (1930), 49-67 [Assesses O'Casey as a dramatist; and comments on The Shadow of a Gunman, Juno and the Paycock, The Plough and the Stars, and The Silver Tassie]. See reference to this article by Séamus O Donnabháin in "A Current Commentary," Irish Book Lover (Dublin), 18 (May-June 1930), 74.

1845 Biaggi, Mario, "Sean O'Casey: Visionary Playwright and Irish Patriot Honored on the Centenary of His Birth," Congressional Record, (4 June 1980), p. E2751 [Salutes the memory of O'Casey].

1846 Binchy, Maeve, "Braving Rain and Traffic to Tour O'Casey's Dublin," Irish Times (Dublin), (28 Sep 1976), p. 9. Reprinted in Sean O'Casey Review, 4 (Fall 1977), 54-6 [Describes the tour of "O'Casey's Dublin," conducted by Tom Buggy].

1847 Bird, Alan, "O'Casey's Juno and the Paycock," Notes and Queries, 27 (June 1980), 233-4 [The play contains O'Casey's ironic treatment of the attitudes to literature].

1848 Bishop, G.W., "Sean O'Casey: Poet-Playwright," Theatre Guild Magazine, 7 (Feb 1930), 11-14, 55 [Examines The Silver Tassie and assesses O'Casey as a dramatist].

1849 B[ishop], G.W., "The Silver Tassie: Interview with Mr. Sean O'Casey," Observer (London), (6 Oct 1929), p. 13 [Interview by an English dramatic critic and author].

1850 Blitch, Alice Fox, "O'Casey's Shakespeare," Modern Drama, 15 (Dec 1972), 283-90 [Juno and the Paycock clearly illustrates the formative influence of the two parts of Henry IV].

1851 Blöcker, Günter, "Irische Rhapsodie: Sean O'Casey--Träumer
      und Rebell," Merkur (Stuttgart), 26 (May 1972), 483-90
      [O'Casey is both a dreamer and a rebel].

1852 Boas, Guy, "The Drama of Sean O'Casey," College English, 10
      (Nov 1948), 80-6 [Discusses O'Casey's Autobiographies and
      plays, and concludes: "Towering above all contemporary
      dramatists ... stands Sean O'Casey].

1853 Boland, John, "States of Chassis," Hibernia (Dublin), (10
      April 1980), p. 38 [O'Casey Centenary celebrations on RTE,
      the Irish national radio and television network].

1854 Bonnefoy, Claude, "Sean O'Casey mort en pleine jeunesse,"
      Arts (Paris), no. 973 (23-29 Sep 1964), 6 [Obituary].

1855 "Book Ends," Sunday Independent (Dublin), (9 Mar 1980), p.
      13 [Calls for more celebrations to mark the O'Casey Centenary].
      See replies by Deirdre McQuillan, "O'Casey at the Abbey,"
      (16 Mar 1980), p. 15 [On the Abbey Theatre's plans for the
      Centenary]; and by Christopher Murray, (16 Mar 1980), p.
      15 [Draws attention to a special issue on O'Casey published
      by the Irish University Review].

1856 Brady, Bennie Phelim, "O'Casey Salute," Evening Herald (Dub-
      lin), (8 April 1964), p. 6 [Letter to the Editor attacking
      O'Casey's socialism].

1857 Brandstädter, Otto, "Ein sprachgewaltiger Dichter des irischen
      Volkes. Sean O'Casey zum heutigen 80. Geburtstag," Neues
      Deutschland (Berlin), 51 (31 Mar 1960), 4 [A tribute to
      O'Casey on his 80th birthday].

1858 Breathnach, Le Deasun, "Agus Sean O'Casey," Evening Press
      (Dublin), (12 Apr 1980), p. 15 [O'Casey was interested in
      the Irish language]. See reply by David Krause, "Sean
      O'Casey Letters," ibid. (15 May 1980), p. 25.

1859 Brereton-Barry, R., "The Need for a State Theatre," Irish
      Statesman (Dublin), 3 (25 Oct 1924), 210-12 [O'Casey chose
      as his subject a phase of Dublin life which could be faithfully
      represented at the Abbey"]. See correspondence, ibid. (1
      Nov 1924), 238; (8 Nov 1924), 270; and (15 Nov 1924), 301.

1860 Brien, Alan, "O'Casey--Child of Slums," Sunday Telegraph
      (London), (20 Sep 1964), p. 6 [Tribute to O'Casey].

1861 "Broadway Pays Tribute to O'Casey," Irish Times (Dublin),
      (13 Oct 1964), p. 5 [A program on O'Casey at the Imperial
      Theatre was attended by 1,400 persons, including Brooks
      Atkinson and Lillian Gish].

1862 Bromage, Mary Cogan, "Literature of Ireland Today," South Atlantic Quarterly, 42 (Jan 1943), 27-37 [O'Casey's plays "show the seamier side of Dublin," and juxtapose comedy and tragedy].

1863 _____, "The Yeats-O'Casey Quarrel," Michigan Alumnus Quarterly Review (Ann Arbor), 64 (Winter 1958), 135-44 [Deals with the controversy over The Silver Tassie].

1864 Brophy, Eanna, "Oh Casey," Sunday Press (Dublin), (13 Apr 1980), p. 23 [O'Casey Centenary celebrations on RTE].

1865 Brown, Ivor, "The New Bardolatry," Drama (London), no. 64 (Spring 1962), 34-6 ["Shakespeare, like O'Casey, is spared the idiotic accusation of being 'literary'"].

1866 _____, "The High Froth," Drama (London), no. 87 (Winter 1967), 32-4 [When one compares the dialogue of such greats as Synge, O'Casey, and Shaw with that of most contemporary playwrights, one must conclude that mass communications has had a flattening effect upon speech].

1867 Browne, Maurice, "Playwrights and Box Office," Listener (London) 22 (7 Jul 1938), 10-11 [Interview with O'Casey by an English dramatist, manager, and actor].

1868 Browne, Noel, "The Star Turns Red: A Preface." Program note to the Abbey Theatre's production, February 1978.

1869 Brugère, Raymond, "Sean O'Casey et le Théâtre irlandais," Revue anglo-américaine (Paris), 3 (Feb 1926), 206-21 [Examines The Shadow of a Gunman, Juno and the Paycock, Nannie's Night Out, and Kathleen Listens In].

1870 Brunet, David, "The Visual Image: Spectacle in Melodrama and in O'Casey's Plays," Sean O'Casey Review, 5 (Spring 1979), 157-66 [O'Casey did not use spectacle in the same way melodramatists used it; he used it to contribute ironic and metaphoric resonances to his plays].

1871 Bryson, Mary E., "'Our One Philosophical Critic': John Eglinton," Eire-Ireland, 10 (Summer 1975), 81-8 [Eglinton influenced O'Casey and others].

1872 Buggy, Tom, "O'Casey Craft," Beacon (Dublin), (Sep 1979), 28 [Notes that the opening of The Shadow of a Gunman is well-constructed].

1873 _____, "Of Days That Are Gone," Sean O'Casey Review, 5 (Fall 1978), 116-18 [Obituary of Eileen Crowe, with references to her recollections of O'Casey, and to her appearances in Juno and the Paycock, Kathleen Listens In, Nannie's Night Out, The Plough and the Stars, and Red Roses for Me].

1874 _____, "Reminiscence," Sean O'Casey Review, 6 (1980), 65-7 [Barney Mulligan recalls O'Casey].

1875 _____, "Sean O'Casey's Dublin," O'Casey Annual (London), no. 1 (1982), 88-96 [Describes forty points of interest in Dublin associated with O'Casey].

1876 Burrowes, Wesley, "Writers Are Not Encouraged," Irish Times (Dublin), (18 Mar 1968), p. 10 [O'Casey left Ireland because "there is nothing in this country to encourage anybody to write a play, except his own dedication"].

1877 Burton, Philip, "Something to Crow About: An Approach to Cock-a-Doodle Dandy," Theatre Arts (N.Y.), 42 (Nov 1958), 22-4 [Although the Cock is a symbol of the full and happy life, the play is not allegorical in every detail].

1878 Butler, Tony, "Bust of O'Casey Unveiled at Abbey," Evening Herald (Dublin), (25 Aug 1981), p. 3 [The Abbey Theatre is presented with a bust of O'Casey].

1879 _____, "Sean, You Really Never Had It So Bad at All," Evening Herald (Dublin), (1 Apr 1980), p. 9 [Rejects the "old myths of (O'Casey's) slum origin and his youthful poverty"].

1880 Calvet, L.J., and L. Atoun, "Ombres et lumières d'un franc-tireur. Tout ce que créent les grands espirts," Calliope: jeune théâtre (Paris), no. 1 (1965), 56-9 [Obituary].

1881 Candida, "An Irishwoman's Diary," Irish Times (Dublin), (8 Aug 1966), p. 7 [Interview with Eileen O'Casey].

1882 _____, "An Irishwoman's Diary: O'Casey Papers," Irish Times (Dublin), (20 Oct 1969), p. 9 [The New York Public Library acquires O'Casey's papers].

1883 Carens, James F., "Eight O'Casey Holographs and The Letters of Sean O'Casey," Sean O'Casey Review, 5 (Fall 1978), 45-7 [Compares the versions of eight O'Casey letters to Oliver St. John Gogarty as they appear in The Letters, to the original holographs in the Gogarty Collection at Bucknell University]. See reply by David Krause, "A Response to Pettifoggery," ibid., (Fall 1978), 47-50; and counter-reply by James F. Carens, "Correspondence," (Spring 1979), 211-13.

1884 _____, "Four Letters: Sean O'Casey to Oliver St. John
Gogarty," James Joyce Quarterly 8 (Fall 1970), 111-18 [The
letters suggest that by the end of the 1920's O'Casey and
Gogarty knew well how much they had in common].

1885 Carey, Edw., "Self-Respect," Standard (Dublin), 27 (4 Mar
1955), 12 [Letter to the Editor on The Bishop's Bonfire].

1886 Carroll, Paul Vincent, "Can the Abbey Theatre Be Restored?"
Theatre Arts (N.Y.), 36 (Jan 1952, 18-19, 79 [O'Casey's
plays evoke the Abbey Theatre's past glory].

1887 Carwood, Jim, "Today's Highlights, Sunday Press (Dublin),
(30 Mar 1980), p. 31 [O'Casey Centenary celebrations on
RTE].

1888 Cary, Richard, "Two O'Casey Letters," Colby Library Quarterly, 9 (June 1972), 547-55 [Two hitherto unpublished letters
by O'Casey discuss his works, his wife, and his motherland].

1889 Casey, Paul Foley, "The Knocking Motif in Sean O'Casey's
The Shadow of a Gunman," Literatur in Wissenschaft und Unterricht (Kiel, W. Germany), 13 (1980), 170-5 [Focuses on
some of the nonverbal means of communication in the play].

1890 Cassidy, Ces, "English to Tour O'Casey in U.S.A.," Irish Press
(Dublin), (1 Nov 1979), p. 9 [O'Casey's Centenary will re-
ceive due attention from the BBC and the RTE, and the Royal
Shakespeare Company are intending to take a production of
Juno and the Paycock on tour to the United States].

1891 Caswell, Robert W., "Unity and the Irish Theatre," Studies
(Dublin), 49 (Spring 1960), 63-7 ["O'Casey opened newer
ground, but writers have taken from him only the more superficial elements of his comedy"].

1892 "Cathedral Sermon Praises O'Casey," Irish Times (Dublin), (16
Nov 1964), p. 11 [Dr. N.D. Emerson, Dean of Christ Church,
Dublin, praises O'Casey at a service in the cathedral to com-
memorate him].

1893 Chappelow, Allan, "Appointment with Sean O'Casey," Times Pictorial [formerly Weekly Irish Times] (Dublin), 78 (13 Sep
1952), p. 14 [Interview by an author and journalist].

1894 Clurman, Harold, "O'Casey: For All His Curses, a Yea-Sayer,"
New York Times, (23 Nov 1969), p. 8 [Reflections on O'Casey
by an American theatre director, manager, and critic].

1895 Coakley, James, and Marvin Felheim, "Thalia in Dublin: Some

Suggestions about the Relationships between O'Casey and Classical Comedy," Comparative Drama, 4 (Winter 1970), 265-71 [There are specific parallels between Juno and the Paycock and Plautus].

1896　Coffey, Brian, "In Dublin," Commonweal (N.Y.), 46 (3 Oct 1947), 597-8 [Includes reference to Ria Mooney's production of The Silver Tassie].

1897　Colum, Padraic, "Ibsen in Irish Writing," Irish Writing (Cork), no. 7 (Feb 1949), 66-70 [O'Casey was not influenced by Ibsen].

1898　_____, "The Narrative Writings of Sean O'Casey," Irish Writing (Cork), no. 6 (Nov 1948), 60-9 [In his Autobiographies, O'Casey has been unjust to many of the public figures of his epoch]. See O'Casey's reply, ibid., no. 7 (Feb 1949), 87.

1899　_____, "Sean O'Casey," Theatre Arts Monthly (N.Y.), 9 (June 1925), 397-404 [Discusses The Shadow of a Gunman and Juno and the Paycock].

1900　"Come-Back in Erin," Sunday Times (London), (6 Mar 1955), p. 3 [O'Casey is honored once more in his own country by the production of The Bishop's Bonfire].

1901　Conacher, W.M., "The Irish Literary Movement," Queen's Quarterly, 45 (Spring 1938), 56-65 [The Plough and the Stars represents the real Irish better than Juno and the Paycock].

1902　Coogan, Beatrice, "The Prophecy of Sean O'Casey," Irish Digest (Dublin), (Apr 1960), 80-93 [Recollections of O'Casey].

1903　Corry, John, "O'Casey Centenary Fans Flames of His Works," New York Times, (26 Mar 1980), section 3, p. 26 [Describes the celebrations to commemorate the 100th anniversary of O'Casey's birth].

1904　Coston, Herbert H., "Sean O'Casey: Prelude to Playwriting," Tulane Drama Review, 5 (Sep 1960), 102-12 [Deals with O'Casey's first literary efforts].

1905　Coulter, Carol, "O'Casey: Shadow of a Revolution," Irish Press (Dublin), (29 Mar 1980), p. 9 [Looks at the life and work of O'Casey and assesses his literary achievement].

1906　_____, "Stages in Being Miss O'Casey," Irish Times (Dublin), (18 Apr 1980), p. 9 [Interview with Shivaun O'Casey, O'Casey's daughter].

1907 _____, "Women in O'Casey Plays," Abbey Theatre Souvenir Programme (Dec 1979), pp. 9-13.

1908 Cowasjee, Saros, "An Evening with Sean O'Casey," Illustrated Weekly of India (Bombay), (17 May 1959), p. 43. Also in Irish Times (Dublin), (25 Jul 1959), p. 8 [Interview].

1909 _____, "The Juxtaposition of Tragedy and Comedy in the Plays of Sean O'Casey," Wascana Review, 2 (Spring-Summer 1967), 75-89 [The Shadow of a Gunman, Juno and the Paycock, and The Plough and the Stars best exemplify O'Casey's unique gift of mingling comedy with tragedy].

1910 _____, "O'Casey Seen Through Holloway's Diary," Review of English Literature, 6 (Jul 1965), 58-69 [Joseph Holloway's voluminous diary includes a number of anecdotes on O'Casey].

1911 Coxhead, Elizabeth, "Mr. Sean O'Casey," Times (London), (22 Sep 1964), p. 15 [Tribute].

1912 Craig, H.A.L., "A Burning Man," Irish Times (Dublin), (30 Mar 1960), p. 8 [A tribute to O'Casey on his 80th birthday].

1913 Croft-Cooke, Rupert, "The Real Sean O'Casey," Theatre World (London), 5 (Oct 1926), 10. Reprinted in his The Numbers Came (London: Putnam, 1963), 159-60 [Interview with O'Casey].

1914 Crone, John S., "Sgéala O Chathair na gCeó," Irish Book Lover, 16 (May-June 1928), 67 [Public opinion is divided about the Yeats-O'Casey controversy re The Silver Tassie].

1915 _____, "Sgéala O Chathair na gCeó," Irish Book Lover, 17 (Sep-Oct 1929), 98 [Irish dramatists, like O'Casey "seem much more in evidence" than Irish poets or novelists].

1916 Cronin, Sean, "Joe Papp and Sean O'Casey," Irish Times (Dublin), (14 June 1972), p. 10 [Recollections of O'Casey and of Joseph Papp, the theatrical producer].

1917 Crowther, Bosley, "Who Is Then the Gentleman?" New York Times, (14 Oct 1934), section 10, p. 1 [Interview with O'Casey in New York on the occasion of the American premiere of Within the Gates].

1918 Cusack, Cyril, "In Terms of Theatre," Iris Hibernia (Fribourg), 4 (1960), 20-6 [The self-critical drama, like the latter-day O'Casey plays, are "likely to be met with suspicion" in Ireland].

1919   , "In the Beginning Was O'Casey," Irish University Review (Dublin), 10 (Spring 1980), 17-24 [Recollections by the Abbey Theatre actor].

1920   , "The Irish Actor," Prompts: Bulletin of the Irish Theatre Archive (Dublin), no. 2 (Sep 1981), 3-14 [Contrasts two productions of Juno and the Paycock by the Abbey Theatre and by the Royal Shakespeare Company].

1921 "Cyril Cusack Gives Lecture on O'Casey," Irish Times (Dublin), (14 Apr 1980), p. 9 [Reports the lecture which the Irish actor gave the RTE as part of the celebrations to commemorate O'Casey Centenary].

1922 D., O.G., "O'Casey Season," Evening Herald (Dublin), (10 Mar 1955), p. 5 [Radio Eireann is planning a season of O'Casey plays].

1923 Dafoe, Christopher, "The Green Cow Remembered--100 Years On," Vancouver Sun, (26 Apr 1980), p. D3 [O'Casey Centenary celebrated].

1924 Daniel, Walter C., "The False Paradise Pattern in Sean O'Casey's Cock-a-Doodle Dandy," CLA Journal (Baltimore, Maryland), 13 (Dec 1969), 137-43 [Michael Marthraun in the play is an ingenious character creation in his ironic contrast to Archangel Michael in Milton's Paradise Lost].

1925   , "Patterns of Greek Comedy in O'Casey's Purple Dust," Bulletin of the New York Public Library, 66 (Nov 1962), 603-12 [As in Aristophanic comedy, this play initially sets up a conflict (agon) between the quixotic and the pragmatic].

1926   , "Public vs. Private Commitment in Two Plays of W.B. Yeats and Sean O'Casey," CLA Journal (Baltimore, Maryland), 23 (Dec 1979), 213-19 [The difference between Yeats and O'Casey may be seen in Kathleen ni Houlihan and The Plough and the Stars].

1927 Danker, Trevor, "Fantastic O'Casey Interest in U.S.," Sunday Independent (Dublin), (13 Apr 1980), p. 15 [Michael Mullen, ITGWU General Secretary, reports on the O'Casey Centenary celebrations in America].

1928 Dantanus, Ulf, "Time for a New Irish Playwright?" Moderna Språk (Stockholm), 71 (1977), 37-47 [It was O'Casey's strong imaginative powers that made his Dublin Trilogy "transcend the narrowly Irish to strike a more universal note"].

1929 Darlington, W.A., "London Economics: West End Managers

Complain of Tax Burden in Slumping Market," New York Times, (8 June 1947), section 2, p. 1 [On the difficulties of presenting O'Casey's plays].

1930 _____, "Stormy Genius," Daily Telegraph (London), (28 Sep 1964), p. 17 [Tribute to O'Casey by a drama critic].

1931 Davidson, Richard, "Drums Under the Windows: Some Words for Sean O'Casey," Sean O'Casey Review, 7 (1981), 12-13 [Poem].

1932 Davies, M. Bryn, "A Few Thoughts About Milk Wood," Literary Half-Yearly, 5 (Jan 1964), 41-4 [Dylan Thomas is not in the same tradition as O'Casey, Brendan Behan, and J.M. Synge].

1933 Davies, Stan Gebler, "Happiness and Mrs. O'Casey," Evening Standard (London), (30 Sep 1971), p. 19 [Interview with Eileen O'Casey].

1934 Davison, P.H., "Three Australian Plays," Southerly, 23 (1963), 110-27 [Summer of the Seventeenth Doll, The Shifting Heart, and The One Day of the Year adopt O'Casey's method of combining melodrama and humor].

1935 Deane, Seamus, "Exemplary Dramatists: Yeats and O'Casey," Threshold (Belfast), 30 (Spring 1979), 21-8 [Yeats is a more profoundly political dramatist than O'Casey].

1936 _____, "Irish Politics and O'Casey's Theatre, Threshold (Belfast), 24 (Spring 1973), 5-16 [O'Casey is certainly the Irish dramatist who, more than any other, paid tribute (of whatever kind) to Irish politics].

1937 "Death of One of the Great Irish Dramatists: Mr. Sean O'Casey," Illustrated London News, 245 (26 Sep 1964), 475 [Tribute to O'Casey].

1938 "Death of Sean O'Casey," Manchester Guardian, (19 Sep 1964), p. 1 [Obituary].

1939 DeBaun, Vincent, "Sean O'Casey and the Road to Expressionism" Modern Drama, 4 (Dec 1961), 254-9 [O'Casey's application of expressionistic techniques began not with The Silver Tassie, but with The Plough and the Stars].

1940 Deegan, Liam, "Comments on O'Casey," Evening Herald (Dublin), (11 Apr 1980), p. 6 [Letter to the Editor on the conflicting accounts of the early life of O'Casey].

1941 Dessner, Lawrence J., "Art and Anger in the Autobiographies of Sean O'Casey," Eire-Ireland, 10 (Autumn 1975), 46-61 [The relationship between historical events and his own early life gave O'Casey a ready-made chronological form which sustained and controlled the first two volumes of his Autobiographies].

1942 "DeValera as Play Censor," Manchester Guardian Weekly, 30 (13 Apr 1934), 296 [O'Casey comments on DeValera's objection to certain Irish plays being presented in America].

1943 "'Dole' Dramatist: Out-of-Work Irishman's Climb to Fame," Daily Herald (London), (6 Mar 1926), p. 1 [Interview with O'Casey].

1944 Dorcey, Donal, "No Bouncing About in the Abbey Bed," Irish Times (Dublin), (1 Apr 1980), p. 9 [Tells how a backstage row nearly closed the Abbey Theatre, and how Yeats joined in having The Plough and the Stars censored].

1945 Doyle, Jacqueline, "Liturgical Imagery in Sean O'Casey's The Silver Tassie," Modern DRama, 21 (Mar 1978), 29-38 [Examines the play's religious symbolism].

1946 "Drama," Encore (London), 3 (Easter 1956), 4, 29-30 ["There is no more irreverent, no more joy-stricken dramatist writing today" than O'Casey].

1947 Drummond, Angus, "O'Casey Says," Courier (London), 42 (Apr 1964), 40-1 [Interview with O'Casey].

1948 Druzina, M.V., "O Scenicnosti Dramaturgii Shona O'Kejsi," Teatr (Moscow), 23 (Nov 1962), 180-4 [The theatrical effectiveness of O'Casey's plays].

1949 "A Dublin Tempest," Literary Digest (N.Y.), 98 (4 Aug 1928), 24-5 [The quarrel over The Silver Tassie].

1950 Duffus, R.L., "Dublin--Story of Two Cities," New York Times Magazine, (17 Mar 1957), pp. 28, 39, 41 ["The Irish of today's Dublin are not necessarily those of Sean O'Casey's plays"].

1951 Dukes, Ashley, "The Irish Scene: Dublin Plays and Playhouses," Theatre Arts Monthly (N.Y.), 14 (May 1930), 378-84 [Discusses The Shadow of a Gunman and The Silver Tassie].

1952 "Dull Gaelic Plough," Newsweek, 30 (24 Nov 1947), 84 [Valentin Iremonger and others protest at a performance of The Plough and the Stars].

1953   Dumay, Emile Jean, "Enter O'Cathasaigh," Etudes Irlandaises
        (Lille), no. 1 (Dec 1976), 85-98 [Discusses The Harvest Fes-
        tival].

1954   _____, "A Few Remarks about French Audiences," Sean
        O'Casey Review, 2 (Spring 1976), 215-16 [Deals with the re-
        ception of The Shadow of a Gunman and The Plough and the
        Stars in France].

1955   _____, "Histoire et fiction dans la trilogie dublinoise de Sean
        O'Casey," Etudes Irlandaises (Lille), no. 5 (Dec 1980), 23-
        35 [History and fiction in the Dublin Trilogy].

1956   _____, "Merriment and Celebration in Sean O'Casey's Plays,"
        Sean O'Casey Review, 2 (Fall 1975), 12-21. Partly reprinted
        in French in Dossiers du théâtre de l'est Parisien (1975) [Mer-
        riment and celebration are used by O'Casey to express the
        joy of life throughout his plays].

1956a   _____, "Notes d'après l'Autobiographie d'O'Casey et sa Cor-
        respondance," T.N.S. actualité (Bulletin d'Information du
        Théâtre National de Strasbourg), no. 30 (Feb 1978), 3 [In-
        troduction to A Pound on Demand and Hall of Healing].

1957   _____, "Notes on the French Premiere of The Silver Tassie,"
        Sean O'Casey Review, 5 (Fall 1978), 19-21 [Points out the
        features of the play on which the staging was founded; and
        quotes some critical reviews].

1958   _____, "Quelques remarques sur le Comique de Sean O'Casey,"
        T.B. actualités (Journal du Théâtre de Bourgogne), (Beaune),
        no. 2 (Jan-Mar 1968), 6-7 [The End of the Beginning].

1959   _____, "Sean O'Casey in France," Cahiers irlandais (Paris:
        Editions Universitaires--Publications de l'Université de Lille
        III), nos. 2/3 (1974): France-Ireland: Literary Relations,
        241-7 [Surveys the productions of O'Casey's plays in France].

1960   _____, "Sean O'Casey in France," Sean O'Casey Review,
        3 (Fall 1976), 33-9 [Surveys the productions of O'Casey's
        plays in France].

1961   _____, "Some Loved the Plough, Others Preferred the Stars,"
        Sean O'Casey Review, 2 (Spring 1976), 214-15 [Deals with
        the reception of The Plough and the Stars in France].

1962   _____, "Une tragi-comédie du cléricalisme," La Vie du centre
        dramatique de l'est (Strasbourg), no. 39 (Dec 1965), 16-17
        [The Bishop's Bonfire].

1963 _____, "Vivons malgré Eux," Préfaces (Journal du Théâtre
      de Nice), (Nice), no. 5 (Mar-Apr 1971), 4-5 [Cock-a-Doodle
      Dandy].

1964 Duranteau, Josane, "Notes sur le théâtre de Sean O'Casey,"
      Critique (Paris), 16 (Nov 1960), 935-40 [Comments on Juno
      and the Paycock, Red Roses for Me, Bedtime Story, The
      Plough and the Stars, The Bishop's Bonfire, and A Pound
      on Demand].

1965 Durbach, Errol, "Peacocks and Mothers: Theme and Dramatic
      Metaphor in O'Casey's Juno and the Paycock," Modern Drama,
      15 (May 1972), 15-25 [Recognizes dramatic qualities in the
      play inconsistent with "slice-of-life" drama and the "photo-
      graphic realism" with which O'Casey has frequently been
      credited].

1966 Durkan, Michael J., "The First American Production of The
      Plough and the Stars," Sean O'Casey Review, 3 (Fall 1976),
      40-5 [Gives details of the production at the Hudson Theatre
      on 28 November 1927].

1967 Earp, T.W., "Irish and English," New Statesman (London), 35
      (5 Jul 1930), 409 [In presenting Ireland to the outer world,
      O'Casey "mixed black and tan with his emerald green"].

1968 "Editorial," Catholic Bulletin (Dublin), 16 (Mar 1926), 242-9
      [O'Casey and Irish nationalism].

1969 "Editorial," Catholic Bulletin, (Dublin), 16 (May 1926), 463-8
      [O'Casey is awarded the Hawthornden Prize for Juno and the
      Paycock].

1970 "Editorial," Catholic Bulletin, (Dublin), 16 (Aug 1926), 803-4
      [O'Casey makes permanent home in London].

1971 "Editorial," Catholic Bulletin, (Dublin), 18 (Jul 1928), 676-7
      [The Silver Tassie is rejected by the Abbey Theatre].

1972 Edwards, A.C., ed., "The Lady Gregory Letters to Sean
      O'Casey," Modern Drama, 8 (May 1965), 95-111 [Publishes
      23 letters, with introduction and annotations].

1973 Edwards, Owen Dudley, "America's Image of Ireland," Irish
      Times (Dublin), (11 Jan 1963), p. 8 ["It is the bitter, unfair
      vituperation by O'Casey rather than the reflective, dispas-
      sionate, ironic tone of O'Connor that one hears echoed"].

1974 Elistratova, A[nne], "Sean O'Casey," Soviet Literature (Moscow),
      no. 11 (Nov 1952), 164-9. Reprinted in Neues Deutschland,
      30 (June 1953), 4 [Deals with O'Casey as a pacifist].

1975 Ervine, St. John, "The Wars and the Drama," Fortnightly,
      154 (Jul 1940), 61-70 [O'Casey "came out of a Dublin slum
      to remind us that poetic speech still lingers on workmen's
      lips"].

1976 Esslinger, Patricia M., "The Irish Alienation of Sean O'Casey,"
      Eire-Ireland, 1 (Spring 1966), 18-25 [O'Casey's alienation
      from Ireland resulted not in a decrease of scope, but in a
      widening of horizons].

1977- _____, "Sean O'Casey and the Lockout of 1913: Materia
8   Poetica of the Two Red Plays," Modern Drama, 6 (May 1963),
      53-63 [The Great Lockout of 1913 was not only responsible
      for The Star Turns Red and Red Roses for Me, but was also
      the origin of the Communistic views which O'Casey held].

1979 Fallon, Gabriel, "The Abbey Theatre Today," Threshold (Bel-
      fast), 3 (1959), 24-32 [In the twenties, critics said that the
      plays of O'Casey were "mere reportage"; today, they complain
      that the Abbey Theatre has not produced a dramatist of his
      calibre].

1980 _____, "Afterword," Irish University Review (Dublin), 10
      (Spring 1980), 159-61 [Recollections of the productions of
      O'Casey's first four plays at the Abbey Theatre].

1981 _____, "The Ageing Abbey," Irish Monthly (Dublin), 66
      (Apr 1938), 265-72 [Refers to O'Casey's association with the
      Abbey Theatre].

1982 _____, "All This and the Abbey Too," Studies (Dublin), 48
      (Winter 1959), 434-42 [O'Casey's relationship with Barry
      Fitzgerald and his views on stagecraft].

1983 _____, "A Child Among Them," Bonaventura (Dublin), 1
      (Autumn 1937), 74-80 [Recollections of O'Casey and others].

1984 _____, "Dublin's Fourth Theatre Festival," Modern Drama,
      5 (May 1962), 21-6 [O'Casey refuses permission for the pres-
      entation of The Drums of Father Ned].

1985 _____, "The First Production of The Plough and the Stars,"
      Sean O'Casey Review, 2 (Spring 1976), 167-75 [Gives details
      of the Abbey Theatre production and of the controversy over
      the play].

1986 _____, "A Forgotten O'Casey Play," Irish Bookman, 2 (Jan
      1948), 12-16 [Recollections of the first production of Kathleen
      Listens In].

1987 _____, "The House on the North Circular Road: Fragments from a Biography," Modern Drama, 4 (Dec 1961), 223-33 [Recollections of O'Casey during the years 1924-28].

1988 _____, "Juno and Joxer and Fluther: They Were All Born in the House with the Sycamore Tree," Sunday Independent (Dublin), (24 Dec 1950), p. 6 [Recollections of O'Casey].

1989 _____, "Maritain Was Wrong," Commonweal (N.Y.), 52 (26 May 1950), 175-6 [Like O'Casey, Seamus Byrne mixes the richest of comedy with his tragedy].

1990 _____, "My Friend Sean O'Casey," Irish Digest (Dublin), 26 (Nov 1946), 33-6 [Recollections of O'Casey].

1991 _____, "My Friend Sean O'Casey," Sunday Independent (Dublin), (30 Mar 1980), pp. 11, 17 [Recollections of the first meeting with O'Casey].

1992 _____, "The Nonsense About O'Casey," Hibernia (Dublin), 22 (Sep 1958), 4-6 [On The Bishop's Bonfire].

1993 _____, "O'Casey," Catholic Standard (Dublin), 2 (2 Oct 1964), I, p. 4 [Tribute].

1994 _____, "O'Casey, the Dramatist in Search of an Author," Evening Press (Dublin), (12 Feb 1955), p. 5 [The rejection of The Silver Tassie had the effect of turning O'Casey out of the theatre workshop which had helped to mold his earlier work].

1995 _____, "Pathway of a Dramatist," Theatre Arts (N.Y.), 34 (Jan 1950), 36-9 [O'Casey "took the hard road, and took it defiantly"].

1996 _____, "Profiles of a Poet," Modern Drama 7 (Dec 1964), 329-44 [Recollections of the first production of The Plough and the Stars].

1997 _____, "We Loved Him Better Than We Knew," Evening Press (Dublin), (19 Sep 1964), p. 4 [Tribute to O'Casey].

1998 _____, "Why Is There No Irish Caludel or Mauriac?" Evening Press (Dublin), (5 Feb 1955), p. 5 [Irish audiences liked O'Casey's plays].

1999 Farragher, Bernard, "Brendan Behan's Unarranged Realism," Drama Critique (N.Y.), 4 (Feb 1961), 38-9 [The Hostage apparently uses O'Casey's method].

2000 Farren, Ronan, "O'Casey: Haunted by a Stigma of Rejection,"

Evening Herald (Dublin), (28 Mar 1980), p. 10 [O'Casey was hardly an overnight success story].

2001 Fast, Howard, "Red Roses and Brotherhood," Daily Worker (N.Y.), (26 Jan 1956), p. 6 [Red Roses for Me shows that O'Casey wants socialism].

2002 Fay, Gerard, "The Irish Theatre," Drama (London), no. 84 (Spring 1967), 33-5 [O'Casey "at one time said that his great ambition was to write a play good enough for the Queen's which used to flourish on Boucicault"].

2003 _____, "Sean O'Casey, Saint and Devil," Guardian (London), (21 Sep 1964), p. 5 [Recollections of O'Casey by a journalist and the son of the Abbey actor Frank Fay].

2004 _____, "Stephens: The Gnome of Genius," Irish Digest, 81 (Aug 1964), 21-4 [James Stephens was a preeminent conversationalist; O'Casey is preeminently a lover of everybody].

2005 _____, "They Made Me an Abbey Theatre 'Rioter,'" Irish Digest (Dublin), 82 (Jan 1965), 13-15 [Recollections of shooting the film Young Cassidy].

2006 Fay, Stephen, "'The Fame of O'Casey is Born Tonight.'" Program note to the National Theatre's production of The Plough and the Stars (Sep 1977).

2007 Fehlmann, Guy, "La pensée politique de Sean O'Casey," Etudes irlandaises (Lille), (Nov 1975), 39-52 [The political views of O'Casey as revealed in his plays].

2008 _____, "La pensée politique de Sean O'Casey," Cahiers du centre de recherches sur les pays du nord et du nord-ouest (Caen), 1 (1978), 45-52 [The political views of O'Casey as revealed in his plays].

2008a Feinstein, Dianne, "San Francisco Proclamation on Sean O'Casey's Centenary," Sean O'Casey Review, 7 (1981), 6 [The Mayor of San Francisco proclaims Sunday, 30 March 1980, as Sean O'Casey Day].

2009 Ferrar, Harold, "Robert Emmet in Irish Drama," Eire-Ireland, 1 (Summer 1966), 19-28 [Boucicault's characterization of misbegotten Irish rebellion "finds enduring expression in ... The Plough and the Stars"].

2010 Fielding, Henry, "Truth About Sean," Daily Herald (London), (27 Apr 1964), p. 6 [Interview with Eileen O'Casey].

2011 "Fighting Genius of O'Casey," Irish Times (Dublin), (19 Feb 1959), p. 5 [Report on a lecture on O'Casey by Gabriel Fallon].

2012 Finegan, J[ohn] J., "The Abbey Will Go It Alone," Evening Herald (Dublin), (16 Nov 1963), p. 13 [O'Casey relaxes ban on his plays so that the Abbey Theatre could take part in the festivities to mark the 400th anniversary of Shakespeare's birth]. See reply by T.F.B. and counterreply by J.J. Finegan, (23 Nov 1963), p. 8.

2013 _____, "O'Casey Love Letters Still Embargoed," Evening Herald (Dublin), (29 Mar 1980), p. 6 [The National Library of Ireland has what is believed to be a large collection of unpublished letters and poems by O'Casey, written between 1917 and 1926 to Maura Keating].

2014 _____, "The Signs Are Encouraging," Evening Herald (Dublin), (22 Feb 1964), p. 8 [Hopes are high that O'Casey's ban on the professional performance of his plays in Ireland will be removed after the Abbey Theatre's season in London]. See reply by Reamonn O Corcorain, (26 Feb 1964), p. 8.

2015 "Fionn MacCool," "O'Casey Centenary Tribute," Irish Post (London), (5 Apr 1980), p. 8 ["A Celebration of Sean O'Casey" on B.B.C.].

2016 Fitzgerald, Jim, "Sean O'Casey," Irish Democrat (London), (Dec 1964), 2 [Interview with Anthony Coughlan].

2017 Fitzgerald, John J., "Sean O'Casey's Dramatic Slums," Descant, 10 (Fall 1965), 26-34 [In his plays set in the slums of Dublin, O'Casey makes the constant squabbling serve a dramatic purpose].

2018 Fitzgerald, Marion, "Playwriting Is Agony, Says Hugh Leonard," Irish Digest, 79 (Jan 1964), 34-6 [Leonard's favorite playwrights are Harold Pinter, Tennessee Williams, and Sean O'Casey--in descending order].

2019 FitzGerald, Mary, "How the Abbey Said No: Readers' Reports and the Rejection of The Silver Tassie," O'Casey Annual (London), no. 1 (1982), 73-87 [Examines the incident again, against the broader context of Abbey history and reading policy].

2020 FitzGerald, Prudence, "O'Casey Centenary," Irish Times (Dublin), (19 Apr 1980), p. 9 [Letter to the Editor concerning the celebration of the 100th anniversary of O'Casey's birth by RTE, the Irish national radio and television network].

2021 Fitz-Simon, Christopher, "The Theater in Dublin," Modern Drama, 2 (Dec 1959), 289-94 ["It is a common error, especially in America, to believe that O'Casey was the mainstay of the Abbey about twenty years ago and that his works are still the most important part of the national repertoire"].

2022 Foley, Donal, "The Centenary," Irish Times (Dublin), (19 Apr 1980), p. 14. [A meeting with Shivaun O'Casey].

2023 _____, "O'Casey Ambassador," Irish Times (Dublin), (22 Mar 1980), p. 14 [Tomas MacAnna is lecturing on O'Casey in Russia and America].

2024 _____, "O'Casey Out to Make Them Laugh," Irish Press (Dublin), (18 Sep 1957), p. 6 [Interview with O'Casey by an Irish journalist].

2025 _____, "O'Casey's Centenary," Irish Times (Dublin), (5 Apr 1980), p. 14 [Celebrations marking the centenary of O'Casey's birth].

2026 _____, "O'Casey's Popularity," Irish Times (Dublin), (5 Jan 1980), p. 12 [O'Casey has been very successfully translated into Norwegian].

2027 "Forsaking Ireland: The Beginnings of Exile," Irish Independent (Dublin), (7 Jul 1926), p. 9; and Daily Sketch (London), (7 Jul 1926), p. 2 [O'Casey makes permanent home in London].

2028 "Forthcoming Works," Irish Book Lover (Dublin), 10 (Apr-May 1919), 94 [The Story of the Irish Citizen Army to be published by Maunsel of Dublin].

2029 Fox, R.M., "Abbey Theatre," Aryan Path (Bombay), 36 (May 1965), 225-27 [Starting in 1923, O'Casey's realistic plays changed the policy of play selection at the Abbey Theatre].

2030 _____, "The Drama of the Dregs," New Statesman (London), 27 (21 Aug 1926), 525-6 [Juno and the Paycock deals faithfully with problems of individual character].

2031 _____, "Foundations of the Abbey," Aryan Path (Bombay), 35 (Jan 1964), 14-16 [Yeats probably objected not to O'Casey's slum characters as such, but to urban-worker characters whose souls lacked poetry].

2032 _____, "Irish Drama Knocks at the Door," Life and Letters (London), 61 (Apr 1949), 16-21 ["After the first World War and Ireland's own battles, drama became increasingly critical, realistic and bitter. Sean O'Casey expressed this phase"].

2033 _____, "The Machine Drama," New Statesman (London), 26 (9 Jan 1926), 383-4. Reprinted in Living Age (Boston), 328 (20 Feb 1926), 421-2 [On Juno and the Paycock].

2034 _____, "Modern Irish Drama," Theatre Arts (N.Y.), 24 (Jan 1940), 22-5 ["Undoubtedly the man who revitalised Irish drama (after 1922) was Sean O'Casey"].

2035 _____, "The O'Casey I Knew," Aryan Path (Bombay), 35 (Dec 1964), 546-8 [Recollections of O'Casey].

2036 _____, "Portrait of O'Casey as a Young Man," Irish Times (Dublin), (1 Dec 1964), p. 8 [Recollections of O'Casey. Expanded version of his earlier piece, "Sean O'Casey's Dublin"].

2037 _____, "Realism in Irish Drama," Irish Statesman (Dublin), 10 (23 June 1928), 310-12 [Examines O'Casey as an "outstanding example" of realism in Irish Drama].

2038 _____, "Sean O'Casey: A Worker Dramatist," New Statesman (London), 26 (10 Apr 1926), 805-6 [Recollections of O'Casey by an Irish historian].

2039 _____, "Sean O'Casey and the Soul of Man," Aryan Path (Bombay), 34 (Aug 1963), 366-9 [Explains how O'Casey's social plays are more than valid today].

2040 _____, "Sean O'Casey's Dublin," Irish Times (Dublin), (2 May 1960), p. 8 [Recollections of O'Casey].

2041 _____, "Social Criticism in the Irish Theatre," Aryan Path (Bombay), 38 (Apr 1967), 179-81 [The effects of Yeats' policy of banning plays containing social criticism and beginning a trend towards plays emphasizing poetry and rhetoric, can be seen in the works of O'Casey].

2042 _____, "The Theatre Goes on in Ireland," Theatre Arts (N.Y.), 24 (Nov 1940), 783-6 [Includes brief discussion on the production of The Star Turns Red at the Unity Theatre, London].

2043 _____, "Twilight over Irish Drama," Theatre Arts (N.Y.), 30 (Dec 1946), 706-8 [Includes brief discussion on Red Roses for Me].

2044 _____, "What Next in Irish Drama?" Theatre Arts (N.Y.), 26 (Apr 1942), 245-9 ["Without O'Casey's strain of passionate poetry it is doubtful if his slum plays would have been looked at by the Abbey"].

2045 _____, "Wild Riders of Irish Drama," Theatre Arts (N.Y.),

28 (May 1944), 301-4 [Includes brief discussion on Red Roses for Me].

2046   Freedman, Morris, "The Modern Tragicomedy of Wilde and O'Casey," College English, 25 (Apr 1964), 518-22, 527. Reprinted in The Moral Impulse (Carbondale and Edwardsville: Southern Illinois University Press, 1967), pp. 63-73 [What connects Wilde and O'Casey most meaningfully is their tone of tragicomedy].

2047   "Freedom of Dublin for O'Casey?" Irish Times (Dublin), (26 Apr 1960), p. 4 [A suggestion in the National Observer that the freedom of Dublin should be conferred on O'Casey has been welcomed].

2048   Freundlich, Elisabeth, "Der Dramatiker Sean O'Casey," Theater der Zeit (Berlin), 3 (June 1956), 181-3 [Discusses The Bishop's Bonfire].

2049   _____, "The Silver Tassie and the Cold War," Sean O'Casey Review, 4 (Spring 1978), 113-19 [Describes European reception to the performances of the play].

2050   Friel, Brian, "O'Casey," Abbey Theatre Souvenir Programme (Dec 1979), p. 26 [Introductory note on the occasion of the production of Juno and the Paycock].

2051   "From Starvation to Success: The Dramatic Career of Sean O'Casey," John O'London's Weekly, 18 (19 Nov 1927), 200 [Biographical essay].

2052   "From the Editor's Chair," Irish Book Lover (Dublin), 14 (Sep-Oct 1924), 122 [Juno and the Paycock is refused a hearing in Cork].

2053   Funke, Lewis, "News and Gossip of the Rialto," New York Times, (27 Mar 1960), section 2, p. 1 [Interview with O'Casey on the occasion of his 80th birthday].

2054   Gardner, Paul, "1,400 Pay Tribute to O'Casey Artistry," New York Times, (12 Oct 1964), p. 35 [A tribute to O'Casey was given at the Imperial Theater, New York].

2055   Gardner, Raymond, "Arm in Arm with Eileen," Guardian (London), (5 Oct 1976), p. 11 [Interview with Eileen O'Casey].

2056   Gassner, John, "The Possibilities and Perils of Modern Tragedy," Tulane Drama Review, 1 (June 1957), 3-14 [Makes few references to O'Casey].

2057 _____, "The Prodigality of Sean O'Casey," Theatre Arts
(N.Y.), 35 (June 1951), 52-3; (Jul 1951), 54-5; (Aug 1951),
48-9. Reprinted in The Theatre in Our Times (New York:
Crown Publishers, 1954), pp. 240-8 [O'Casey's "prodigal
creativity" sets him apart from the "largely trivial and con-
stricted" contemporary theater].

2058 _____, "The Winter of Our Discontent," Theatre Arts (N.Y.),
39 (Aug 1955), 22-4, 86 [O'Casey is one of the two "major
playwrights alive in the world"].

2059 Geneson, Paul, "The Yeats-O'Casey Relationship: A Study in
Loyal Opposition," Sean O'Casey Review, 2 (Fall 1975), 52-7
[An abiding sense of loyalty in the relationship of Yeats and
O'Casey has generally been overlooked by the critics].

2060 Gheorghiu, Mihnea, "O'Casey: Menestrel al irlandei eroice,"
Secolul 20 (Bucharest), 1 (1961), 144-50 [O'Casey is a "singer
of heroic Ireland"].

2061 _____, "Sean O'Casey: Trandafiri fara piine" [Sean O'Casey:
Roses Without Bread], Secolul 20 (Bucharest), 4 (1964), 92-
103 [Tribute to O'Casey].

2062 Gibbon, Monk, "In Defence of Censorship," Bell (Dublin), 9
(Jan 1945), 313-22; (Feb 1945), 395-409; (Mar 1945), 528-35;
10 (Apr 1945), 81 [O'Casey disagrees with Gibbon's views on
Literary censorship].

2063 Gibbons, Renée, and Lew Gibbons, "The Heart of San Francisco,"
Sean O'Casey Review, 7 (1981), 2-3 [Gives an account of the
celebrations in San Francisco to mark the O'Casey Centenary].

2064 Goldstone, Herbert, "O'Casey in '74: Or Has Everything Been
Said?" Sean O'Casey Review, 1 (Fall 1974), 6-10 [While a
great deal has been said about O'Casey, still possibilities for
new direction, new emphasis, new assessments exist].

2065 _____, "The Unevenness of O'Casey: A Study of Within the
Gates," Forum (Houston), 4 (Winter-Spring 1965), 37-42 [The
play provides good examples of the best and the worst in
O'Casey's later plays].

2066 Good, J.W., "A New Irish Dramatist," New Statesman (London),
22 (29 Mar 1924), 731 [Assesses O'Casey as a dramatist and
discusses The Shadow of a Gunman and Juno and the Paycock].

2067 Gould, Jack, "TV: Sean O'Casey Is Interviewed," New York
Times, (23 Jan 1956), p. 49 [Interview with O'Casey by Robert Emmett Ginna on N.B.C.].

2068 Grant, Lee, "Eileen O'Casey Looks Back," Sean O'Casey Review,
      1 (Spring 1975), 30-7. Reprinted from the Los Angeles Times
      [Interview with Eileen O'Casey].

2069 Gray, Ken, "Edna O'Brien States Case," Irish Times (Dublin),
      (17 Nov 1966), p. 10 [O'Casey neglected his real work to be-
      come embroiled in public controversy over censorship and
      kindred matters which involves much writing to the Irish
      Times]. See reply by John O'Riordan, "O'Casey, Letter-
      Writer," ibid. (23 Nov 1966), p. 9.

2070 Greany, Helen T., "Some Interesting Parallels: Pope and the
      Paycock," Notes and Queries, 103 (June 1958), 253 [The last
      act of Juno and the Paycock quotes Pope's Essay on Man IV.
      248].

2071 "Great Love for Ireland," Newsweek, 64 (28 Sep 1964), 91
      [Obituary of O'Casey].

2072 Greaves, C. Desmond, "Denigration of O'Casey," Hibernia
      (Dublin), (30 Aug 1979), p. 4 [Letter to the Editor on
      O'Casey's criticism of Connolly].

2073 "Greaves on O'Casey," Irish Socialist (Dublin), (Jul 1980), 4
      [Report on a lecture on O'Casey by Desmond Greaves to com-
      memorate the O'Casey Centenary].

2074 Gregory, Lady, "How Great Plays Are Born: The Coming of
      Mr. O'Casey," Daily News (London), (27 Mar 1926), p. 6
      [Tells how O'Casey became a dramatist].

2075 Guidi, Augusto, "'Le rose rossi' di S. O'Casey," L'Italia che
      scrive (Rome), 50 (Feb-Mar 1967), 27 [Analysis of Red Roses
      for Me].

2076 Gulliver 7: Literatur und Politik in Irland: Sean O'Casey zum
      100. Geburtstag. Gulliver, Bd. 7 (Berlin: Argument 1980)
      [Contents: Thomas Metscher, "Bürgerliche und sozialistische
      Literatur in Ireland, von Swift bis O'Casey"; Jack Mitchell,
      "In Defence of Sean O'Casey's One-Acters"; Manfred Pauli,
      "Eine Herausforderung an die Künste des Theaters. Zur
      Aneignung der Werke Sean O'Casey's in der DDR"; Rüdiger
      Hillgärtner, "Der Anspruch auf ein erfülltes Leben. Zum
      Verhältnis von Biographie und Autobiographie bei Sean
      O'Casey"; Reiner Lehberger, "Der Irlandkonflikt als Thema
      einer Unterrichtseinheit für die Sekundarstufe II. Vorschläge
      zu einer Verquickung landeskundlicher und literarischner
      Texte unter besonderer Berücksichtigung von Sean O'Casey's
      The Plough and the Stars"; and reviews of books on O'Casey].

2077 Gunn, John, "'Telly? Count Me Out,' Says O'Casey," Sunday Review (Dublin), 5 (13 Aug 1961), 28 [O'Casey bans future TV productions of his plays].

2078 Habart, Michel, "Introduction à Sean O'Casey," Théâtre populaire (Paris), no. 34 (2nd Quarter 1959), 5-37 [Comprehensive study].

2079 _____, "Une mère et deux fils," Cahiers de la companie Madeleine Renaud-Jean-Louis Barrault (Paris), no. 37 (Feb 1962), 17-31 [Although Shaw and O'Casey are different writers, the "Irishism ... is omni-present in their dramatic works"].

2080 _____, "Sean O'Casey," L'Avant-scène (Paris), no. 230 (Nov 1960), 34-5 [Discusses Bedtime Story].

2081 _____, "Sean O'Casey," Lettres françaises, no. 1047 (23-30 Sep 1964), pp. 11, 13 [Obituaries by Michel Habart, André Clavé, Jean Dasté, and Stellio Lorenzi].

2082 _____, "Sean O'Casey: Théâtre et réalité," Nouvelle critique (Paris), no. 127 (June 1961), 71-82 [Gives an assessment of O'Casey as a dramatist].

2083 _____, "Le Théâtre irlandais," Théâtre populaire (Paris), no. 9 (Sep-Oct 1954), 24-43 [Discusses The Shadow of a Gunman, Juno and the Paycock and The Plough and the Stars].

2084 _____, "Le théâtre irlandais et Sean O'Casey," Bref (Paris), no. 43 (Feb 1961), 4-5 [Gives an assessment of O'Casey as a dramatist].

2085 Hall, Gus, "'He Would Have Felt at Home,'" Daily World (N.Y.), (10 Mar 1978), p. 8 [Greetings by the General Secretary of the American Communist Party].

2086 Hamburger, Maik, "Sean O'Casey in the Theatre," Sean O'Casey Review, 6 (1980), 45-61 [Some notes prompted by stagings of O'Casey's plays in the German Democratic Republic].

2087 Hardie, Margaret, "Contemporary British Dramatists," Cizi jazyky ve skole, 10 (1967), 97-104 [Discusses The Shadow of a Gunman, Juno and the Paycock, and The Plough and the Stars].

2088 Harkness, Marguerite, "The Silver Tassie: No Light in the Darkness," Sean O'Casey Review, 4 (Spring 1978), 131-7 [The play depicts O'Casey's starkest perception of the oppressed cooperating willingly with their oppressors].

2089 Harman, Bill J., and Ronald G. Rollins, "Mythical Dimensions in O'Casey's Within the Gates," West Virginia University Philological Papers, 16 (Nov 1967), 72-8 [The play uses mythical prototypes to interpret contemporary history].

2090 Harmon, Maurice, "The Era of Inhibitions: Irish Literature 1920-60," Emory University Quarterly, 22 (Spring 1966), 18-28 ["O'Casey faced official opposition by a native, predominantly Catholic government"].

2091 _____, "Juno and the Paycock," Era Review (The Curragh, Co. Kildare), no. 3 (1977), 34-8 [Some literary references in the play].

2092 Harvey, Anthony E., "Letters from Sean O'Casey to a Randolph-Macon Senior," Randolph-Macon Bulletin, 26 (Sep 1954), 7-9, 23-6 [Describes how O'Casey helped and corresponded with a senior student at Randolph-Macon College].

2093 Harvey, Francis, "O'Casey," Irish Times (Dublin), (2 Apr 1960), p. 9 [Letter to the Editor greeting O'Casey on his 80th birthday].

2094 Hawkins, A. Desmond, "The Poet in the Theatre," Criterion: A Literary Review (London), 14 (Oct 1934), 29-39 [O'Casey is "in danger of collapsing into a pretentious pseudo-poetic drama based on a crude use of Symbolism"].

2095 "Hawthornden Prize Awarded: Lord Oxford's Tribute to Mr. Sean O'Casey," Times (London), (24 Mar 1926), p. 11 [O'Casey is awarded the Hawthornden Prize for Juno and the Paycock].

2096 H[ayes], J.J., "On Foreign Stages," New York Times, (15 Nov 1925), section 8, p. 2 [The Secretary of the Irish Dramatists League says that "even Sean O'Casey, repeated too often, began to pall"]. See O'Casey's reply, "To the Dramatic Editor," ibid. (27 Dec 1925), section 7, p. 2.

2097 Hays, Peter C., "Raisin in the Sun and Juno and the Paycock," Phylon, 33 (Summer 1972), 175-6 [There are many parallels between Juno and the Paycock and Raisin in the Sun by Lorraine Hansberry, who states in her autobiography, To Be Young, Gifted and Black, that she was intensely moved by a production of O'Casey's play].

2098 "He Called O'Casey 'Unsavoury': Ex-Fun Fair Man Puts Foot in It," Daily Worker (London), (20 Feb 1954), p. 3 [J. Carlton, Chingford Council's Entertainments Manager, objects to Chingford's Unity Theatre performing Bedtime Story].

2099 Heidenreich-Krawschak, Regina, "Critical Reception of Sean
      O'Casey in Berlin Since 1953," Sean O'Casey Review, 5 (Fall
      1978), 55-62 [Surveys the productions of O'Casey's plays and
      looks at their critical reviews].

2100 Henahan, John F., "The Abbey: Waiting for O'Casey," Boston
      Globe Magazine, (16 March 1980), 13, 36, 41 [The Abbey The-
      atre celebrated its 75th anniversary by reviving Juno and the
      Paycock].

2101 Henderson, Gordon, "An Interview with Denis Johnston," Jour-
      nal of Irish Literature, 2 (May-Sep 1973), 30-44 [Comments
      on acting in Juno and the Paycock].

2102 Henn, T.R., "The Bible in Relation to the Study of English
      Literature Today," Hermathena (Dublin), no. 100 (Summer
      1965), 29-43 [Examines The Silver Tassie].

2103 _____, "A Note on the Irish Theatre," Cambridge Review,
      58 (12 Feb 1937), 250-1; (19 Feb 1937), 269-70 [O'Casey and
      Synge compared].

2104 Hennigan, Aidan, "O'Casey Plays Not for TV," Irish Press
      (Dublin), (9 May 1961), p. 3 [Interview with O'Casey].

2105 _____, "O'Casey Rejects Plea," Irish Press (Dublin), (20
      Mar 1962), p. 3 [O'Casey's embargo on professional produc-
      tions of his plays in Ireland not lifted].

2106 Hennigan, Tony, "Remembering Sean O'Casey," Irish Independ-
      ent (Dublin), (28 Mar 1980), p. 8 [Interview with Gabriel
      Fallon, O'Casey's friend].

2107 Herbert, Edward T., "Eugene O'Neill: An Evaluation by Fel-
      low Playwrights," Modern Drama, 6 (Dec 1963), 239-40 [Short
      comments by O'Casey and others].

2108 Herring, Thelma, "Maenads and Goat-Song," Southerly, 25
      (1965), 219-33 [O'Casey influenced Patrick White].

2109 Hethmon, Robert, "Great Hatred, Little Room," Tulane Drama
      Review, 5 (June 1961), 51-5 [Discusses Kathleen Listens In].

2110 Hewes, Henry, "American Playwrights Self-Appraised," Satur-
      day Review (N.Y.), 38 (3 Sep 1955), 18-19 [O'Casey is cited
      as a favorite playwright by some American playwrights].

2111 _____, "Broadway Postscript: Dublin," Saturday Review
      (N.Y.), 40 (18 May 1957), 34-5 [Ernst Blythe gives reasons
      for not producing O'Casey's later plays].

2112 _____, "Mirror in the Hallway," Saturday Review (N.Y.),
39 (22 Sep 1956), 30 [Interview with O'Casey on the occasion
of the Broadway dramatization of Pictures in the Hallway].

2113 _____, "Seventeen Playwrights Self-Appraised," Saturday
Review (N.Y.), 38 (7 May 1955), 48-9 [O'Casey is cited as
a favorite playwright by some British playwrights].

2114 Hickey, Des, "O'Casey's Hidden Dublin," Sunday Independent
(Dublin), (30 Mar 1980), p. 11 [Tom Buggy has launched a
literary bus tour of the landmarks for O'Casey pilgrims].

2115 _____, "The Truth About Sean O'Casey," Sunday Independent (Dublin), (13 Apr 1980), p. 13 [Refutes the allegations
that O'Casey was "a dyed-in-the-wool Communist, a black
atheist, a bad-tempered recluse, and a liar about his not-
so-hard times"].

2116 Hingerty, Kay, "Eileen O'Casey Remembers," Irish Times (Dublin), (1 Apr 1980), p. 9 [Interview with Eileen O'Casey].

2117 Hodson, J.L., "The Strange Mystery of Sean O'Casey," News
Chronicle (London), (21 Dec 1931), p. 6 [Interview with
O'Casey by an English journalist, dramatist, and novelist].

2118 Hogan, Robert, "Dublin: The Summer Season and the Theatre
Festival, 1967," Drama Survey, 6 (Spring 1968), 315-23 [In-
cludes brief discussions on the productions of Red Roses for
Me and Pictures in the Hallway].

2119 _____, "The Experiments of Sean O'Casey," Dublin Magazine,
33 (Jan-Mar 1958), 4-12 [Refutes misconceptions about O'Casey's
later plays]. Cf. "Riches Scorned," Times Literary Supplement (London), (31 Jan 1958), p. 61; and Robert Hogan,
ibid. (21 Mar 1958), p. 153.

2120 _____, "The Haunted Inkbottle: A Preliminary Study of
Rhetorical Devices in the Late Plays of Sean O'Casey," James
Joyce Quarterly, 8 (Fall 1970), 76-95 [The style of the late
plays is a complex mixture of most of the elements of O'Casey's
early style, plus the addition of a few new devices].

2121 _____, "In Sean O'Casey's Golden Days," Dublin Magazine,
5 (Autumn-Winter 1966), 80-93. Reprinted in his After the
Irish Renaissance (London: Macmillan, 1967), pp. 235-52;
rev. version reprinted in Sean O'Casey, ed. Ronald Ayling
(London: Macmillan, 1969), pp. 162-76 [Examines O'Casey's
place in the pastoral tradition].

2122 _____, "O'Casey, Influence and Impact," Irish University

Review (Dublin), 10 (Spring 1980), 146-58 [O'Casey had more impact than influence].

2123 _____, "O'Casey's Dramatic Apprenticeship," Modern Drama, 4 (Dec 1961), 243-53 [Discusses The Robe of Rosheen, The Frost in the Flower, Nipped in the Bud, The Harvest Festival, The Crimson in the Tri-Colour, Kathleen Listens In, and Nannie's Night Out].

2124 _____, and Gordon Henderson, eds., "A Sheaf of Letters," Journal of Irish Literature, 3 (Jan 1974), 65-92 [These letters were written by Brian O'Nolan to O'Casey and others].

2125 Hone, J.M., "A Letter from Ireland," London Mercury, 14 (June 1926), 189-91 ["Of late, the big 'draw' at the Abbey Theatre has been Mr. O'Casey"].

2126 "Honour for O'Casey Next?" Times Pictorial (Dublin), 72 (30 Mar 1946), 4 [Suggests that the Freedom of Dublin be bestowed on O'Casey after having been bestowed on Bernard Shaw].

2127 Houlihan, Con, "O'Casey--The First Careful Rapture," Evening Press (Dublin), (8 Apr 1980), p. 6 [Argues that the earlier plays contain more of the "real" O'Casey than the later ones and the autobiographical volumes].

2128 _____, "Sean O'Casey--A Giant with the Killer Instinct," Evening Press (Dublin), (28 Mar 1980), p. 8 [Assesses O'Casey's work].

2129 Howard, John, "'Abbey Has Been Deteriorating for Years,' Says Sean O'Casey," Irish Times (Dublin), (4 Jul 1964), pp. 1, 11 [Interview with O'Casey].

2130 Howard, Milton, "Orwell or O'Casey?" Masses and Mainstream (N.Y.), 8 (Jan 1955), 20-6 [O'Casey loved humanity].

2131 Howarth, William L., "Some Principles of Autobiography," New Literary History, 5 (Winter 1974), 363-81 [Includes brief discussion on O'Casey's Autobiographies].

2132 Humbert, Michel, "1916--La Charrue et les Etoiles--1968," Sean O'Casey Review, 2 (Spring 1976), 216-17 [Recollections of a production of The Plough and the Stars at Rouen, France].

2133 Hunt, Hugh, "'To Buried Merit Raise the Tardy Bust ...,'" Hibernia (Dublin), (17 April 1980), p. 18 [Discusses the changing critical attitudes towards O'Casey].

2134 Hynes, Malachy, "A Burrow of Culture: The Two Jims," Irish Times (Dublin), (6 May 1959), p. 10 [Recollections of O'Casey].

2135 "'I Won't Write for Abbey'--O'Casey," Sunday Press (Dublin), (4 Mar 1962), p. 5 [Interview with O'Casey].

2136 Igoe, Vivien, "Dublin Days and Places," Irish Times (Dublin), (1 Apr 1980), p. 9 [Describes the early days of O'Casey and the houses in which he lived].

2137 Igoe, W.J., "Sean O'Casey: At Home Only with People," Catholic Herald (London), (25 Sep 1964), p. 10 [O'Casey's self-imposed exile was tragic for him and for the drama]. See reply by John O'Riordan, ibid. (2 Oct 1964), p. 5 [Letter to the Editor].

2138 _____, "Sean O'Casey, Tragic Jester," Critic (Chicago), 19 (June-July 1961), 15-16, 67-9 [O'Casey's war against Ireland has had tragic consequences for him as a playwright].

2139 Ingalls, Leonard, "Drive on Censor Gains in Britain: Butler Tells Commons Close Attention Will Be Given to Stage Reform Bid," New York Times (9 May 1958), p. 19 [O'Casey supports the Theatre Censorship Reform Committee formed under the chairmanship of Sir Gerald Barry].

2140 Inouye, Chizouko, "The Irish Theme of Sean O'Casey," Baika Review (Ibaraki), no. 8 (1975), 27-39 [In Japanese].

2141 _____, "Realistic Symbolism in Sean O'Casey's Cock-A-Doodle Dandy," Baika Review (Ibaraki), no. 9 (1976), 25-38 [In Japanese].

2142 "Insight to O'Casey's Character," Irish Independent (Dublin), (12 May 1980), p. 8 [Report on Robert Hogan's lecture on RTE to commemorate the O'Casey Centenary].

2143 "International Notes," Sean O'Casey Review, 4 (Fall 1977), 30-40 [O'Casey items of interest from Austria, England, France, Iceland, Ireland, Portugal, and the United States].

2144 "International Notes," Sean O'Casey Review, 4 (Spring 1978), 173-9 [O'Casey items of interest from Austria, England, France, Ireland, and the United States].

2145 "International Notes," Sean O'Casey Review, 5 (Fall 1978), 34-9 [O'Casey items of interest from Cuba, England, the German Democratic Republic, Ireland, and the United States].

2146 "International Notes," Sean O'Casey Review, 5 (Spring 1979),

187-92 [O'Casey items of interest from England, Germany, and the United States].

2147 "International Notes," Sean O'Casey Review, 6 (1980), 62-4 [O'Casey items of interest from England and the United States].

2148 "Invalids," Times (London), (26 Apr 1947), p. 4 [O'Casey is recovering from influenza at his home at Totnes, Devon].

2149 "Invalids," Times (London), (27 Feb 1956), p. 8 [O'Casey is recovering from a minor operation in Torbay Hospital, Torquay].

2150 "Invalids," Times (London), (1 Mar 1956), p. 8 [O'Casey undergoes a second operation at Torbay Hospital].

2151 "Invalids," Times (London), (20 Mar 1956), p. 10 [O'Casey leaves Torbay Hospital].

2152 "Ireland's New Playwright," Literary Digest (N.Y.), 89 (17 Apr 1926), 27-8 [Compares Juno and the Paycock with The Plough and the Stars, and includes several quotations from the press reviews].

2153 "Irish Academy of Letters: Names of the First Members," Times (London), (20 Sep 1932), p. 10 [O'Casey has been nominated by Bernard Shaw and W.B. Yeats].

2154 "Irish Literary Shillalahs," New York Times (6 Feb 1930), p. 22 [Editorial on the dispute between O'Casey and George Russell over art]. See O'Casey's reply, ibid. (20 Mar 1930), p. 26.

2155 "The Irish Theatre: Sick or Sound?" Aquarius (Benburb, County Tyrone), 4 (1971), 17-25, passim [Micheál MacLiammóir, Tyrone Guthrie, and Eugene McCabe make references to O'Casey at a symposium].

2156 Isaacs, Stan, "Dinner with a Grande 'Gloriously Human' Dame," Newsday (Garden City, N.Y.), (5 Feb 1976), p. 7 [Sean O'Casey's Festival at Hofstra University].

2157 Izakov, Boris, "Five Meetings," Sovetskaya Kultura (Moscow), no. 153 (15 Dec 1955), p. 4 [Interview with O'Casey by an author, translator, and friend of O'Casey].

2158 J., W., "Wonderful London Yesterday," Daily Graphic (London), (24 Mar 1926), p. 5 [Report on the reception at which O'Casey was awarded the Hawthornden Prize for Juno and the Paycock].

2159 Jacque, Valentina, "Soviet Critics on Modern English Writing," Soviet Literature, no. 4 (1963), 163-7 [Most frequently translated into Russian are books by those authors, like O'Casey and others, whose attitudes coincide with those of the Soviets].

2160 Johnston, Denis, "Humor-Hibernian Style," New York Times (5 Feb 1961), Drama Section, p. 3 [O'Casey's use of adjectives makes his plays easily recognized as Irish].

2161 _____, "A Hundred Years Old," Irish Times (Dublin), (1 Apr 1980), p. 9 [A tribute to O'Casey to commemorate his Centenary].

2162 _____, "Joxer in Totnes: A Study in Sean O'Casey," Irish Writing (Cork), no. 13 (Dec 1950), 50-3 [Discusses O'Casey as a man and as a writer].

2163 _____, "O'Casey," Abbey Theatre Souvenir Programme (Dec 1979), p. 25 [Introductory note on the occasion of the production of Juno and the Paycock].

2164 _____, "Sean O'Casey," Nation (N.Y.), 199 (5 Oct 1964), 198 [Tribute to O'Casey, pointing out that his vitality and his style are his greatest merits].

2165 _____, "Sean O'Casey: An Appreciation," Daily Telegraph (London), (11 Mar 1926), p. 15. Reprinted in Living Age (Boston), 329 (17 Apr 1926), 161-3 [Compares O'Casey to Toller and O'Neill, and stresses that he has never written for popularity].

2166 _____, "What Has Happened to the Irish?" Theatre Arts (N.Y.), 43 (Jul 1959), 11-12, 72 ["O'Casey has no opinions whatever, apart from certain mechanical reactions to his own personal history"].

2167 _____, "Writer Recalls O'Casey Exile," Irish Times (Dublin), (31 Mar 1980), p. 5 [Report on his lecture on RTE to mark the O'Casey Centenary].

2168 Jones, Mervyn, "In Commemoration," Listener (London), (10 Apr 1980), p. 473 [O'Casey Centenary celebrated on B.B.C.].

2169 Jordan, John, "The Passionate Autodidact: The Importance of Litera Scripta for O'Casey," Irish University Review (Dublin), 10 (Spring 1980), 59-76 [Establishes the weight of literary reference in O'Casey's plays as well as his lifelong love and respect for books].

2170 _____, "A World in Chassis," University Review (Dublin), 1

(Spring 1955), 21-8 [Finds that there are two O'Caseys:
the early happy Sean of Dublin and the later unhappy Sean
of Devon].

2171 "Journal Focuses on O'Casey," Irish Times (Dublin), (1 Apr
1980), p. 6 [The Irish University Review publishes a special
issue on O'Casey to mark his centenary].

2172 Kargova, A.M., "Image of the Author in Sean O'Casey's Work
Mirror in the Hallway," Literaturovedcheskiy Sbornik (Ryazan), (1972), 139-58 [In Russian].

2173 _____, "Interpretation of Sean O'Casey's Novel Sunset and
Evening Star," Voprosy Istorii Literatury (Chelibinska),
(1971), 146-62 [In Russian].

2174 _____, "Metaphysical Style in the Autobiographies of Sean
O'Casey," Literaturovedcheskiy Sbornik (Ryazan), (1972),
102-38 [In Russian].

2175 _____, "Sean O'Casey and Leo Tolstoy," Tolstovskiy Sbornik
(Tula), 5 (1973), 275-85 [In Russian].

2176 _____, "Walt Whitman and Sean O'Casey," Literaturovedcheskiy Sbornik (Ryazan), (1972), 159-69 [In Russian].

2177 Kaufman, Michael W., "O'Casey's Structural Design in Juno and
the Paycock," Quarterly Journal of Speech, 58 (Apr 1972),
191-8 [The concluding scenes of the play epitomize its central
dialectic between actuality and illusion].

2178 _____, "The Position of The Plough and the Stars in O'Casey's
Dublin Trilogy," James Joyce Quarterly, 8 (Fall 1970), 48-63
[The meaning of the play is the folly of glorified illusions
about war and heroism, and its position in the Trilogy sug-
gests that the cycle of death and destruction will be repeated
endlessly].

2179 Kavanagh, Jim, "My Friend O'Casey," Irish Democrat (London),
(Nov 1964), p. 4. Reprinted in Sean O'Casey Review, 2
(Fall 1975), 58-61 [Recollections of O'Casey, as told to An-
thony Coughlan].

2180 Kawano, Tomiaki, "O'Casey's Women in the 'Dublin Trilogy,'"
Eigo Eibubgaku (Kumamato University), 23 (1979), 36-57 [In
Japanese].

2181 Kellerson, Philippe, "Sean O'Casey," Courrier dramatique de
l'ouest (Rennes), no. 39 (Jan 1961) [Five-unnumbered-page
article preceding p. 1].

2182 Kelly, Seamus, "Dublin," Holiday (Philadelphia), 19 (Jan 1956), 38-43 [O'Casey left Dublin "because he couldn't make himself understood in his own city"].

2183 _____ , "Greatest Playwright in a Half-Century," Irish Times (Dublin), (19 Sep 1964), p. 5 [Tribute to O'Casey].

2184 Kenneally, Michael, "Autobiographical Revelation in O'Casey's I Knock at the Door," Canadian Journal of Irish Studies, 7 (Dec 1981), 21-38 [Though this book contains the biographical highlights of O'Casey's early years, the manner of presenting those experiences provides key insights into the autobiographer's contemporary character].

2185 _____ , "The Changing Contents of O'Casey's Autobiography," O'Casey Annual (London), no. 1 (1982), 148-66 [Examines the shift in emphasis in the last two volumes of Autobiographies].

2186 _____ , "Principles of Organization in O'Casey's Drums Under the Windows," Canadian Journal of Irish Studies, 6 (Dec 1980), 34-57 [An examination of the autobiographical book reveals that the organization of material is significant on several levels].

2187 Kennelly, Brendan, "The Two Irelands of Synge and O'Casey," New Knowledge (London), 6 (1966), 961-5 [Assesses O'Casey as a playwright].

2188 Kerr, Walter, "Where O'Casey's Career Went Wrong," New York Times (2 Feb 1969), pp. 1, 11 [Discusses O'Casey's later plays]. See "The Crow for Sean O'Casey," ibid. (2 Mar 1969), pp. 15, 40 [Letter to the Editor].

2189 Kevin, "Far and Near," Catholic Bulletin (Dublin), 16 (Mar 1926), 279-82 [O'Casey and Irish nationalism].

2190 Kiely, Benedict, "Joe the Post," Northwest Review, 9 (Fall-Winter 1967), 110-16 [O'Casey described Joseph Holloway's Journal as an "impossible pile of rubbish"].

2191 Kilroy, Thomas, "O'Casey," Abbey Theatre Souvenir Programme (Dec 1979), p. 27 [Introductory note on the occasion of the production of Juno and the Paycock].

2192 K[irwan], H.N., "Evolution of a Playwright," Freeman's Journal (Dublin), (15 Mar 1924), p. 5 [Discusses O'Casey's works and his outlook].

2193 _____ , "Sean O'Casey: The Man and the Dramatist," Crystal (Dublin), 1 (Feb 1926), 5, 20 ["It is certain that Sean

O'Casey has brought the art of the Abbey another step forward"].

2194 Kleiman, Carol, "O'Casey's 'Debt' to Toller: Expressionism in
The Silver Tassie and Red Roses for Me," Canadian Journal
of Irish Studies, 5 (June 1979), 69-86 [In these two plays,
O'Casey is not working in the manner of Toller].

2195 _____, "The Silver Tassie and Others: A Revaluation in the
Light of the Absurd," Sean O'Casey Review, 4 (Spring 1978),
139-72 [Examines O'Casey's relationship to the Theatre of the
absurd].

2196 Knepler, Henry W., "The 1961 MLA Conference in Modern
Drama," Modern Drama, 4 (Feb 1962), 339-42 [David Krause
is preparing an edition of O'Casey's letters and asks members for information].

2197 Knight, G. Wilson, "Ever a Fighter: On Sean O'Casey's The
Drums of Father Ned," Stand, 4 (Summer 1960), 15-18 [In
this play O'Casey is doing rather differently what he did in
Within the Gates; he is deliberately tidying up his sense of
forces and values, and this tidying up is his governing con-
cern].

2198 Kolozsvári, Emil, "Sean O'Casey," Nagyvilág (Budapest), 13
(Jan 1968), 112-18 [Discusses The Shadow of a Gunman,
Juno and the Paycock, and The Plough and the Stars. In
Hungarian].

2199 Kornilova, E[lena], "Vsegda s irlandieĭ, vsegda s narodom,"
Teatr (Moscow), 20 (May 1959), 167-78 [O'Casey always deals
with Ireland and with people].

2200 Kosok, Heinz, "The Revision of The Silver Tassie," Sean O'Casey
Review, 5 (Fall 1978), 15-18 [Notes the differences between
the 1928 edition and that included in volume II of Collected
Plays].

2201 _____, "Sean O'Casey: 1880-1964," Die Neueren Sprachen,
13 (Oct 1964), 453-68 [O'Casey's basic themes are poverty
and social injustice, the Anglo-Irish conflict, and his own
alienation from Ireland].

2202 _____, "Sean O'Casey's Hall of Healing," Die Neueren Sprachen, 19 (Apr 1970), 168-79 [Although the play is almost naturalistic in its setting, there is a generalizing tendency in
its treatment of character which, together with elements of
farce and paradox, precludes sentimentality. In German].

2203 _____, "The Three Versions of Red Roses for Me," O'Casey Annual (London), no. 1 (1982), 141-7 [Examines the three versions and concludes that the Collected Plays text is "decidedly superior"].

2204 _____, "Unity Theatre and The Star Turns Red," Sean O'Casey Review, 6 (1980), 68-74 [The two productions of The Star Turns Red at the Unity Theatre, London, in 1940 and 1946, seem to have made O'Casey aware of a number of weaknesses in his play].

2205 Krajewska, Wanda, "Irlandskość Eugene' a O'Neill," Przeglad humanistyczny (Warsaw), 10 (1966), 51-66 [The influence of O'Casey and other Irish dramatists on O'Neill].

2206 _____, "Sean O'Casey i Ekspresjonizm," Kwartalnik neofilologiczny (Warsaw), 12 (1965), 363-79 [O'Casey's expressionism is always combined with other elements: lyricism, poetic symbolism, and straight realism].

2207 Krause, David, "Antiphonies: Twelve Poems and a Tilly," Irish University Review (Dublin), 10 (Spring 1980), 98-102.

2208 _____, "The Barbarous Sympathies of Antic Irish Comedy," Malahat Review, 22 (Apr 1972), 99-117 [The desecrating laughter we find in O'Casey's plays is a celebration].

2209 _____, "The Comic Mythology of O'Casey," James Joyce Quarterly, 18 (Fall 1980), 11-22 [O'Casey knew that a comic mythology can serve as a powerful defense against the forces of repression].

2210 _____, "The Hidden Oisín," Studia Hibernica (Dublin), no. 6 (1966), 7-24 [Connects O'Casey's works with the tragicomic tradition of Gaelic myth, particularly the medieval Celtic dialogues between Oisín and St. Patrick].

2211 _____, "The Ironic Victory of Defeat in Irish Comedy," O'Casey Annual (London), no. 1 (1982), 33-63 [Discusses comic irony in the plays of O'Casey].

2212 _____, "The Maiming of Sean O'Casey," Evening Herald (Dublin), (26 Nov 1976), p. 8 [A reply to the attacks on O'Casey by Anthony Butler].

2213 _____, "O'Casey and Yeats and the Druid," Modern Drama, 11 (Dec 1968), 252-62 [O'Casey had too much integrity to engage in petty vindictiveness after Yeats severely damaged his career by rejecting The Silver Tassie for the Abbey Theatre].

2214   , "The Playwright's Not for Burning," <u>Virginia Quarterly Review</u>, 34 (Winter 1958), 60-76 [Examines <u>The Silver Tassie</u> and the controversy over it].

2215   , "The Principle of Comic Disintegration," <u>James Joyce Quarterly</u>, 8 (Fall 1970), 3-12 [It is the "instinctive ability to transform the raw material of high tragedy into low comedy" which characterizes the work of O'Casey].

2216   , "'The Rageous Ossean': Patron-Hero of Synge and O'Casey," <u>Modern Drama</u>, 4 (Dec 1961), 268-91 [Just as Cuchulain was Yeats's patron-hero, Oisín indirectly served in a similar role for Synge and O'Casey].

2217   , "Sean O'Casey," <u>Spectator</u> (London), 209 (28 Sep 1962), 435 [Letter to the Editor seeking information on the letters of O'Casey for the authorized edition].

2218   , "Sean O'Casey: 1880-1964," <u>Massachusetts Review</u> 6 (Winter-Spring 1965), 233-51. Reprinted in <u>Irish Renaissance</u>, ed. Robin Skelton and David R. Clark (Dublin: Dolmen Press, 1965), pp. 139-57 [Recollections].

2219   , "Sean O'Casey: Word-Fighter and Word-Painter," <u>Ireland Today</u> (Dublin), no. 964 (Mar 1980), 11-13 [It is time to remember that O'Casey was also a poetic word-painter].

2220   , "Some Truths and Jokes About the Easter Rising," <u>Sean O'Casey Review</u>, 3 (Fall 1976), 3-23 [Examines O'Casey's nationalism].

2221 Krehayn, Joachim, "Dichter des irischen Proletariats. Zum 80 Geburtstag Sean O'Casey," <u>Berliner Zeitung</u>, (1 Apr 1960), p. 7 [Pays tribute to O'Casey on the occasion of his 80th birthday].

2222   , "Sean O'Casey zum 80 Geburtstag," <u>Börsenblatt für den Deutschen Buchhandel</u> (Leipzig), 127 (2 Apr 1960), 220-1 [Pays tribute to O'Casey on the occasion of his 80th birthday].

2222a Kreps, Barbara, "The Meaning of Structure and Images in Sean O'Casey's <u>The Silver Tassie</u>," <u>Studi dell' Istituto Linguistico</u> (Florence), 2 (1979), 195-210 [An analysis of the play's curious structure makes it clear that O'Casey intentionally focuses on war and its effects].

2223 L., E., "Mr. O'Casey and 'Love on the Dole,'" <u>Adelphi</u> (London), 9, N.S. (1935), 371-2 [Replies to O'Casey's criticism of <u>Love on the Dole</u>, by Ronald Gow and Walter Greenwood].

2224 "Labourer Wins a Literary Prize: Mr. O'Casey Eulogised by
Lord Oxford," Daily Express (24 Mar 1926), p. 9 [O'Casey is
awarded the Hawthornden Prize for Juno and the Paycock].

2225 Larson, Gerald A., "An Interview with Mrs. Sean O'Casey,"
Educational Theatre Journal, 17 (Fall 1965), 234-9 [Eileen
O'Casey talks about her husband].

2226 "Latest Wills," Times (London), (1 Dec 1964), p. 19 [O'Casey
left £1,702].

2227 Lennon, Michael J., "Sean O'Casey and His Plays," Catholic
World (N.Y.), 130 (Dec 1929), 295-301; (Jan 1930), 452-61
[A biographical sketch and a critique of O'Casey's plays,
commencing with Kathleen Listens In and ending with The
Silver Tassie].

2228 Lentin, Louis, "O'Casey on RTE," Irish Times (Dublin), (11
Apr 1980), p. 11 [Letter to the Editor on the recognition of
the O'Casey Centenary by the Irish national radio and television network]. See reply by Fergus Pyle, ibid. (11 Apr
1980), p. 11.

2229 Leonard, Dymphna, "Sean O'Casey's Gift to Dublin," America
(N.Y.), 143 (11 Oct 1980), 209-10 [Describes Dublin's Celebrations to mark the O'Casey Centenary].

2230 Leonard, Hugh, "Drama: The Turning Point," Etudes irlandaises (Lille), no. 3 (Dec 1978), 77-85 [The Irish theatre was
"founded on the bedrock of Yeats, Synge and O'Casey"].

2231 _____, "O'Casey," Abbey Theatre Souvenir Programme (Dec
1979), pp. 26-7 [Introductory note on the occasion of the production of Juno and the Paycock].

2232 _____, "O'Casey's Centenary Celebrates a 'People's Playwright,'" New York Times, (30 Mar 1980), section 2, pp. 1,
6 [An assessment of O'Casey's achievement by an Irish dram-
atist].

2233 _____, "Sean the Proud," Evening Herald (Dublin), (28 Mar
1980), p. 10 [An assessment of O'Casey's achievement].

2234 Levander, Marianne, "O'Casey and Realism," Moderna Språk
(Stockholm), 69 (May-June 1975), 121-6 [The Shadow of a
Gunman, Juno and the Paycock, and The Plough and the Stars
seem more realistic than O'Casey's Autobiographies].

2235 Levett, Jack, "A Great 'Hurrah' for Life," Daily Worker (London), (30 Mar 1964), p. 2 [Interview with O'Casey].

2236 Levin, Bernard, "The Green Crow Folds His Wings," Daily Mail (London), (21 Sep 1964), p. 8 [Tribute to O'Casey].

2237 Lewis, Allan, "Sean O'Casey's World," Nation (N.Y.), 181 (24 Dec 1955), 555-6 [O'Casey's place in the development of the modern theatre].

2238 Lewis, Peter, "O'Casey Wishes the Money Had Come Earlier," Irish Digest, 76 (Nov 1962), 43-5 [Interview with O'Casey].

2239 Lewis, Robert, "Visiting Sean O'Casey in Devon: Informal Talks with Irish Playwright," New York Herald Tribune, (29 Jul 1951), section 4, p. 2 [Interview with O'Casey].

2240 Liddy, James, "For Sean O'Casey," Poetry Ireland (Dublin), no. 3 (Spring 1964), 111-12 [Poem].

2241 _____, "For Sean O'Casey," Sean O'Casey Review, 6 (1980), 75 [Poem].

2242 Lindsay, Jack, "The Plough and the Stars Reconsidered," Sean O'Casey Review, 2 (Spring 1976), 187-95 [Examines the content of the play].

2243 "Liverpool Meeting on Sean O'Casey," Irish Democrat (London), (Jan 1967), p. 8 [The Liverpool branch of the Connolly Association held a meeting on O'Casey].

2244 "London at His Feet," Daily Graphic (London), (8 Mar 1926), p. 5 [Interview with O'Casey].

2245 "London Letter: Dr. Soper," Irish Times (Dublin), (16 Jan 1956), p. 5 [O'Casey praises The Very Rev. Dr. Donald Soper, former President of the Methodist Conference]. See reply by C.W. Griffin, "Sean O'Casey," (19 Jan 1956), p. 7 [Letter to the Editor].

2246 "London Letter: 'O'Casey Speaks," Irish Times (Dublin), (3 Mar 1962), p. 9 [Interview with O'Casey]. See replies by Gabriel Fallon, (6 Mar 1962), p. 7; by Robert Hogan, (10 Mar 1962), p. 7; by Gabriel Fallon, (13 Mar 1962), p. 7; by Sean O'Casey and Robert Hogan, (21 Mar 1962), p. 7; by 'Criticus,' (26 Mar 1962), p. 7; by Ronald Ayling, (25 Apr 1962), p. 9; by Gabriel Fallon and A. Sherlock, (27 Apr 1962), p. 7; and by Padraic Fallon, (7 May 1962), p. 7 [Letters to the Editor].

2247 "London Notes," Irish Democrat (London), (Dec 1966), p. 8 [Report on a meeting on O'Casey at the Conway Hall].

2248 "The Londoner's Diary: No Smooth Talk," Evening Standard (London), (22 Jul 1961), p. 6 [Telephone comments from O'Casey on the eve of the London premiere of The Bishop's Bonfire].

2249 Lowery, Robert G., "The Autobiographies: An Historical Approach," O'Casey Annual (London), no. 1 (1982), 97-140 [Examines in detail the various historical aspects of the Autobiographies].

2250 _____, "Early O'Casey Play Published This Month," Daily World (N.Y.), (5 Dec 1979), p. 12 [The Harvest Festival].

2251 _____, "Editorial," Sean O'Casey Review, 5 (Fall 1978), 4-5 [Similarities between Sean O'Casey and Paul Robeson].

2252 _____, "Greaves Revisited," Sean O'Casey Review, 7 (1981), 14-21 [Disagrees with the evaluations of Sean O'Casey: Politics and Art, by C. Desmond Greaves].

2253 _____, "Mr. Lowery Objects," Irish Democrat (London), (Mar 1981), p. 7 [Letter to the Editor on the journal The Sean O'Casey Review]. See reply by Feicrednach, ibid. pp. 7-8.

2254 _____, "Obituaries," Sean O'Casey Review, 7 (1981), 23-5 [Of Gabriel Fallon, Richard Watts, and Alan Simpson].

2255 _____, "O'Casey, Critics, and Communism," Sean O'Casey Review, 1 (Fall 1974), 14-18 [Analyzes O'Casey's Communism, which has been the source of great controversy].

2256 _____, "The O'Casey Centenary," James Joyce Quarterly, 18 (Fall 1980), 7-9 [Views the celebrations marking the O'Casey Centenary].

2257 _____, "O'Casey's 'Silver Tassie': Challenge to U.S. Theatre," Daily World (N.Y.), (6 Sep 1978), p. 8 [Evaluates the play on its 50th anniversary].

2258 _____, "Prelude to Year One: Sean O'Casey Before 1916," Sean O'Casey Review, 2 (Spring 1976), 92-102 [Tries to illustrate O'Casey's political state of mind in the days and months prior to the Easter Rising].

2259 _____, "The Relevance of The Silver Tassie," Sean O'Casey Review, 4 (Spring 1978), 84 [The play will continue to be relevant as long as there are wars].

2260 _____, "A Salute to Sean O'Casey," Workers Life (Dublin), (Oct 1980), 25-7 [In the United States, the major celebrations of the O'Casey Centenary were noteworthy for their working class orientation].

2261 _____, "Sean O'Casey and New York," Irish Echo (N.Y.), (15 Mar 1980), p. 8 [Examines O'Casey's views on the U.S.].

2262 _____, "Sean O'Casey: 'Culture Is the Life We Live,'" Daily World (N.Y.), (13 Mar 1980), p. 16 [Evaluates O'Casey's views on culture and drama].

2263 _____, "Sean O'Casey in 1980," Ais-Eiri: The Magazine of Irish-America (N.Y.), 2 (1979), 3-4 [Tribute to O'Casey on the occasion of his Centenary].

2264 _____, "Sean O'Casey's Early London Residences," Sean O'Casey Review, 4 (Fall 1977), 51-3 [Gives details of O'Casey's residences in London between March 1926 and January 1928].

2265 _____, "'The Silver Tassie'--Contemporaneous Classic," Daily World (N.Y.), (10 Aug 1978), p. 20 [A 50th anniversary perspective on The Silver Tassie shows the continued relevance of O'Casey's great anti-war play].

2266 _____, "A Storm in the Fair City," Sean O'Casey Review, 3 (Spring 1977), 127-43 [Deals with the truth of O'Casey's origin; and reproduces a review article by Anthony Butler in the Evening Herald (Dublin), a reply by David Krause, and a counter-reply by Anthony Butler].

2267 _____, "A Tribute," Sean O'Casey Review, 1 (Fall 1974), 4 [On the occasion of the 10th anniversary of O'Casey's death].

2268 _____, "What Whitman Taught O'Casey," Daily World (N.Y.), (12 June 1980), p. 16 [Whitman pervaded the consciousness of O'Casey].

2269 Lustig, Irma S., "America and Apollonian Temples: Conversations and Correspondence with Sean O'Casey," Colby Library Quarterly, 9 (June 1972), 537-46 [The merits of the New World versus the Old are the theme of an interview with O'Casey and three letters from him].

2270 Lynch, John, "O'Casey Kept Best Character Roles for Women," Womens View (Dublin), no. 2 (Summer 1980), 22-4 [Women play a very important part in The Shadow of a Gunman, Juno and the Paycock, and The Plough and the Stars].

2271 Lynch, Kevin, "O'Casey and the World Working-Class Struggle," Daily World (N.Y.), (17 Nov 1978), p. 12 [Assesses the journal The Sean O'Casey Review].

2272 Lyons, J.B., "Play-Going in the 'Forties," Dublin Magazine, 9, no. 4 (1972), 80-6 [O'Casey revivals "have been overdone"].

2273 Lyttleton, E., "Sean O'Casey's Story," Time and Tide (London), 14 (27 May 1933), 640-1 [Letter to the Editor on "I Wanna Woman"].

2274 MacAnna, Tomas, "In Interview About the Later O'Casey Plays at the Abbey Theatre," Irish University Review (Dublin), 10 (Spring 1980), 130-45 [The director of the Abbey Theatre is interviewed by Christopher Murray].

2275 _____, "O'Casey: The Genius of Chassis," Irish Times (Dublin), (12 Jan 1971), p. 10 [Reassesses O'Casey's achievement].

2276 _____, "The Old Man Said 'Truflais!'" Sean O'Casey Review, 5 (Fall 1978), 51-4 [Discusses O'Casey's later plays].

2277 _____, "Preface to Glittering Spears," Sean O'Casey Review, 8 (1982), 3-4 [Gives an account of the controversy over The Silver Tassie on which Glittering Spears is based].

2278 MacAvock, J. D., "Public Opinion," Bell (Dublin), 10 (Apr 1945), 81 [Letter to the Editor in reply to O'Casey's statement that he had "never yet heard a whisper of the banning of play, poem, or novel by the officials of the U.S.S.R."].

2279 McCormack, Susan Allison, "The Moral Impulse in Sean O'Casey's Fiction," Sean O'Casey Review, 5 (Fall 1978), 69-73 [O'Casey's short stories are interesting primarily because they help crystallize our image of him as a reformer and as a social critic].

2280 McCormick, Jane L., "Drive That Man Away: The Theme of the Artist in Society in Celtic Drama, 1890-1950," Susquehanna University Studies (Selingrove, Pennsylvania), 8 (June 1969), 213-29 [The relationship of the artist to society is an important theme in The Shadow of a Gunman, Red Roses for Me, and Cock-a-Doodle Dandy].

2281 McDonagh, John, "Acting in Dublin," Commonweal (N.Y.), 10 (19 June 1929), 185-6 ["Nowadays the Abbey has become very popular, mainly through the success of the Sean O'Casey plays which raised the box-office receipts and hell at the same time"].

2282 MacDonogh, Steve, "Letters to the Editor," Books Ireland (Dublin), No. 61 (Mar 1982), 30 [On the editions of The Story of the Irish Citizen Army].

2283 McEligot, Garry, "A Last Letter from O'Casey," Irish Independent (Dublin), (21 Sep 1964), p. 6. Also in Irish Times (Dublin), (21 Sep 1964), p. 11 [O'Casey was "as gentle and helpful in private correspondence as he was vitriolic and destructive in public discussion"].

2284 MacGrior, D., "Indignation and Selectivity," Standard (Dublin), 27 (11 Mar 1955), 11 [Letter to the Editor supporting the Standard for its denunciation of O'Casey's "persistent vilification of the Irish Catholic clergy"].

2285 McHugh, Roger, "Always Complainin': The Politics of Young Sean," Irish University Review (Dublin), 10 (Spring 1980), 91-7 [The division in O'Casey's mind about nationalism and socialism began to manifest itself about 1912-13].

2286 _____, "Counterparts: Sean O'Casey and Samuel Beckett," Modern Språk (Stockholm), 67 (1973), 217-22 [For all their obvious differences and a few superficial similarities, O'Casey and Beckett reveal together something about the nature of dramatic literature and of its theatrical function].

2287 _____, "The Legacy of Sean O'Casey," Texas Quarterly, 8 (Spring 1965), 123-37 [O'Casey's plays are his chief legacy; the six-volume autobiography is of mixed value].

2288 _____, "Sean O'Casey and Lady Gregory," James Joyce Quarterly, 8 (Fall 1970), 119-23 [The friendship between O'Casey and Lady Gregory was unusual in that normally they would have been separated by barriers of class, belief, and location].

2289 _____, "Sean O'Casey: Fifty Years After The Plough," Etudes irlandaises (Lille), no. 2 (Dec 1977), 109-15. Also in Threshold (Belfast), no. 29 (Autumn 1978), 49-56 [The continuing production of O'Casey's plays shows their endurance through the changes of a half-century].

2290 _____, "Sean O'Casey: Ideology or Artistic Value?" Inostrannaia literatura [Foreign literature] (Moscow), 5 (1978), 208-11 [In Russian].

2291 _____, "Tradition and the Future of Irish Drama," Studies (Dublin), 40 (1951), 469-74 [Argues that O'Casey's "deliberate widening of his focus in a search for new dramatic forms has somehow coincided with a diffusion of energy and of effect"].

2292 Macken, Ultan, "To Welcome the Bishop," RTE Guide (Dublin), (29 Feb 1980), 19 [O'Casey Centenary celebrated on RTE].

2293 _____, "Eileen: 'The Pulse of My Heart,'" Irish Press (Dublin), (29 Mar 1980), p. 9 [Interview with Eileen O'Casey].

2294 _____, "O'Casey on Radio & Television," RTE Guide (Dublin), (29 Feb 1980), 19 [Details of the O'Casey Centenary celebrations by the Irish national radio and television network].

2295 McKenna, David, "The Word and the Flesh: A Veiw of Theatre as Performance," The Crane Bag (Holmsdale, Co. Wicklow), 6, no. 1 (1982), 90-1 ["Yeats dealt a body-blow to the future of the Irish theatre by deciding that Sean O'Casey was getting out of hand and that his plays were a bit much"].

2296 McLaughlin, John, "Political Allegory in O'Casey's Purple Dust," Modern Drama, 13 (May 1970), 47-53 [Beneath the ripples of surface laughter in the play runs a political allegory of the destruction of capitalism and the victory of militant socialism].

2297 _____, "A Tired-Out Oul' Blatherer," America (N.Y.), 100 (7 Mar 1959), 653-5 [Discusses Cock-a-Doodle Dandy and assesses O'Casey as a dramatist].

2298 MacLiammóir, Micheál, "Always the Giant," Irish Times (Dublin), (30 Mar 1960), p. 8 [Tribute to O'Casey on his 80th birthday].

2299 MacMághnais, Peadar, "O'Casey at the Mermaid," Focus: A Monthly Review (Belfast), 5 (Oct 1962), 233-4 [On the O'Casey festival at the Mermaid Theatre, London].

2300 McManus, John T., "James Cagney Dreams of O'Casey," New York Times, (27 Dec 1936), section 10, p. 4 [Interview with Cagney during which he aired his views on participating in the current trend toward Irish drama in the cinema].

2301 McQuillan, Deirdre, "O'Casey at the Abbey," Sunday Independent (Dublin), (16 Mar 1980), p. 15 [Letter to the Editor on the Abbey Theatre plans for the O'Casey Centenary].

2302 Magalaner, Marvin, "O'Casey's Autobiography," Sewanee Review, 65 (Winter 1957), 170-4 [O'Casey's six autobiographical books are the man, and they emphasize the considerable success of the full life which they embody].

2303 Maitra, Lila, "O'Casey's Autobiographies," Calcutta Review, 151 (Apr 1959), 53-7 [Discusses the various qualities of the six volumes of Autobiographies].

2304 _____, "Sean O'Casey--The Man and the Dramatist," Calcutta Review, 153 (Oct 1959), 71-6 [Discusses O'Casey's dramatic achievement].

2305   Malone, Andrew E., "The Abbey Theatre Season," Dublin Maga-
        zine, 2 (Oct-Dec 1927), 30-8 ["To some extent the advent of
        this newer audience coincides with the emergence of Sean
        O'Casey, and that it is a less critical and less discriminating
        audience there can be no doubt"].

2306   _____, "The Coming of Age of the Irish Drama," Dublin Re-
        view, 181 (Jul 1927), 101-14 [O'Casey "has yet to prove him-
        self equal" to Synge].

2307   _____, "The Decline of the Irish Drama," Nineteenth Century
        and After (London), 97 (Apr 1925), 578-88 [There has been
        "little of dramatic technique" in O'Casey's Dublin Trilogy].

2308   _____, "Ireland," Drama Magazine (Chicago), 21 (Dec 1930),
        19, 24 ["O'Casey's characters are merely peasants in the en-
        vironment of a Dublin Slum"].

2309   _____, "Ireland Gives a New Playwright to the World," The-
        atre Magazine (N.Y.), 43 (Apr 1926), 9, 58, 62 [Assesses
        O'Casey as a dramatist; and comments on The Shadow of a
        Gunman, Juno and the Paycock and The Plough and the Stars].

2310   _____, "The Irish Theatre in 1933," Dublin Magazine, 9 (Jul-
        Sep 1934), 45-54 [Joxer Daly, Captain Boyle, and Fluther
        Good now occupy the places vacated by the Stage Irishman].

2311   _____, "The Shadow of Sean O'Casey," Bookman (London),
        70 (May 1926), 104-7 [Assesses O'Casey as a dramatist; and
        comments on The Shadow of a Gunman, Juno and the Paycock,
        and The Plough and the Stars].

2312   _____, "Synge and O'Casey," Tribune (Cork), (12 Mar 1926),
        pp. 17-19 ["In their methods Synge and O'Casey are poles
        apart"].

2313   Malone, Maureen, "Red Roses for Me: Fact and Symbol," Mod-
        ern Drama, 9 (Sep 1966), 147-52 [Traces the historical and
        autobiographical foundations of the play, and discovers how
        this factual mass is illuminated by the dramatist's art].

2314   "Mandrake," "Jewels from Mr. O'Casey," Sunday Telegraph
        (London), (8 Apr 1979), p. 6 [On Breon O'Casey].

2315   _____, "Sunday Morning with 'Mandrake': Last Thoughts
        from O'Casey," Sunday Telegraph (London), (20 Sep 1964),
        p. 13 [Interview with O'Casey by John Summers].

2316   Manning, Mary, "In Dublin Today," Saturday Review of Litera-
        ture (N.Y.), 6 (17 May 1930), 1048-50 [Includes a brief dis-
        cussion of the production of The Silver Tassie].

2317 Margulies, Martin B., "Historical Note," Theatre Programme on The Plough and the Stars. The Repertory Theater of Lincoln Center, (Jan 1973), 8-9.

2318 Maroldo, William J., "A Darwinian Garden of Eden: A Major Emphasis in Sean O'Casey's Autobiographies," Sean O'Casey Review, 5 (Spring 1979), 167-76 [Discusses "Green Fire on the Hearth," the eleventh chapter of Drums Under the Windows].

2319 _____, "Lines from Torquay: Letters by and about Sean O'Casey," Sean O'Casey Review, 3 (Spring 1977), 117-26 [Describes his correspondence with O'Casey, and includes seven letters from him].

2320 _____, "O'Casey's Tributes to Joyce in the First Irish Book," O'Casey Annual (London), no. 1 (1982), 17-32 [O'Casey pays tribute to Joyce through his particular use of language, stream-of-consciousness narrations, interior monologue, and Joycean epiphany in the first book of his Autobiographies].

2321 "Marriage of Mr. Sean O'Casey," Times (London), (24 Sep 1927), p. 7 [O'Casey marries Eileen Reynolds (Carey) at the Church of our Most Holy Redeemer, Cheyne-row, Chelsea, London].

2322 Marriott, R.B., "Sean O'Casey," Stage and Television Today (London), (24 Sep 1964), 8 [Obituary].

2323 Martin, Augustine, "Inherited Dissent: The Dilemma of the Irish Writer," Studies (Dublin), 54 (Spring 1965), 1-20 [O'Casey, like other Irish writers, makes comments in his writings on the apparent difficulty which the literary artist finds in living among and writing about his countrymen].

2324 _____, "O'Casey: Prophet and Artist." Programme-note to the Abbey Theatre's production of Cock-a-Doodle Dandy, August 1977.

2325 _____, "The Star Turns Red--The Playwright as Visionary." Program note to the Abbey Theatre's production, February 1978.

2326 Martin, Robert, "Playwright O'Casey Better Provider Dead Than Alive," Globe and Mail (Toronto), (17 Feb 1973), p. 25 [Interview with Eileen O'Casey].

2327 Maxwell, Sean, "Conversation with O'Casey," Irish Digest, 80 (June 1964), 37-9 [O'Casey said he had never lost his love for Ireland and her people].

2328 Meachean, Patrick, "Two Irish Dramatists," Library Assistant
      (London), 20 (June 1927), 123-34 [Compares O'Casey with
      Yeats; and discusses The Shadow of a Gunman, Juno and
      the Paycock, and The Plough and the Stars].

2329 Mercier, Vivian, "Decline of a Playwright: The Riddle of Sean
      O'Casey," Commonweal (N.Y.), 64 (13 Jul 1956), 366-8 [Com-
      pares the Dublin Trilogy with O'Casey's later plays].   See
      reply by Robert Hogan, (24 Aug 1956), 517; and "Correction"
      by Vivian Mercier, (21 Sep 1956), 612.

2330 "Mermaid O'Casey," Plays and Players (London), 9 (Sep 1962),
      46 [Peter Duguid talks about the O'Casey Festival at the Mer-
      maid Theatre, London].

2331 "Messages Pouring in for Sean O'Casey," Irish Times (Dublin),
      (17 Feb 1956), p. 3 [Hundreds of telegrams wishing a quick
      recovery have been received by Torquay Hospital for O'Casey,
      who will undergo a major kidney operation].

2332 Mikhail, E.H., "The Personal Element in The Plough and the
      Stars," Sean O'Casey Review, 2 (Spring 1976), 137-40 [Of
      all his plays, The Plough and the Stars comes closest to
      O'Casey's own experience].

2333 Miles, Bernard, "Sean O'Casey: Sources of His Greatness,"
      Daily Worker (London), (18 Aug 1962), p. 3 [The founder
      of the Mermaid Theatre, London, discusses why it is pre-
      senting three of O'Casey's plays in a two-month festival].

2334 "Milestones: Sean O'Casey," Time, 84 (25 Sep 1964), 70
      [Obituary].

2335 Mili, Gjon, "Tea and Memories and Songs at a Last Fond Visit,"
      Life (Chicago), 57 (9 Oct 1964), 92-3; International Edition,
      37 (2 Nov 1964), 53 [Recollections of O'Casey by the photog-
      rapher who was responsible for the camera-work for the film
      Young Cassidy].

2336 _____, "O'Casey in Search of a Stage," Irish Digest (Dublin),
      52 (Nov 1954), 52-4 [Surveys O'Casey's life and works].

2337 Milstead, John, "The Structure of Modern Tragedy," Western
      Humanities Review, 12 (Autumn 1958), 365-9 [Tennessee Wil-
      liams, Sean O'Casey, and Arthur Miller delineate man as the
      pawn of fate and the product of his environment; thus man
      is incapable of manifesting greatness in tragic circumstances].

2338 Mitchell, Jack, "The Theatre of Sean O'Casey," Zeitschrift für
      Anglistik und Amerikanistik (Leipzig), 26 (1978), 28-47
      [O'Casey depicts the development of Irish politics].

2339 Mitchison, Naomi, "Sean O'Casey's Story," Time and Tide (London), 14 (27 May 1933), 641 [Letter to the Editor on "I Wanna Woman"].

2340 Mooney, Ria, "Playing Rosie Redmond: An Autobiographical Essay," Journal of Irish Literature, 6 (May 1977), 21-7 [Recollections of the first production of The Plough and the Stars].

2341 Moore, John Rees, "Now Yeats Has Gone," Hollins Critic, 3 (Apr 1966), 6-12 [The Contemporary Irish poet faces a bewildering variety of masks from which to choose; the great shadows of Yeats, Joyce, O'Casey and others loom over him].

2342 "Moscow Conference on Sean O'Casey's Centenary," Sean O'Casey Review, 7 (1981), 22 [The Institute of World Literature to hold a conference on the occasion of the centenary of O'Casey's birth].

2343 Moses, Robert, "A Toast to O'Casey," New York Times Magazine, (1 Feb 1959), p. 30 [A comment on O'Casey's article "The Harp in the Air Still Sings"].

2344 Moya, Carmela, "The Mirror and the Plough," Sean O'Casey Review, 2 (Spring 1976), 141-53 [O'Casey used similar dramaturgic techniques in the Autobiographies and in The Plough and the Stars].

2345 _____, "Sean O'Casey: d'après deux livres récents," Etudes anglaises (Paris), 20 (Apr–June 1967), 160-4 [O'Casey's writings as seen by Saros Cowasjee and Gabriel Fallon].

2346 _____, "Sean O'Casey's Autobiographies: Literary Aspects," Etudes irlandaises (Lille), no. 4 (Nov 1975), 53-75 [O'Casey forges his own language to express his intensely personal vision of the world].

2347 "Mr. Sean O'Casey," Irish Times (Dublin), (18 Feb 1956), p. 1 [O'Casey is stated to be quite comfortable in Torbay Hospital after undergoing an operation].

2348 "Mr. Sean O'Casey: Controversial Dramatist of Genius," Times (London), (21 Sep 1964), p. 16 [Obituary].

2349 "Mr. Sean O'Casey's Refusal," Times (London), (22 Aug 1964), p. 7 [O'Casey refuses permission for use of recorded extracts from his works at World Fair in New York].

2350 "Mrs. O'Casey Explains," Times (London), (24 Aug 1964), p. 5 [Comment on O'Casey's refusal to permit the Irish Government to use recorded excerpts from his works at New York World Fair].

2351 "Mrs. O'Casey in Dublin," Irish Times (Dublin), (3 Aug 1966), p. 6 [Eileen O'Casey denies that her husband was a voluntary exile; and expresses a preference for his later plays].

2352 "Mrs. O'Casey Undisturbed by Sniping," Irish Times (Dublin), (8 Aug 1967), p. 7 [Eileen O'Casey talks about her husband at a press conference at the Abbey Theatre during a new production of Red Roses for Me].

2353 Mulhern, Francis, "'Ideology and Literary Form'--A Comment," New Left Review, (May-June 1975), 80-7 ["O'Casey's political criticisms of the Dublin Rising of 1916 were profoundly at variance with his theatrical treatment of that event"].

2354 Mulkerns, Val, "Who's Afraid of O'Casey?" Evening Press (Dublin), (12 Apr 1980), p. 6 [O'Casey centenary is celebrated on RTE].

2355 Mullane, Dermot, "Sean O'Casey Dies Aged 84 After Heart Attack: A Man Who Was True to Himself," Irish Times (Dublin), (19 Sep 1964), p. 1.

2356 _____, "O'Casey's Funeral Passed Unnoticed," Irish Times (Dublin), (23 Sep 1964), p. 4.

2357 Mullen, Michael, "The World Is Still in a State of Chassis: Sean O'Casey--A Personal View," Liberty (Dublin), (Apr 1980), 6, 8 [Deals with O'Casey as a socialist].

2358 Murphy, Maureen, "Sean O'Cathasaigh agus Conradh na Gaelige," Sean O'Casey Review, 1 (Fall 1974), 18-19 [An early Gaelic League enthusiast, O'Casey broke with it over its reluctance to interfere in religious or political issues, a policy too narrow for his broader interests in social and national reform].

2359 Murphy, R[obert] Patrick, "Sean O'Casey and the Avant-Garde," Colby Library Quarterly, 11 (Dec 1975), 235-48 [According to the theory developed by Renato Poggioli in The Theory of the Avant-Garde, the term may be applied to O'Casey].

2360 _____, "Sean O'Casey and 'The Bald Primaqueera,'" James Joyce Quarterly, 8 (Fall 1970), 96-110 [The heart of O'Casey's article is an attack on Antonin Artaud's theatre of cruelty, which O'Casey does not seem to understand].

2361 Murray, Christopher, "A Dickens Parallel," Sean O'Casey Review, 6 (1980), 42-4 [Draws attention to a marked similarity in language between Captain Boyle in Juno and the Paycock and Captain Edward Cuttle in Dombey and Son].

2362 _____, "Introduction," Irish University Review (Dublin) 10, (Spring 1980), 9-16 [Introduction to the Sean O'Casey Special Issue dealing with the situation of O'Casey criticism].

2363 _____, "O'Casey at War," RTE Guide (Dublin), 4 (28 Mar 1980), 12 [Comments on The Silver Tassie].

2364 _____, "Three Letters from Lady Gregory," Prompts: Bulletin of the Irish Theatre Archive (Dublin), no. 1 (June 1981), 5-7 [Makes references to O'Casey's association with Lady Gregory and Michael J. Dolan].

2365 _____, "Two More Allusions in Cock-a-Doodle Dandy," Sean O'Casey Review, 4 (Fall 1977), 6-18 [Suggests that allusiveness is a distinct and important quality of O'Casey's imagination].

2366 Nagin, Rick, "Youngstown & O'Casey," Daily World (N.Y.), (10 Mar 1978), p. 8 [Report on the Second Sean O'Casey Festival held at Youngstown State University, Ohio, 2-4 March 1978].

2367 Nagy, Peter, "Sean O'Casey, a Drámairó," Nagyvilág (Budapest), (1977), 100-9 [O'Casey as a dramatist].

2368 Nason, Richard W., "Shyre Batting for O'Casey," New York Times, (3 Mar 1957), section 2, p. 3 [Actor-producer Paul Shyre ignites interest in O'Casey after his adaptation for dramatic reading of the first two volumes of Autobiographies].

2369 Nathan, George Jean, "The Best of the Irish," Newsweek, 15 (29 Jan 1940), 33 [O'Casey is the best of the living Irish dramatists].

2370 _____, "Lament for Irish Playwrights," American Mercury (N.Y.), 52 (Apr 1941), 483-9 ["Except for O'Casey ... the quondam rich vein appears to have run dry"].

2371 "New Play in Dublin," Time, 65 (14 Mar 1955), p. 74 [Includes O'Casey's comments to Time on the nature of his political faith, on the occasion of the premiere of The Bishop's Bonfire].

2372 "New Theatre Director Is 'Excited but Terrified,'" Times (London), (10 Jan 1977), p. 3 [Clare Venables to produce The Silver Tassie].

2373 "New York Buys O'Casey Papers," Times (London), (31 Jul

1969), p. 8 [New York Public Library acquires O'Casey's literary papers for the Berg Collection].

2374 "New York State Proclamation on Sean O'Casey's Centenary," Sean O'Casey Review, 7 (1981), 7 [The Senate salutes the memory of O'Casey].

2375 "No 80 Candles for O'Casey," Sunday Review (Dublin), 4 (20 Mar 1960), 3 [O'Casey does not plan to celebrate his 80th birthday becuase he "does not like any fuss about birthdays"].

2376 North, Joseph, "No Men Are Strangers: O'Casey Philosophy," Daily Worker (N.Y.), (25 Oct 1964), p. 7 [Tribute].

2377 Norwood, Gilbert, "English Drama Between Two Wars," Dalhousie Review, 22 (Jan 1943), 405-20 [Juno and the Paycock and The Plough and the Stars are among the important plays of the 1920s that handle "contemporary fact"].

2378 _____, "The New Writers, 4: Sean O'Casey," Canadian Forum, 10 (Apr 1930), 250-1 [O'Casey's "one merit is skillful photography, his peculiarity a predilection for anguish"].

2379 "Notes and News," Library Review (Glasgow), 20 (Spring 1965), 62 [Obituary of O'Casey].

2380 Nowlan, David, "Man of No False Modesty," Irish Times (Dublin), (1 Apr 1980), p. 8 [Tribute to O'Casey on the occasion of his centenary].

2381 O'Brien, Conor Cruse, "Thoughts on Commitment," Listener (London), 86 (16 Dec 1971), 834-6 [O'Casey lost political effect by being an effective playwright].

2382 O Broin, Seamus, "Sean O'Casey," Standard (Dublin), 27 (25 Feb 1955), 23 [Letter to the Editor suggesting that O'Casey's "failure to rise in the Rising has doomed him to attempt to 'rise' ever since"].

2383 "Observer," "Press Cuttings," Irish Book Lover (Dublin), 15 (Jan 1925), 16 [O'Casey had submitted four plays to the Abbey Theatre before The Shadow of a Gunman was accepted].

2384 O'Casey, Breon, "Sean O'Casey: A Portrait," Threshold (Belfast), no. 26 (Autumn 1975), 95-9. Reprinted in Sean O'Casey Review, 3 (Fall 1976), 53-7 [The domestic O'Casey is sketched by his son].

2385 O'Casey, Eileen, "London and The Plough and the Stars," Sean O'Casey Review, 2 (Spring 1976), 154-6 [Recollections of the London premiere of the play].

2386 _____, "Red Roses for Sean," in the theatre program for the production of Red Roses for Me at the Lyric Players Theatre, Belfast, March 1972 [Recollections of the origins of the play].

2387 _____, and Brenna Katz, "A Bunch of Blue Ribbons," Arts in Ireland (Dublin), 1 (1972), 13-23 [Interview on the women in O'Casey's plays].

2388 O'Casey, Sean, "Behind the Ban, " New York Times, (5 Jan 1964), section 2, pp. 1, 3 [The Drums of Father Ned in retrospect].

2389 _____, "From Within the Gates," New York Times, (21 Oct 1934), section 9, pp. 1, 3.

2390 _____, "Memories of a Farewell to Ireland," New York Times (4 Dec 1960), section 2, pp. 1, 5 [The Plough and the Stars in Retrospect].

2391 _____, "Mr. O'Casey's Play: Author's Rejoinder," Irish Independent (Dublin), (26 Feb 1926), p. 8 [On The Plough and the Stars].

2392 _____, "O'Casey's Credo," New York Times (9 Nov 1958), section 2, pp. 1, 3 [Introduction to Cock-a-Doodle Dandy].

2393 _____, "The Plough and the Stars: A Reply to the Critics," Irish Times (Dublin), (19 Feb 1926), p. 6. Also in Irish Independent (Dublin), (20 Feb 1926).

2394 O'Casey, Shivaun, "Correspondence," Sean O'Casey Review, 6 (1980), 64 [Letter to the Editor in reply to a statement made by Alan Simpson in which he said that O'Casey's widow "is likely to be grateful with any success solidly reflected in the box-office returns"].

2395 "O'Casey," Irish Times (Dublin), (25 Aug 1961), p. 7 [Editorial stating that the time was long overdue for ending the quarrel between O'Casey and his fellow countrymen]. See replies by Gabriel Fallon, (26 Aug 1961), p. 7; by Liam Mac-Aoidh, (29 Aug 1961), p. 5; by Brendan Behan, (29 Aug 1961), p. 5; by J.O.G. Macnamara, (31 Aug 1961), p. 7; and by Anthony Mangan, (4 Sep 1961), p. 7.

2396 "O'Casey Adopted Larkin Vision," Irish Times (Dublin), (21 Apr 1980), p. 11 [On James Plunkett's lecture on RTE to mark the O'Casey centenary].

2397 "O'Casey and the Trade Unions," Irish Press (Dublin), (21 Apr 1980), p. 5 [Report on a lecture by James Plunkett on the occasion of the O'Casey centenary].

2398 "O'Casey Angry about Strike Call Now," Irish Times (Dublin),
(14 Apr 1964), p. 1 [Abbey Players' threatened strike in
support of a pay dispute jeopardizes their participation in the
World Theatre season in London].

2399 "O'Casey Bans Works at World's Fair," Irish Times (Dublin),
(22 Aug 1964), p. 11 [O'Casey refuses to permit the Irish
Government to use recorded excerpts from his works at New
York World Fair].

2400 "O'Casey Celebrations," Evening Press (Dublin), (29 Mar 1980),
p. 4 [The BBC and the RTE celebrate the O'Casey centenary].

2401 "O'Casey Did Not Celebrate 80th Birthday," Irish Times (Dublin), (31 Mar 1960), p. 9 [Interview with O'Casey].

2402 "O'Casey Doing Well," Irish Times (Dublin), (6 Mar 1956), p.
9 [O'Casey is rapidly recovering at Torbay Hospital, Torquay,
after two operations].

2403 "O'Casey Gives Play to Telefis," Sunday Press (Dublin), (24
June 1962), p. 4 [Permission given by O'Casey in an interview with Edward Roth at Torquay for Telefis Eireann to
broadcast The Moon Shines on Kylenamoe].

2404 "O'Casey Goes Home," Irish Times (Dublin), (20 Mar 1956),
p. 5 [O'Casey leaves Torbay Hospital after undergoing two
minor operations].

2405 "O'Casey Has 81st Birthday," New York Times, (31 Mar 1961),
p. 21 [O'Casey says, "I just don't like birthdays. I am not
interested"].

2406 "O'Casey Honoured: Lord Oxford on Most Moving Drama in 20
Years," Daily Sketch (London), (24 Mar 1926), p. 3 [O'Casey
is awarded the Hawthornden Prize for Juno and the Paycock].

2407 "O'Casey Is No Longer a Fair Playwright," Sunday Independent
(Dublin), (19 Oct 1958), p. 7 [Report on a debate in Dublin
in which David Krause and Gabriel Fallon participated].

2408 "O'Casey May Let the Abbey Stage His Plays," Sunday Press
(Dublin), (20 Sep 1959), p. 5 [Following a visit by Ernest
Blythe to O'Casey in Torquay].

2409 "O'Casey on Air Again," Irish Press (Dublin), (23 May 1955),
p. 6 [Radio Eireann plans "O'Casey Festival"].

2410 "O'Casey on Theatre Censor Body," Irish Press (Dublin), (2
May 1958), p. 1 [O'Casey supports a theatre censorship

reform committee formed under the chairmanship of Sir Gerald Barry].

2411 "O'Casey Papers Acquired," Bulletin of the New York Public Library, 73 (June 1969), 356-8 [Describes the contents of O'Casey's literary papers recently acquired by the Berg Collection of the New York Public Library].

2412 "O'Casey Plans Broadcast of Four Plays," Irish Times (Dublin), (28 Feb 1955), p. 9 [from Radio Eireann].

2413 "O'Casey Progressing," Irish Times (Dublin), (2 Mar 1956), p. 1 [after operation].

2414 "O'Casey Records Talks for Radio Eireann," Irish Times (Dublin), (8 Mar 1955), p. 3 [O'Casey records four talks to be used to introduce a festival of his plays].

2415 "O'Casey Riddle Finally Solved," Irish Press (Dublin), (31 Mar 1980), p. 3 [Denis Johnston explains the riddle of the inclusion in The Plough and the Stars of the upper class lady from Rathmines who has lost her way in the tumult].

2416 "O'Casey Service Tuesday," New York Times, (20 Sep 1964), p. 88 [A private funeral service will be held in Torquay for O'Casey].

2417 "O'Casey--The Style Was the Man," Irish Press (Dublin), (12 May 1980), p. 5 [Report on Robert Hogan's lecture on RTE on the occasion of the O'Casey centenary].

2418 "O'Casey Will Be Buried Today," Irish Times (Dublin), (22 Sep 1964), p. 9 [Only members of O'Casey's family will attend his funeral in Torquay].

2419 "O'Casey Will Be Cremated," Evening Herald (Dublin), (19 Sep 1964), p. 1 [Tribute by Ernest Blythe, Gabriel Fallon, May Craig, and John McCann].

2420 "O'Casey Will Be Cremated Tomorrow," Irish Times (Dublin), (21 Sep 1964), p. 1.

2421 "O'Casey Withdraws All Plays from TV," Irish Times (Dublin), (19 Sep 1957), p. 1 [O'Casey bans his plays from British television].

2422 "O'Casey Writing New Play," New York Times, (28 Jan 1927), p. 15 [O'Casey announces that he is writing a new play entitled The Red Lily].

2423 "O'Casey's Choice," Irish Independent (Dublin), (18 Apr 1980),
p. 24 [Recollections of O'Casey by Shelah Richards].

2424 "O'Casey's Court," Irish Writing (Cork), no. 13 (Dec 1950),
5-6 [Preface to O'Casey's autobiographical piece, "A Gate
Clangs Shut," published in the same issue].

2425 "O'Casey's Letters," Sean O'Casey Review, 1 (Spring 1975),
19-25 [Letters to Edith Segal and Jack Lindsay, with com-
ments].

2426 "O'Casey's Letters," Sean O'Casey Review, 2 (Fall 1975), 61-3
[Letters to Jim Kavanagh].

2427 "O'Casey's Letters," Sean O'Casey Review, 2 (Spring 1976),
164-6 [Letters to the Hudson Guild Players, Ronald Rollins,
and Edward H. Mabley].

2428 "O'Casey's Letters," Sean O'Casey Review, 3 (Fall 1976), 50-2
[Letters to Helen Kiok].

2429 "O'Casey's Letters," Sean O'Casey Review, 3 (Spring 1977),
117-26 [Letters to William J. Maroldo, with an introductory
note].

2430 "O'Casey's Return to Irish Stage," Daily Worker (N.Y.), (30
Mar 1955), p. 7 [O'Casey's championship of freedom for the
individual and hatred of oppression, as occasioned by the
Dublin premiere of The Bishop's Bonfire].

2431 O'Connor, Brother Antony Cyril, "The Successors of Synge,"
Unitas (Manila), 27 (Jul-Sep 1954), 444-51 [O'Casey's later
plays "have become progressively weaker in dramatic vigor"
than his Dublin Trilogy].

2432 O'Connor, Frank, "O'Casey and the Ghosts," Holiday (Philadelphia), 19 (Jan 1956), 65, 109-11 [Discusses The Plough
and the Stars, The Silver Tassie, The Bishop's Bonfire, and
Autobiographies].

2433 O'Connor, Patrick, "Theatre," Furrow (Maynooth), 15 (1964),
242-5 [Deals with various aspects of O'Casey's plays and
comments on his anti-clericalism and communism].

2434 O'Connor, T.P., "Men, Women, and Memories: The Hawthornden Prize Winner," Sunday Times (London), (4 Apr 1926),
p. 9 [O'Casey wins the prize for Juno and the Paycock].

2435 O'Connor, Ulick, "Dublin's Dilemma," Theatre Arts (N.Y.),
40 (Jul 1956), 64-5, 96 [Yeats, Synge and O'Casey "tower
over the other dramatists of their time"].

2436 O Corcorain, Reamonn, "Abbey Directors Congratulated," Evening Herald (Dublin), (3 Sep 1963), p. 6 [Letter to the Editor congratulating the directors of the Abbey Theatre on inviting O'Casey to attend the laying of the foundation stone of the new national theatre].

2437 _____, "Ask O'Casey to Return," Evening Herald (Dublin), (7 Nov 1963), p. 13 [Letter to the Editor thanking O'Casey for relaxing the ban on the professional presentation of his plays; and renewing his suggestion that some steps be taken to try to persuade O'Casey to return to his native land].

2438 _____, "Bringing Back Sean O'Casey," Evening Herald (Dublin), (9 Apr 1963), p. 10 [Letter to the Editor suggesting the formation of an "O'Casey Come Back Association"]. See following correspondence (15 Apr 1963), p. 4; (17 Apr 1963), p. 6; (23 Apr 1963), p. 10; (27 Apr 1963), p. 6; (1 May 1963), p. 6; (2 May 1963), p. 4; (3 May 1963), p. 8; (6 May 1963), p. 6; and (15 May 1963), p. 8.

2439 _____, "Come Back O'Casey," Evening Press (Dublin), (11 Sep 1964), p. 10 [Letter to the Editor persuading O'Casey to return to Ireland].

2440 _____, "O'Casey: Dead One Year," Evening Press (Dublin), (14 Sep 1965), p. 10 [Letter to the Editor: O'Casey tribute].

2441 O'Direain, Martin, "O'Casey," Sean O'Casey Review, 5 (Fall 1978), 43-4. Reprinted from Cloch Choirneil (1966) [Poem].

2442 O'Donnell, Donat, "The Abbey: Phoenix Infrequent," Commonweal (N.Y.), 57 (30 Jan 1953), 423-4 ["O'Casey's language was always much nearer real speech than was, for all its beauty, the hysterical-pastoral of Synge"].

2443 [O'Donnell, Peadar], "Ghosts," Bell (Dublin), 15 (Feb 1948), 1-2 [O'Casey "speaks Larkin almighty to men who followed Larkin only in his coffin"].

2444 O'Donovan, John, "Who Is the Stars?" RTE Guide (Dublin), (29 Feb 1980), 18 [Explains why O'Casey's Dublin plays have become distanced from us].

2445 O'Faolain, Sean, "The Abbey Festival," New Statesman and Nation (London), 16 (20 Aug 1938), 281-2 ["The new dramatists, like O'Casey, ... write on the offensive"].

2446 _____, "The Case of Sean O'Casey," Commonweal (N.Y.), 22 (11 Oct 1935), 577-8 [Discusses O'Casey's exile and The Silver Tassie affair]. See reply by Terence L. Connolly, ibid. 23 (14 Feb 1936), 442.

2447 _____, "The Dilemma of Irish Letters," Month (London), 2 (Dec 1949), 366-79 [O'Casey "worked best at home"].

2448 _____, "Ireland after Yeats," Bell (Dublin), 18 (Summer 1953), 37-48. Reprinted in Books Abroad, 26 (Autumn 1953), 325-33 [O'Casey's plays are "an exactly true statement of the Irish Revolution whose flag should be, not the tricolour, but the plough and the stars of the labouring classes"].

2449 O hAodha, Micheál, "O'Casey and the Abbey Theatre," Irish Times (Dublin), (1 Apr 1980), p. 8 [Tribute on the occasion of the O'Casey centenary].

2450 _____, "O'Casey in the Abbey," Irish Literary Supplement, 1 (Fall 1982), p. 26 [Comments made at a presentation of a sculpture of O'Casey to the Abbey Theatre on 29 August 1981].

2451 _____, "O'Casey on the Air," Irish University Review (Dublin), 10 (Spring 1980), 118-26 [O'Casey broadcasts on RTE, the Irish national radio and television network].

2452 _____, "75th Birthday Greetings to the Abbey Theatre, Dublin 1904-1979," Ireland of the Welcomes (Dublin), 28 (Nov-Dec 1979), 21-8 [Refers to O'Casey's contribution to the Theatre].

2453 O'Hegarty, P.S., "The Abbey Theatre," Irish Times (Dublin), (6 Sep 1944), p. 3 ["O'Casey has not written a good play since Juno, and he will not write one until he again tries to portray men and women, and recognises that he is neither a prophet nor a philosopher"].

2454 _____, "A Dramatist of New-Born Ireland," North American Review (N.Y.), 224 (June-Aug 1927), 315-22 [Examines The Shadow of a Gunman, Juno and the Paycock, and The Plough and the Stars].

2455 O'Keeffe, Timothy, "Poets' Sobriquets," Times Literary Supplement, (12 Nov 1971), p. 1422 [Letter to the Editor denying that O'Casey was poor].

2456 O'Leary, Con, "'Abbey Can't Have My Plays'--O'Casey," Sunday Press (Dublin), (27 Jul 1958), p. 1 [O'Casey bans all professional productions of his plays in Ireland after the withdrawal of The Drums of Father Ned from the Dublin Drama Festival earlier in the year].

2457 Olivier, Sir Laurence, "Meditations on Juno," National Theatre program, London, April 1966 [Relates O'Casey's tragicomic technique to the performance of counterpoint one experiences in the popular tradition of Irish ballad singing].

2458 O'Mahony, T.P., "Theatre in Ireland," Eire-Ireland, 4 (Summer 1969), 93-100 ["O'Casey, for all his proximity to the Labour movement, was anything but an apologist for it in the manner, say, of Brecht vis-à-vis Marxism"].

2459 O'Malley, Conor, "Sean O'Casey at the Lyric Theatre, Belfast," Sean O'Casey Review, 6 (1980), 33-41 [Surveys the performances of O'Casey's plays at the Lyric Players Theatre, and gives a list of the productions].

2460 O Maoláin, Micheál, "An Ruathar Ud Agus A nDeachaigh Leis," Feasta (Dublin), 8 (May 1955), 2-4, 6, 24-5 [Deals with O'Casey's attack on the clergy in The Bishop's Bonfire].

2461 O Maolain, Tomas, "Pitiable O'Casey," Standard (Dublin), 27 (25 Feb 1955), 23 [Letter to the Editor attributing O'Casey's attacks on Ireland and her priests to his failure at a debate organized by a Republican club in the Mills Hall].

2462 "Omen," "Mr. O'Maolain Was There!" Standard (Dublin), 27 (11 Mar 1955), 11 [Letter to the Editor condemning the "hate-purveying of O'Casey in his literary works"].

2463 O Murcada, Padraig, "Impressed by Army Parade," Evening Herald (Dublin), (20 Apr 1963), p. 8 [Letter to the Editor on O'Casey and Irish nationalism].

2464 O N., C., "Bhi Neart Gaelilge Ag O Cathasaigh," Inniu (Dublin), (4 Apr 1980), p. 5 [O'Casey had forceful Irish].

2465 O'Neill, Padraig, "Why Not Sean O'Casey Theatre?" Sunday Independent (Dublin), (16 Mar 1980), p. 15 [Letter to the Editor expressing surprise that Ireland has no theatre named after O'Casey].

2466 O'Neill-Barna, Anne, "O'Casey at 80: More Rebel Than Ever," New York Times Magazine, (27 Mar 1960), pp. 26, 90-1 [Interview with O'Casey].

2467 "An Open Letter to David H. Greene," Sean O'Casey Review, 3 (Fall 1976), 48-9 [Appealing to him to give permission to David Krause to see O'Casey's letters to Jack Carney].

2468 O'Reilly, John, "On View," Evening Press (Dublin), (11 Apr 1980), p. 21 [O'Casey centenary celebrated on RTE].

2469 O'Riordan, John, "[Sean O'Casey's] Birthday," Bookseller

(London), (20 Feb 1960), 1080 [Letter to the Editor on
O'Casey's correct age]. See reply by Timothy O'Keeffe of
MacGibbon and Kee, (27 Feb 1960), 1138.

2470   _____, "The Cult of Yeats," Catholic Standard (Dublin), 2
(30 Oct 1964), 5 [Letter to the Editor in reply to hostile
criticism of Yeats and O'Casey]. See reply by R. Donnellan,
(6 Nov 1964), 5; and counter-reply by John O'Riordan, (20
Nov 1964), 5.

2471   _____, "Exclusive Tea-Time Chat with Playwright Sean
O'Casey," Enfield Weekly Herald, (19 Apr 1963), p. 4. Ex-
tracted as "2-Hour Chat with Sean O'Casey," Enfield Gazette
and Observer, (31 May 1963), p. 7. Reprinted in The Sting
and the Twinkle, ed. E. H. Mikhail and John O'Riordan (London: Macmillan, 1974), pp. 133-5 [Interview].

2472   _____, "The Garlanded Horror of War: Reflections on The
Silver Tassie," Sean O'Casey Review, 5 (Fall 1978), 23-8
[Deals with O'Casey's views as expressed in the play].

2473   _____, "Inoffensive Tune," Spectator (London), (24 Oct
1981), 17 [Letter to the Editor refuting the suggestion that
'Lilliburlero,' as the anthem of Protestant Ireland, is offensive to Irish Roman Catholics by citing its appearance in The
Drums of Father Ned]. See correspondence by Patrick Bury,
(31 Oct 1981), 20; and Stan Gebler Davies, (7 Nov 1981), 30.

2474   _____, "National Theatre Omission," Sunday Times (London),
(27 Oct 1968), p. 14 [Letter to the Editor chiding Sir Laurence Olivier and the National Theatre for not performing
The Silver Tassie instead of Juno and the Paycock in 1966
after O'Casey's death].

2475   _____, "O'Casey in Exile," Irish Times (Dublin), (12 Oct
1971), p. 11 [Letter to the Editor in reply to critics who
argue that O'Casey lost contact with Ireland when he went to
live in England].

2476   _____, "O'Casey, the Peerless Ploughman," Sean O'Casey Review, 2 (Spring 1976), 177-86 [Examines O'Casey's views on
the Irish Labour movement, as reflected in The Plough and
the Stars].

2477   _____, "O'Casey's Dublin Critics," Library Review (Glasgow),
21 (Summer 1967), 59-63 [O'Casey has suffered at the hands
of Dublin critics].

2478   _____, "O'Casey's Plays," Irish Times (Dublin), (12 Oct
1967) p. 9 [Letter to the Editor rebuking Tyrone Guthrie

for his derogatory remarks, 'O'Casey Dated,' at the International Theatre Seminar, Abbey Theatre, as reported in Irish Times (5 Oct 1967) p. 8]. An acrimonious correspondence followed: by Mrs. Kay Quinlan (20 Oct 1967) p. 15; Peadar Mac Maghnais (27 Oct 1967) p. 11; John O'Riordan (30 Oct 1967) p. 14; Donal O'Sullivan (3 Nov 1967) p. 14; and John O'Riordan (15 Nov 1967) p. 13.

2479 _____, "Re: The Letters; O'Casey's Bow of Burning Gold," Sean O'Casey Review, 3 (Spring 1977), 157-62 [Discusses critical reaction to O'Casey's letters and works].

2480 _____, "Sean O'Casey's Centenary in England," Sean O'Casey Review, 7 (1981), 10-11 [Gives details of the celebrations to mark the Centenary].

2481 _____, "Stage O'Casey," Irish Times (Dublin), (9 Oct 1968), p. 11 [Letter to the Editor chiding the Abbey Theatre and producers for neglecting O'Casey's later plays].

2482 _____, "Sean O'Casey: Colourful Quixote of the Drama," Library Review (Glasgow), 22 (Spring 1970), 235-42 [Views "the remarkable achievements of a dramatist of universal distinction"].

2483 _____, "Sean O'Casey's Legacy," Tribune (London), 34 (18 Sep 1970), 11 [Assesses O'Casey's achievement on the occasion of the 90th anniversary of his birth].

2484 O'Riordan, Michael. "O'Casey's Red Star Still Shining Bright," Irish Socialist (Dublin), (May 1980), 4 [Communist Party of Ireland's greeting on the occasion of the O'Casey centenary].

2485 O'Shannon, Cathal, "He Shared His Room with Sean O'Casey," Evening Press (Dublin), (6 May 1955), p. 5 [Micheál O Maoláin].

2486 O'Toole, Michael, "A 'Shadow' of O'Casey Is Now in the Abbey," Evening Press (Dublin), (25 Aug 1981), p. 7 [A bas-relief of O'Casey presented to the Abbey Theatre].

2487 "An Outstanding Artist of Year," Irish Times (Dublin), (31 Dec 1952), p. 1 [O'Casey is selected as one of the outstanding artists of the year by the United States National Arts Foundation].

2488 O'Valle, Violet M., "Melville, O'Casey, and Cock-a-Doodle Dandy," O'Casey Annual (London), no. 1 (1982), 167-79 [Examines the similarities between the play and Herman Melville's short story "Cock-A-Doodle Doo!"].

2489 Page, Malcolm, "The Early Years at Unity," Theatre Quarterly,
1 (Oct-Dec 1971), 60-6 [Makes references to O'Casey's relationship with the Unity Theatre, London, and to the first
production of The Star Turns Red].

2490 Page, Sean, "The Abbey Theatre," Dublin Magazine, 5 (Autumn-
Winter 1966), 6-14 [Discusses the production of The Plough
and the Stars].

2491 "'Page 1 Awards' Made by Newspaper Guild," New York Times,
(29 Mar 1949), p. 21 [The non-fiction award goes to O'Casey
for his Inishfallen, Fare Thee Well].

2492 Palmer, M.G., "Writers at Odds on Art: Literary Brickbats
Exchanged by A.E. and Sean O'Casey on Moderns," New York
Times, (26 Jan 1930), section 3, p. 3 [George Russell and
O'Casey on modern art]. See also O'Casey's letter to the
Editor, (20 Mar 1930), p. 26.

2493 Papke, Mary, "Juno and the Paycock as a Larkinite Stage Parable," Sean O'Casey Review, 3 (Spring 1977), 105-16 [Ana-
lyzes the play as an artistic correlation to the Irish working-
class group consciousness].

2494 Parker, R.B., "Bernard Shaw and Sean O'Casey," Queen's
Quarterly, 73 (Spring 1966), 13-34. Reprinted in Shaw Seminar Papers (Toronto), 65 (1966), 1-29 [Explores the influence of Shaw on O'Casey].

2495 Pasachoff, Naomi S., "O'Casey's Not Quite Festive Comedies,"
Eire-Ireland, 12 (Fall 1977), 41-61 [Within the Gates, Purple
Dust, and Cock-a-Doodle Dandy are all dominated by a single
concern: the celebration of life].

2496 _____, "Unity of Theme, Image, and Diction in The Silver
Tassie," Modern Drama, 23 (Mar 1980), 58-64 [Proves that
W.B. Yeats was wrong in his criticism of the play].

2497 Paul-Dubois, L[ouis], "Le théâtre irlandais: M. Sean O'Casey,"
Revue des deux mondes (Paris), 27 (1 June 1935), 644-52
[Comments on The Shadow of a Gunman, Juno and the Paycock,
The Plough and the Stars, The Silver Tassie, and Within the
Gates].

2498 Pauli, Manfred, "'Mein Freund Billy Shakespeare': Ammerkun-
gen über Sean O'Caseys Verhältnis zur Tradition," Shakes-
peare-Jahrbuch (Weimar), 113 (1977), 135-48 [Comments on
O'Casey's relation to tradition].

2499 Peinert, Dietrich, "Sean O'Casey," Praxis des neusprachlichen

Unterrichts (Dortmund), 15 (1968), 182-6 [Gives a biographical sketch of O'Casey, an assessment of his works, and a
select bibliography. In English].

2500 _____ , "Sean O'Casey: The Shadow of a Gunman," Praxis
des neusprachlichen Unterrichts (Dortmund), 15 (1968), 32-
45 [Examines the play in depth].

2501 Pellegrini, Alessandro, "Dalla tragedia irlandese e di Sean
O'Casey," Convegno (Milano), 17 (29 Oct 1936), 329-42 [Dis-
cusses The Shadow of a Gunman, Juno and the Paycock,
The Plough and the Stars, The Silver Tassie and Within the
Gates].

2502 "Personality Cult Scorned by O'Casey: Author, in Phone Interview, Talks of Many Things--Working on a 'Frolic,'" New
York Times (25 Aug 1957), section 1, p. 112 [Provoked by
the success of Purple Dust in New York, with plans later
that year to stage Cock-a-Doodle Dandy].

2503 "Personality of the Month," Plays and Players (London), 7 (Oct
1959), 5 [Describes O'Casey as "the greatest living dramatist
in the English language," and hopes that theatre managements
will bring his neglected plays to the London stage].

2504 Peter, John, "Jack MacGowran on O'Casey and Beckett," Times
(London), (18 Mar 1967), p. 7 [Comments on O'Casey's later
plays].

2505 Peterson, Richard F., "Polishing Up The Silver Tassie Controversy: Some Lady Gregory and W.B. Yeats Letters to Lennox Robinson," Sean O'Casey Review, 4 (Spring 1978), 121-9
[Makes use of the Lennox Robinson Collection at Southern Illinois University].

2506 Phillipson, Dom Wulstan, O.S.B., "Two Glimpses of O'Casey,"
Westminster Cathedral Chronicle (London), 59 (Mar 1965), 46
[Recollections of O'Casey].

2507 Pixley, Edward E., "The Plough and the Stars--The Destructive Consequences of Human Folly," Educational Theatre Journal, 22 (Mar 1971), 75-82 [The play is O'Casey's most intri-
cately designed attempt to reveal the havoc wreaked by the
seemingly innocent actions of foolish characters upon themselves and those around them].

2508 Platt, David, "O'Casey Honored Despite Witchhunt," Daily People's World (San Francisco), (8 Jan 1953), p. 7 [The National
Arts Foundation names O'Casey as one of the outstanding artists of 1952].

2509 _____, "Sean O'Casey's Letter About Artists Who 'Face Front and Fear Little,'" Daily Worker (N.Y.), (25 May 1955), p. 6 [O'Casey's letter of 19 May 1955 to the Bronx American Labor Party].

2510 _____, "U.S. Arts Group Names Communist as One of Outstanding Artists of Year," Daily Worker (N.Y.), (5 Jan 1953), p. 8 [The National Arts Foundation names O'Casey as one of the outstanding artists of 1952].

2511 "Playwright's Last Shilling," Daily News (London), (6 Mar 1926), p. 5 [Interview with O'Casey].

2512 Plunkett, James, "The Old Spot by the River," Irish Times (Dublin), (20 Feb 1960), p. 6 [O'Casey was the first secretary of the Irish Citizen Army].

2513 Porter, Raymond J., "O'Casey and Pearse," Sean O'Casey Review, 2 (Spring 1976), 104-14 [Examines O'Casey's views on Pearse's ideals].

2514 Porter, Thomas E., "Samuel Beckett: Dramatic Tradition and Ausländer," Eire-Ireland, 4 (Sep 1969), 62-75 [As Ausländer, Beckett does not share the belief of O'Casey and Anouilh in humankind's infinite progress].

2515 Potter, Rosanne G., "Toward a Syntactic Differentiation of Period Style in Modern Drama: Significant Between-Play Variability in 21 English Language Plays," Computers and the Humanities, 14 (Nov 1980), 187-96 [Investigates the rhetoric of the first act of Juno and the Paycock].

2516 Prescott, Joseph, ed., "Sean O'Casey Concerning James Joyce," Massachusetts Review, 5 (Winter 1964), 335-6 [Three letters by O'Casey to Prescott on Joyce].

2517 "Profile: Sean O'Casey," Observer (London), (10 Mar 1946), p. 6 [Biographical essay].

2518 "Pro-Quidnunc," "An Irishman's Diary: O'Casey on Connolly," Irish Times (Dublin), (22 Sep 1964), p. 7 [O'Casey never liked James Connolly and believed that he would have been nowhere without Larkin]. See replies by Cathal O'Shannon, (24 Sep 1964), p. 9; and by Thomas A. Browne, (2 Oct 1964), p. 9.

2519 Purser, S., "O'Casey Centenary," Irish Times (Dublin), (11 Apr 1980), p. 11 [Letter to the Editor praising the acting of Maureen Delany and Shelah Richards].

2520 "Quidnunc," "An Irishman's Diary: O'Casey's Kisser," Irish Times (Dublin), (3 Mar 1956), p. 10 [O'Casey gives reasons for turning down a request for an article on Bernard Shaw for Icarus].

2521 _____, "An Irishman's Diary: Speculation," Irish Times (Dublin), (29 March 1960), p. 6 [Suggests that O'Casey be honored on his 80th birthday].

2522 _____, "An Irishman's Diary: Sympathy," Irish Times (Dublin), (5 Jan 1957), p. 8 [Offers condolences to O'Casey on the death of his son Niall].

2523 _____, "An Irishman's Diary: What's in a Name?" Irish Times (Dublin), (12 Feb 1958), p. 5 [Comments on O'Casey's ban on his plays].

2524 _____, "An Irishman's Diary: Broadway Tribute-Consummation," Irish Times (Dublin), (21 Oct 1964), p. 9 [Report on the tribute to O'Casey which was staged at the Imperial Theatre, New York]. See reply by Ronald Ayling, (10 Nov 1964), p. 11.

2525 Quirke, James, "G.B.S. or O'Casey," Irish Times (Dublin), (28 Sep 1968), p. 9 [Letter to the Editor in reply to a leading article (25 Sep 1968) saying that Shaw is Ireland's most famous dramatist].

2526 Rafroidi, Patrick, "Dramaturges irlandais d'hier et d'avant-hier," Langues modernes (Paris), 60 (May-June 1966), 320-4 [Reviews some recent publications on O'Casey].

2527 _____, "La Scène littéraire irlandaise contemporaine," Langues modernes (Paris), 61 (Mar 1967), 84-9 [O'Casey and Brendan Behan have just "quit the scene"].

2528 Raftery, A., "Salute to Sean O'Casey," World News (London), (9 Apr 1960), p. 176 [Greets O'Casey on his 80th birthday].

2529 Ramsey, Roger, "The Making of an Angry Old Playwright," English Record (Binghamton, N.Y.), 22 (Winter 1971), 19-25 [O'Casey's independence and idealism were consistently mistaken for treachery to the Irish cause].

2530 "Records Say His 70th Birthday But--'I Don't Know How Old I Am,' O'Casey Declares," Irish Press (Dublin), (1 Apr 1954), p. 5 [Interview with Sean and Eileen O'Casey].

2531 Rees, Leslie, "Remembrance of Things Past: On Meeting Sean O'Casey," Meanjin Quarterly (Melbourne), 24 (Dec 1964), 414-20 [Interview with O'Casey].

2532 Regnault, Maurice, "Sean O'Casey: le poète de la rose rouge,"
      Lettres françaises (Paris), no. 810 (4-10 Feb 1960), 9 [Com-
      ments on Juno and the Paycock, Red Roses for Me, and Bed-
      time Story].

2533 Reid, Alec, "Dublin's Abbey Theatre Today," Drama Survey,
      3 (Fall 1964), 507-19 ["Synge and O'Casey gave us English
      enriched for all English speakers by its Irish cadences and
      imagery"].

2534 _____, "The Legend of the Green Crow: Observations on
      Recent Work By and About Sean O'Casey," Drama Survey,
      3 (May 1963), 155-64 [As one reads recent studies of O'Casey,
      "one finds those emotional and misleading assertions, those
      over-simplifications which are the very stuff of literary leg-
      end"].

2535 Rest, Jaime, "O'Casey: Adios al Teatro de la Abadia," Teatro
      XX (Buenos Aires), no. 6 (1964), p. 7 [Obituary].

2536 Reynolds, Stanley, "No Gift for the Irish," Guardian (London),
      (31 Mar 1980), p. 11 [Recollections of what O'Casey stood
      for].

2537 Richards, Shelah, "Extract from Proposed Autobiography,"
      Sean O'Casey Review, 2 (Spring 1976), 175-6 [Recollections
      of the first production of The Plough and the Stars].

2538 "Riches Scorned," Times Literary Supplement (London), (31
      Jan 1958), p. 61 [Editorial on the neglect of O'Casey]. See
      reply by Robert Hogan, ibid., (21 Mar 1958), p. 153.

2539 Ritchie, Harry M., "The Influence of Melodrama on the Early
      Plays of Sean O'Casey," Modern Drama, 5 (Sep 1962), 164-
      73 [Attempts to establish the exact relationship of O'Casey's
      technique to that of Boucicault].

2540 Robinson, Eric, "Juno and the Paycock: An Introduction,"
      Use of English (London), 11 (Winter 1959), 111-18 [A critical
      study of the play].

2541 Robinson, Lennox, "Recipe for a National Theatre," Realist
      (London), (June 1929), 130-41 ["O'Casey's work can spring
      from Dublin and no other city in the world but Dublin"].

2542 Rocke, William, "May Craig Recalls That Abbey Uproar," Irish
      Digest (Dublin), 80 (Mar 1964), 71-3 [Recollections of the
      first productions of The Plough and the Stars].

2543 _____, "O'Casey--The Man Who Came to Dinner," Sunday

Press (Dublin), (20 Jul 1980), p. 16 [O'Casey Centenary
marked in Wexford].

2544 Rodgers, W.R., "A Good Word for Sean," Sunday Times (London), (20 Sep 1964), p. 15 [Tribute to O'Casey by an Irish
poet and critic].

2545 Rogoff, Gordon, "Sean O'Casey's Legacy," Commonweal (N.Y.),
81 (23 Oct 1964), 128-9 [Deals with the contradictions of
O'Casey's life of exile, and concludes that the right director
and the right theatre have not yet been found to produce
O'Casey's later plays properly].

2546 _____, "Wasp Against the Criticonians," Encore (London), 3
(Easter 1956), 5-6, 25-6, 29 [O'Casey has been upsetting the
equilibrium of critics ever since he began writing].

2547 Rollins, Ronald G., "Clerical Blackness in the Green Garden:
Heroine as Scapegoat in Cock-a-Doodle Dandy," James Joyce
Quarterly, 8 (Fall 1970), 64-72 [Appropriation and manipula-
tion of ancient myth for satiric indictment is apparent in
O'Casey's dark comedy and fantasy].

2548 _____, "Desire Versus Damnation in O'Casey's Within the
Gates and Donleavy's The Ginger Man," Sean O'Casey Review,
1 (Spring 1975), 41-7 [Traces the similarities in the careers
of Jannice in O'Casey's Within the Gates and Miss Lily Frost
in Donleavy's The Ginger Man].

2549 _____, "Dramatic Symbolism in Sean O'Casey's Dublin Trilogy,"
West Virginia University Bulletin Philological Papers, 15 (June
1966), 49-56 [O'Casey, in The Shadow of a Gunman, Juno and
the Paycock, and The Plough and the Stars, develops symbols out of the movement of the plays rather than imposing
symbols on the work].

2550 _____, "Finn Again: O'Casey Resurrects Celtic Heroes in
Red Roses for Me," Irish University Review (Dublin), 10
(Spring 1980), 52-8 [O'Casey uses Finn MacCool and his Fian
to teach his countrymen how to behave].

2551 _____, "Form and Content in Sean O'Casey's Dublin Trilogy,"
Modern Drama, 8 (Feb 1966), 419-25 [Close examination of
The Shadow of a Gunman, Juno and the Paycock, and The
Plough and the Stars, reveals that the dramas are adroitly
designed].

2552 _____, "From Ritual to Romance in Within the Gates and
Cock-a-Doodle Dandy," Modern Drama, 17 (Mar 1974), 11-18
[In these two plays, O'Casey simultaneously mimics and mod-
ifies some distinguishing dimensions of myth].

2553 _____, "O'Casey and Johnston: Different Reactions to the 1916 Easter Rising," Sean O'Casey Review, 4 (Fall 1977), 19-29 [Compares O'Casey's The Plough and the Stars with Denis Johnston's The Scythe and the Sunset].

2554 _____, "O'Casey and Synge: The Irish Hero as Playboy and Gunman," Arizona Quarterly, 22 (Autumn 1966), 216-22 [The Shadow of a Gunman and The Playboy of the Western World both contain heroes who illustrate a common theme: the imaginative Irishman's obsession with the heroic personality and his deception by the false and flamboyant personality].

2555 _____, "O'Casey, O'Neill and Expressionism in The Silver Tassie," Bucknell Review, 10 (May 1962), 364-9 [O'Casey's chance acquaintance with O'Neill's The Hairy Ape impelled him to abandon the inadequacies of his earlier realism and to integrate the symbolism of expressionism into a penetrating critique of war in The Silver Tassie].

2556 _____, "O'Casey, O'Neill, and Expressionism in Within the Gates," West Virginia University Bulletin Philological Papers, 13 (Dec 1961), 76-81 [O'Casey's play reflects the expressionism of The Hairy Ape in its psychoanalytical approach and symbolism].

2557 _____, "O'Casey, Yeats and Behan: A Prismatic View of the 1916 Easter Week Rising," Sean O'Casey Review, 2 (Spring 1976), 196-207 [Examines O'Casey's attitude toward the Rising as reflected in The Plough and the Stars].

2558 _____, "O'Casey's Cock-a-Doodle Dandy," Explicator, 23 (Sep 1964), item 8 [The stage properties in Scene I represent Ireland "as a bleak, backward, and superstitious island"].

2559 _____, "O'Casey's Purple Dust," Explicator, 26 (Oct 1967), item 19 [O'Casey resorts to mythical patterns to impart provocative dimensions to his satiric drama].

2560 _____, "O'Casey's The Silver Tassie," Explicator, 20 (Apr 1962), item 62 [The first act of the play is built around a sacrificial theme].

2561 _____, "Pervasive Patterns in The Silver Tassie," Eire-Ireland, 6 (Winter 1971), 29-37 [O'Casey uses many of the same symbols--the tassie, cross, medals, and guns--to provide continuity and to intensify his indictment of war].

2562 _____, "Portraits of Four Irishmen As Artists: Verisimilitude and Vision," Irish University Review, 1 (Spring 1971), 189-97 [Joyce, Yeats, O'Casey, and Synge comprise an Irish gathering

that was endlessly fascinated by the relationship between illusion and reality, fact and dream, or verisimilitude and vi-
sion].

2563 _____, "Sean O'Casey's Mental Pilgrimage," Arizona Quarterly,
17 (Winter 1961), 293-302 [O'Casey's mental pilgrimage through
his plays has been a tortuous, erratic voyage in which he
has been pulled by the polar magnets of Communism and
Christianity].

2564 _____, "Sean O'Casey's The Star Turns Red: A Political
Prophecy," Mississippi Quarterly, 16 (Spring 1963), 67-75
[O'Casey's play is "a propagandistic drama with a blatant
political prediction revealing his intense, abiding interest in
international communism"].

2565 _____, "O'Casey's Within the Gates," Explicator, 29 (Oct
1970), item 8 [O'Casey identifies Jannice with Janus, the
Roman god of doorways, and Diana, the Roman goddess of
the hunt].

2566 _____, "Shaw and O'Casey: John Bull and His Other Island,"
Shaw Review, 10 (May 1967), 60-9 [Purple Dust is remarkably
like Shaw's John Bull's Other Island in subject matter, but
differs from it in technique].

2567 _____, "Unpublished Letters of Sean O'Casey," Eire-Irland,
6 (Summer 1971), 43-7 [Two letters from O'Casey dealing
with influences on his work, with his development as a playwright, and with his response to comment on his work].

2568 _____, and Llewellyn Rabby, "The Silver Tassie: The Post-
World-War-I Legacy," Modern Drama, 22 (June 1979), 125-35
[The Silver Tassie is a protest play which transparently be-
longs to the large category of post-World-War-I Expressionistic
drama].

2569 "Roots," Times Literary Supplement (London), (26 Feb 1960),
p. 129 [Something has gone wrong after The Silver Tassie:
"natural speech has become rhetoric, pathos sentiment, humour farce, the sense of reality the sense of propaganda"].

2570 "Roses Rouges pour Lui," Lettres françaises (Paris), no. 1047
(24-30 Sep 1964), 11 [Obituaries by Michel Habart, André
Clavé, Stellio Lorenzi, and Jean Dasté].

2571 Ross, Don, "O'Casey, 78, Says Hurrah to Life," New York
Herald Tribune, (16 Nov 1958), section 4, p. 1 [A transatlantic telephone conversation between a reporter and O'Casey
on the gala occasion of two of his plays being staged the same

month in New York: The Shadow of a Gunman and Cock-a-Doodle Dandy].

2572 Ross, Malcolm Mackenzie, "The Theatre and the Social Confusion," University of Toronto Quarterly, 5 (Jan 1936), 197-215 [Includes brief discussion of the ending of Within the Gates].

2573 Roy, Gregor, "Sean O'Casey: Genius of the Theater," Catholic World (N.Y.), 200 (Jan 1965), 259-60 [Obituary].

2574 Rudin, Seymour, "Playwright to Critic: Sean O'Casey's Letters to George Jean Nathan," Massachusetts Review, 5 (Winter 1964), 326-34 [Describes them, with excerpts].

2575 Rushe, Desmond, "O'Casey's Hundredth," Eire-Ireland, 15 (Summer 1980), 123-7 [There were two O'Caseys: The Public O'Casey who heaped scorn and abuse on Ireland and her institutions; and the Private O'Casey who was a person of striking gentleness, compassion, tolerance, and generosity].

2576 _____, "O'Casey's Spartan Life-Style," Irish Independent (Dublin), (8 Apr 1980), p. 8 [On the special issue of the Irish University Review to mark the O'Casey centenary].

2577 "Russian Magazine's Tribute to O'Casey," Irish Times (Dublin), (20 Oct 1964), p. 6 [New Times, published in Moscow, pays tribute to O'Casey].

2578 "Russians Like Sean O'Casey," Irish Times (Dublin), (1 Apr 1955), p. 1 [Soviet citizens like O'Casey because his writings "are true to life"].

2579 Ryan, Desmond, "Some Thoughts on Sean O'Casey," Tribune (Cork), (26 Mar 1926), pp. 10-11 [In The Plough and the Stars O'Casey "has gone astray in his facts"].

2580 Ryan, Ken, "Day O'Casey Got the Sack for Union Backing," Irish Independent (Dublin), (21 Apr 1980), p. 7 [Report on a lecture on RTE by James Plunkett to mark the O'Casey centenary].

2581 Ryan, Stephen P., "Crisis in Irish Letters," Commonweal (N.Y.), 71 (18 Dec 1959), 347-9 [Includes a comparison between Brendan Behan and O'Casey].

2582 _____, "Ireland and Its Writers," Catholic World (N.Y.), 192 (Dec 1960), 149-55 ["Despite the potent arguments now being waged to the contrary, Sean O'Casey is something less the artist than he was thirty-five years ago when he came to England"].

2583 Sagarra, Juan de, "En la Muerte de Sean O'Casey y Otras No-
tas," El Noticiero Universal (Barcelona), (2 Oct 1964), p. 24
[Obituary].

2584 Saroyan, William, "Some Frank Talk with William Saroyan," New
York Times (4 Jan 1953), section 2, pp. 1, 3 [On the lack
of support for O'Casey's plays].

2585 Sarukhanian, Alla, "Sean O'Casey," Voprosy Literatury [The
Problems of Literature] (Moscow), 4 (1979), 176-201 [Letters
and interviews. In Russian].

2586 _____, "Sean O'Casey: Ideology Plus Artistic Value," Inostrannaia Literatura (Foreign Literature] (Moscow), 5 (1978),
211-15 [In Russian].

2587 _____, "Sean O'Casey Is Seventy-Five," Soviet Literature
(Moscow), 3 (1955), 144-5 [Salutes O'Casey on his birthday].

2588 Schoen, Ernst, "Sean O'Casey--ein Dramatiker unserer Zeit,"
Theater der Zeit (Berlin), 15 (Mar 1960), 53-64 [Irish life
as illustrated in O'Casey's plays and autobiographies.]

2589 Schrank, Bernice, "Dialectical Configurations in Juno and the
Paycock," Twentieth Century Literature (Denver), 21 (Dec
1975), 438-56 [The play goes beyond domestic melodrama to
make a larger statement about the nature of existence].

2590 _____, "The Low and the Lofty: A Comparison of Sean
O'Casey's The Plough and the Stars and Denis Johnston's
The Scythe and the Sunset," Modern Language Studies, 11,
no. 1 (1980-81), 12-16.

2591 _____, "'Th' nakedness o' th' times'" Dressing-up in The
Plough and the Stars," Canadian Journal of Irish Studies,
7 (Dec 1981), 5-20 [In this play O'Casey uses the characters'
concern about clothing to indicate their inarticulate aspira-
tions].

2592 _____, "The Naturalism of O'Casey's Early Plays," Sean
O'Casey Review, 4 (Fall 1977), 41-8 [Shows that the central
concern of The Shadow of a Gunman, Juno and the Paycock,
and The Plough and the Stars, is the interaction of language
and time].

2593 _____, "Poets, Poltroons and Platitudes: A Study of Sean
O'Casey's The Shadow of a Gunman," Mosaic (Winnipeg, Manitoba), 11 (Fall 1977), 53-60 [The play has not received the
critical attention it deserves].

2594 _____, "'You needn't say no more': Language and the

Problems of Communication in Sean O'Casey's The Shadow of a Gunman," Irish University Review, 8 (Spring 1978), 23-37 [In this play O'Casey examines the manifestations of chaos].

2595 Scrimgeour, James, "O'Casey's Street People: Characterization in the Autobiographies," Sean O'Casey Review, 4 (Fall 1977), 57-65 [O'Casey's Autobiographies deal not only with heroic figures, but also with ordinary human beings].

2596 "Sean May End Ban on Abbey," Sunday Review (Dublin), 3 (20 Sep 1959), 28 [Speculation as to whether O'Casey would have a change of heart following a visit by Ernest Blythe to O'Casey in Torquay].

2597 "Sean O'Casey," Irish Times (Dublin), (21 Sep 1964), p. 7 [Editorial tribute].

2598 "Sean O'Casey," Irish Independent (Dublin), (21 Sep 1964), p. 10 [Editorial tribute].

2599 "Sean O'Casey," New York Times, (25 Sep 1964), p. 40 [Editorial tribute].

2600 "Sean O'Casey," Publishers Weekly (Philadelphia), 186 (28 Sep 1964), 96 [Obituary].

2601 "Sean O'Casey," New Republic (N.Y.), 151 (3 Oct 1964), 6 [Editorial tribute].

2602 "Sean O'Casey Centenary Greetings and Photos," Sean O'Casey Review, 6 (1980), 3-21 [Received on the occasions of the "Labour Salute to Sean O'Casey" in New York City, 25 March 1980; and the "Sean O'Casey: A Centenary Conference" at Hofstra University, 27-28 March 1980].

2603 "Sean O'Casey Dies at 84," Daily Mail (London), (19 Sep 1964), p. 1.

2604 "Sean O'Casey Dies: Heart Attack in Nursing Home," Times (London), (19 Sep 1964), p. 8.

2605 "The Sean O'Casey Festival," Sean O'Casey Review, 3 (Spring 1977), 144-8 [Remarks and messages received during the first Sean O'Casey Festival and Conference held at Hofstra University on Long Island, N.Y., to commemorate the 50th anniversary of The Plough and the Stars].

2606 "Sean O'Casey 'Getting along Fine,'" Irish Times (Dublin), (25 Aug 1964), p. 5 [O'Casey is convalescing at his home after a recent illness].

2607 "Sean O'Casey Greets Gurley Flynn Event," Daily Worker (N.Y.),
(26 Mar 1963), p. 5 [O'Casey sends greetings to the Elizabeth
Gurley Flynn reception which was held in conjunction with the
publication of her book The Anderson Story].

2608 "Sean O'Casey Greets N.Y. Connolly Rally," Daily Worker
(N.Y.), (4 May 1950), p. 4 [O'Casey sends a message to the
Connolly Commemoration Committee for its invitation to him to
appear at its rally].

2609 "Sean O'Casey Has Second Operation," Irish Times (Dublin),
(1 Mar 1956), p. 5 [O'Casey undergoes a second operation
at Torbay Hospital, Torquay].

2610 "Sean O'Casey Ill on Birthday," New York Times (31 Mar 1962),
p. 16 [O'Casey spends his 82nd birthday in bed with influ-
enza].

2611 "Sean O'Casey in Hospital," Irish Times (Dublin), (15 Feb 1956),
p. 1 [O'Casey is to undergo a major operation in Torbay Hospital, Torquay].

2612 "Sean O'Casey, Irish Playwright, Is Dead at 84," New York
Times, (19 Sep 1964), pp. 1, 12.

2613 "Sean O'Casey Left £1,702," Irish Times (Dublin), (1 Dec 1964),
p. 9.

2614 "Sean O'Casey, Playwright of Genius," Daily Telegraph (London), (19 Sep 1964), p. 18 [Obituary].

2615 "Sean O'Casey Recuperating," New York Times, (15 Feb 1956),
p. 3 [O'Casey is recuperating from an operation in a hospital
in Torquay].

2616 "Sean O'Casey R.I.P.," National Review (N.Y.), 16 (6 Oct
1964), 859 [Obituary].

2617 "Sean O'Casey Sees London: Irish Dramatist's First Visit to
England," Evening Standard (London), (5 Mar 1926), p. 4
[Interview with O'Casey].

2618 "Sean O'Casey: Study in Class and National Betrayal," New
Literature and Ideology (Toronto: Norman Bethune Institute),
n. 20 (May 1976), 51-3 [O'Casey's "so-called realism is merely
a cover for the imperialist propaganda that it is the people
themselves who are to blame for the hardship they suffer"].

2619 "Sean O'Casey Talks," Daily Sketch (London), (6 Mar 1926),
p. 5 [Interview with O'Casey].

2620 "Sean O'Casey's Story," Time and Tide (London), 14 (27 May 1933), 640-1 [Letters to the Editor by W.B. Yeats, Sylvia Townsend Warner, and E. Lyttleton on the printer's refusal to set up O'Casey's story "I Wanna Woman"].

2621 Seaton, George, "A Dublin Experience," Sean O'Casey Review, 1 (Spring 1975), 38-40 [The director of the production of Juno and the Paycock at the Mark Taper Forum in Los Angeles tells of his trip to Dublin to capture all the pathos of that war-torn nation].

2622 Sedgwick, Ruth Woodbury, "O'Casey: Laborer--Playwright--Poet," Stage (N.Y.), 12 (Nov 1934), 29-31 [Biographical and critical essay].

2623 Seehase, Georg, "Zum neuen Typ des künstlerischen Bewusstseins in Sean O'Casey's Dramen," Zeitschrift für Anglistik und Amerikanistik, 27 (1979), 101-7 [Deals with the new type of artistic consciousness in the plays of O'Casey].

2624 Selezneva, L., "The Bishop's Bonfire by Sean O'Casey," Research Papers of the Sverdlovsk Pedagogical Institute, 259 (1976), 120-39 [Examines "the problem of the nature of the genre." In Russian].

2625 _____, "The Comedy Cock-a-Doodle Dandy," Law of Genre (Tambov), 3 (1978), 102-6 [Discusses the problem of the genre].

2626 _____, "Sean O'Casey's Comedy The Drums of Father Ned," Research Papers of the Sverdlovsk Pedagogical Institute, 280 (1976), 132-48 [Discusses the problem of the genre. In Russian].

2627 Selz, Jean, "Sean O'Casey," Lettres nouvelles (Paris), no. 31 (Nov 1959), 15-17 [Discusses Juno and the Paycock, Red Roses for Me, and Bedtime Story].

2628 Sexton, Máire, "W.B. Yeats, Wilfred Owen and Sean O'Casey," Studies (Dublin), 70 (Spring 1981), 88-95 [Yeats disliked the war poetry of Owen, and this may have in turn been responsible for his rejection of The Silver Tassie].

2629 Shaw, Iain, "O'Casey's Hurrah for Life Echoes Louder than Guns," Tribune (London), (17 Aug 1962), p. 5 [Discusses Purple Dust, Red Roses for Me, and The Plough and the Stars].

2630 Shchepilova, L., "Vsegda Plug i Zvezdy [Always the Plough and the Stars]," Teatr (Moscow) 28 (Nov 1967), 151-4 [General comments on O'Casey's writings].

2631 Shenker, Israel, "Refusal of Examination or Publication of 126 Sean O'Casey Letters Owned by N.Y.U. Stirs a Literary Dispute," New York Times, (23 Jan 1977), p. 37 [Professor David H. Greene of New York University refuses access to the letters, and the University over-rules the refusal].

2632 Shepard, Richard F., "O'Casey's Wife Carries on the Glory," New York Times, (6 Apr 1980), p. 39 [Interview with Eileen O'Casey].

2633 Shyre, Paul, "Talk with Two Titans [O'Casey and Edward Gordan Craig]," New York Times, (8 Sep 1957), section 2, pp. 1, 3 [Recollections by an American theatre director and adapter who produced dramatized versions of O'Casey's autobiographies and directed Purple Dust and Cock-a-Doodle Dandy].

2634 Siegmeister, Elie, "A Long, Long Road: An American Composer Tells Why His The Plough and the Stars Was a Decade in the Making," Sean O'Casey Review, 1 (Fall 1974), 22-32. Reprinted from Opera News, 34 (14 Mar 1970), 27-29 [Discusses the difficulty of making an opera out of the play].

2635 "The Silver Tassie 1928-1978," Sean O'Casey Review, 4 (Spring 1978), 85-93 [Messages received at the Sean O'Casey Conference at Youngstown, Ohio on the occasion of the 50th anniversary of the publication of the play].

2636 Simpson, Alan, "O'Casey and the East Wall Area in Dublin," Irish University Review (Dublin), 10 (Spring 1980), 41-51 [O'Casey's environment influenced his personality and his writings].

2637 _____, "The Unwanted Director," Irish Times (Dublin), (1 Apr 1980), p. 8 [An Irish director gives his views on the production of O'Casey's plays].

2638 Sinko, Grzegorz, "Irlandia--daleka i bliska" [Ireland--Far and Near]," Dialog (Warsaw), 6 (Oct 1961), 106-17 [Particularly on O'Casey].

2639 Skeffington, O. Sheehy, "Senator Sheehy Skeffington," Standard (Dublin), 27 (4 Mar 1955), 11 [Letter to the Editor denouncing the Standard for its attacks on O'Casey].

2640 Skelton, Robin, "Jack Coughlin: Irish Portraits," Malahat Review, 22 (Apr 1972), 63-72 [The most complex of Coughlin's etchings is the one entitled "Studies of Sean O'Casey"].

2641 Slavov, Atanas, "Ideyna nasochenost i kompozitsionna teknika v Az Chukam na Vratata na Shon O'Keysi i Odisey na Dzheyms

Dzhoys," Literaturna Misul (Sofia), 14 (1970), 72-83 [Ideological thrust and technique of composition in I Knock at the Door and in Joyce's Ulysses. In Bulgarian].

2642 "Slum Child Who Became World Famed Dramatist," Irish Times (Dublin), (19 Sep 1964), p. 5 [Obituary].

2643 Smith, Bobby L., "From Athlete to Statue: Satire in Sean O'Casey's The Silver Tassie," Arizona Quarterly, 27 (Winter 1971), 347-61 [The play satirizes a war and the values that made that war inevitable].

2644 _____, "The Hat, The Whore, and The Hyprocrite in O'Casey's Bedtime Story," Serif: Kent State University Library Quarterly, 4 (June 1967), 3-5 [The play is an exposé of what O'Casey calls "the drab and malicious menace of puritanism"].

2645 _____, "O'Casey's Satiric Vision," James Joyce Quarterly, 8 (Fall 1970), 13-28 ["O'Casey's satiric vision gives both continuity and unity to the kaleidoscopic variety of his work"].

2646 _____, "Satire in O'Casey's Cock-a-Doodle Dandy," Renascence, 19 (Winter 1967), 64-73 [O'Casey uses farcical satire inspired by the Cock's magical powers to reduce to absurdity the stultified, superstitious religion of the Irish parish of Nyadnanave].

2647 _____, "Satire in The Plough and the Stars," Ball State University Forum, 10 (Summer 1969), 3-11 [In this play, O'Casey satirizes the vanity and madness of war, particularized in the Easter Rising].

2648 Smith, Gus, "Clash with Yeats," Sunday Independent (Dublin), (30 Mar 1980), p. 11 [Recalls the controversy over O'Casey's plays, especially The Silver Tassie].

2649 _____, "Gabriel Never Forgot O'Casey," Sunday Independent (Dublin), (15 June 1980), p. 30 [Obituary of Gabriel Fallon, with references to his friendship with O'Casey].

2650 _____, "Great Family Man," Sunday Independent (Dublin), (30 Mar 1980), p. 11 [Interview with Eileen O'Casey].

2651 Smith, Paul, "Dublin's Lusty Theater," Holiday (Philadelphia), 33 (Apr 1963), 119, 123, 157 [O'Casey is "the most performed Irish playwright outside Ireland"].

2652 Smith, Winifred, "The Dying God in the Modern Theatre," Review of Religion (N.Y.), 5 (Mar 1941), 264-75 [Discusses

The Silver Tassie, which has been "strangely misinterpreted and then neglected by critics"].

2653 Snoddy, Oliver, "Sean O'Casey as Troublemaker," Eire-Ireland, 1 (Winter 1966), 23-38 [Deals with O'Casey's republicanism].

2654 Snowden, J.A., "Dialect in the Plays of Sean O'Casey," Modern Drama, 14 (Feb 1972), 387-91 [O'Casey's use of dialect is always conscious and he exploits it for the purposes of mood and attitude].

2655 _____, "Sean O'Casey and Naturalism," Essays and Studies, 24 (1971), 56-58 [O'Casey was not strictly a naturalist at all in his Dublin Trilogy].

2656 "Son of Sean O'Casey Dies," New York Times, (8 Jan 1957), p. 31 [Niall O'Casey dies of leukemia].

2657 "Stage Censorship Reform," Times (London), (2 May 1958), p. 6 [O'Casey supports a theatre censorship reform committee formed under the chairmanship of Sir Gerald Barry].

2658 "The Staging of Sean O'Casey's Plays: A Symposium," Sean O'Casey Review, 5 (Spring 1979), 131-56 [Contributions by Heinz Moog, Alan Simpson, Sylvia O'Brien, Vincent Dowling, Ingeborg Pietzsch, Philip Burton, and Emile Jean Dumay].

2659 Staples, Hugh B., "Mirror in His House," Wake Newslitter, 8 (June 1971), 44-5 [Eight references in O'Casey's Autobiography show strong roots in Finnegans Wake].

2660 Starkie, Walter, "Den irländska nationalteatern," Ord och bild (Stockholm), 38 (Oct 1929), 529-48; (Nov 1929), 593-608 [Comments on The Shadow of a Gunman, Juno and the Paycock, The Plough and the Stars, and The Silver Tassie].

2661 _____, "The Plays of Sean O'Casey," Nineteenth Century and After (London), 104 (Aug 1928), 225-36 [Highly compliments O'Casey's first three full-length plays, but is cautious and equivocal about his latest one, The Silver Tassie]. See O'Casey's reply, ibid. (Sep 1928), 399-402.

2662 Stein, Joseph, "'It Was Fun,' Said Sean O'Casey," Irish Digest (Dublin), 45 (May 1959), 50-2 [Recollections of O'Casey by the librettist who adapted Juno and the Paycock into a musical].

2663 Stephens, James, "Dublin Letter," Dial (Chicago), 77 (Aug 1924), 155-7 [Report on the success of Juno and the Paycock].

2664 Stewart, Andrew J., "The Acting of the Abbey Theatre,"
Theatre Arts Monthly (N.Y.), 17 (Mar 1933), 243-5 [Acting
Captain Boyle in Juno and the Paycock is easier for an Irish
actor].

2665 Stokes, Leslie, "The English Spotlight: A Joyful Birth," Theatre Arts (N.Y.), 30 (16 Feb 1946), 111-16 [Shaw and O'Casey
are "the outstanding dramatists of this century"].

2666 "Strike Hits O'Casey Centenary Record," Sunday Press (Dublin),
(6 Apr 1980), p. 5 [A strike at EMI holds up the release of
"The Green Crow Caws," a centenary celebration record].

2667 "Successful Realist Determined to Be Fanciful," Guardian (London), (21 Sep 1964), p. 5 [Obituary].

2668 Summerfield, H., ed., "Unpublished Letters from AE to John
Eglinton," Malahat Review, no. 14 (Apr 1970), 84-107 [O'Casey
is among the literary figures mentioned in the letters].

2669 Sutherland, Jack, "O'Casey, Bard of Common Folk," Daily
Worker (London), (21 Sep 1964), p. 2 [Obituary].

2670 Swander, Homer D., "Shields at the Abbey: A Friend of Cathleen," Eire-Ireland, 5 (Summer 1970), 25-41 [Arthur Shields
believed that the greatness of the Abbey Theatre rested primarily with its writers: Lady Gregory, Yeats, Synge, O'Casey,
and others].

2671 Taborski, Boleslaw, "Jeszcze o Seanie O'Casey," Dialog (Warsaw),
(1962), 100-7 [An assessment of O'Casey's achievement. In
Polish].

2672 Talbott, Earl G., "For Playwright O'Casey, Long Was the Staff
of Life," New York Herald Tribune, (19 Sep 1964), pp. 1, 8
[Obituary].

2673 "'Tassie' Rejection Recalled," Irish Times (Dublin), (7 Apr
1980), p. 13 [Report on Tomas MacAnna's lecture on RTE to
mark the O'Casey Centenary].

2674 Taubman, Howard, "Sean O'Casey: 1880-1964," New York
Times, (27 Sep 1964), section 2, p. 3 [Obituary].

2675 Taylor, John Russell, "An Irish Patchwork of Folksy Vigour
and Colourfulness," Times (London), (19 Feb 1980), p. 15
[On Breon O'Casey].

2676 Templeton, Joan, "Sean O'Casey and Expressionism," Modern
Drama, 14 (May 1971), 47-62 [The techniques of Expressionist

Drama are found throughout O'Casey's plays, and his early
attempts at Expressionism become a kind of proving ground
for his last plays].

2677 Terres celtiques (Lyon), (1965). An O'Casey issue. [Contents:
      Patrick O'Connor, "Sean O'Casey," 21-24; F. de Rocquois,
      "Le prêtre et l'homme," 25-33; Francoise Hanriot, "Le com-
      munisme de O'Casey," 35-36; Gisèle Bissuel, "La muse tragi-
      comique," 37-38; Roland Ronzière, "Juno et le paon," 39-48;
      Jean-Claude Rolland, "Les tambours du Père Ned," 49-51;
      Monique Payrand, "Le trivial et le sublime," 53-54].

2678 Thacher, Molly Day, "Bentley on Theater," New Leader (N.Y.),
      38 (10 Jan 1955), 26-7 [It was not Expressionism but Commun-
      ism that undermined O'Casey's later plays].

2679 "Thersites," "Private Views," Irish Times (Dublin), (5 Feb
      1955), p. 6 [Quotes Gabriel Fallon's and Richard Findlater's
      views on O'Casey]. See reply by Denis Johnston, "Who Cod-
      dled Donizetti?" (10 Mar 1955), p. 5 [Letter to the Editor].

2680 "They Stand Out from the Crowd: Sean O'Casey," Literary Di-
      gest (N.Y.), 118 (6 Oct 1934), 12 [O'Casey in New York for
      the production of Within the Gates].

2681 Thompson, Laurence, "The Rebel Who Never Retired," News
      chronicle (London), (3 Mar 1955), p. 6. Condensed in Irish
      Digest (Dublin), 53 (May 1955), 8-10. Extracts appeared in
      Evening Herald (Dublin), (5 Mar 1955), under the title of
      "Melodrama Defended" [Interview with O'Casey by an English
      journalist and author].

2682 Thompson, Ralph, "In and Out of Books," New York Times
      Magazine, (26 Dec 1948), p. 12 [Discusses Inishfallen Fare
      Thee Well].

2683 Tindemans, C., "Requiem voor Sean O'Casey," Streven, 18
      (Nov 1964), 171-7 [Obituary].

2684 Tobin, Michael, "The Pondering of a Playgoer," Iris Hibernia
      (Fribourg), 4 (1960), 27-39 [Juno, in Juno and the Paycock,
      in the "nearest approach to the truly Christian character"].

2685 Todd, R. Mary, "The Two Published Versions of Sean O'Casey's
      Within the Gates," Modern Drama, 10 (Feb 1968), 346-55 [The
      changes made in O'Casey's other plays are a simple form of
      revision, while in Within the Gates the alterations are on a
      larger scale and often of another order].

2686 "Too Shy to See His Own Play: Sean O'Casey's First Night in

London," Daily Graphic (London), (6 Mar 1926), p. 2 [Interview with O'Casey].

2687 "Tragic Artist," Irish Catholic (Dublin), 77 (24 Sep 1964), 3 [Editorial tribute].

2688 Trewin, J.C., "Memories of the First Production of The Star Turns Red." Program note to the Abbey Theatre's production, February 1978.

2689 _____, "O'Casey the Elizabethan," New Theatre (London), 3 (June 1946), 2-3 [O'Casey follows Yeats and Synge, but his work surpasses theirs on the stage "because he is more prodigal, more various, more exciting"].

2690 _____, "Shaw and the Rest," Plays and Players (London), 16 (Jul 1969), 66-71 [Shaw and O'Casey are unquestionably the principal dramatists of this century].

2691 _____, "Sean O'Casey on the English Stage," Sean O'Casey Review, 3 (Fall 1976), 24-32 [Discusses the productions of O'Casey's plays in England].

2692 "Tribute to O'Casey," Irish Times (Dublin), (5 Oct 1964), p. 6 [The current weekly Bulletin of the Department of External Affairs in Ireland is completely devoted to a tribute to O'Casey and an assessment of his work].

2693 "Tributes Paid to Playwright," Irish Times (Dublin), (19 Sep 1964), p. 5 [By Hilton Edwards, Micheál MacLiammóir, Gabriel Fallon, Brendan Smith, and Phyllis Ryan].

2694 "TV Show Drops O'Casey Interview," Irish Times (Dublin), (15 Mar 1960), p. 11 [Ed Sullivan Program cancels excerpt of Barry Fitzgerald-O'Casey from the Abbey Theatre filmed documentary Cradle of Genius because of alleged hostility in America to O'Casey as a true representative of Ireland].

2695 "Twelve British Actors Start Campus Tour," New York Times, (30 Jan 1965), p. 17 [Theatre Group 20, including Shivaun O'Casey].

2696 " £200-a-Week Ex-Navvy Sees London: Motor Tour in a Cap and Dusty Clothes," Daily Express (London), (6 Mar 1926), p. 9 [Interview with O'Casey].

2697 "U.S. Congress Proclamation on Sean O'Casey's Centenary. Congressional Record," Sean O'Casey Review, 7 (1981), 8-9 [Salutes the memory of O'Casey].

2698 Ussher, Arland, "Irish Literature," Zeitschrift für Anglistik und Amerikanistik, 14 (1966), 30-55 [The works of O'Casey are among the highlights of Irish literature].

2699 Van Druten, John, "O'Casey as Phenomenon for Dublin," Boston Evening Transcript, (13 Feb 1926), part 3, pp. 4, 5, 7. Reprinted from the New York Evening Post [O'Casey is the only Irish playwright who reflected the conditions which obtained during the Irish wars].

2700 Vaughan, Constance, "O'Casey Explains Himself," Daily Sketch (London), (24 Mar 1926), p. 7 [Interview with O'Casey by an English journalist].

2701 Verity, Christine, "Life with the O'Caseys," Sunday Telegraph (London), (26 Sep 1971), p. 11 [Interview with Eileen O'Casey].

2702 Vilaça, Mário, "Sean O'Casey e o movimento dramático irlandès," Vertice: Revista de Cultura e Arte (Coimbra), 11 (June 1951), 293-9; (July 1951), 369-72; (Aug 1951), 399-406; (Sep 1951), 479-83; (Oct 1951), 553-6 [O'Casey and the Irish Dramatic Movement. In Portuguese].

2703 "V.I.P.," "Sean O'Casey," Standard (Dublin), 27 (4 Mar 1955), 12 [Letter to the Editor remarking that Juno and the Paycock is "a great Catholic play" despite O'Casey's being a Protestant].

2704 Vitte, Oksana, "'Zrobyty svit svitlišym i kraščym': Do 100-riččja z dnja narodžennja Sona O'Kejsi," Vsesvit, 3 (1980), 159-65 [A study of O'Casey's dramas, on the occasion of his centenary].

2705 Vosey, Michael, "Sean O'Casey: A Personal View," Irish Times (Dublin), (18 Apr 1980), p. 10 [Conflict in the world might come to an end if people listened to O'Casey, who stresses humanity rather than nationality in his work].

2706 Wall, Mervyn, "O'Casey: The Devon Years," Evening Press (Dublin), (26 Apr 1980), p. 6 [The O'Casey centenary is marked by RTE, the Irish national radio and television network].

2707 Walsh, Caroline, "Literary Landmarks--20: Sean O'Casey's Dublin," Irish Times (Dublin), (12 Jul 1977), p. 8 [Biographical sketch of O'Casey, describing the houses in which he lived].

2708 Walsh, Louis J., "A Catholic Theatre for Dublin," Irish Rosary (Dublin), 39 (Oct 1935), 749-54 [Denounces The Silver Tassie "for its obscenities and its blasphemies"].

2709   ,, "The Defiance of the Abbey," Irish Rosary (Dublin), 39 (Sep 1935), 650-4 [The Abbey Theatre defies Catholic and Irish sentiment and opinion by putting on The Silver Tassie].

2710 Wardle, Irving, "The Tragedy of Sean O'Casey," Observer (London), (20 Sep 1964), p. 27 [Obituary]. See replies by John Arden and John O'Riordan, (27 Sep 1964), p. 37.

2711 Warner, Sylvia Townsend, "Sean O'Casey's Story," Time and Tide (London), 14 (27 May 1933), 640 [Letter to the Editor on "I Wanna Woman"].

2712 Washburn, A.M., "Form and Effect: Mr. O'Casey's Within the Gates," Harvard Advocate, 121 (Christmas 1934), 73-6 [Examines various aspects of the play].

2713 Weatherby, W.J., "Figure in the Shadows," Manchester Guardian, (10 Sep 1959), p. 6 [Interview with O'Casey by an English author, journalist, and novelist].

2714   , "The Sting and the Twinkle," Manchester Guardian, (15 Aug 1962), p. 7. Also in Irish Times (Dublin), (15 Aug 1962), p. 8 [Interview with O'Casey].

2715 Webb, Clifford, "Shaw and the Twentieth Century Theatre," Shavian, 2 (June 1964), 13-17 [Since 1920, O'Casey and others have exhibited "signs of Shavian influence"].

2716 Weiler, A.H., "By Way of Report: O'Casey Autobiography Acquired," New York Times, (13 Aug 1961), section 2, p. 7 [Sextant, Inc. has acquired film rights to O'Casey's Autobiographies].

2717 Weissman, David L., "Writer Condemns Producers for Failure to Offer O'Casey Plays," New York Times, (7 Dec 1952), section 2, p. 7 [Letter to the Drama Editor].

2718 White, Terence de Vere, "C'est le même journal," Irish Times (Dublin), (7 Jan 1967), p. 8 ["I believe O'Casey to have been overrated"]. See reply by "Quidnunc," "An Irishman's Diary," (10 Jan 1967), p. 9.

2719 Whittaker, Herbert, "O'Casey's Widow Says Poets 'Hit the Core,'" Globe and Mail (Toronto), (23 Nov 1976), p. 18 [Interview with Eileen O'Casey].

2720 Williams, Simon, "The Unity of The Silver Tassie," Sean O'Casey Review, 4 (Spring 1978), 99-112 [Examines the reasons why the play is rarely performed].

2721 Williams, Stephen, "How O'Casey Wrote a Great Play," Irish
Digest (Dublin), 39 (June 1951), 32-4 ["With a sixpenny dictionary by his side, and by the light of a guttering candle,
O'Casey immortalised in Juno and the Paycock the tenement
life that surrounded him"].

2722 Wilson, Cecil, "From Squalor Grew the Genius of Juno," Daily
Mail (London), (19 Sep 1964), p. 11 [Obituary].

2723 Winkler, Elizabeth Hale, "The Clown in O'Casey's Drama,"
Irish University Review (Dublin), 10 (Spring 1980), 77-90
[Critical justice cannot be done to the plays of O'Casey unless the elements of knockabout clowning and low comedy in
his drama are fully analyzed and accepted as an integral part
of his many-faceted playwriting technique].

2724 Winnington, Alan, "O'Casey Life Story," Morning Star (London),
(16 May 1966), p. 2 [Eileen O'Casey to write her memoir of
her husband].

2725 Wojewoda, Cecylia, "Spotkanie z Seanem O'Casey," Dialog (Warsaw), (1962), 108-12. Reprinted in English as "Remembering
Sean," Sean O'Casey Review, 1 (Fall 1974), 33-7 [The translator of O'Casey's works into Polish recollects a meeting with
him in 1926].

2726 Wood, J. Bertram, "The Irish Drama," Humberside (Manchester),
6 (Oct 1938), 99-116 [In the realism of O'Casey's early plays
Irish drama reached the uttermost limit of divergence from
Yeats's romantic conception].

2727 Woodbridge, Homer E., "Sean O'Casey," South Atlantic Quarterly, 40 (Jan 1941), 50-9 [Discusses The Shadow of a Gunman, Juno and the Paycock, The Plough and the Stars, The
Silver Tassie, and Within the Gates].

2728 "Works by O'Casey Published in Russia," Irish Times (Dublin),
(11 Mar 1957), p. 5 [Autobiographies, The Shadow of a Gunman, and Juno and the Paycock have been published in Russian editions].

2729 "The World of Sean O'Casey," Life (Chicago), 37 (26 Jul 1954),
68-77, 79-80. International Edition, 17 (23 Aug 1954), 45-
55 [A pictorial feature which formed the impetus for the making of the film Young Cassiday].

2730 Worth, Katharine, "In Celebration of Sean O'Casey's Centenary,"
Royal Shakespeare Company (London) Special Programme for
the performance of Juno and the Paycock (1980).

2731 _____, "The O'Casey Centenary," Times Literary Supplement (London), (9 May 1980), p. 527 [Surveys the celebrations to mark the occasion].

2732 _____, "O'Casey, Synge and Yeats," Irish University Review (Dublin), 10 (Spring 1980), 103-17 [Discusses O'Casey's relation to Synge and Yeats].

2733 _____, "O'Casey's Dramatic Symbolism," Modern Drama, 4 (Dec 1961), 260-7 [Symbolism is an intrinsic part of the dramatic process in O'Casey's plays, whether it functions in a fantastic or realistic context].

2734 "Writer Recalls O'Casey Exile," Irish Times (Dublin), (31 Mar 1980), p. 5 [Report on Denis Johnston's lecture on RTE to mark the O'Casey Centenary].

2735 Yeats, W.B., "The Plough and the Stars: Mr. Sean O'Casey's New Play," Irish Times (Dublin), (12 Jan 1926), p. 9 [Interview during which Yeats defends the play].

2736 _____, "Sean O'Casey's Story," Time and Tide (London), 14 (27 May 1933), 640 [Letter to the Editor on "I Wanna Woman"].

2737 _____, "To Sean O'Casey," Observer (London), (3 June 1928), p. 19. Reprinted in Irish Statesman (Dublin), 10 (9 June 1928), 268-72 [Letter on The Silver Tassie]. See O'Casey's reply, "W.B. Yeats and The Silver Tassie," ibid.

[This section is arranged chronologically under each play.]

THE SHADOW OF A GUNMAN

2738 "Abbey Theatre: The Shadow of a Gunman," Irish Times (Dublin), (13 Apr 1923) p. 4.

2739 McH., M. F., "A Good Play. Last Piece of the Season at the Abbey. A 'Gunman,'" Freeman's Journal (Dublin), (13 Apr 1923) p. 8.

2740 O'D., F.J.H., "Treat at the Abbey: The Shadow of a Gunman," Evening Herald (Dublin), (13 Apr 1923) p. 1.

2741 "New Abbey Play," Irish Independent (Dublin), (14 Apr 1923) p. 3.

2742 Mac, "Too Much Laughter at the Abbey," Irish Statesman (Dublin), 3 (20 Sep 1924) 46.

2743 "Court Theatre: The Shadow of a Gunman by Sean O'Casey," Times (London), (28 May 1927) p. 10.

2744 "Court Theatre: The Shadow of a Gunman, by Sean O'Casey," Daily Telegraph (London), (28 May 1927) p. 12.

2745 "Irish Players Back: Sean O'Casey's Humour and Tragedy," Daily Mail (London), (28 May 1927) p. 9.

2746 P., A., "New O'Casey Play: The Shadow of a Gunman at the Court Not Up to Standard," Daily Sketch (London), (28 May 1927) p. 2.

2747 E., M., "The Shadow of a Gunman: Early O'Casey Play Comes to London," Daily Herald (London), (28 May 1927) p. 2.

2748 "London Theatres: The Shadow of a Gunman," Scotsman (Edinburgh), (28 May 1927) p. 2.

2749 Griffith, Hubert, "The Shadow of a Gunman: Mr. Sinclair's

Brilliant Comedy in Another O'Casey Play," Evening Standard (London), (28 May 1927) p. 4.

2750 P., W., "Mr. Sean O'Casey's First Play. And How He Slipped Away When the Curtain Fell. His Goad to Work," Evening News (London), (28 May 1927) p. 7.

2751 Agate, James, "Court: The Shadow of a Gunman," Sunday Times (London), (29 May 1927) p. 6.

2752 H., H., "Court: The Shadow of a Gunman, by Sean O'Casey," Observer (London), (29 May 1927) p. 15.

2753 "The Court: The Shadow of a Gunman," Stage (London), (2 June 1927) p. 16.

2754 Birrell, Francis, "Court Theatre: The Shadow of a Gunman by Sean O'Casey," Nation and Athenaeum (London), 41 (4 June 1927) 304.

2755 "The Shadow of a Gunman at the Court," Illustrated London News, 170 (4 June 1927) 1022.

2756 T.[Joseph Thorp], "At the Play," Punch (London), 172 (8 June 1927) 637.

2757 "A Troubled Ireland in The Shadow of a Gunman," Illustrated Sporting and Dramatic News (London), 115 (11 June 1927) 725.

2758 Farjeon, Herbert, "The London Stage: The Shadow of a Gunman," Graphic and National Weekly (London), 116 (11 June 1927) 441.

2759 Horsnell, Horace, "Early Sean O'Casey: The Shadow of a Gunman. Court Theatre," Outlook (London), 59 (11 June 1927) 770.

2760 Grein, J. T., "The World of the Theatre: The Shadow of a Gunman," Illustrated London News, 170 (18 June 1927) 1104.

2761 Brown, Ivor, "The Shadow of a Gunman by Sean O'Casey: The Court Theatre," Saturday Review (London), 143 (18 June 1927) 938.

2762 Jennings, Richard, "The Shadow of a Gunman at the Court Theatre," Spectator (London), 88 (18 June 1927) 1062.

2763 Charques, R. D., "The London Stage--Various New Productions," New York Times (26 June 1927) section 8, p. 1.

2764 Sutton, G[raham], "The Shadow of a Gunman," Bookman (London), 72 (Jul 1927) 248.

2765 S., W. N., "Court: The Shadow of a Gunman," Theatre World (London), 6 (Jul 1927) 10.

2766 Shipp, Horace, "Reality and the Theatre," English Review (London), 45 (1927) 110-12.

2767 D[onaghey], F[rederick], "Theatre," Chicago Daily Tribune (11 Apr 1929), p. 33 [at the Blackstone Theater].

2768 Atkinson, Brooks, "Sean O'Casey's First Drama Acted for First Time in New York: The Shadow of a Gunman," New York Times (31 Oct 1932) p. 18.

2769 O Meadhra, Sean, "Theatre: Poet and Peasant," Ireland Today (Dublin), I, no. 2 (1936), 62-5.

2770 Pollock, Arthur. "Theater Time: O'Casey's 'Shadow of Gunman' Done Creditably in Village," Daily Compass (N.Y.), (17 Jul 1951) p. 10 [At the Provincetown Playhouse].

2771 "Irish Theatre Club: The Shadow of a Gunman by Sean O'Casey," Times (London), (26 Jan 1953) p. 2.

2772 "Sean O'Casey Play to Open," Daily Worker (N.Y.), (11 Dec 1953) p. 7 [by Studio 8:40].

2773 Raymond, Harry, "The Shadow of a Gunman by Sean O'Casey," Daily Worker (N.Y.), (23 Feb 1954) p. 7.

2774 Eylau, Hans Ulrich, "Helden vom grossen Geschwätz," Berliner Zeitung (1 June 1954) p. 3.

2775 Rühle, Jürgen, "Schatten über der grünen Insel: Sean O'Caseys Harfe und Gewehr in den Kammerspielen des Deutschen Theaters," Sonntag (Berlin), (6 June 1954) p. 4.

2776 Schoen, Ernst, "Der Dramatiker Sean O'Casey," Theater der Zeit (Berlin), 9, no. 4 (1954) 19-21.

2777 Sander, H.-D., "Harfe und Gewehr von Sean O'Casey," Theater der Zeit (Berlin), 9, no. 7 (1954) 47-50.

2778 "Stage Group Scores with O'Casey," Daily People's World (San Francisco), (10 Jan 1955) p. 7 [By the Stage Society, Los Angeles].

2779 Olden, G. A., "Radio Review: Plays of O'Casey," Irish Times (Dublin), (19 May 1955) p. 8 [Radio Eireann].

2780 Wirth, A., "Warsztat rexyserki meodych," Po Prostu (Warsaw), no. 39 (27 Nov 1955) 4.

2781 "Dramatic By-Ways of Edinburgh," Times (London), (27 Aug 1956) p. 6 [By the Irish Festival Players].

2782 "The New Lindsey Theatre Club: A New Irish Company," Times (London), (10 Oct 1956) p. 3.

2783 B[aker], F. G., "The Shadow of a Gunman. By Sean O'Casey. First London Performance of This Revival by the Irish Players at the New Lindsey Theatre," Plays and Players (London), 4 (Nov 1956) 17.

2784 "Lyric Theatre, Hammersmith: The Shadow of a Gunman by Sean O'Casey," Times (London), (15 Jan 1957) p. 9.

2785 "London Letter: O'Casey in London," Irish Times (Dublin), (16 Jan 1957) p. 5.

2786 Hobson, Harold, "Irish Drama," Sunday Times (London), (20 Jan 1957) p. 13.

2787 Grahame, Paul, "The Poet and the Playboy," Daily Worker (London), (22 Jan 1957) p. 2.

2788 Conrad, Derek, "The Shadow of a Gunman. By Sean O'Casey. First Performance of This Revival at Lyric Theatre, Hammersmith," Plays and Players (London), 4 (Mar 1957) 17.

2789 Peck, Seymour, "Three with a Dream: Co-Producers and Directors of O'Casey Play Bring New Venture to Bijou," New York Times (16 Nov 1958) section 2, pp. 1, 3.

2790 Atkinson, Brooks, "A Prologue to Greatness: Shadow of a Gunman by O'Casey at Bijou," New York Times (21 Nov 1958) p. 26.

2791 Chapman, John, "O'Casey's The Shadow of a Gunman Stirringly Staged at the Bijou," New York Daily News (21 Nov 1958) p. 72.

2792 "O'Casey Play Divides New York Critics," Irish Times (Dublin), (22 Nov 1958) p. 4.

2793 Atkinson, Brooks, "Two by O'Casey: Cock-a-Doodle Dandy and The Shadow of a Gunman Open Within 9 Days," New York Times (23 Nov 1958) section 2, p. 1.

2794 Atkinson, Brooks, "Theatre Prose," New York Times (30 Nov 1958) section 2, p. 1.

2795 Hewes, Henry, "Where Is Fancy Bred?" Saturday Review of
      Literature (N.Y.), 41 (6 Dec 1958) 37.

2796 Tynan, Kenneth, "The Troubles in the Studio," New Yorker
      (N.Y.), 34 (6 Dec 1958) 112. Reprinted in Curtains (New
      York: Atheneum, 1961) pp. 285-8.

2797 "N.Y. Theatre Goes Irish: O'Casey Too Much for the Actors,"
      Times (London), (10 Dec 1958) p. 3.

2798 Driver, Tom F., "Studio Portrait: The Shadow of a Gunman
      by Sean O'Casey," Christian Century (Chicago), 75 (17 Dec
      1958) 1463.

2799 "The Shadow of a Gunman," America (N.Y.), 100 (20-27 Dec
      1958) 382.

2800 "The Shadow of a Gunman," Theatre Arts (N.Y.), 43 (Feb
      1959) 22-3.

2801 Wyatt, Euphemia van Rensselaer, "The Shadow of a Gunman,"
      Catholic World (N.Y.), 188 (Feb 1959) 417.

2802 Colin, Saul, "Plays and Players in New York: Tenement Trag-
      edy," Plays and Players (London), 6 (Feb 1959) 24.

2803 Kerr, Walter, "The Shadow of a Gunman and Cock-a-Doodle
      Dandy," Cincinnati Daily Enquirer (30 Nov 1959) p. 50.

2804 Pessemesse, Pierre, "Sean O'Casey au Theatre Quotidien de
      Marseille," Lettres françaises (Paris) no. 881 (22-28 June
      1961) 9.

2805 "Abbey Theatre's Comeback. Abbey Theatre, Dublin: The
      Shadow of a Gunman," Times (London), (20 Aug 1964) p. 12.

2806 Addison, Alan, "Two O'Casey Revivals: The Shadow of a Gun-
      man (Mermaid)," Morning Star (London), (7 Apr 1967) p. 2.

2807 Brien, Alan, "Challenge to Chaplin," Sunday Telegraph (Lon-
      don), (9 Apr 1967) p. 10.

2808 "Two Comedies by Sean O'Casey," Observer (London), (9 Apr
      1967) p. 25 [picture only].

2809 Hobson, Harold, "Triumphs Unforeseen," Sunday Times (Lon-
      don), (9 Apr 1967) p. 49.

2810 Sutherland, Jack, "Understanding O'Casey's Stature," Morning
      Star (London), (11 Apr 1967) p. 2.

2811 "Shadow of a Gunman in Belfast," Irish Times (Dublin), (5 Oct 1967) p. 8 [at the Grove Theatre].

2812 "Five European Cities Will See Abbey Players Next Year," Irish Times (Dublin), (15 Dec 1967) p. 1.

2813 Quidnunc, "An Irishman's Diary," Irish Times (Dublin), (8 Feb 1968) p. 11.

2814 "Abbey Players to Perform in Florence," Irish Times (Dublin), (20 Apr 1968) p. 1. See also picture, p. 13.

2815 Kelly, Seamus, "Florence Welcomes the Abbey Players," Irish Times (Dublin), (22 Apr 1968) p. 1.

2816 Kelly, Seamus, "14 Curtain Calls for Abbey Players," Irish Times (Dublin), (23 Apr 1968) pp. 1, 8 [at the Teatro della Pergola].

2817 Kelly, Seamus, "Italian Accolade for Abbey Players," Irish Times (Dublin), (27 Apr 1968) p. 6.

2818 Kelly, Henry, "Synge and O'Casey in the Abbey," Irish Times (Dublin), (14 May 1968) p. 8.

2819 Evans, Gareth Lloyd, "The Shadow of a Gunman," Guardian (London), (25 Feb 1978) p. 13 [At the Nottingham Playhouse].

2820 Young, B.A., "The Shadow of a Gunman," Financial Times (London), (27 Feb 1978) p. 11.

2821 Chaillet, Ned, "The Shadow of a Gunman," Times (London), (2 Mar 1978) p. 8.

2822 Seligsohn, Leo, "The Shadow of a Gunman from Sean O'Casey," Newsday (Long Island), (21 Sep 1979) 11, p. 16.

2823 Gussow, Mel, "Stage: O'Casey's The Shadow of a Gunman," New York Times (23 Sep 1979) p. 56.

2824 Gordon, Eric, "Viable production of Shadow," Daily World (N.Y.), (28 Sep 1979) p. 9.

2825 Roman, Robert, "O'Casey's Play Gets a Good Production," Irish Echo (N.Y.), (29 Sep 1979) p. 7.

2826 Fox, Terry Curtis, "Shadow of a Production," Village Voice (N.Y.), (1 Oct 1979) p. 90 [At the Symphony Space, New York].

2827 O'Clery, Conor, "O'Casey Play Staged in Tehran," Irish Times
      (Dublin), (28 Jan 1980) p. 7.

2828 Wardle, Irving, "The Shadow of a Gunman," Times (London),
      (2 Apr 1980) p. 11 [By the Royal Shakespeare Company at
      the Other Place, Stratford-upon-Avon].

2829 Billington, Michael, "When Poet and Killer Wear the Same Hat,"
      Guardian (London), (2 Apr 1980) p. 9.

2830 Coveney, Michael, "The Shadow of a Gunman," Financial Times
      (London), (2 Apr 1980) p. 19.

2831 Shorter, Eric, "The O'Casey Enigma," Daily Telegraph (London),
      (2 Apr 1980) p. 15.

2832 Billington, Michael, "A Tragic Dream," Guardian (London), (3
      Apr 1980) p. 11.

2833 Cushman, Robert, "On the Razor's Edge," Observer (London),
      (6 Apr 1980) p. 14.

2834 Fenton, James, "Theatre (The Shadow of a Gunman)," Sunday
      Times (London), (6 Apr 1980) p. 39.

2835 Matheson, T. P., "The Knocks and Blows of Irish History,"
      Times Literary Supplement (London), (11 Apr 1980), p. 413.

2836 Sennett, Graham, "Giving a Role Something Fresh," Evening
      Press (Dublin), (26 Apr 1980) p. 6 [To be presented at the
      Abbey Theatre on 8 May 1980].

2837 Aire, Sally, "The Shadow of a Gunman," Plays and Players
      (London), 27 (May 1980) 29.

2838 "His First Gunman," Evening Press (Dublin), (3 May 1980)
      p. 6.

2839 Finegan, John, "It's a Pedlar Hat-Trick for Donal McCann,"
      Evening Herald (Dublin), (3 May 1980) p. 6.

2840 "O'Casey Again," Hibernia (Dublin), (8 May 1980) p. 36.

2841 Nowlan, David, "The Shadow of a Gunman at the Abbey,"
      Irish Times (Dublin), (9 May 1980) p. 8.

2842 Rushe, Desmond, "MacAnna's Incisive Gunman," Irish Inde-
      pendent (Dublin), (9 May 1980) p. 6.

2843 [Sheridan, Michael], "Abbey's Brilliant Shadow," Irish Press
      (Dublin), (9 May 1980) p. 3.

2844 Houlihan, Con, "O'Casey Gets the Full Treatment," Evening Press (Dublin), (9 May 1980) p. 5.

2845 Finegan, John, "Abbey's 'Gunman' Topical As Ever," Evening Herald (Dublin), (9 May 1980) p. 24.

2846 Smith, Gus, "Best 'Gunman' I've Seen," Sunday Independent (Dublin), (11 May 1980) p. 30.

2847 Kehoe, Emmanuel, "Theatre," Sunday Press (Dublin), (11 May 1980) p. 19.

2848 Boland, John, "Theatre: Shades and Shadows," Hibernia (Dublin), (15 May 1980) p. 31.

2849 McKenna, David, "Drama & Dance," In Dublin, No. 102 (16-29 May 1980) 39.

2850 O Gallchóir, Dónall, "Drama: An Cathasach Og," Irish Press (Dublin), (17 May 1980) p. 8.

2851 MacAnna, Tomas, "The Shadow of a Gunman: A Note on the Political Background," Abbey Theatre Programme (May 1980) no page numbers. See also his "A Word or Two About 'Glittering Spears,'" ibid.

2852 Finegan, John, "The Shadow of a Gunman Tops the O'Casey List," Evening Herald (Dublin), (28 June 1980) p. 6.

2853 Evans, G. L., "Plays in Performance," Drama (London), no. 137 (July 1980) 58.

2854 "Off to Baltimore," Irish Times (Dublin), (19 June 1981) p. 9 [Editorial].

2855 Harriss, R. P., "Make Theater Festival an Annual Event," News-American (Baltimore), (21 June 1981).

2856 Dawson, Jack, "Echoes of Modern Gunfire for Abbey Theatre," Sun (Baltimore), (21 June 1981) pp. D1, D8.

2857 Roades, Toni, "Abbey Actor Gets His First U.S. Curtain," Sun (Baltimore), (22 June 1981) pp. B1, B6 [Micheal O Briain].

2858 Kernan, Michael, "Ringside at the Abbey," Washington Post (23 June 1981) pp. C1, C4.

2859 Lardner, James, "Abbey's 'Gunman' Calling Everyone's Bluff," Washington Post (24 June 1981) p. B3.

2860 Gedrone, Lou, "O'Casey's Play Is a Bit Dated But Still Power-
      ful and Relevant," Evening Sun (Baltimore), (23 June 1981)
      p. B5.

2861 Schoettler, Carl, "Eileen O'Casey, Reflections of 'My Sean,'
      17 Years after His Death," Evening Sun (Baltimore), (23
      June 1981) pp. B1, B7.

2862 Nowlan, David, "Abbey Encounters Language Barrier at U.S.
      Festival," Irish Times (Dublin), (24 June 1981) p. 11.

2863 Wilson, Craig, "Abbey Theatre: Superb," Saratogian (30 June
      1981) p. B6.

2864 Leonard, Mary Anne, "'Shadow of a Gunman': Timely and
      Timeless," Knickerbocker News (30 June 1981) p. C1.

2865 O'Brien, Jack, "A Bittersweet Masterpiece," Delmarva Farmer
      (30 June 1981) p. 19.

2866 Barnes, Clive, "International Theatre Fete a Milestone," New
      York Post (4 Jul 1981) p. 15.

2867 Kroll, Jack, "Bonanza in Baltimore," Newsweek (6 Jul 1981)
      p. 83.

2868 Vadeboncoeur, Joan E., "'Gunman' Tame for Dublin's Reputa-
      tion," Syracuse Herald-Journal (7 Jul 1981) p. D6.

2869 Haas, Barbara, "Dublin Abbey Players Give Spirited Perform-
      ance," Syracuse Post-Standard (7 Jul 1981) p. B8.

2870 Dunning, Jennifer, "Stage: Abbey Theatre Presents the 'Shadow
      of a Gunman,'" New York Times (14 Jul 1981) p. C12 [Rpt.
      in Irish Press (Dublin), 16 Jul 1981].

2871 Barnes, Clive, "Abbey's 'Gunman' Off-Target," New York Post
      (18 Jul 1981) p. 14.

2872 Connelly, Maureen, "O'Casey, the Abbey and Boston," Boston
      Irish Echo (18 Jul 1981) pp. 8, 9.

2873 Wardle, Irving, "Rivers of Ink," Times (London), (25 Jul 1981)
      p. 9 [By the Royal Shakespeare Company at the Warehouse
      Theatre, London].

2874 Billington, Michael, "'Shadow of a Gunman,'" Guardian (Lon-
      don), (25 Jul 1981) p. 11.

2875 Barber, John, "Gunman Without Guts," Daily Telegraph (Lon-
      don), (25 Jul 1981) p. 7.

2876 Carne, Rosalind, "'The Shadow of a Gunman,'" Financial Times (London), (27 Jul 1981) p. 11.

2877 Shulman, Milton, "A Poet Cornered," New Standard (London), (27 Jul 1981) p. 22.

2878 Marriott, R. B., "Warehouse: The Shadow of a Gunman," Stage & Television Today (London), (6 Aug 1981) p. 15.

2879 Nightingale, Benedict, "Theatre," New Statesman (London), (7 Aug 1981) p. 23.

2880 Trewin, J. C., "New Plays," Lady (London), (13 Aug 1981) p. 271.

CATHLEEN LISTENS IN

2881 C[ox], J. H., "Cathleen Listens In: A Topical Extravaganza," Irish Independent (Dublin), (2 Oct 1923) p. 6 [At the Abbey Theatre].

2882 O'D., F. J. H., "Cathleen Listens In: Topical Extravaganza at the Abbey Theatre," Evening Herald (Dublin), (2 Oct 1923) p. 2.

2883 Prior, "Abbey Theatre: Cathleen Listens In," Irish Times (Dublin), (2 Oct 1923) p. 4.

2884 McH., M. F., "Abbey Theatre: New One-Act Phantasy Produced," Freeman's Journal (Dublin), (2 Oct 1923) p. 4.

2885 "The Abbey: New One-Act Phantasy Produced. A Delightful Piece," Evening Telegraph (Dublin), (2 Oct 1923) p. 2.

2886 M[itchell], S[usan] L., "Dramatic Notes," Irish Statesman (Dublin), 1 (6 Oct 1923) 122.

2887 "Notes and News of Dublin Productions," Evening Telegraph (Dublin), (6 Oct 1923) p. 4.

2888 "Abbey Theatre," Irish Times (Dublin), (4 Mar 1925) p. 9.

2889 "Abbey Theatre," Irish Independent (Dublin), (4 Mar 1925) p. 8.

JUNO AND THE PAYCOCK

2890 "Abbey Theatre: Juno and the Paycock," Irish Times (Dublin), (4 Mar 1924) p. 8.

2891 Jacques, "Truth and Tragedy in a Realistic Play: Ireland's Civil War," Irish Independent (Dublin), (4 Mar 1924) p. 6.

2892 M., H. L., "Master of Irony: Success of Mr. O'Casey's New Play at Abbey," Freeman's Journal (Dublin), (4 Mar 1924) p. 4.

2893 Jacques, "Truth and Tragedy. Realistic Play Produced at the Abbey Theatre," Evening Herald (Dublin), (4 Mar 1924) p. 2.

2894 Lawrence, W. J., "Juno and the Paycock at the Abbey," Irish Statesman (Dublin), 2 (15 Mar 1924) 16.

2895 Gwynn, Stephen, "A Brilliant Irish Play," Living Age (Boston), 321 (3 May 1924) 869-70.

2896 Jewell, Edward Alden, "Juno and the Paycock," Nation (N.Y.), 118 (28 May 1924) 617-19.

2897 "Royalty Theatre: Juno and the Paycock by Sean O'Casey," Times (London), (17 Nov 1925) p. 12.

2898 B., I., "Dublin Fair City," Manchester Guardian (17 Nov 1925) p. 14.

2899 B., G., "Juno and the Paycock: Harrowing Realism in Play by Former Bricklayer," Daily Graphic (London), (17 Nov 1925) p. 2.

2900 P., A., "New Irish Play: Clever Presentation of Juno and the Paycock," Daily Sketch (London), (17 Nov 1925) p. 3. Pictures, p. 13.

2901 "London Theatres: Juno and the Paycock," Scotsman (Edinburgh), (17 Nov 1925) p. 9.

2902 "Juno and the Paycock: Mr. Arthur Sinclair's Delightful Acting," Daily Mail (London), (17 Nov 1925) p. 10.

2903 "Royalty Theatre: Juno and the Paycock, by Sean O'Casey," Daily Telegraph (London), (17 Nov 1925) p. 12.

2904 E., M., "Juno and the Paycock: Fine Irish Play Comes to London," Daily Herald (London), (17 Nov 1925) p. 5.

2905 G[riffith], H[ubert], "A Brilliant Irish Play," Evening Standard (London), (17 Nov 1925) p. 3.

2906 M., A. E., "A Page of Life from Dublin. Irish Players in Juno and the Paycock. An Unusual Medley," Evening News (London), (17 Nov 1925) p. 7.

2907 "The Royalty: Juno and the Paycock," Stage (London), (19 Nov 1925) p. 18.

2908 J., R., "A New Irish Dramatist," Spectator (London), 135 (21 Nov 1925) 923-4.

2909 Brown, Ivor, "Life by the Liffey: Juno and the Paycock by Sean O'Casey. Royalty Theatre," Saturday Review (London), 140 (21 Nov 1925) 594.

2910 Agate, James, "Royalty: Juno and the Paycock, a Tragedy by Sean O'Casey. Monday, November 16," Sunday Times (London), (22 Nov 1925) p. 6. Reprinted in The Contemporary Theatre, 1925 (London: Chapman & Hall, 1926) pp. 114-18; in Red Letter Nights (London: Jonathan Cape, 1944) pp. 230-3; in James Agate: An Anthology, ed. Herbert Van Thal (London: Rupert Hart-Davis, 1961) pp. 76-8; and in Sean O'Casey, ed. Ronald Ayling (London: Macmillan, 1969) pp. 76-8.

2911 H., H., "Royalty: Juno and the Paycock by Sean O'Casey," Observer (London), (22 Nov 1925) p. 11.

2912 Omicron, "From Alpha to Omega," Nation and Athenaeum (London), 38 (28 Nov 1925) 320-1.

2913 MacCarthy, Desmond, "Juno and the Paycock," New Statesman (London), 26 (28 Nov 1925) 207.

2914 "Juno and the Paycock at the Royalty," Illustrated London News, 167 (28 Nov 1925) 1104.

2915 St. John, Christopher, "The Irish Bubble," Time and Tide (London), 6 (4 Dec 1925) 1195-6.

2916 B., C. H., "Royalty: Juno and the Paycock," Theatre World and Illustrated Stage Review (London), 2 (Dec 1925) 65.

2917 Shipp, Horace, "Juno and the Paycock, by Sean O'Casey (Royalty Theatre)," English Review (London), 42 (Jan 1926) 112-15.

2918 Waldman, Milton, "Juno and the Paycock, by Sean O'Casey: Royalty Theatre," London Mercury, 13 (Feb 1926) 422-3.

2919   Atkinson, Brooks, "Irish Folk Life in a Tragedy: Juno and the Paycock. A Play in Three Acts by Sean O'Casey," New York Times (16 Mar 1926) p. 22 [At the Mayfair Theater, New York].

2920   Mantle, Burns, "Juno and the Paycock: A Sad Irish Drama," New York Daily News (17 Mar 1926) p. 30.

2921   Atkinson, Brooks, "O'Casey at the Bat: Juno and the Paycock --His First American Production," New York Times (21 Mar 1926) section 8, pp. 1-2.

2922   "The Irish Prize Play," New York Times (26 Mar 1926) p. 20.

2923   B., D. W., "Broad Comedy. Stark Realism out of Dublin: O'Casey's Play of Juno and the Paycock," Boston Evening Transcript (26 Mar 1926) p. 8.

2924   G., G. W., "The Theatre," New Yorker, 2 (27 Mar 1926) 25.

2925   Krutch, Joseph Wood, "A Dublin Success," Nation (N.Y.), 122 (31 Mar 1926) 348.

2926   Nathan, George Jean, "Judging the Shows," Judge (N.Y.), 90 (10 Apr 1926) 15.

2927   "The Talk of the Town," Dublin Opinion, 5 (Apr 1926) 38.

2928   Carb, David, "Juno and the Paycock," Vogue (N.Y.), 67 (15 May 1926) 98, 140.

2929   Skinner, R. Dana, "From Triumph to Illusion," Independent (N.Y.), 116 (15 May 1926) 580.

2930   Stone, Melville E., "A New View of Juno," New York Times (23 May 1926) section 8, p. 1.

2931   Barrett, Larry, "The New Yorker," Bookman (N.Y.), 58 (May 1926) 343-4.

2932   Kalonyme, Louis, "Paycocks Under the Moon," Arts and Decoration (N.Y.), 25 (May 1926) 64, 92.

2933   Brown, John Mason, "The Rush Hour on Broadway," Theatre Arts Monthly (N.Y.), 10 (May 1926) 286-9.

2934   Hornblow, Arthur, "Mr. Hornblow Goes to the Play," Theatre Magazine (N.Y.), 43 (May 1926) 15.

2935   Atkinson, Brooks, "Again the Irish Players: Juno and the

Paycock. A Play in Three Parts by Sean O'Casey," New York Times (20 Dec 1927) p. 32 [By the Irish Players at the Gallo Theater, New York].

2936 Krutch, Joseph Wood, "Poet Laureate," Nation (N.Y.), 125 (21 Dec 1927) 718.

2937 Brackett, Charles, "Humble Pie with a Drop of Vinegar," New Yorker, 3 (31 Dec 1927) 23.

2938 Doyle, Mary Agnes, "Sean O'Casey Comes to Chicago," Drama (Chicago), 118 (Dec 1927) 68-70.

2939 "A New York Diary," New Republic (N.Y.), 53 (4 Jan 1928) 191-2.

2940 Carb, David, "Juno and the Paycock," Vogue (N.Y.), 71 (15 Feb 1928) 87, 122.

2941 Brown, John Mason, "The Laughter of the Gods: Broadway in Review," Theatre Arts Monthly (N.Y.), 12 (Feb 1928) 91-5.

2942 D[onaghey], F[rederick], "Juno and the Paycock: Comedy in Three Acts by Sean O'Casey," Chicago Tribune (5 Mar 1928) p. 33 [At the Blackstone Theater, Chicago].

2943 Seldes, Gilbert, "The Theatre," Dial (Chicago), 84 (Mar 1928) 259-60.

2944 "Abbey Theatre's American Tour," Manchester Guardian Weekly, 25 (7 Aug 1931) 114.

2945 P., H. T., "O'Casey Gains Place at Last on Our Stage: Juno and the Paycock Acted by the Abbey Company to Answering Audience," Boston Evening Transcript (13 Apr 1932) pt 2, p. 5.

2946 G., W. E., "Hollis Street: Juno and the Paycock," Boston Herald (13 Apr 1932) p. 20.

2947 Atkinson, Brooks, "Tatterdemalions of Dublin in Juno and the Paycock," New York Times (20 Oct 1932) p. 24.

2948 [Ould, Herman], "No Bricks for Irish Players This Time," Literary Digest (N.Y.), 114 (19 Nov 1932) 17-18.

2949 "Little Theatre: Juno and the Paycock by Sean O'Casey," Times (London), (2 Mar 1934) p. 12.

2950 C., J., "Juno and the Paycock: Blarney, Humour and Sentiment in Revival of Charming Irish Play," <u>Daily Sketch</u> (London), (2 Mar 1934) p. 2.

2951 Darlington, W. A., "Notable Irish Play Revived: <u>Juno and the Paycock</u>," <u>Daily Telegraph</u> (London), (2 Mar 1934) p. 10.

2952 Disher, Willson, "<u>Juno and the Paycock</u>: Fine Acting in Revival," <u>Daily Mail</u> (London), (2 Mar 1934) p. 21.

2953 "The 'Paycock' Returns," <u>Evening Standard</u> (London), (2 Mar 1934) p. 11.

2954 "<u>Juno and the Paycock</u>: First-Rate Acting by the Irish Players," <u>Evening News</u> (London), (2 Mar 1934) p. 3.

2955 Brown, Ivor, "Little: <u>Juno and the Paycock</u>, by Sean O'Casey," <u>Observer</u> (London), (4 Mar 1934) p. 17.

2956 "The Little: <u>Juno and the Paycock</u>," <u>Stage</u> (London), (8 Mar 1934) p. 10.

2957 B., C., "<u>Juno and the Paycock</u>. Sean O'Casey. Little," <u>Time and Tide</u> (London), 15 (10 Mar 1934) 326.

2958 "Embassy Theatre: <u>Juno and the Paycock</u> by Sean O'Casey," <u>Times</u> (London), (27 June 1934) p. 14.

2959 "An O'Casey Revival," <u>New Statesman and Nation</u> (London), 7 (30 June 1934) 995.

2960 Gregory, Russell, "Embassy Theatre: <u>Juno and the Paycock</u> by Sean O'Casey," <u>Saturday Review</u> (London), 157 (30 June 1934) 774.

2961 Mantle, Burns, "Abbey Players Turn to O'Casey: True Picture of the Dublin Tenement Is Colorfully Acted," <u>New York Daily News</u> (24 Nov 1934) p. 23.

2962 Ervine, St. John, "At the Play," <u>Observer</u> (London), (27 Jan 1935) p. 15.

2963 "Q Theatre: <u>Juno and the Paycock</u> by Sean O'Casey," <u>Times</u> (London), (13 Jul 1937) p. 12.

2964 H[art]-D[avis], R[upert], "<u>Juno and the Paycock</u> by Sean O'Casey: At the Haymarket Theatre," <u>Spectator</u> (London), 158 (13 Aug 1937) 275.

2965 "<u>Juno and the Paycock</u> at the Haymarket," <u>New Statesman and Nation</u> (London), 14 (14 Aug 1937) 252.

2966 Brown, Ivor, "Theatre Royal, Haymarket: Juno and the Paycock by Sean O'Casey," Observer (London), (15 Aug 1937) p. 11.

2967 Morgan, Charles, "Juno and the O'Casey," New York Times (29 Aug 1937) section 10, p. 2.

2968 Cookman, A. V., "Juno and the Paycock: By Sean O'Casey," London Mercury, 36 (Sep 1937) 469.

2969 Atkinson, Brooks, "Sean O'Casey's Juno and the Paycock Acted by the Abbey Theatre Troupe," New York Times (7 Dec 1937) p. 32 [At the Ambassador Theatre, New York].

2970 Atkinson, Brooks, "The Play: Barry Fitzgerald and Sara Allgood Resume Their Original Parts in Juno and the Paycock," New York Times (17 Jan 1940) p. 24 [At the Mansfield Theater].

2971 Atkinson, Brooks, "Box Office Now Open: Juno and the Paycock," New York Times (21 Jan 1940) section 9, p. 1.

2972 Atkinson, Brooks, "Juno and the Paycock," New York Times (28 Jan 1940) section 9, p. 1.

2973 "Old Play in Manhattan," Time (N.Y.), 35 (29 Jan 1940) 36.

2974 Nathan, George Jean, "The Best of the Irish," Newsweek (N.Y.), 15 (29 Jan 1940) 33.

2975 Vernon, Grenville, "Juno and the Paycock," Commonweal (N.Y.), 31 (2 Feb 1940) 327-8.

2976 Jordan, Elizabeth, "Juno and the Paycock," America (N.Y.), 62 (10 Feb 1940) 502.

2977 Connolly, Terence L., "No Hypersensitiveness," America (N.Y.), 62 (2 Mar 1940) 578 [Letter to the Editor in reply to Elizabeth Jordan's review].

2978 Gassner, John, "Stage," Direction (N.Y.), 3 (Mar 1940) 16.

2979 Wyatt, Euphemia van Rensselaer, "Juno and the Paycock," Catholic World (N.Y.), 150 (Mar 1940) 730-1.

2980 Gilder, Rosamond, "Juno and the Paycock," Theatre Arts (N.Y.), 24 (Mar 1940) 162, 165.

2981 Fallon, Gabriel, "Sitting at the Play. The Month's Theatre: Arthur Sinclair in Sean O'Casey's Juno and the Paycock,"

Irish Monthly (Dublin), 69 (Jul 1941) 403-6 [At the Abbey Theatre].

2982 Fallon, Gabriel, "The Nobility and Dignity of Juno," Standard (Dublin), 23 (16 Mar 1951) 5 [At the Abbey Theatre].

2983 Arundel, Honor, "Radio: Two Rebellions," Daily Worker (London), (19 Mar 1951) p. 2 [Broadcast play].

2984 "Irving Theatre: Juno and the Paycock by Sean O'Casey," Times (London), (11 Sep 1953) p. 2.

2985 "New Lindsey Theatre: Juno and the Paycock by Sean O'Casey," Times (London), (31 Mar 1954) p. 5.

2986 Igoe, W. J., "London Letter," America (N.Y.), 91 (14 Aug 1954) 480-1.

2987 "Sean O'Casey Play Next at Greenwich Mews," Daily Worker (N.Y.), (13 Jan 1955) p. 7.

2988 Atkinson, Brooks, "O'Casey's Dublin Tenements: Juno and the Paycock Revived Downtown," New York Times (24 Feb 1955) p. 20 [At the Greenwich Mews Theatre, as a community project sponsored by the Village Presbyterian Church and the Brotherhood Synagogue].

2989 Raymond, Harry, "Juno and the Paycock at the Mews Theatre," Daily Worker (N.Y.), (28 Feb 1955) p. 7.

2990 Leventhal, A. J., "Dramatic Commentary: Juno and the Paycock. By Sean O'Casey. Radio Eireann," Dublin Magazine, 31 (Jul-Sep 1955) 53.

2991 "The Gramophone: Irish Drama on Record. Juno and the Paycock," Times (London), (18 Aug 1956) p. 9.

2992 Macleod, Alison, "Radio & TV: If Only We Could See It," Daily Worker (London), (1 Mar 1957) p. 2.

2993 Garrick, D., "Green Room," Plays and Players (London), 5 (Jul 1958) 23.

2994 Quidnunc, "An Irishman's Diary," Irish Times (Dublin), (19 Aug 1958) p. 6 [Juno as musical on Broadway soon].

2995 "Sean O'Casey on Broadway," Daily Worker (London), (11 Sep 1958) p. 3.

2996 Schumach, Murray, "O'Casey's Juno, Singing," New York Times (1 Mar 1959) section 2, p. 1 [At Winter Garden Theatre].

2997 Atkinson, Brooks, "A Musical Juno Arrives: Show Based on Play by O'Casey Opens," New York Times (10 Mar 1959) p. 41.

2998 "Sean O'Casey Play as Musical: Juno and the Paycock," Times (London), (11 Mar 1959) p. 13.

2999 Atkinson, Brooks, "Musical Juno: O'Casey Play Converted into Another Medium," New York Times (15 Mar 1959) section 2, p. 1.

3000 "Juno Posts Closing Notice," New York Times (17 Mar 1959) p. 42.

3001 Driver, Tom F., "O'Casey's Juno as Musical," New Republic (N.Y.), 140 (30 Mar 1959) 20-1.

3002 "O'Casey-Hansberry," New York Times (28 June 1959) section 2, p. 3 [Raisin in the Sun owes much to Juno and the Paycock].

3003 Muller, André, "O'Casey--Zu Selten gespielt: Juno und der Pfau in Wuppertal," Theater der Zeit (Berlin), no. 5 (1959) 50-2.

3004 Marcel, Gabriel, "Le Théâtre," Nouvelles littéraires (Paris), (20 Apr 1961) p. 10.

3005 L., J., "Au Théâtre de la Renaissance: Junon et le paon de Sean O'Casey par la Comédie de l'Ouest," Figaro littéraire (Paris), (22 Apr 1961) p. 16.

3006 Bourget-Pailleron, Robert, "Revue dramatique. Renaissance: La Comédie de l'Ouest: Jean Goubert et Guy Parigot présentent Junon et le paon," Revue des deux mondes (Paris), (1 May 1961) pp. 154-6.

3007 "O'Casey to Allow 2 Plays to Be Performed in Dublin," New York Times (6 Nov 1963) p. 35 [Juno and the Paycock and The Plough and the Stars as a preview for London].

3008 O'Casey, Sean, "Behind the Ban," New York Times (5 Jan 1964) section 2, pp. 1, 3 [Lifting the ban on Juno and the Paycock and The Plough and the Stars].

3009 "O'Casey Angry About Strike Call Now," Irish Times (Dublin), (14 Apr 1964) p. 1.

3010 Shorter, Eric, "O'Casey Old Rogues at Their Best," Daily Telegraph (London), (21 Apr 1964) p. 18.

3011 "Abbey-O'Casey Reunion. Aldwych Theatre: Juno and the Paycock," Times (London), (21 Apr 1964) p. 14.

3012 Hope-Wallace, Philip, "Juno and the Paycock at the Aldwych," Guardian (London), (21 Apr 1964) p. 9.

3013 Kelly, Seamus, "Juno Is Received Coolly in London," Irish Times (Dublin), (21 Apr 1964) p. 1.

3014 Shulman, Milton, "Begorra! Where's That Irish Sparkle?" Evening Standard (London), (21 Apr 1964) p. 5.

3015 Brien, Alan, "Theatre: Juno at the Aldwych," Sunday Telegraph (London), (26 Apr 1964) p. 12.

3016 Lenoir, Jean-Pierre, "Abbey Troupe Gives Juno at Paris Fete," New York Times (6 May 1964) p. 41 [At Sarah Bernhardt Theatre].

3017 "Abbey Reply to O'Casey: In No Position to Pronounce Judgment," Irish Times (Dublin), (3 Jul 1964) p. 1. See "Abbey Has Been Deteriorating for Years" (4 Jul 1964) p. 1.

3018 Shaw, Iain, "Juno and The Plough," Encore (London), 2 (Jul-Aug 1964) 52-4.

3019 "Derry Visit Subject of O'Casey's Letter to Abbey," Irish Times (Dublin), (3 Nov 1964) p. 11.

3020 W[endt], E[rnst], "Gespenstische Clowns: Hans Mahnke und Bruno Hübner in O'Caseys Juno und der Pfau," Theater heute (Hannover), 6 (May 1965) 46-7.

3021 "O'Casey: Victim of His Own Legend. The National Theatre: Juno and the Paycock by Sean O'Casey," Times (London), (27 Apr 1966) p. 7.

3022 Lewis, Peter, "O'Casey Seen for the First Time. Juno and the Paycock, by Sean O'Casey. National Theatre Company, Old Vic," Daily Mail (London), (27 Apr 1966) p. 18.

3023 Kretzmer, Herbert, "English Beat the Irish. Old Vic: Juno and the Paycock," Daily Express (London), (27 April 1966) p. 4.

3024 Hope-Wallace, Philip, "Juno and the Paycock at the National Theatre," Guardian (London), (27 Apr 1966) p. 9.

3025 Darlington, W. A., "Joyce Redman Achieves Wonders as Juno," Daily Telegraph (London), (27 Apr 1966) p. 19.

3026 Shulman, Milton, "Juno and the Paycock at the National The-
     atre," Evening Standard (London), (27 Apr 1966) p. 4.

3027 Barker, Felix, "It's a Darlin' Thing--This Paycock," Evening
     News (London), (27 Apr 1966) p. 5.

3028 Sutherland, Jack, "National Theatre Honours O'Casey's Memory:
     Juno and the Paycock," Morning Star (London), (28 Apr 1966)
     p. 2.

3029 H., P., "O'Casey Triumphs at the National Theatre," Stage and
     Television Today (London), (28 Apr 1966) p. 15.

3030 Bryden, Ronald, "Sir Laurence's Line," Observer (London), (1
     May 1966) p. 24.

3031 Hobson, Harold, "Theatre," Sunday Times (London), (1 May
     1966) p. 29.

3032 Brien, Alan, "Theatre," Sunday Telegraph (London), (1 May
     1966) p. 12.

3033 V., L., "A New Tribute to O'Casey. Juno and the Paycock:
     Old Vic," Time and Tide (London), 47 (5-11 May 1966) 29.

3034 Jones, Mervyn, "O'Casey's Pessimism," Tribune (London), 30
     (6 May 1966) 14.

3035 Jones, D. A. N., "Designs for Dying," New Statesman and Na-
     tion (London), 71 (6 May 1966) 662.

3036 Spurling, Hilary, "A Darlin' Paycock: Juno and the Paycock
     (Old Vic)," Spectator (London), 216 (6 May 1966) 570.

3037 Trewin, J. C., "Theatre," Illustrated London News (7 May
     1966) p. 38.

3038 Leonard, Hugh, "Olivier's O'Casey," Plays and Players (Lon-
     don), 13 (June 1966) 25.

3039 Quidnunc, "An Irishman's Diary," Irish Times (Dublin), (21
     Jul 1966) p. 7.

3040 Kelly, Seamus, "O'Casey's Juno at the Gaiety," Irish Times
     (Dublin), (2 Aug 1966) p. 8.

3041 Quidnunc, "An Irishman's Diary: At the Play," Irish Times
     (Dublin), (17 Aug 1966) p. 7.

3042 Bastable, Adolphus, "Our Theatres in the Sixties," Shavian
     (London), 3 (winter 1966-7) 20.

3043 Kelly, Seamus, "Abbey: A Gallant Juno Lacked the Old Magic,"
      Irish Times (Dublin), (7 Oct 1969) p. 8.

3044 Colgan, Gerald, "Dublin," Plays and Players (London), 17
      (Dec 1969) 54.

3045 Mastroianni, Tony, "Characters star in O'Casey Play," Cleve-
      land Press (13 Jul 1979) p. 56 [At Great Lakes Shakespeare
      Festival, Lakewood, Ohio].

3046 Maupin, Betsey, "Great Lakes' 'Juno' Is a Powerful Play,"
      Chronicle-Telegram (Elyria, Ohio), (13 Jul 1979) p. 1.

3047 Ward, Leah, "Sense of Endurance," Journal (Lorain, Ohio),
      (13 Jul 1979) p. 18.

3048 Ward, Michael, "O'Casey's Play Shows It Still Has Relevance,"
      Plain Dealer (Cleveland), (14 Jul 1979) p. 4D.

3049 Lowery, Robert G., "Traveling to Ohio for a Classic," Daily
      World (N.Y.), (26 Jul 1979) p. 24.

3050 Finegan, John, "Prestigious," Evening Herald (Dublin), (15
      Dec 1979) p. 8 [To be presented at the Abbey Theatre on
      27 Dec 1979].

3051 Rocke, William, "Gala Headache," Sunday Press (Dublin), (16
      Dec 1979) p. 22.

3052 Smith, Gus, "Theatre," Sunday Independent (Dublin), (16 Dec
      1979) p. 1.

3053 Cassidy, Ces, "Play Notes," Irish Press (Dublin), (20 Dec 1979)
      p. 9.

3054 Sennett, Graham, "What Is the Stars?" Evening Press (Dublin),
      (22 Dec 1979) p. 6.

3055 Smith, Gus, "Gabriel Will Miss the Celebration," Sunday Inde-
      pendent (Dublin), (23 Dec 1979) p. 2 [Gabriel Fallon].

3056 "The Abbey's 75 Years Call Up Memories," Irish Times (Dublin),
      (28 Dec 1979) p. 5.

3057 "The Abbey Celebrates Its 75th," Irish Press (Dublin), (28
      Dec 1979) p. 3.

3058 "Hillery Hails Vigour of the Abbey," Irish Times (Dublin), (28
      Dec 1979) p. 5.

3059 Dryson, Sean, "Juno Jubilee for the Great Old Lady," Irish Press (Dublin), (28 Dec 1979) p. 3.

3060 "Hyde's Link with Theatre Recalled," Irish Times (Dublin), (28 Dec 1979) p. 5.

3061 Sheridan, Michael, "'Juno' Muted by Stage Fright," Irish Press (Dublin), (28 Dec 1979) p. 3.

3062 Nowlan, David, "Juno and the Paycock at the Abbey," Irish Times (Dublin), (28 Dec 1979) p. 5.

3063 Walsh, Caroline, "Theatre's Past Recalled," Irish Times (Dublin), (28 Dec 1979) p. 5.

3064 Sheridan, Michael, "Grande Dame of the Irish Theatre Back on Familiar Ground," Irish Press (Dublin), (28 Dec 1979) p. 3.

3065 Finegan, John, "Eloquent 'Juno' at the Abbey," Evening Herald (Dublin), (28 Dec 1979) p. 9.

3066 O'Sullivan, Terry, "Gabriel, the Last Survivor of the First 'Juno,'" Evening Press (Dublin), (28 Dec 1979) p. 11 [Gabriel Fallon].

3067 Rushe, Desmond, "Lustrous Lost in O'Casey Classic," Irish Independent (Dublin), (29 Dec 1979) p. 7.

3068 Kehoe, Emmanuel, "Theatre: Juno and the Paycock," Sunday Press (Dublin), (30 Dec 1979) p. 8.

3069 Brophy, Eanna, "A Lack Lustre Juno," Sunday Press (Dublin), (30 Dec 1979) p. 8.

3070 Smith, Gus, "Theatre: This 'Juno' Left Me Unmoved," Sunday Independent (Dublin), (30 Dec 1979) p. 2.

3071 Fenton, James, "How the Paycock Lost His Passion," Sunday Times (London), (30 Dec 1979) p. 43.

3072 Houlihan, Con, "Juno: Is It a Good Play?" Evening Press (Dublin), (31 Dec 1979) p. 3.

3073 Chaillet, Ned, "Juno and the Abbey Habit," The Times (London), (31 Dec 1979) p. 11.

3074 Cronin, Colm, "Theatre: Pace by Pace," Hibernia (Dublin), (3 Jan 1980) p. 27.

3075 Foley, Donal, "The Abbey's Night," Irish Times (Dublin), (5 Jan 1980) p. 12.

3076 O Gallchóir, Dónall, "Drama: 75 bliain ag dul i dtreise," Irish Press (Dublin), (5 Jan 1980) p. 8.

3077 O'F., P., "Theatre Topics," Westmeath Examiner (Mullingar), (12 Jan 1980) p. 2.

3078 Bradley, Richard, "Abbey 75th Anniversary: O'Casey's Juno and the Paycock Still a Play of Enormous Impact," Irish Tatler (Dublin), (Jan-Feb 1980) 22.

3079 Hennessy, Liam, "Delusion & Despair," USI News (Dublin), 9 (Feb 1980) 8.

3080 Chaillet, Ned, "Juno and the Paycock," The Times (London), (8 Oct 1980) p. 9 [By the Royal Shakespeare Company at the Aldwych Theatre, London].

3081 Billington, Michael, "Juno and the Paycock," Guardian (London), (8 Oct 1980) p. 10.

3082 Barber, John, "Authentic Slum," Daily Telegraph (London), (8 Oct 1980) p. 13.

3083 Tinker, Jack, "Stunning Centenary Tribute to O'Casey," Daily Mail (London), (8 Oct 1980) p. 3.

3084 Barker, Felix, "A Great Night for the Irish," Evening News (London), (8 Oct 1980) p. 13.

3085 Shulman, Milton, "Mrs. Boyle's Law," Evening Standard (London), (8 Oct 1980) p. 22.

3086 Cushman, Robert, "Feathered Friends," Observer (London), (12 Oct 1980) p. 37.

3087 Fenton, James, "Theatre: Juno and the Paycock," Sunday Times (London), (12 Oct 1980) p. 40.

3088 King, Francis, "Flying into Reality," Sunday Telegraph (London), (12 Oct 1980) p. 16.

3089 Morley, Sheridan, "Dublin Troubles," Punch (London), (15 Oct 1980) p. 655.

3090 Elsom, John, "Hymn Against Hate," Listener (London), (16 Oct 1980) p. 518.

3091 Marriott, R. B., "Juno and the Paycock at the Aldwych," Stage (London), (16 Oct 1980) p. 11.

3092 Mahon, Derek, "When Irish Eyes Are Shutting," Times Literary Supplement (London), (17 Oct 1980) p. 1172.

3093 Nightingale, Benedict, "Women Pay," New Statesman (London), 100 (17 Oct 1980) p. 33.

3094 Robertson, Bryan, "Melodic," Spectator (London), 245 (18 Oct 1980) p. 27.

3095 Trewin, J. C., "Juno and the Paycock," Lady (London), (23 Oct 1980) p. 687.

3096 Christiansen, Richard, "Masterpiece 'Juno and the Paycock' Is Brought to Life," Chicago Tribune (28 Mar 1981), section 1, p. 15 [At the Court Theatre of the University of Chicago].

3097 Taylor, John Russell, "London," Drama (London), no. 139 (First Quarter 1981) 36.

NANNIE'S NIGHT OUT

3098 C[ox], J. H., "Abbey Activities: Mr. Sean O'Casey's New Play," Irish Independent (Dublin), (30 Sep 1924) p. 6.

3099 "Abbey First Night: S. O'Casey's New Picture of Slum Life. Curious Humour," Evening Telegraph (Dublin), (30 Sep 1924) p. 2.

3100 "New Comedy at the Abbey: Nannie's Night Out," Irish Times (Dublin), (30 Sep 1924) p. 4.

3101 Lonndubh, An, "The Worker at the Abbey: Mr. O'Casey's New Play," Voice of Labour (Dublin), (4 Oct 1924) p. 7.

3102 O., Y. [George Russell], "Nannie's Night Out," Irish Statesman (Dublin), 3 (11 Oct 1924) 144-5.

3103 Buggy, Bertha, "From the Back Seats," Irish Statesman (Dublin), 3 (18 Oct 1924) 175.

3104 Malone, A.E., "From the Stalls," Dublin Magazine, 2 (Nov 1924) 221-2.

THE PLOUGH AND THE STARS

3105 "The Plough and the Stars: Mr. Sean O'Casey's New Play,"

Irish Times (Dublin), (12 Jan 1926) p. 9 [At the Abbey Theatre, Dublin].

3106 "The Plough and the Stars: Mr. Sean O'Casey's New Play," Irish Times (Dublin), (9 Feb 1926) p. 7.

3107 G., J. W., "Sean O'Casey's New Play: The Plough and the Stars," Irish Independent (Dublin), (9 Feb 1926) p. 9.

3108 "Plough and Stars: Sean O'Casey's New Play at the Abbey," Evening Herald (Dublin), (9 Feb 1926) p. 2.

3109 "Abbey Theatre Scene: An Attempt to Stop Mr. O'Casey's New Play. Fight on Stage," Irish Times (Dublin), (12 Feb 1926) pp. 7-8.

3110 "Riotous Scenes in Abbey Theatre. Fights with Actors on the Stage. Women Engage in Fierce Fistic Battles. Hours of Uproar," Irish Independent (Dublin), (12 Feb 1926) p. 7.

3111 "New Play Resented. Last Night's Scenes in the Abbey Theatre. 1916 Memories. Onlooker's Impressions of People's Protest," Evening Herald (Dublin), (12 Feb 1926) p. 1.

3112 S[tarkie], W[alter], "The Plough and the Stars," Irish Statesman (Dublin), 5 (13 Feb 1926) 716-17.

3113 "Cant and Facts," Irish Times (Dublin), (13 Feb 1926) p. 6 [Leading article].

3114 Lonndubh, An, "The Plough and the Stars: Sean O'Casey's New Play at the Abbey," Voice of Labour (Dublin), (13 Feb 1926) p. 4.

3115 Gwynn, Stephen, "The Dublin Play Riots: Accounts by Eye-Witnesses," Observer (London), (14 Feb 1926) p. 16.

3116 McQueen, John, "Letter to the Editor," Irish Independent (Dublin), (15 Feb 1926) p. 8.

3117 Sheehy-Skeffington, Mrs. H[annah], "Letter to the Editor," Irish Independent (Dublin), 15 Feb 1926) p. 8. See O'Casey's reply (20 Feb 1926) p. 8.

3118 O'Shea, Sean, "Letter to the Editor," Irish Independent (Dublin), (15 Feb 1926) p. 8.

3119 Perrin, J. H., "Letter to the Editor," Irish Independent (Dublin), (15 Feb 1926) p. 8.

3120 O'Casey, Sean, "The Plough and the Stars: A Reply to the Critics," Irish Times (Dublin), (19 Feb 1926) p. 6.

3121 M., A. N., "A Bookman's Notes: Art and the Patriot," Manchester Guardian Weekly, 14 (19 Feb 1926) 152.

3122 Spectator, "Politics and People," Irish Statesman (Dublin), 5 (20 Feb 1926) 736-7.

3123 O'Flaherty, Liam, "The Plough and the Stars," Irish Statesman (Dublin), 5 (20 Feb 1926) 739-40 [Letter to the Editor].

3124 Clarke, Austin, "The Plough and the Stars," Irish Statesman (Dublin), 5 (20 Feb 1926) 740 [Letter to the Editor].

3125 "At Home and Abroad," Illustrated London News (London), 168 (20 Feb 1926) 322.

3126 Malone, Andrew E., "Shattered Dreams," Voice of Labour (Dublin), 8 (20 Feb 1926) 1.

3127 "At the Abbey," Voice of Labour (Dublin), 8 (20 Feb 1926) 4.

3128 Sheehy-Skeffington, Mrs. H[annah], "The Plough and the Stars: Reply to Mr. O'Casey," Irish Independent (Dublin), (23 Feb 1926) p. 9.

3129 O'Casey, Sean, "Mr. O'Casey's Play: Author's Rejoinder," Irish Independent (Dublin), (26 Feb 1926) p. 8 [Letter to the Editor in reply to Mrs. Sheehy-Skeffington's letter of 15 Feb].

3130 O'Higgins, Brigid, "The Plough and the Stars: As a Woman Saw It," Irish Statesman (Dublin), 5 (27 Feb 1926) 770-1.

3131 Fallon, Gabriel, "The Plough and the Stars," Irish Statesman (Dublin), 5 (27 Feb 1926) 768 [Letter to the Editor].

3132 Donaghy, Lyle, "The Plough and the Stars," Irish Statesman (Dublin), 5 (27 Feb 1926) 767-8 [Letter to the Editor].

3133 "O'Casey and The Voice," Voice of Labour (Dublin), 8 (27 Feb 1926) p. 5 [Letter to the Editor by O'Casey and the Editor's reply].

3134 "The Plough and the Stars: Criticism in a Lecture. The Author's Reply," Irish Times (Dublin), (2 Mar 1926) p. 5.

3135 Higgins, F. R., "The Plough and the Stars," Irish Statesman (Dublin), 5 (6 Mar 1926) 797-8 [Letter to the Editor].

3136 Spectator, "Politics and People," Irish Statesman (Dublin), 5 (6 Mar 1926) 794.

3137 O'Sullivan, Kathleen, "The Plough and the Stars," Irish Statesman (Dublin), 6 (13 Mar 1926) 11-12 [Letter to the Editor].

3138 A Seeker of Truth, "The Plough and the Stars," Irish Statesman (Dublin), 6 (13 Mar 1926) 12 [Letter to the Editor].

3139 Hayes, J. J., "Another by O'Casey," New York Times (21 Mar 1926) section 8, p. 2.

3140 "Dramatic Unrest in Ireland," Living Age (Boston), 328 (27 Mar 1926) 693-4.

3141 "Editorial," Catholic Bulletin (Dublin), 16 (Mar 1926) 242-8.

3142 "The Plough and the Stars," Catholic Bulletin (Dublin), 16 (Mar 1926), 279-82.

3143 Booth, Arthur, "Lies and Libels," Dublin Opinion, 5 (Mar 1926), 1.

3144 K., L., "The Plough and the Stars: The Play of the Season," Crystal (Dublin), 1 (Mar 1926) 47-8, 51.

3145 "The Talk of the Town," Dublin Opinion, 5 (Mar 1926) 6.

3146 "Fortune Theatre: The Plough and the Stars by Sean O'Casey," Times (London), (14 May 1926) p. 4.

3147 "Wonderful London Yesterday," Daily Graphic (London), (14 May 1926) p. 2.

3148 Agate, James, "Fortune: The Plough and the Stars," Sunday Times (London), (16 May 1926) p. 3. Reprinted in Red Letter Nights (London: Jonathan Cape, 1944) pp. 233-6; and in Sean O'Casey, ed. Ronald Ayling (London: Macmillan, 1969) pp. 79-81.

3149 E., St. J., "The Plough and the Stars, by Sean O'Casey," Observer (London), (16 May 1926) p. 4.

3150 Atkinson, Brooks, "Disillusion in Irish Drama," New York Times (16 May 1926) section 8, pp. 1-2.

3151 "The Fortune: The Plough and the Stars," Stage (London), (20 May 1926) p. 19.

3152 Royde-Smith, N. G., "The Drama: The Plough and the Stars by Sean O'Casey. Fortune," Outlook (London), 57 (22 May 1926) 359.

3153 Brown, Ivor, "The Plough and the Stars by Sean O'Casey: The Fortune Theatre," Saturday Review (London), 141 (22 May 1926) 614-15.

3154 MacCarthy, Desmond, "The Plough and the Stars," New Statesman (London), 27 (29 May 1926) 170.

3155 "Plays and Pictures," Nation and Athenaeum (London), 39 (29 May 1926) 207.

3156 A., E. S., "Mr. O'Casey Again: The Plough and the Stars by Sean O'Casey. Fortune Theatre," Spectator (London), 136 (29 May 1926) 904.

3157 "London Letter: The Plough and the Stars," Irish Times (Dublin), (21 June 1926) p. 6 [To be transferred from the Fortune Theatre to the New Theatre].

3158 Shipp, Horace, "The Art of Sean O'Casey," English Review (London), 42 (June 1926) 851-3.

3159 Waldman, Milton, "The Plough and the Stars by Sean O'Casey: Fortune Theatre," London Mercury, 14 (July 1926) 299-300.

3160 Nathan, George Jean, "The London Season," American Mercury (N.Y.), 9 (Oct 1926) 245-6.

3161 E[rvine], St. J[ohn], "At the Play," Observer (London), (16 May 1927) p. 32.

3162 Atkinson, Brooks, "O'Casey and the Irish Players: The Plough and the Stars," New York Times (29 Nov 1927) p. 30 [At the Hudson Theatre, New York].

3163 Mantle, Burns, "The Plough and the Stars: Irish Players Begin Their Season at the Hudson," New York Daily News (29 Nov 1927) p. 33.

3164 Atkinson, Brooks, "Sean O'Casey's The Plough and the Stars Performed by the Irish Players," New York Times (4 Dec 1927) section 10, p. 1.

3165 O'F., T. J., "O'Casey on the Gat The Plough and the Stars at the Hudson: a Homily on Violence," Daily Worker (N.Y.), (9 Dec 1927) p. 4.

3166 Brackett, Charles, "Art Attack," New Yorker, 3 (10 Dec 1927) 34.

3167 Sayler, Oliver M., "The Play of the Week: The Plough and the Stars, a Tragedy in Four Acts by Sean O'Casey. Produced by the Irish Players for George C. Taylor at the Hudson Theatre, New York," Saturday Review of Literature (N.Y.), 4 (10 Dec 1927) 427.

3168 Nathan, George Jean, "Judging the Shows," Judge (N.Y.), 92 (17 Dec 1927) 18.

3169 Krutch, Joseph Wood, "Poet Laureate," Nation (N.Y.), 125 (21 Dec 1927) 718.

3170 "Irish Players Amuse and Irritate," Literary Digest (N.Y.), 95 (24 Dec 1927) 20-1.

3171 "A New York Diary," New Republic (N.Y.), 53 (4 Jan 1928) 191-2.

3172 Jordan, Elizabeth, "The Stage in Mid-Season," America (N.Y.), (7 Jan 1928) 324.

3173 Maxwell, Perriton, "The Plough and the Stars," Theatre Magazine (N.Y.), 48 (Feb 1928) 58.

3174 Carb, David, "The Plough and the Stars," Vogue (N.Y.), 71 (1 Feb 1928) 100.

3175 B., F. R., "Lights Down," Outlook (N.Y.), 148 (1 Feb 1928) 187.

3176 Brown, John Mason, "The Laughter of the Gods: Broadway in Review," Theatre Arts Monthly (N.Y.) 12 (Feb 1928) 91-5.

3177 Waters, Arthur B. "Irish Players Seen in Sean O'Casey," Philadelphia Public Ledger, (7 Feb 1928) p. 16 [At the Broad Street Theatre].

3178 D[onaghey], F[rederick], "The Plough and the Stars," Chicago Daily Tribune (21 Feb 1928) p. 25 [At the Blackstone Theatre].

3179 Dale, Virginia, "Great Performance by Irish Players," Chicago Daily Journal (21 Feb 1928) p. 8.

3180 Seldes, Gilbert, "The Theatre," Dial (Chicago), 85 (Apr 1928) 259-60.

3181 "Duchess Theatre: The Plough and the Stars by Sean O'Casey," Times (London), (4 June 1930) p. 14.

3182 H., H., "Duchess: The Plough and the Stars by Sean O'Casey," Observer (London), (8 June 1930) p. 11.

3183 Omicron, "The Plough and the Stars: Duchess Theatre," Nation and Athenaeum (London), 47 (14 June 1930) 247-8.

3184 P., M. E., "The Irish Players and Sean O'Casey: The Plough and the Stars As It Is Acted at Providence," Boston Evening Transcript (11 Oct 1934) p. 11.

3185 Atkinson, Brooks, "Return of the Abbey Theatre Players in O'Casey's The Plough and the Stars," New York Times (13 Nov 1934) p. 22.

3186 Vernon, Grenville, "The Plough and the Stars," Commonweal (N.Y.), 21 (23 Nov 1934) 122.

3187 Reynolds, Horace, "Riot in the Abbey," American Spectator (N.Y.), 3 (Dec 1934) 14.

3188 Isaacs, Edith J. R., "The Abbey Players," Theatre Arts Monthly (N.Y.), 19 (Jan 1935) 10-11.

3189 Melvin, Edwin F., "Rich Humors and Tragedy from O'Casey: His Plough and the Stars for First Performance in Boston," Boston Evening Transcript (3 June 1935) p. 10.

3190 "Q Theatre: The Plough and the Stars by Sean O'Casey," Times (London), (27 June 1939) p. 12.

3191 Quidnunc, "An Irishman's Diary," Irish Times (Dublin), (10 Nov 1947) p. 5.

3192 Hollway, Frank, "The Plough and the Stars: Sean O'Casey. Nothing Derogatory," Tyneside Phoenix (Newcastle upon Tyne), 8 (Summer 1949) 5-6.

3193 Rubin, Barnard, "Good Production of O'Casey's 'Plough and the Stars,'" Daily Worker (N.Y.), (6 Feb 1950) p. 11.

3194 O'Casey, Sean, "O'Casey Reports: Irish Author Discusses His Own Play," New York Times (12 Mar 1950) section 2, p. 2 [Letter to the Hudson Guild Players on their production of the play].

3195 Cronin, Anthony. "Theatre," Bell (Dublin), 17 (Jul 1951) 43-6 [At the Abbey].

3196 Clurman, Harold, "Theatre," Nation (N.Y.), 176 (25 Apr 1953) 353-4 [At the Cherry Lane Theater, Greenwich Village].

3197 Hewes, Henry, "Broadway Postscript: The Plough and the Stars," Saturday Review of Literature (N.Y.), 36 (6 June 1953) 25.

3198 "New Lindsey Theatre: The Plough and the Stars by Sean O'Casey," Times (London), (28 May 1954) p. 2.

3199 Igoe, W. J., "A Handful of Dubliners: The Plough and the Stars," Catholic Herald (London), (11 June 1954) p. 5.

3200 Igoe, W. J., "London Letter," America (N.Y.), 91 (14 Aug 1954) 480-1.

3201 Carroll, Niall, "New Actor in Old Robe," Irish Press (Dublin), (14 Mar 1955) p. 6 [By the Abbey Theatre at the International Festival, in the Sarah Bernhardt Theatre, in Paris].

3202 Carroll, Niall, "O'Casey Didn't Get Mad at Me," Irish Press (Dublin), (25 Apr 1955) p. 4.

3203 "Abbey Players in Paris," Irish Times (Dublin), (17 May 1955) p. 5.

3204 "Abbey Won Paris with a 'Plough,'" Irish Press (Dublin), (20 May 1955) p. 7.

3205 Triolet, Elsa, "De Dublin à Pékin: Introduction au IIe Festival International d'Art Dramatique de la Ville de Paris," Lettres françaises (Paris), no. 570 (26 May-2 June 1955) 1, 7.

3206 Burton, Bernard, "'Plough and Stars,'" Daily People's World (San Francisco), (20 Oct 1955) p. 7 [At the Ivar Theater, Hollywood].

3207 R. H., "'Plough and the Stars' Stimulating Dublin Story," Daily Worker (N.Y.), (9 Apr 1956) p. 7 [By the Craftsmen at the Barbizon-Plaza].

3208 Canright, Margery, "Workshop Wins Cheers in O'Casey's 'Plough,'" Daily People's World (San Francisco), (18 Oct 1956) p. 5 [By the Actor's Workshop at the Marine's Memorial Theater, San Francisco].

3209 S., R., "Hilarious and Tragic O'Casey: The Plough and the Stars (Tower Theatre)," Daily Worker (London), (2 Mar 1959) p. 3.

3210 Taubman, Howard, "Easter Rising: O'Casey's The Plough and the Stars Opens," New York Times (7 Dec 1960) p. 56 [At the Phoenix Theater].

3211   Balliett, Whitney, "Groucho in Dublin," New Yorker, 36 (17 Dec 1960) 96-8.

3212   Clurman, Harold, "Theatre," Nation (N.Y.), 91 (24 Dec 1960) 510-11.

3213   "The Plough and the Stars," Theatre Arts (N.Y.), 45 (Feb 1961) 11.

3214   Sullivan, A. M., "The Off-Broadway Phoenix Theater," Catholic World (N.Y.), 92 (Feb 1961) 320.

3215   Leclerc, Guy, "Au Théâtre Montparnasse: La Charrue et les étoiles," L'Humanité (Paris), (4 May 1962) p. 2.

3216   Poirot-Delpech, B. "La Charrue et les étoiles d' O'Casey," Monde (Paris), (8 May 1962) p. 12.

3217   Marcabru, Pierre, "La Charrue et les étoiles," Arts (Paris), (9 May 1962) p. 8.

3218   Lemarchand, J., "La Charrue et les étoiles de Sean O'Casey au Théâtre Montparnasse," Figaro littéraire (Paris), (12 May 1962) p. 20.

3219   Olivier, Claude, "La Charrue et les étoiles de Sean O'Casey au Montparnasse-Gaston Baty," Lettres françaises (Paris), no. 927 (17-23 May 1962) 8.

3220   Camp, André, "La Quinzaine Dramatique: La Charrue et les étoiles, de Sean O'Casey, par la Comédie de Saint-Etiènne," Avant-Scène (Paris), no. 267 (15 June 1962) 40-2.

3221   Saurel, Renée, "Un dramaturge incomparable," Temps modernes (Paris), 17 (June 1962) 1938-44.

3222   "Pleasant End to Theatre Season," Times (London), (28 June 1962) p. 10 [At the Théâtre Montparnasse-Gaston Baty in Paris].

3223   "Mere Sketch of The Plough. Uphill Struggle: Mermaid Theatre," Times (London), (26 Sep 1962) p. 8.

3224   Levin, Bernard, "Well, the Things We've Seen Here: The Plough and the Stars, by Sean O'Casey. Mermaid Theatre," Daily Mail (London), (26 Sep 1962) p. 3.

3225   Kretzmer, Herbert, "Irish Heresy Becomes Museum Piece," Daily Express (London), (26 Sep 1962) p. 9.

3226 Darlington, W. A., "Richness of O'Casey Lost in Space," <u>Daily Telegraph</u> (London), (26 Sep 1962) p. 14.

3227 Fay, Gerard, "<u>The Plough and the Stars</u> at the Mermaid," <u>Guardian</u> (London), (26 Sep 1962) p. 9.

3228 Shulman, Milton, "A Fitting Climax to the O'Casey Festival," <u>Evening Standard</u> (London), (26 Sep 1962) p. 14.

3229 Barker, Felix, "Shadow of 'The Trouble,'" <u>Evening News</u> (London), (26 Sep 1962) p. 5.

3230 M., M., "The Harsh Truth: <u>The Plough and the Stars</u> (Mermaid)," <u>Daily Worker</u> (London), (27 Sep 1962) p. 2.

3231 H., P., "Mermaid Reaches Zenith of O'Casey Festival," <u>Stage and Television Today</u> (London), (27 Sep 1962) p. 13.

3232 Tynan, Kenneth, "Theatre: On the Trail of the True Self," <u>Observer</u> (London), (30 Sep 1962) p. 25.

3233 Lambert, J. W., "London Theatre," <u>Sunday Times</u> (London), (30 Sep 1962) p. 41.

3234 Churchill, Andrew, "The Plough and the Stars: Sean O'Casey (Mermaid)," <u>Time and Tide</u> (London), 43 (4-11 Oct 1962) 28.

3235 Gellert, Roger, "Sportive Peer," <u>New Statesman</u> (London), 64 (5 Oct 1962) 464.

3236 Gascoigne, Bamber, "Organised Blarney: <u>The Plough and the Stars</u>. (Mermaid)," <u>Spectator</u> (London), 209 (5 Oct 1962) 513.

3237 Trewin, J. C., "Men of the Hour," <u>Illustrated London News</u>, 241 (6 Oct 1962) 530.

3238 Brien, Alan, "O'Casey for Today," <u>Sunday Telegraph</u> (London), (7 Oct 1962) p. 10.

3239 Goldsworthy, E., "Gascoigne on O'Casey," <u>Spectator</u> (London), 209 (12 Oct 1962) 555 [Letter to the Editor].

3240 S., F., "Mermaid: <u>The Plough and the Stars</u>," <u>Theatre World</u> (London), 58 (Nov 1962) 6.

3241 Esslin, Martin, "The Plough and the Stars," <u>Plays and Players</u> (London), 10 (Dec 1962) 58.

3242 Wehmeier, Jörg, "Muss O'Casey uns fremd bleiben?" <u>Theater heute</u> (Hannover), 4 (Aug 1963) 16-17.

3243 Leutner, Gert Omar, "Umgang mit Sean O'Casey," Theater heute (Hannover), 4 (Aug 1963) 17-20.

3244 "O'Casey to Allow 2 Plays to Be Performed in Dublin," New York Times (6 Nov 1963) p. 35 [Juno and the Paycock and The Plough and the Stars as a preview for World Theatre Season, London].

3245 O'Casey, Sean, "Behind the Ban," New York Times (5 Jan 1964) section 2, pp. 1, 3 [Lifting ban on Juno and the Paycock and The Plough and the Stars].

3246 "O'Casey Play in Rehearsal at Abbey," Irish Times (Dublin), (29 Jan 1964) p. 5.

3247 "The O'Casey Truce," Irish Times (Dublin), (29 Jan 1964) p. 7 [Leader].

3248 "O'Casey Play Opens at the Abbey Theatre," Irish Times (Dublin), (12 Feb 1964) p. 9.

3249 K., "The Plough and the Stars Returns to the Abbey," Irish Times (Dublin), (12 Feb 1964) p. 9.

3250 "Abbey Scores with Second O'Casey Play," Irish Times (Dublin), (28 Apr 1964) p. 1.

3251 "Abbey Make Amends. Aldwych Theatre: The Plough and the Stars," Times (London), (28 Apr 1964) p. 15.

3252 Shorter, Eric, "'Plough and Stars' Is Not Moving Enough," Daily Telegraph (London), (28 Apr 1964) p. 18.

3253 Levin, Bernard, "This Time, a Better Deal for the 'Heroes,'" Daily Mail (London), (28 Apr 1964) p. 14.

3254 Mortimer, John, "O'Casey Triumphs in This Test of a Great Play," Evening Standard (London), (28 Apr 1964) p. 4.

3255 Baker, Bert, "More to O'Casey Than Comedy: The Plough and the Stars (World Theatre Season, Aldwych)," Daily Worker (London), (29 Apr 1964) p. 2.

3256 Gascoigne, Bamber, "Living Through the Troubles," Observer (London), (3 May 1964) p. 25.

3257 Hobson, Harold, "Who'd Be a Patriot?" Sunday Times (London), (3 May 1964) p. 33.

3258 Brien, Alan, "Theatre: It's Hard to Listen," Sunday Telegraph (London), (3 May 1964) p. 14.

3259 "Abbey Reply to O'Casey: In No Position to Pronounce Judgment," Irish Times (Dublin), (3 Jul 1964) p. 1. See "Abbey
Has Been Deteriorating for Years" (4 Jul 1964) p. 1.

3260 Shaw, Iain, "Juno and The Plough," Encore (London), 11 (Jul-
Aug 1964) 52-4.

3261 "O.U.D.S. True to O'Casey. Oxford Playhouse: The Plough
and the Stars," Times (London), (12 May 1965) p. 15.

3262 Kelly, Seamus, "The Plough and the Stars at the Abbey,"
Irish Times (Dublin), (16 Aug 1966) p. 6.

3263 Kelly, Henry, "The Plough and the Stars," Irish Times (Dublin), (14 Feb 1968) p. 10 [By 66 Theatre Company, Dun
Laoghaire].

3264 Quidnunc, "An Irishman's Diary: The Scene Changes," Irish
Times (Dublin), (6 Apr 1968) p. 11.

3265 Clurman, Harold, "Theatre," Nation (N.Y.), 203 (11 Dec 1976)
634 [The Abbey Theatre (Dublin) production of The Plough
and the Stars at the Brooklyn Academy of Music, then on
tour].

3266 Wardle, Irving, "Too Lonely to Group of Characters," Times
(London), (21 Sep 1977) p. 10 [At the National Theatre,
London, 20 Sep 1977]. See reply by John O'Riordan,
"O'Casey as Socialist," ibid. (5 Oct 1977) p. 15.

3267 Billington, Michael, "Olivier: Plough and the Stars," Guardian
(London), (21 Sep 1977) p. 10.

3268 Young, B. A., "Olivier: The Plough and the Stars," Financial
Times (London), (21 Sep 1977) p. 3.

3269 Shulman, Milton, "Irish Times," Evening Standard (London),
(21 Sep 1977) p. 19.

3270 Barber, John, "Fine War Play Is Ironical Throughout," Daily
Telegraph (London), (22 Sep 1977) p. 15.

3271 Cushman, Robert, "Stars That Don't Shine," Observer (London), (25 Sep 1977) p. 26.

3272 Levin, Bernard, "The NT Takes a Shot at O'Casey's War,"
Sunday Times (London), (25 Sep 1977) p. 37.

3273 Marcus, Frank, "Ploughing Sean O'Casey: As Irish as the Ham
of Dublin," Sunday Telegraph (London), (25 Sep 1977) p. 16.

3274 Morley, Sheridan, "Theatre," Punch (London), (28 Sep 1977) 566.

3275 Elsom, John, "Over the Top: The Plough and the Stars. National," Listener (London), (29 Sep 1977) pp. 421-2. See reply by John O'Riordan, "O'Casey's Drama," ibid. (13 Oct 1977) p. 476.

3276 Morley-Priestman, Anne, "The Plough and the Stars," Stage and Television Today (London), (29 Sep 1977) p. 11.

3277 Nightingale, Benedict, "The Plough and the Stars (Olivier)," New Statesman (London), (30 Sep 1977) 456.

3278 Hurren, Kenneth, "Worth Doing Badly," What's On in London, (30 Sep 1977) p. 34.

3279 Whitehead, Ted, "Lost Worlds: The Plough and the Stars (Olivier)," Spectator (London), (1 Oct 1977) p. 27. See reply by John O'Riordan, "An 'Overpowering' Play," ibid. (22 Oct 1977) p. 15; and counter-play by Ted Whitehead, "Irish Joke," ibid. (28 Jan 1978) pp. 25-26.

3280 Trewin, J. C., "New Plays," Lady (London), (6 Oct 1977) 483.

3281 "Dublin's Mini-Festival," Times (London), (13 Oct 1977) p. 11, passim.

3282 Stewart, Ian, "The Old Struggle," Country Life (London), (27 Oct 1977) 1193.

3283 Esslin, Martin, "The Plough and the Stars," Plays and Players (London), 25 (Nov 1977) 18-19.

3284 Morley, Sheridan, "'I Believe in the Power of the Actor,'" Times (London), (19 Sep 1977) p. 12 [Interview with Cyril Cusack, who opened as Fluther Good].

3285 Nordell, Roderick, "Reconsideration: The Plough and the Stars by Sean O'Casey," New Republic, 178 (18 Feb 1978) 38-39.

3286 MacCool, Fionn, "Birmingham Festival Does Us Proud," Irish Post (London), (29 Mar 1980) p. 8 [The Plough is included in a nine-day festival titled "Salute to Ireland"].

3287 Naughton, Lindie, "The Plough Comes to the Suburbs," Irish Press (Dublin), (11 Apr 1980) p. 5 [By Lissadell Players].

THE SILVER TASSIE

3288 "Mr. O'Casey's New Play. Why It Was Rejected. Mr. Yeats
on the Dramatist's Job. The War and the Stage," Observer
(London), (3 June 1928) p. 19 [Correspondence on the play
by O'Casey, Yeats, Lennox Robinson, and Walter Starkie].
Reprinted in Irish Statesman (Dublin), 10 (9 June 1928)
268-72. Yeats's letter also reprinted in The Letters of W. B.
Yeats, ed. A. Wade (London: Rupert Hart-Davis, 1954) pp.
740-2.

3289 "O'Casey's New Play Rejected: Severe Criticism by Abbey Directors," Irish Times (Dublin), (4 June 1928) p. 8 [Corre-
spondence].

3290 "Ploughing the Star," Manchester Guardian (4 June 1928) p. 8
[leader]. See O'Casey's reply (12 June 1928) p. 22 [Letter
to the Editor].

3291 "Our London Letter: The Silver Tassie," Irish Independent
(Dublin), (5 June 1928) p. 6.

3292 "Mr. Sean O'Casey Angry: Abbey Rejects His New Play,"
Irish Independent (Dublin), (5 June 1928) p. 9.

3293 "Mr. O'Casey Replies to His Critics: Strong Comment on
Treatment of His Play. The Big Four," Irish Times (Dublin), (9 June 1928) p. 7 [Correspondence].

3294 O'Casey, Sean, "The Rejected Play: O'Casey and the Big Four,"
Irish Independent (Dublin), (9 June 1928) p. 10 [Letter to
the Editor].

3295 Webb, Arthur, "Abbey Rejects Sean O'Casey's New Play," New
York Times (10 June 1928) section 3, p. 1.

3296 T., M. A., "O'Casey and the Critics," Sunday Independent
(Dublin), (10 June 1928) p. 2.

3297 O'Casey, Sean, "Mr. O'Casey's 'Last Word,'" Irish Times
(Dublin), (21 June 1928) p. 4 [Letter to the Editor].

3298 O'Casey, Sean, "Tying Things Together: Mr. O'Casey's Rejected Play," Irish Independent (Dublin), (21 June 1928)
p. 9 [Letter to the Editor].

3299 B., G. W., "The Silver Tassie: Interview with Mr. Sean
O'Casey," Observer (London), (6 Oct 1929) p. 13.

3300 Morgan, Charles, "Apollo Theatre: The Silver Tassie, a Tragic

Comedy by Sean O'Casey," Times (London), (12 Oct 1929) p. 8. Reprinted in The English Dramatic Critics: An Anthology 1660–1932, ed. James Agate (London: Arthur Barker, 1932; New York: Hill & Wang, n.d. [1958]) pp. 347–9; and Sean O'Casey, ed. Ronald Ayling (London: Macmillan, 1969) pp. 88–90.

3301 D[arlington], W. A., "Sean O'Casey's New Play. An Author Worth a Message. Originality and Purpose. The Silver Tassie," Daily Telegraph (London), (12 Oct 1929) p. 8.

3302 "London Theatres: The Silver Tassie," Scotsman (Edinburgh), (12 Oct 1929) p. 14.

3303 Parsons, Alan, "Mr. S. O'Casey's War Play. Girl and V.C. in a Poignant Scene. Mr. Bernard Shaw's Praise," Daily Mail (London), (12 Oct 1929) p. 21.

3304 E., M., "Irishman's War Play. Mr. Sean O'Casey Tries an Experiment Not a Success. Chanting Soldiers at the Front," Daily Herald (London), (12 Oct 1929) p. 5.

3305 Griffith, Hubert, "Sean O'Casey's New Play. War Disillusionment and a Tragic Irish Aftermath. A Scenic Triumph. "Behind the Lines" as rendered by Mr. Augustus John," Evening Standard (London), (12 Oct 1929) p. 8.

3306 B., J. G., "Mr. Sean O'Casey's War Play: The Silver Tassie an Ambitious Work," Evening News (London), (12 Oct 1929) p. 7.

3307 Agate, James, "Apollo: The Silver Tassie," Observer (London), (13 Oct 1929) p. 6.

3308 Ervine, St. John, "Mr. Sean O'Casey's Passion Play. Apollo: The Silver Tassie," Observer (London), (13 Oct 1929) p. 15.

3309 "The Silver Tassie," Irish Independent (Dublin), (14 Oct 1929) p. 6 [Editorial].

3310 "The Apollo: The Silver Tassie," Stage (London), (17 Oct 1929) p. 18.

3311 "Dublin and O'Casey: 'Silver Tassie' Still Taboo [in Dublin]," Irish News (Belfast), (17 Oct 1929) p. 5.

3312 "Dublin Letter: The Silver Tassie," Cork Examiner, (17 Oct 1929) p. 8.

3312a St. John, Christopher, "Another Irish Victory," Time and Tide (London), 10 (18 Oct 1929) 1254.

3312b B., I., "The Silver Tassie: Mr. O'Casey's New Play," Manchester Guardian Weekly, 21 (18 Oct 1929) 318.

3312c Brown, Ivor, "The Silver Tassie by Sean O'Casey: Apollo Theatre," Saturday Review (London), 148 (19 Oct 1929) 446-7.

3312d B.-W., J., "The Silver Tassie," New Statesman (London), 34 (19 Oct 1929) 52-3.

3313 Jennings, Richard, "The Silver Tassie, by Sean O'Casey: At the Apollo Theatre," Spectator (London), 143 (19 Oct 1929) 523.

3314 "The Silver Tassie at the Apollo," Illustrated London News, 175 (19 Oct 1929) 696.

3315 O'F[aolain], S[ean], "The Silver Tassie Staged," Irish Statesman (Dublin), 13 (19 Oct 1929) 134-5.

3316 "The Silver Tassie," Edinburgh Evening News (19 Oct 1929) p. 5.

3317 "Theatrical Gossip: Sean O'Casey's Fourth Success," Western Independent (20 Oct 1929) p. 14.

3318 T. [Joseph Thorp], "At the Play," Punch (London), 177 (23 Oct 1929) 470.

3319 "The Silver Tassie," Truth (London), (23 Oct 1929) 702.

3320 Atkinson, Brooks, "O'Casey's War Drama: The Silver Tassie," New York Times (25 Oct 1929) p. 26.

3321 Norgate, Matthew, "Mr. O'Casey's Experiment. Apollo Theatre: The Silver Tassie," Nation and Athenaeum (London), 46 (26 Oct 1929) 138-9.

3322 "Our London Letter: The Silver Tassie," Eastern Daily Press (30 Oct 1929) p. 7.

3323 "What Dublin Missed," Liverpool Post and Mercury (30 Oct 1929) p. 6.

3324 "The Silver Tassie," John O'London's Weekly (2 Nov 1929) p. 153.

3325 Dannhorn, A. John, "Our Friend the Drama," Musical Standard (London), (2 Nov 1929) p. 145.

3326 Morgan, Charles, "As London Sees O'Casey," New York Times (3 Nov 1929) section 9, p. 4.

3327 Atkinson, Brooks, "Making or Breaking O'Casey," New York Times (10 Nov 1929) section 10, p. 1.

3328 Barton, Ralph, "Theatre," Life (Chicago), 94 (15 Nov 1929) 24.

3329 Shaw, George Bernard, "Letter to the Producer of The Silver Tassie," Times (London), (26 Nov 1929) p. 14. Reprinted in Sean O'Casey, ed. Ronald Ayling (London: Macmillan, 1969) p. 91.

3330 Young, Stark, "The Silver Tassie, by Sean O'Casey," New Republic (N.Y.), 61 (27 Nov 1929) 17-18 [At the Irish Theater, New York].

3331 Shipp, Horace, "The Silver Tassie," English Review (London), 49 (Nov 1929) 639.

3332 H., T., "Apollo: The Silver Tassie," Theatre World (London), 10 (Nov 1929) 14.

3333 Gwynn, Stephen, "Ebb and Flow: Mr. O'Casey's Play," Fortnightly Review (London), 126 (2 Dec 1929) 851-3.

3334 MacDonell, A. G., "The Silver Tassie by Sean O'Casey: Apollo Theatre," London Mercury, 21 (Dec 1929) 166-7.

3335 R[eilly], J[oseph] J., "The Silver Tassie," Catholic World (N.Y.), 130 (Dec 1929) 334-5.

3336 "The World and the Theatre: The Silver Tassie," Theatre Arts Monthly (N.Y.), 14 (Jan 1930) 6-10.

3337 S., J. E., "Suspense," New Statesman (London), 35 (10 May 1930) 148-9.

3338 MacCarthy, Desmond, "Very Much on the Spot," New Statesman (London), 35 (17 May 1930) 180-1 [Charles Laughton's performance in the play].

3339 Levy, Benn, "Mr. Morgan Shudders at the Theatre," Theatre Arts Monthly (N.Y.), 15 (Aug 1931) 648-52.

3340 Bottomley, Gordon, "To the Editor," Theatre Arts Monthly (N.Y.), 15 (Oct 1931) 790-2.

3341 "Mr. Sean O'Casey and the Abbey Theatre," Times (London), (26 June 1935) p. 14 [To be produced by the Abbey Theatre].

3342 "Dublin Drama Feud Ends: Abbey Theatre to Let O'Casey Produce Silver Tassie," New York Times (26 June 1935) p. 17.

3343 O'Casey, Sean, "Mr. O'Casey Dissents," New York Times (11 Aug 1935) section 9, p. 1.

3344 B., M., "O'Casey Obscenity: Play That May Shock Christians," Evening Herald (Dublin), (13 Aug 1935) p. 6 [At the Abbey].

3345 P., J. A., "O'Casey Play at the Abbey: Packed House for The Silver Tassie," Irish Independent (Dublin), (13 Aug 1935) p. 8.

3346 "The Silver Tassie: Abbey Players Produce O'Casey Play," Irish Press (Dublin), (13 Aug 1935) p. 2. See O'Casey's reply (20 Aug 1935) p. 6; and counter-reply (20 Aug 1935) p. 6.

3347 "An Outrage of Our Faith," Standard (Dublin), 8 (Aug 1935), 8.

3348 Ulad, Cu, "The Abbey Theatre," Irish Independent (Dublin), (21 Aug 1935) p. 10 [Letter to the Editor].

3349 "The Silver Tassie at Abbey Theatre," Catholic Herald (London), (24 Aug 1935) p. 5. See reply by Robert Speaight, "In Defence of Sean O'Casey" (30 Aug 1935) p. 13.

3350 "Galway Critics of the Abbey," Irish Independent (Dublin), (28 Aug 1935) p. 9.

3351 Starkie, Walter, "Dr. Starkie's Reply to Galway's Critics," Irish Independent (Dublin), (29 Aug 1935) p. 7 [Letter to the Editor].

3352 MacNamara, Brinsley, "Abbey Production of O'Casey Play: Revelations by a Director of the Theatre," Irish Independent (Dublin), (29 Aug 1935) p. 7.

3353 MacNamara, Brinsley, "An Abbey Play: Views of Three Directors," Irish Times (Dublin), (29 Aug 1935) p. 7.

3354 "Cleanse the Theatre," Standard (Dublin), 8 (30 Aug 1935) 8.

3355 "Abbey Directors Reply to Mr. MacNamara," Evening Herald (Dublin), (3 Sep 1935) p. 4.

3356 "The Abbey Theatre," Irish Times (Dublin), (3 Sep 1935) p. 6 [Leading article].

3357 Murphy, J., "The Abbey Theatre," Irish Times (Dublin), (3 Sep 1935) p. 6 [Letter to the Editor].

3358 Costelloe, J., "The Silver Tassie: Reply to Mr. Brinsley Mac-
Namara by His Fellow Directors," Irish Press (Dublin), (3
Sep 1935) p. 2 [Letter to the Editor].

3359 Murphy, J., "Abbey Theatre Productions," Irish Press (Dublin),
(3 Sep 1935) p. 6 [Letter to the Editor].

3360 "Unchristian and Pagan: The Silver Tassie. Voice of Galway
Protests," Irish Catholic (Dublin), 48 (7 Sep 1935) 2.

3361 Costelloe, John, "To the Editor," Irish Catholic (Dublin), 48
(7 Sep 1935) 2.

3362 O'Casey, Sean, "Mr. O'Casey and the Abbey Theatre: "Defen-
sive Words" on The Silver Tassie," Irish Press (Dublin), (11
Sep 1935) p. 8 [Letter to the Editor].

3363 Smith, Hugh, "Dublin Is Harrassed Again," New York Times
(22 Sep 1935) section 10, p. 3.

3364 Leventhal, A. J. "Dramatic Commentary," Dublin Magazine,
22 (1947), 53-6 [At the Gaiety Theatre, Dublin].

3365 F[unke], L[ewis], "O'Casey's Silver Tassie: A Criticism of
War and Effect on Youth. Given in Carnegie Hall," New York
Times (22 Jul 1949) p. 16.

3366 Atkinson, Brooks, "The Silver Tassie: Interplayers' Revival
Is Signal Service," New York Times (4 Sep 1949) section 2,
p. 1.

3367 Clurman, Harold, "Theatre: Off Broadway," New Republic
(N.Y.), 121 (19 Sep 1949) 21-2.

3368 Phelan, Kappo, "A Note on O'Casey," Commonweal (N.Y.), 50
(7 Oct 1949) 631-2.

3369 K., "The Silver Tassie at the Queen's," Irish Times (Dublin),
(25 Sep 1951) p. 6.

3370 M., I., "Abbey Players' First Night at the Queen's Theatre,"
Irish Independent (Dublin), (25 Sep 1951) p. 7.

3371 C., N., "First Abbey Play in New Home," Irish Press (Dublin)
(25 Sep 1951) p. 9.

3372 "O'Casey Drama of Soccer Star," Evening Herald (Dublin), (25
Sep 1951) p. 4.

3373 Fallon, Gabriel, "The Fatal Rejection," Standard (Dublin), 23
(28 Sep 1951) 5.

3374 Kennedy, Maurice, "Shadow of a Playwright," Sunday Press (Dublin), (30 Sep 1951) p. 9.

3375 E., H.U., "Theater zwischen Krieg und Frieden," Berliner Zeitung (11 Dec 1953) p. 9.

3376 "The Silver Tassie: A Broadcast Full of Atmosphere," Times (London), (9 Apr 1957) p. 3.

3377 Smith, R. D., "The Silver Tassie," Radio Times (London), 171 (7 Apr 1966) 58 [B.B.C. Third Program].

3378 Rundall, Jeremy, "Ballet in Sound," Sunday Times (London), (17 Apr 1966) p. 32. See reply by John O'Riordan, "Sentimental?" (24 Apr 1966) p. 15 [Letter to the Editor].

3379 Ayling, Ronald, "Stage History of The Silver Tassie," Program note to Nottingham Playhouse production, 5 Apr 1967.

3380 Addison, Alan, "Two O'Casey Revivals: The Silver Tassie (Nottingham Playhouse)," Morning Star (London), (7 Apr 1967) p. 2.

3381 Hastings, Ronald, "O'Casey after 40 Years," Daily Telegraph (London), (6 Sep 1969) p. 15 [At the Aldwych].

3382 Sutherland, Jack, "Sean O'Casey and The Silver Tassie," Morning Star (London), (9 Sep 1969) p. 2.

3383 "The Silver Tassie," Irish Times (Dublin), (10 Sep 1969) p. 11 [Leader].

3384 Lewis, Peter, "O! What a Lovely O'Casey," Daily Mail (London), (11 Sep 1969) p. 14.

3385 Kretzmer, Herbert, "A Brave Cry Against War. The Silver Tassie: Aldwych," Daily Express (London), (11 Sep 1969) p. 18.

3386 Brahms, Caryl, "Aldwych Theatre: The Silver Tassie," Guardian (London), (11 Sep 1969) p. 8.

3387 Wardle, Irving, "Welcome Revival. Aldwych Theatre: The Silver Tassie," Times (London), (11 Sep 1969) p. 15.

3388 Barber, John, "Non-Irish Cast Shine in O'Casey," Daily Telegraph (London), (11 Sep 1969) p. 21.

3389 Nathan, David, "Dusting Off the Beauty of O'Casey," Sun (London), (11 Sep 1969) p. 9.

3390 Shulman, Milton, "At the Theatre," Evening Standard (London), (11 Sep 1969) p. 19.

3391 Barker, Felix, "The O'Casey Genius Comes Across--In Flashes. The Silver Tassie: Royal Shakespeare Company, Aldwych," Evening News (London), (11 Sep 1969) p. 2.

3392 Young, B. A., "Aldwych: The Silver Tassie," Financial Times (London), (12 Sep 1969) p. 3.

3393 Sutherland, Jack, "Memorable O'Casey Revival: The Silver Tassie (Aldwych)," Morning Star (London), (12 Sep 1969) p. 2.

3394 Wardle, Irving, "A Neglected Masterpiece," Times (London), (13 Sep 1969) Saturday Review Section, p. 3.

3395 Marcus, Frank, "No Tarnish on the Tassie," Sunday Telegraph (London), (14 Sep 1969) p. 14.

3396 Lambert, J. W., "O'Casey Says Yes," Sunday Times (London), (14 Sep 1969) p. 58.

3397 Bryden, Ronald, "O'Casey and His Raw Torso," Observer (London), (14 Sep 1969) p. 26.

3398 Kingston, Jeremy, "At the Theatre," Punch (London), 257 (17 Sep 1969) 469-70.

3399 Blake, Douglas, "The Silver Tassie: Forty Years On," Stage and Television Today (London), (18 Sep 1969) p. 15.

3400 Nightingale, Benedict, "Without Apology," New Statesman (London), 78 (19 Sep 1969) 389-90.

3401 Spurling, Hilary, "Nut-and-Apple Case," Spectator (London), (20 Sep 1969) p. 381.

3402 Jones, D. A. N., "Known Warriors," Listener (London), (25 Sep 1969) p. 431.

3403 Trussler, Simon, "Theatre," Tribune (London), (26 Sep 1969) p. 15.

3404 Trewin, J. C., "O'Casey Speaks Again," Illustrated London News (27 Sep 1969) p. 35.

3405 Trewin, J. C., "The New Plays: The Silver Tassie (Aldwych)," Lady (London), 170 (2 Oct 1969) 500.

3406 O'Brien, Kate, "Long Distance," Irish Times (Dublin), (6 Oct 1969) p. 10.

3407 "Punch Choice: The Silver Tassie," Punch (London), 257 (22 Oct 1969) 7.

3408 Leonard, Hugh, "Aldwych: The Silver Tassie," Plays and Players (London), 17 (Nov 1969) 20-3.

3409 Manning, Mary, "The Abbey Theatre Tour," Arts in Ireland, 2 (Autumn 1973) 47-53.

3410 Wardle, Irving, "The Silver Tassie. Theatre Royal, Stratford East," Times (London), (10 Feb 1977) p. 13 [Presented by Theatre Workshop].

3411 Coveney, Michael, "Theatre Royal: The Silver Tassie," Financial Times (London), (10 Feb 1977) p. 3.

3412 Billington, Michael, "Stratford East: The Silver Tassie," Guardian (London), (10 Feb 1977) p. 8.

3413 Shulman, Milton, "Words of War," Evening Standard (London), (10 Feb 1977) p. 18. See reply by John O'Riordan, "Close Shavianism," (17 Feb 1977) p. 22.

3414 Barber, John, "Good Omen from New Theatre Royal Team," Daily Telegraph (London), (11 Feb 1977) p. 13.

3415 Cushman, Robert, "The Curse on Thebes," Observer (London), (13 Feb 1977) p. 34.

3416 Levin, Bernard, "Theatre," Sunday Times (London), (13 Feb 1977) p. 37.

3417 Marcus, Frank, "Round Again," Sunday Telegraph (London), (13 Feb 1977) p. 18.

3418 Morley-Priestman, Anne, "Theatre Workshop: The Silver Tassie," Stage and Television (London), (17 Feb 1977) p. 19.

3419 Trewin, J. C., "New Plays: The Silver Tassie," Lady (London), (24 Feb 1977) 315.

3420 Nightingale, Benedict, "Theatre," New Statesman (London), 93 (25 Feb 1977) 264.

3421 Gooch, Steve, "The Silver Tassie," Plays and Players (London), 24 (Apr 1977) 35-7.

3422 Curtis, Anthony, "Plays in Performance," Drama (London),
      no. 124 (Spring 1977) 44-5.

3423 Lowery, Robert G., "'E' for Effort," Daily World (N.Y.), (30
      Oct 1982) p. 13 [By Soho Repertory Theatre, New York].

WITHIN THE GATES

3424 Stewart, M.C., "Mr. Sean O'Casey's New Play," Times (London),
      (2 Dec 1933) p. 8 [Letter to the Editor].

3425 Ervine, St. John, "At the Play: Mr. O'Casey's Apocalypse,"
      Observer (London), (7 Jan 1934) p. 15.

3426 "Dramatis Personae," Observer (London), (4 Feb 1934) p. 13.

3427 B[eckles], G[ordon], "A Challenge to Sean O'Casey," Daily
      Express (London), (8 Feb 1934) p. 3.

3428 "Royalty Theatre: Within the Gates by Sean O'Casey," Times
      (London), (8 Feb 1934) p. 12.

3429 Darlington, W. A., "Sean O'Casey's New Play. Prose Poem on
      the Stage: Within the Gates," Daily Telegraph (London), (8
      Feb 1934) p. 8.

3430 C., J., "Last Night's First Nights: Sordid Parade. Sean
      O'Casey's Biting Satire of Modern Life," Daily Sketch (Lon-
      don), (8 Feb 1934) p. 13.

3431 M., P. L., "O'Casey Mocks World in Hyde Park. Odd Experi-
      ment in Symbolism. Royalty Theatre: Within the Gates,"
      Daily Herald (London), (8 Feb 1934) p. 11.

3432 "London Theatres: Within the Gates," Scotsman (Edinburgh),
      (8 Feb 1934) p. 8.

3433 Disher, Willson, "A New Sort of Play. Sean O'Casey's Genius.
      Raw Life," Daily Mail (London), (8 Feb 1934) p. 17.

3434 B., I., "Within the Gates: Sean O'Casey's New Play," Man-
      chester Guardian (8 Feb 1934) p. 12.

3435 Baughan, E. A., "Sean O'Casey Epic of Pessimism: Play That
      Will Distress Many," News Chronicle (London), (8 Feb 1934)
      p. 11.

3436 P., P., "Mr. Sean O'Casey Loses His Way," Evening Standard
      (London), (8 Feb 1934) p. 9.

3437 B., J. G., "An Irish Man's General Grouse: Sean O'Casey's Play on a London Park Theme," Evening News (London), (8 Feb 1934) p. 9.

3438 "New Play by O'Casey Produced in London: Within the Gates," New York Times (8 Feb 1934) p. 14.

3439 Agate, James, "Royalty: Within the Gates. A Play, by Sean O'Casey," Observer (London), (11 Feb 1934) p. 6.

3440 Agate, James, "The Dramatic World: Beyond the Agates. A Difficult Play. Royalty: Within the Gates," Sunday Times (London), (11 Feb 1934) p. 6.

3441 Brown, Ivor, "Royalty: Within the Gates by Sean O'Casey," Observer (London), (11 Feb 1934) p. 15.

3442 "The Royalty: Within the Gates," Stage (London), (15 Feb 1934) p. 10.

3443 Verschoyle, Derek, "Within the Gates by Sean O'Casey: At the Royalty Theatre," Spectator (London), 152 (16 Feb 1934) 235.

3444 Bosanquet, Theodora, "Within the Gates. Sean O'Casey. Royalty Theatre," Time and Tide (London), 15 (17 Feb 1934) 222.

3445 MacCarthy, Desmond, "Hyde Park," New Statesman and Nation (London), 7 (17 Feb 1934) 226-7. Reprinted in Drama (London and New York: Putnam, 1940) pp. 349-54.

3446 "Within the Gates at the Royalty," Illustrated London News, 184 (17 Feb 1934) 264.

3447 T. [Joseph Thorp], "At the Play," Punch (London), 186 (21 Feb 1934) 216-17.

3448 Galitzine, Prince Nicolas, "The Theatre," Saturday Review (London), 157 (24 Feb 1934) 219.

3449 Morgan, Charles, "Within the Gates: Further Thoughts on Sean O'Casey's Recently Shown Play," New York Times (25 Feb 1934) section 9, p. 3.

3450 Grein, J. T., "The World of the Theatre,," Illustrated London News, 184 (3 Mar 1934) 320.

3451 Reynolds, Horace, "Sean O'Casey's Symbolic Drama: Within the Gates," Saturday Review of Literature (N.Y.), 10 (3 Mar 1934) 519.

3452 Hughes, Elinor, "The Irish Drama Contributes Sean O'Casey's Within the Gates," Boston Herald (25 Mar 1934) p. 9.

3453 "Broadway to See New O'Casey Play: Within the Gates Will Be Produced by Bushar and Tuerk Next Season," New York Times (26 Mar 1934) p. 18.

3454 Grein, J. T., "The World of the Theatre," Illustrated London News, 184 (31 Mar 1934) 498.

3455 D., F. J., "Royalty: Within the Gates," Theatre World (London), 21 (Mar 1934) 120.

3456 Codman, Florence, "Sean O'Casey," Nation (N.Y.), 138 (25 Apr 1934) 476-7.

3457 Dukes, Ashley, "The English Scene," Theatre Arts Monthly (N.Y.), 18 (Apr 1934) 258-9.

3458 "Irish Playwright, Sean O'Casey, Here: Author of Within the Gates Comes to Be Present at Play's Rehearsal," New York Times (18 Sep 1934) p. 23.

3459 O'Casey, Sean, "From Within the Gates," New York Times (21 Oct 1934) section 9, pp. 1, 3.

3460 Atkinson, Brooks, "The Play: Fantasy of the Seasons in Hyde Park in Sean O'Casey's Within the Gates," New York Times (23 Oct 1934) p. 23 [At the National Theatre, New York].

3461 Brown, John Mason, "Within the Gates," New York Post (23 Oct 1934) p. 17. Reprinted in Two on the Aisle (New York: W. W. Norton, 1938) pp. 126-30.

3462 Mantle, Burns, "Within the Gates Thru a Pink Haze," New York Daily News (23 Oct 1934) p. 41.

3463 Ruhl, Arthur, "The Theatres: Within the Gates by Sean O'Casey," New York Herald Tribune (23 Oct 1934) p. 14.

3464 Alexander, Leon, "Sean O'Casey Tilts a Dull Lance Against Puritanism in Play Within the Gates," Daily Worker (N.Y.), (27 Oct 1934) p. 5.

3465 "Not Good Enough for Ireland," Literary Digest (N.Y.), 118 (27 Oct 1934) 26.

3466 Atkinson, Brooks, "Within the Gates: Sean O'Casey's Fantasy of Hyde Park--Drama of Life as They Lead It Out-of-Doors," New York Times (28 Oct 1934) section 9, p. 1.

3467 "An Irishman Looks at England, and Beyond," Saturday Review (N.Y.), 11 (3 Nov 1934) 256 [Editorial].

3468 "Stage: Sean O'Casey Brings His Within the Gates to N.Y.," Newsweek (N.Y.) 4 (3 Nov 1934) 27.

3469 Benchley, Robert, "A Big Week for Everybody," New Yorker, 10 (3 Nov 1934) 29-30.

3470 "New Plays in Manhattan: Within the Gates," Time (N.Y.) 24 (5 Nov 1934) 30.

3471 Krutch, Joseph Wood, "Mr. O'Casey's Charade," Nation (N.Y.), 139 (7 Nov 1934) 546.

3472 Young, Stark, "Theatre Gates: Within the Gates by Sean O'Casey, National Theatre," New Republic (N.Y.), 80 (7 Nov 1934) 369.

3473 Vernon, Grenville, "The Play and Screen: Within the Gates," Commonweal (N.Y.), 21 (9 Nov 1934) 66.

3474 Blankfort, Michael, "The Theatre," New Masses (N.Y.), (13 Nov 1934) 28.

3475 Jordan, Elizabeth, "Sean O'Casey's Crawling World," America (N.Y.), 52 (24 Nov 1934) 160-1.

3476 Mannes, Marya, "Vogue's Spotlight," Vogue (N.Y.), 84 (15 Dec 1934) 51, 72.

3477 Wyatt, Euphemia van Rensselaer, "Within the Gates," Catholic World (N.Y.), 140 (Dec 1934) 338-40.

3478 Fadiman, Clifton, "Within the Gates," Stage (N.Y.), 12 (Dec 1934) 13.

3479 Sedgwick, Ruth Woodbury, "Within the Gates: An Appreciation," Stage (N.Y.), 12 (Dec 1934) 18-19.

3480 Blake, Ben, "Within the Gates," New Theatre (N.Y.), 1 (Dec 1934) 19.

3481 Isaacs, Edith J. R., "Playhouse Gates: Broadway in Review," Theatre Arts Monthly (N.Y.), 18 (Dec 1934) 894-9. Reprinted in Theatre Arts Anthology (New York, 1950).

3482 Farma, William J., "The New York Stage: Concerning Elmer Rice, and Sean O'Casey's New Play," Players Magazine (Racine, Wis.) 11 (Dec 1934) 10.

3483 Nathan, George Jean, "Within the Gates," American Spectator (N.Y.), 3 (Dec 1934) 12.

3484 C., A. V., "The Theatre," Time and Tide (London), 16 (5 Jan 1935) 20.

3485 Reynolds, Horace, "Sean O'Casey and Within the Gates," Boston Evening Transcript (5 Jan 1935) part 2, pp. 4-5.

3486 "Watch-Ward Head Says Friends OK O'Casey Play," Boston Traveler (16 Jan 1935) pp. 1, 25.

3487 "O'Casey's Play 'Not Bad Enough to Be Banned,'" Boston Evening Transcript (16 Jan 1935) pp. 1, 3.

3488 "Mansfield Bans "Within the Gates" on Clergy Protest; Quincy Will Bar It," Boston Herald (16 Jan 1935) pp. 1, 4.

3489 "Fr. [Terence L.] Connolly Condemns Play by Sean O'Casey," Boston Traveler (16 Jan 1935) p. 25.

3490 "Appeal Ban on Irish Play," Boston Daily Record (17 Jan 1935) pp. 2, 31.

3491 "Letters That Come on the O'Casey Play," Boston Evening Transcript (17 Jan 1935) pp. 9-10 [Letters to the Editor by Frank Chouteau Brown, Gaylord Parks, Mark Howe, Jr., Stephen Green, Hubert V. Coryell, Jr., John S. Bainbridge, and S.E. Angoff].

3492 "Boston Censors to Hear Appeal," Boston Globe (17 Jan 1935) p. 6.

3493 Norton, Elliot, "Will Hear Theatre Men's Plea," Boston Post (17 Jan 1935) p. 11.

3494 "Thumbs Down on 'Within the Gates,'" Boston Evening Transcript (17 Jan 1935) pp. 1, 5.

3495 "Harvard Dramatic Club Against Ban," Boston Evening Transcript (17 Jan 1935) p. 5.

3496 "Mayor Moves to Ban O'Casey in Book Form," Boston Traveler (17 Jan 1935) pp. 1, 9.

3497 "O'Casey Play Ban Stays; Foes Heard by Mayor," Boston American (17 Jan 1935) p. 1.

3498 "Telegrams in Brief," Times (London), (17 Jan 1935) p. 11.

3499 "Move to Bar O'Casey Book in Hub," Boston Post (18 Jan 1935) p. 1, 2.

3500 "Playwrights Plead for Lifting of Ban," Boston Post (18 Jan 1935) p. 2.

3501 Sprague, George, "Mayor Bans Book of O'Casey Play," Boston Record (18 Jan 1935) pp. 2, 14.

3502 " 'Within Gates' Book Sold Out, Police Are Told," Boston Evening Transcript (18 Jan 1935) p. 2.

3503 "O'Casey Play Sought by Petition to Mayor," Harvard Crimson (Cambridge, Mass.), (18 Jan 1935) p. 1.

3504 "Ban Now Sought on O'Casey Book," Boston Globe (18 Jan 1935) p. 19.

3505 "Agrees with Mayor on Book," Boston Globe (18 Jan 1935) p. 19.

3506 "Cambridge Police to Study 'Within the Gates,'" Boston Globe (18 Jan 1935) p. 19.

3507 "O'Casey Book Faces 2 Police Drives," Boston American (18 Jan 1935) p. 15.

3508 "O'Casey Book Ban Ordered by Leonard," Boston Traveler (18 Jan 1935) pp. 1, 3.

3509 "Copy of Book on O'Casey Play Can't Be Found," Boston Daily Record (19 Jan 1935) p. 4.

3510 Connolly, Terence L., S.J., "Critics, Interviews, and Sean O'Casey," America (N.Y.), 52 (19 Jan 1935) 357-8.

3511 Dieffenbach, Albert C., "Religion Today: Clergy Bans the Play 'Within the Gates,'" Boston Evening Transcript (19 Jan 1935) section 5, p. 4.

3512 Hughes, Elinor, "'Within the Gates'; Gilbert & Sullivan and Others," Boston Herald (20 Jan 1935) p. 20.

3513 "Banned Play Showing Sean," Boston Traveler (21 Jan 1935) p. 14.

3514 "Police Censor Sermon in Hub," Boston Post (21 Jan 1935) pp. 1, 9.

3515 "Banned Play Read in Pulpit," Boston Herald (21 Jan 1935) p. 5.

3516 "'Within the Gates' to Reopen in N.Y.," Boston Herald (21 Jan 1935) p. 5.

3517 "Sees 'Medievalism' in Banning of Play; Anita Block Says 'Within the Gates' Has Purpose," Boston Globe (21 Jan 1935) p. 2.

3518 "Police Note Down Sermon," Boston Globe (21 Jan 1935) pp. 1, 2.

3519 "Play Banned Here to Reopen in New York," Boston Globe (21 Jan 1935) p. 2.

3520 "O'Casey Banned in Cambridge," Boston Traveler (19 Jan 1935) p. 4.

3521 "Calls 'Within the Gates' Book of Common Smut," Boston Globe (21 Jan 1935) p. 2.

3522 "Manhattan Levity on O'Casey Play," Boston Evening Transcript (21 Jan 1935) p. 4.

3523 "Letters to the Editor," Boston Evening Transcript (21 Jan 1935) p. 12 [By Homer Lockwood and Thaddeus Clapp].

3524 "Mayor's Threat to Close Church Hall Halts Public Reading of Banned Play," Boston Herald (22 Jan 1935) pp. 1, 4.

3525 "Play Ban by Mayor Contested," Boston American (22 Jan 1935) p. 11.

3526 "To Contest Banning of O'Casey Play," Boston Evening Transcript (22 Jan 1935) p. 6. See also Letters to the Editor, ibid., part 2, p. 12.

3527 "No O'Casey Reading by Prof. [H.W.L.] Dana; Byron [Street] House People Fearing Action, Put End to Meeting," Boston Post (22 Jan 1935) p. 9.

3528 Rogers, Robert E., "This Is Life," Boston American (22 Jan 1935) p. 11.

3529 "Ultimatum on 'Within the Gates,'" Boston Globe (23 Jan 1935) p. 13.

3530 "'Within the Gates' Banned in Somerville," Boston Globe (23 Jan 1935) p. 13.

3531 "Tufts School Dean Assails O'Casey Ban; Rev. Dr. Skinner Will Discuss Issue at Community Church Sunday--No Copy of Book on Sale," Boston Globe (23 Jan 1935) p. 15.

3532 "Boston Plays the Clown to a Limit Beyond Defense," Boston Evening Transcript (23 Jan 1935) p. 3.

3533 "Powerful Catholic Group Organized Here for Exertion of United Strength," Boston Herald (23 Jan 1935) pp. 1, 8.

3534 "Women's Clubs in Conference," Boston Herald (23 Jan 1935) p. 16.

3535 "Hub Church to Test Ban on O'Casey," Boston Post (23 Jan 1935) p. 23.

3536 Holland, George, "O'Casey Bank Roll Swelled by Ban," Boston American (23 Jan 1935) p. 15.

3537 "Mansfield Book Ban Warning; Defies Union; 'Within the Gates' Won't Be Read in Hall," Boston American (23 Jan 1935) p. 11.

3538 "Will Discuss Ban on Play in Sermon; Dr. Skinner Will Condemn Censors in Symphony Hall," Boston Globe (24 Jan 1935) p. 15.

3539 "Protest of Students Against Play Ban Bears 300 Names; Hillyer, Atkinson Score Censor of 'Within the Gates,'" Harvard Crimson (Cambridge, Mass.), (25 Jan 1935) pp. 1, 3.

3540 "Dr. Skinner to Speak on 'Within the Gates,'" Boston Herald (26 Jan 1935) p. 9.

3541 M[elvin], E[dwin] F., "Beside Grave Boston's Uncommon Common," New York Times (27 Jan 1935) section 8, p. 1.

3542 Atkinson, Brooks, "Thundering in the Index: In Banning Within the Gates Boston Withdraws from Universe Again-- Religion of O'Casey's Play," New York Times (27 Jan 1935) section 8, pp. 1, 3.

3543 "Stayed Not by Snow," New York Times (27 Jan 1935) section 8, p. 1. [Letters to the Editor by George Bushar, John Tuerk, and Frank Chouteau Brown].

3544 Watts, Richard, Jr., "Sight and Sound," New York Herald-Tribune (27 Jan 1935) section 5, pp. 1, 4.

3545 "Censorship Law Revisions Urged; Dean Skinner of Tufts Takes Issue with Catholics on O'Casey Play," Boston Herald (28 Jan 1935) p. 18.

3546 Melvin, Edwin F., "Miss Gish to Meet Pilgrims from Boston," Boston Evening Transcript (30 Jan 1935) part 2, p. 3.

3547 Nathan, George Jean, "The Theatre: Within the Gates," Vanity Fair (N.Y.), 43 (Jan 1935) 31-2.

3548 Melville, Nina, "Within the Gates," Modern Quarterly (Baltimore), 8 (Jan 1935) 695.

3549 Craven, Thomas, "Within the Gates," Stage (N.Y.), 12 (Jan 1935) 15.

3550 Connolly, Rev. Terence L., S.J., "Catholic View of 'Within the Gates': Analysis of O'Casey's Interpretation of Religion and the Church, and a Critique of Favoring Reviewers," Boston Evening Transcript (2 Feb 1935) part 4, pp. 5-6.

3551 Melvin, Edwin F., "O'Casey Via an Excursion to Manhattan; 'Within the Gates' and the Expedition from Boston to See It," Boston Evening Transcript (4 Feb 1935) p. 10.

3552 Hull, Forrest P., "Mayor to Let All Plays Give Showing Before Ban," Boston Evening Transcript (6 Feb 1935) pp. 1, 3.

3553 "Mayor to Refuse Advance Opinions on Plays of 'Doubtful Propriety,'" Boston Herald (7 Feb 1935) p. 4.

3554 "Theatres to Be Own Censors, But Face Trouble If Judgment Is Poor," Boston Post (7 Feb 1935) p. 4.

3555 "Modern Drama Stresses Sordid Things of Life," Boston Herald (7 Feb 1935) p. 14 [Letter to the Editor by Eric Fessenden].

3556 Guest, Edgar A., "Within the Gates, As Revised for Ultra-Sophisticated Boston Palates," Harvard Lampoon (Cambridge, Mass.), 109 (21 Feb 1935) p. 45.

3557 "Censorship Debate: Others to Address Educators Will Be Mrs. Franklin D. Roosevelt, Dr. Dana, and Dean Holmes," Harvard Crimson (Cambridge, Mass.), (7 Mar 1935) pp. 1, 4.

3558 "Father Sullivan and Dr. Dana in Heated Debate Before N. E. Teachers Association at Continental; Dana Quotes 'Within the Gates' to Demonstrate Its Worth; Sullivan Attacks It," Harvard Crimson (Cambridge, Mass.), (9 Mar 1935) pp. 1, 3.

THE END OF THE BEGINNING

3559 "Abbey Theatre: New Play by Sean O'Casey," Irish Times (Dublin), (9 Feb 1937) p. 8.

3560 S., D., "The Abbey: New Play by Sean O'Casey," Irish Independent (Dublin), (9 Feb 1937) p. 10.

3561 "Sean O'Casey Play. First Production at the Abbey Theatre," Evening Herald (Dublin), (9 Feb 1937) p. 5.

3562 "Q Theatre: A Triple Bill: A Pound on Demand by Sean O'Casey. Pariah by August Strindberg. The End of the Beginning by Sean O'Casey," Times (London), (17 Oct 1939) p. 6.

3563 Barker, Dudley, "Study of the Criminal Mind," Evening Standard (London), (17 Oct 1939) p. 10.

3564 "The Q: One-Act Plays: The End of the Beginning," Stage (London), (19 Oct 1939) p. 8.

3565 Brown, Ivor, "Q: The End of the Beginning," Observer (London), (22 Oct 1939) p. 11.

3566 "Unity Theatre: Sean O'Casey's Short Plays," Times (London), (23 May 1953) p. 8.

3567 Trewin, J. C., "Five Plays," Observer (London), (24 May 1953) p. 11.

3568 "The Unity: Three in a Row," Stage (London), (28 May 1953) p. 9.

3569 Douglas, Donald, "O'Casey Smashes His Targets," Daily Worker (London), (29 May 1953) p. 2.

3570 Harle, Eve, "Irish Life on London Stage," Challenge (London), 18 (6 June 1953) 2.

3571 "O'Casey Tops New Labor Theater Show," Daily People's World (San Francisco), (15 Oct 1954) p. 6 [At the San Francisco Labor Theater].

3572 G., J., "'O'Casey and Others' Offers a Fine Evening's Entertainment," Daily People's World (San Francisco), (26 Oct 1954) p. 7.

3573 Quidnunc, "An Irishman's Diary: O'Casey, Too," Irish Times (Dublin), (12 Jan 1967) p. 7 [At the Carouge, Geneva].

A POUND ON DEMAND

3574 "Q Theatre: A Triple Bill: A Pound on Demand by Sean

O'Casey. Pariah by August Strindberg. The End of the Beginning by Sean O'Casey," Times (London), (17 Oct 1939) p. 6.

3575 Barker, Dudley, "Study of the Criminal Mind," Evening Standard (London), (17 Oct 1939) p. 10.

3576 "The Q: One-Act Plays: A Pound on Demand," Stage (London), (19 Oct 1939) p. 8.

3577 Brown, Ivor, "Q: A Pound on Demand by Sean O'Casey," Observer (London), (22 Oct 1939) p. 11.

3578 Atkinson, Brooks, "The Play," New York Times (20 Dec 1946) p. 29.

3579 "Irishmen and Christians," Newsweek (N.Y.), 28 (30 Dec 1946) 71 [By the American Repertory Theater].

3580 Krutch, Joseph Wood, "Drama," Nation (N.Y.), 164 (4 Jan 1947) 26.

3581 Young, Stark, "Welcome Repertory," New Republic (N.Y.), 116 (6 Jan 1947) 42.

3582 Atkinson, Brooks, "Triple Play," New York Times (16 Apr 1959) p. 28 [At the Playhouse].

3583 Atkinson, Brooks, "Triple Play," New York Times (26 Apr 1959) section 2, p. 1.

3584 "Broadway Plans," New York Times (11 May 1959) p. 30 ["Triple Play" to close].

3585 "Triple Play," Theatre Arts (N.Y.), 43 (June 1959) 9.

3586 Brien, Alan, "Challenge to Chaplin," Sunday Telegraph (London), (9 Apr 1967) p. 10 [At the Mermaid].

3587 "Fifteen Plays for Galway Festival," Irish Times (Dublin), (18 Mar 1968) p. 10.

THE STAR TURNS RED

3588 Nathan, George Jean, "O'Casey Turns Red," Newsweek (N.Y.), 13 (26 June 1939) 25 [Synopsis of the play].

3589 "Unity Theatre: The Star Turns Red," Times (London), (14 Mar 1940) p. 6.

3590 D., A., "Mr. Sean O'Casey's New Play: The Star Turns Red," Manchester Guardian (14 Mar 1940) p. 8.

3591 "Authors Should Not Go to First Nights--Says Sean O'Casey," News Chronicle (London), (14 Mar 1940) p. 7.

3592 "Red Star," News Review (London), 9 (14 Mar 1940) 32.

3593 Moore, L. E., "The Star Turns Red. Sean O'Casey. Unity," Time and Tide (London) 21 (16 Mar 1940) 286-7.

3594 Spender, Stephen, "A Morality Play with No Morals: The Star Turns Red, at the Unity," New Statesman and Nation (London), 19 (16 Mar 1940) 363-4. See O'Casey's reply (30 Mar 1940) 432-3.

3595 Agate, James, "A Masterpiece. Unity: The Star Turns Red--A Play by Sean O'Casey," Sunday Times (London), (17 Mar 1940) p. 3.

3596 Bennett, Eric, "Fun, Moon and Stars," Sunday Chronicle (Manchester), (17 Mar 1940) p. 13.

3597 Brown, Ivor, "Unity: The Star Turns Red, by Sean O'Casey," Observer (London), (17 Mar 1940) p. 11.

3598 P., H. D. C., "We Are Amused: Art As Propaganda," Weekly Review (London), 30 (21 Mar 1940) 466-7.

3599 "Amusements: Unity," Cavalcade (London), 2 (23 Mar 1940) 16.

3600 Brown, Ivor, "The Bright and the Light," Illustrated London News, 196 (6 Apr 1940) 464.

3601 Digges, A. "The Star Turns Red," Irish Freedom (London), (Apr 1940) 2.

3602 "The Star Turns Red," Theatre World (London), 33 (Apr 1940) 95.

3603 Dukes, Ashley, "Social Basis: The English Scene," Theatre Arts (N.Y.), 24 (June 1940) 409-14.

3604 Lynd, Sheila, "This Is a Play for Our Time: The Star Turns Red (Unity Theatre)," Daily Worker (London), (26 Jul 1946) p. 2.

3605 Allen, Johm "An O'Casey Landmark," New Theatre (London), 3 (Aug 1946) 15.

3606 Marcabru, Pierre, "L'Etoile devient rouge," Arts (Paris), (27 June 1962) p. 6 [At the Gymnase d'Aubervilliers].

3607 Ganzl, Serge, "Le Théâtre: L'Etoile devient rouge de Sean O'Casey, au Festival d'Aubervilliers (Eté 1962)," Europe (Paris), année 40, nos. 401-2 (Sep-Oct 1962) 191-4.

3608 Capelle, J.-L., "L'Etoile devient rouge," France nouvelle (Paris), (24-30 Oct 1962) p. 33.

3609 "Minor O'Casey Play Performed in Paris," New York Times (25 Oct 1962) p. 47.

3610 Leclerc, Guy, "Le Théâtre d'Aubervilliers à Paris avec L'Etoile devient rouge de Sean O'Casey," L'Humanité (Paris), (26 Oct 1962) p. 2.

3611 Sandier, Gilles, "L'Etoile devient rouge," Arts (Paris), (31 Oct 1962) p. 8.

3612 "The Star Turns Red in Paris," Times (London), (31 Oct 1962) p. 8.

3613 L., J., "L'Etoile devient rouge. Au Théâtre Récamier," Figaro littéraire (Paris), (3 Nov 1962) p. 20.

3614 Gisselbrecht, André, "Réflexions sur la critique théâtrale (A propos de L'Etoile devient rouge)," L'Humanité (Paris), (3 Nov 1962) p. 2.

3615 Saurel, Renée, "De l'Esthétisme à la réalité: L'Etoile devient rouge, de Sean O'Casey au Théâtre Récamier," Temps modernes (Paris), année 18, no. 199 (Dec 1962) 1137-8.

3616 Forez, Maurice, "L'Etoile devient rouge," Théâtre populaire (Paris), no. 48 (1962) 108-12.

3617 Trilling, Ossia, "East Berlin Arts Festival Let-Down," Stage and Television Today (London), (13 Feb 1969) p. 21.

3618 Rocke, William, "O'Casey Once Again," Sunday Press (Dublin), (22 Jan 1978) p. 18 [Advance notice on the play, to be presented by the Abbey Theatre, Dublin].

3619 Smith, Gus, "Tribute to O'Casey," Sunday Independent (Dublin), (29 Jan 1978) p. 2 [Tomas MacAnna's forthcoming first Irish production].

3620 Kelly, Seamus, "The Star Turns Red at the Abbey," Irish Times (Dublin), (3 Feb 1978) p. 9.

3621 Rushe, Desmond, "Too Long a Wait for This Play," Irish Independent (Dublin), (3 Feb 1978) p. 11.

3622 Martin, Peter, "O'Casey's 'Star' Has Flaws, but Works," Irish Press (Dublin), (3 Feb 1978) p. 6.

3623 Houlihan, Con, "No Flesh and Blood in O'Casey's Crude Parable," Evening Press (Dublin), (3 Feb 1978) p. 3.

3624 Finegan, John, "Abbey Goes with O'Casey," Evening Herald (Dublin), (3 Feb 1978) p. 4.

3625 Smith, Gus, "Abbey Braves the Red Flag," Sunday Independent (Dublin), (5 Feb 1978) p. 2.

3626 Chaillet, Ned, "The Star Turns Red: Abbey, Dublin," Times (London), (8 Feb 1978) p. 9.

3627 Cronin, Colm, "The Plot Thins," Hibernia (Dublin), (10 Feb 1978) p. 19. See reply by Robert G. Lowery, ibid. (2 Mar 1978) p. 2.

3628 O'Connor, Kevin, "Dublin: The Star Turns Red," Stage and Television Today (London), (23 Feb 1978) pp. 22-23.

3629 "Conflict Between Fascism and Socialism Theme of O'Casey Play," United Irishman (Dublin), 36 (Mar 1978) p. 11. See reply by Robert G. Lowery, ibid. (May 1978) p. 7.

3630 Lowery, Robert G., "Sean O'Casey: The Passionate Believer," Daily World (N.Y.), (2 Mar 1978) p. 12. See letters to the editor by Conn O'Grady, "O'Casey Lives," ibid. (4 Mar 1978) p. 6; and by Leon Baya, "Mr. O'Casey's World of Reality," ibid. (21 Mar 1978) p. 6.

3631 "The Star Turns Red," Variety (N.Y.), (5 Apr 1978) p. 92.

3632 Lowery, Robert G., "Theatre Reviews: The Star Turns Red," Sean O'Casey Review, 4 (Spring 1978) 194-9.

RED ROSES FOR ME

3633 "Olympia Theatre: Red Roses for Me," Irish Times (Dublin), (16 Mar 1943) p. 3.

3634 S., D., "New O'Casey Play," Irish Independent (Dublin), (16 Mar 1943) p. 2.

3635 "Red Roses for Me," Evening Herald (Dublin), (16 Mar 1943) p. 2.

3636 Fallon, Gabriel, "Red, Red Roses," Standard (Dublin), 15 (26 Mar 1943) 3.

3637 "Red Roses for Me: Olympia Theatre, Dublin," Theatre Arts (N.Y.), 27 (Oct 1943) 586.

3638 Kelleher, John V., "O'Casey in Boston," New Republic (N.Y.), 110 (20 Mar 1944) 380 [At the Tributary Theatre].

3639 "Red Roses for Me: Design by Matt Horner," Theatre Arts (N.Y.), 28 (Jul 1944) 437.

3640 "Embassy Theatre: Red Roses for Me by Sean O'Casey," Times (London), (27 Feb 1946) p. 6.

3641 D., A., "O'Casey Play with All-Irish Cast: Red Roses for Me. Embassy Theatre," News Chronicle (London), (27 Feb 1946) p. 3.

3642 Darlington, W. A., "Sean O'Casey's Fine Play: Realism with Symbolism," Daily Telegraph (London), (27 Feb 1946) p. 5.

3643 Grant, Elspeth, "Sean O'Casey Gets Away with It," Daily Sketch (London), (27 Feb 1946) p. 3.

3644 Hale, Lionel, "At the Play--O'Casey on the Right Road Back," Daily Mail (London), (27 Feb 1946) p. 3.

3645 Williams, Stephen, "A New Sean O'Casey Play," Evening News (London), (27 Feb 1946) p. 2.

3646 "The Embassy: Red Roses for Me," Stage (London), (28 Feb 1946) p. 4.

3647 Agate, James, "A Poet's Play: Red Roses for Me. Embassy," Sunday Times (London), (3 Mar 1946) p. 2.

3648 T., J. C., "Red Roses for Me," Observer (London), (3 Mar 1946) p. 2.

3649 Redfern, James, "Red Roses for Me at the Embassy Theatre," Spectator (London), 176 (8 Mar 1946) 244.

3650 Potter, Stephen, "Red Roses for Me at the Embassy," New Statesman and Nation (London), 31 (9 Mar 1946) 173.

3651 Hope-Wallace, Philip, "Red Roses for Me. Sean O'Casey. Embassy," Time and Tide (London), 27 (9 Mar 1946) 224.

3652 Darlington, W. A., "O'Casey Scores a Hit," New York Times (10 Mar 1946) section 2, p. 2.

3653 Eric [Keown], "At the Play," Punch (London), 210 (13 Mar 1946) 230.

3654 Trewin, J. C., "Roses for Sean O'Casey," John O'London's Weekly, 54 (22 Mar 1946) 254.

3655 Hope-Wallace, Philip, "Theatre," Time and Tide (London), 27 (30 Mar 1946) 296.

3656 Aickman, Robert Fordyce, "Mr. O'Casey and the Striker. Red Roses for Me: Embassy, Swiss Cottage," Nineteenth Century and After (London), 139 (Apr 1946) 172-5.

3657 M., H. G., "Red Roses for Me," Theatre World (London), 42 (Apr 1946) 7-8.

3658 "New Theatre: Red Roses for Me by Sean O'Casey," Times (London), (29 May 1946) p. 6.

3659 W., T., "Theatre," Irish Press (Dublin), (3 June 1946) p. 4.

3660 Stokes, Sewell, "New Plays at Last! The English Spotlight: Red Roses for Me," Theatre Arts (N.Y.), 30 (June 1946) 355-6.

3661 Fallon, Gabriel, "All Professionals Now," Standard (Dublin), 18 (5 Jul 1946) 5. See reply by O'Casey, 18 (26 Jul 1946) 5; and counter-reply by Fallon, 18 (26 Jul 1946) 5 [Letters to the Editor].

3662 W., A., "Red Roses for Me," Theatre World (London), 42 (Jul 1946) 7 [At the Lyric Theatre, Hammersmith, to which it was transferred from the Embassy Theatre on 9 Apr 1946].

3663 Fallon, Gabriel, "Calling Mr. O'Casey," Standard (Dublin), 18 (9 Aug 1946) 5. See O'Casey's reply, "And Sean O'Casey Wrote," 18 (9 Aug 1946) 5 [Letter to the Editor].

3664 McHugh, Roger, "Dublin Theatre," Bell (Dublin), 12 (Sep 1946) 520-3.

3665 MacLeod, Alison, "Radio and TV: Drama High and Low," Daily Worker (London), (2 Nov 1953) p. 2 [B.B.C.].

3666 Calta, Louis, "O'Casey Play Set for October Bow: Red Roses for Me, Slightly Autobiographical, to Be Produced by [Gordon W.] Pollock," New York Times (29 Mar 1955) p. 33.

3667 Norton, Elliot, "Red Roses for Me," Boston Post (14 Dec 1955) p. 5.

3668 Norton, Elliot, "Second Thoughts of a First-Nighter. Irish Drama Is Good But Actors Not Right: Red Roses for Me," Boston Sunday Post (18 Dec 1955) Dramatic Page.

3669 Lewis, Allan, "Sean O'Casey's World," Nation (N.Y.), 181 (24 Dec 1955) 555-6.

3670 "After 21 Years, Broadway to See a New O'Casey Play," Daily Worker (N.Y.), (26 Dec 1955) p. 8.

3671 Atkinson, Brooks, "Sean O'Casey," New York Times (29 Dec 1955) p. 15 [At the Booth Theater, New York].

3672 Chapman, John, "Red Roses for Me Pure O'Casey, Lilting, Beautiful, and a Bit Dull," New York Daily News (29 Dec 1955) p. 43.

3673 Watts, Richard, "Sean O'Casey's Red Roses for Me," New York Post (29 Dec 1955) p. 12.

3674 Kerr, Walter, "Red Roses for Me," New York Herald Tribune (29 Dec 1955) p. 11.

3675 "O'Casey Back on Broadway after 21 Years," Daily People's World (San Francisco), (29 Dec 1955) p. 7.

3676 Coleman, Robert, "Red Roses for Me," New York Daily Mirror (30 Dec 1955) pp. 23, 25.

3677 "O'Casey's Red Roses Opens in New York," Irish Times (Dublin), (30 Dec 1955) p. 7.

3678 "O'Casey's Play in New York," Times (London), (30 Dec 1955) p. 3.

3679 McClain, John, "O'Casey's Play Follows a Tortuous Course," New York Theatre Critics' Review, 16 (31 Dec 1955) 183.

3680 Coleman, Robert, "Red Roses for Me," New York Theatre Critics' Review, 16 (31 Dec 1955) 184.

3681 Hawkins, William, "Red Roses for Me a Rare and Major Event," New York Theatre Critics' Review, 16 (31 Dec 1955) 184.

3682 Raymond, Harry, "O'Casey's Red Roses for Me a Song of Human Brotherhood," Daily Worker (N.Y.), (3 Jan 1956) p. 7.

3683 Atkinson, Brooks, "Red Roses for Me: O'Casey's Beautiful Ode to the Glory of Life," New York Times (8 Jan 1956) section 2, p. 1.

3684 "New Play in Manhattan," Time (N.Y.), 67 (9 Jan 1956) 41.

3685 "Huzzas for O'Casey: Red Roses for Me: Produced by Gordon W. Pollock. Directed by John O'Shaughnessy," Newsweek (N.Y.), 47 (9 Jan 1956) 44-5.

3686 Gibbs, Wolcott, "Red Roses for Me," New Yorker, 31 (14 Jan 1956) 58-64.

3687 Hewes, Henry, "Sean O'Casey's One-Shilling Opera," Saturday Review of Literature (N.Y.), 39 (14 Jan 1956) 20.

3688 Clurman, Harold, "Red Roses for Me," Nation (N.Y.), 182 (14 Jan 1956) 39-40. Reprinted in Lies Like Truth (New York: Macmillan, 1958) pp. 122-4.

3689 Shipley, Joseph T., "Red Roses for Me. By Sean O'Casey. Presented by Gordon W. Pollock. At the Booth Theatre," New Leader (N.Y.), 39 (16 Jan 1956) 27.

3690 Lewis, Theophilus, "Theatre: Red Roses for Me," America (N.Y.), 94 (21 Jan 1956) 459-60.

3691 Bentley, Eric, "The Politics of Sean O'Casey," New Republic (N.Y.), 134 (30 Jan 1956) 21. Reprinted in What Is Theatre? (London: Dennis Dobson, 1957) pp. 107-11; (New York: Antheneum 1968) pp. 265-8.

3692 Wyatt, Euphemia van Rensselaer, "Red Roses for Me," Catholic World (N.Y.), 182 (Feb 1956) 387-8.

3693 Gassner, John, "Red Roses for Me," Educational Theatre Journal (Ann Arbor, Mich.), 8 (Mar 1956) 37-8.

3694 "Red Roses for Me. December 28, 1955. Booth Theatre," Theatre Arts (N.Y.), 40 (Mar 1956) 15.

3695 Skoumal, Aloys, "Irské drama znovu v Realistickém divadle: Sean O'Casey," Divadlo (Prague), 8 (Dec 1957) 1007-12.

3696 Verdot, Guy, "Paris Fait Connaissance avec l'Irlandais O'Casey," Figaro littéraire (Paris), no. 772 (4 Feb 1961) 3 [At the Théâtre national populaire].

3697 "Théâtre Populaire Performs O'Casey," New York Times (11 Feb 1961) p. 26.

3698 Olivier, C., "Roses Rouges pour moi, de Sean O'Casey," Lettres françaises (Paris), (16-22 Feb 1961) p. 8.

3699 Saurel, Renée, "Vilar sur la brèche," Temps modernes (Paris), 16 (1961), 1237-42.

3700 Lemarchand, Jacques, "Roses Rouges pour moi de Sean O'Casey, au Théâtre national populaire," Figaro littéraire (Paris), no. 774 (18 Feb 1961) 16.

3701 "Roses Rouges pour moi, de Sean O'Casey (T.N.P.)," L'Avant-Scène (Paris), no. 238 (1 Mar 1961) 36.

3702 Bourget-Pailleron, Robert, "Théâtre National Populaire: Roses Rouges pour moi, quatre actes de Sean O'Casey, texte français de Michel Habart," Revue de deux mondes (Paris), (1 Mar 1961) 155-6.

3703 "O'Casey in Epic Style: Vilar Produces Red Roses for Me," Times (London), (25 Apr 1961) p. 20.

3704 Beigbeder, Marc, "Du Sang et des roses," Lettres nouvelles (Paris), (Apr 1961) 143-7.

3705 Taubman, Howard, "Sean O'Casey: Red Roses for Me Is Revived Downtown," New York Times (18 Nov 1961) p. 41 [At Greenwich Mews Theatre].

3706 Oliver, Edith, "Off Broadway: Presses Flowers," New Yorker (N.Y.), 37 (9 Dec 1961) 162-4.

3707 "Irish Worker's Mission. Mermaid Theatre: Red Roses for Me," Times (London), (5 Sep 1962) p. 13.

3708 Lewis, Peter, "On the Boil and All's Well in the O'Caseyland," Daily Mail (London), (5 Sep 1962) p. 3.

3709 Hope-Wallace, Philip, "Red Roses for Me at the Mermaid," Guardian (London), (5 Sep 1962) p. 7.

3710 Kretzmer, Herbert, "Just a Golden Stream of Irish Words," Daily Express (London), (5 Sep 1962) p. 4.

3711 Pacey, Ann, "Red Roses Get No Bouquet," Daily Herald (London), (5 Sep 1962) p. 3.

3712 Darlington, W. A., "O'Casey Play Problems Unsolved," Daily Telegraph (London), (5 Sep 1962) p. 14.

3713 Shulman, Milton, "O'Casey Brought to Shining Life," Evening Standard (London), (5 Sep 1962) p. 4.

3714 Frame, Colin, "Poetry Out of the Grime," Evening News (London), (5 Sep 1962) p. 5.

3715 Cashin, Fergus, "O'Casey Bouquet," Daily Sketch (London), (6 Sep 1962) p. 4.

3716 M., M., "Bright Shilling: Red Roses for Me (Mermaid)," Daily Worker (London), (6 Sep 1962) p. 2.

3717 M., R. B., "Garlands of Beautiful Words," Stage and Television Today (London), (6 Sep 1962) p. 13.

3718 Hobson, Harold, "Responsibility of War," Sunday Times (London), (9 Sep 1962) p. 33.

3719 Brien, Alan, "Mermaid Score," Sunday Telegraph (London), (9 Sep 1962) p. 8.

3720 Tynan, Kenneth, "Theatre. Second Lap: Red Roses for Me (Mermaid)," Observer (London), (9 Sep 1962) p. 22.

3721 Gellert, Roger, "Cold Fry," New Statesman (London), 64 (14 Sep 1962) 334.

3722 Gascoigne, Bamber, "Meccano Drama: Red Roses for Me (Mermaid)," Spectator (London), 209 (14 Sep 1962) 364.

3723 B., D. F., "Mermaid: Red Roses for Me," Theatre World (London), 58 (Oct 1962) 8.

3724 Taylor, John Russell, "Red Roses for Me," Plays and Players (London), 10 (Nov 1962) 66-7.

3725 Rodel, Fritz, "Rote Rosen für mich," Berliner Zeitung (4 May 1963) p. 6.

3726 Kerndl, R., "Rote Rosen für mich: Die optimistische Tragödie des Iren Sean O'Casey auf der Bühne des Deutschen Theaters," Neues Deutschland (Berlin), (10 May 1963) p. 4.

3727 Wendt, Ernst, "O'Caseys Narrenspiele: über Aufführungen in Wuppertal, Ostberlin und Stuttgart," Theater heute (Hannover), 4 (Aug 1963) 20-6.

3728 Kelly, Seamus, "Red Roses for Me at the Abbey," Irish Times (Dublin), (1 Aug 1967) p. 8.

3729 F[inegan], J[ohn] J., "Abbey First Night: Many Echoes in Red Roses," Evening Herald (Dublin), (1 Aug 1967) p. 4.

3730 "Red Roses at Abbey Falls Flat," Irish Independent (Dublin), (2 Aug 1967) p. 10.

3731 Page, Sean, "What Happened to O'Casey?" Sunday Press (Dublin), (6 Aug 1967) p. 19. See reply by John O'Riordan, "The Croak of a Critical Corncrake" (24 Sep 1967) p. 12 [Letter to the Editor].

3732 Coughlan, Aileen, "All-Ireland Drama Festival," Irish Times (Dublin), (30 Apr 1968) p. 10.

3733 Coughlan, Aileen, "Athlone Festival: O'Casey," Irish Times (Dublin), (6 May 1968) p. 10.

3734 Coughlan, Aileen, "Amateur Drama," Irish Times (Dublin), (31 May 1968) p. 10.

3735 Sweeney, Maxwell, "Sean O'Casey's Posthumous Peace Puts 'Red Roses' into the Abbey," Variety (9 Jan 1980) 272 [To be presented at the Abbey Theatre on 10 Apr 1980].

3736 Finegan, John, "Theatres," Evening Herald (Dublin), (8 Mar 1980) p. 6.

3737 Kehoe, Emmanuel, "Killing the White-Washed Kitchen," Sunday Press (Dublin), (30 Mar 1980) p. 11.

3738 Finegan, John, "Theatres," Evening Herald (Dublin), (4 Apr 1980) p. 6.

3739 Sennett, Graham, "The Sean O'Casey Show," Evening Press (Dublin), (4 Apr 1980) p. 6.

3740 Rocke, William, "Easter Eggs!" Sunday Press (Dublin), (6 Apr 1980) p. 18.

3741 Sheridan, Michael, "Playing It Safe," Irish Press (Dublin), (8 Apr 1980) p. 9.

3742 Boland, John, "Here's Sean," Hibernia (Dublin), (10 Apr 1980) p. 36.

3743 Walsh, Caroline, "President Attends O'Casey Tribute," Irish Times (Dublin), (11 Apr 1980) p. 6 [On opening of play].

3744 Kennedy, Maev, "Red Roses for Me at the Abbey," Irish Times (Dublin), (11 Apr 1980) p. 10.

3745 Rushe, Desmond, "Red Roses for Me Lacking in Impact," Irish Independent (Dublin), (11 Apr 1980) p. 11.

3746 Sheridan, Michael, "Script's Flaws Prove a Thorn in 'Red Roses,'" Irish Press (Dublin), (11 Apr 1980) 5.

3747 Finegan, John, "Red Roses--A Play of Echoes," Evening Herald (Dublin), (11 Apr 1980) p. 7.

3748 Brogan, Theresa, "Abbey's 'Red Roses' Lacks Dramatic Impact," Evening Press (Dublin), (11 Apr 1980) p. 3.

3749 Coveney, Michael, "Red Roses for Me," Financial Times (London), (12 Apr 1980) p. 14.

3750 Smith, Gus, "Full Justice to Anton Chekhov," Sunday Independent (Dublin), (13 Apr 1980) p. 30.

3751 "Abbey's O'Casey," Sunday Independent (Dublin), (13 Apr 1980).

3752 Kehoe, Emmanuel, "No Bloom," Sunday Press (Dublin), (13 Apr 1980) p. 23.

3753 Chaillet, Ned, "Theatre," Times (London), (14 Apr 1980) p. 12.

3754 Cronin, Colm, "O Rose, Thou Art Sick," Hibernia (Dublin), (17 Apr 1980) p. 31.

3755 Hunt, Hugh, "Red Roses for Me: The Background," Abbey Theatre Programme (Apr 1980) no page numbers.

3756 O'Casey, Eileen, "Red Roses for Sean," Abbey Theatre Programme (Apr 1980) no page numbers.

3757 Richards, Shelah, "Red Roses for Me: The First Production," Abbey Theatre Programme (Apr 1980) no page numbers.

3758 McKenna, David, "Blossom Time," In Dublin, no. 100 (18 Apr-1 May 1980) 15-17.

3759 O Gallchóir, Dónall, "Red Roses for Me," Irish Press (Dublin), (26 Apr 1980) p. 8.

3760 O'F., P., "Superb O'Casey," Westmeath Examiner (Mullingar), (10 May 1980) p. 2.

3761 "Ireland's Television," America (N.Y.), 142 (31 May 1980) 463.

PURPLE DUST

3762 Agate, James, "A New Challenge," Sunday Times (London),

(19 Apr 1942) p. 2 [To be produced by Alec Clunes at the Arts Theatre]. See replies by O'Casey, "A New Challenge," (26 Apr 1942) p. 4; and "Mr. Agate: A Curt Reply," (10 May 1942) p. 2 [Letters to the Editor].

3763 Hughes, Elinor, "Purple Dust: A Comedy in Three Acts by Sean O'Casey," Boston Herald (7 Dec 1944) p. 23 [At N.E. Mutual Hall by the Boston Tributary Theater].

3764 "London Letter," Irish Times (Dublin), (28 Aug 1945) p. 3 [To open at Liverpool Playhouse].

3765 "London Letter: O'Casey Play," Irish Independent (Dublin), (25 Mar 1953) p. 6 [To open at Theatre Royal, Glasgow].

3766 "Mr. Sean O'Casey's Purple Dust: An Anglo-Irish Comedy New to London," Times (London), (30 Mar 1953) p. 9 [Forthcoming production].

3767 "Advice from Sean O'Casey," Daily Worker (London), (1 Apr 1953) p. 3.

3768 S., N., "Mr. Sean O'Casey's Play: Purple Dust," Manchester Guardian (29 Apr 1953) p. 4.

3769 "Croydon Players: Purple Dust by Sean O'Casey," Times (London), (3 Nov 1954) p. 6.

3770 Thespis, "Plays and Films," English (London), 10 (spring 1955) 139-40.

3771 Atkinson, Brooks, "The O'Casey," New York Times (28 Dec 1956) p. 15 [At the Cherry Lane Theatre, Greenwich Village].

3772 Chapman, John, "Purple Dust," New York Daily News (28 Dec 1956) p. 39.

3773 Raymond, Harry, "O'Casey's Purple Dust in Glowing Production," Daily Worker (N.Y.), (2 Jan 1957) p. 6.

3774 Beaufort, John, "O'Casey Off-Broadway: Purple Dust," Christian Science Monitor (Boston), (5 Jan 1957) p. 10.

3775 Kerr, Walter, "O'Casey, Molière: A Jig and a Minuet," New York Herald Tribune (6 Jan 1957) section 4, pp. 1, 2.

3776 "O'Casey at Play: Purple Dust. Produced by Paul Shyre, Noel Behan, Lewis Manilow, Howard Gottfried. Directed by Philip Burton," Newsweek (N.Y.), 49 (12 Jan 1957) 67.

3777 Hatch, Robert, "Theatre and Films," Nation (N.Y.), 184 (19 Jan 1957) 65-6.

3778 Hewes, Henry, "Purple Dust," Saturday Review of Literature (N.Y.), 40 (19 Jan 1957) 48.

3779 Shipley, Joseph T., "Purple Dust. By Sean O'Casey. At the Cherry Lane Theater," New Leader (N.Y.), 40 (21 Jan 1957) 28.

3780 Aronson, James, "Sean O'Casey," National Guardian (N.Y.), (18 Feb 1957) p. 9.

3780a "Purple Dust," New York Times Magazine (24 Feb 1957) p. 24 [picture].

3781 Wyatt, Euphemia van Rensselaer, "Purple Dust," Catholic World (N.Y.), 184 (Mar 1957) 469-70.

3782 Colin, Saul, "Plays and Players in New York," Plays and Players (London), 4 (Apr 1957) 17.

3783 "Cast's Support for Mr. O'Casey: Demands Well Met in Wayward Comedy," Times (London), (19 Mar 1960) p. 8 [At the Tower Theatre].

3784 "O'Casey Festival Is Set for London. Mermaid Theatre to Offer 3 of Irish Playwright's Works," New York Times (15 Aug 1962) p. 37 [Purple Dust, Red Roses for Me and The Plough and the Stars].

3785 "Bright and Dusty Bits in O'Caseyland. Mermaid Theatre: Purple Dust," Times (London), (16 Aug 1962) p. 5.

3786 Worsley, T. G., "The Mermaid: Purple Dust," Financial Times (London), (16 Aug 1962) p. 16.

3787 Shorter, Eric, "Snook Cocked at English: Mermaid Miss Full O'Casey," Daily Telegraph (London), (16 Aug 1962) p. 12.

3788 Nathan, David, "First Night: Sad Time for Sean O'Casey," Daily Herald (London), (16 Aug 1962) p. 3.

3789 Levin, Bernard, "It's an Uncontrolled Shambles: And As for the Irish Accents!" Daily Mail (London), (16 Aug 1962) p. 3.

3790 Kretzmer, Herbert, "A Bitter Joke Behind the Laughter," Daily Express (London), (16 Aug 1962) p. 8.

3791 Hope-Wallace, Philip, "Purple Dust," Guardian (London), (16 Aug 1962) p. 5.

3792 Shulman, Milton, "The English Can't Be Irish," Evening Standard (London), (16 Aug 1962) p. 4.

3793 Cashin, Fergus, "A Dust-up over Nothing," Daily Sketch (London), (17 Aug 1962) p. 8.

3794 M., M., "A Flying Start for O'Casey Season: Purple Dust (Mermaid)," Daily Worker (London), (17 Aug 1962) p. 2.

3795 Brien, Alan, "Graves and Guffaws," Sunday Telegraph (London), (19 Aug 1962) p. 8.

3796 Hobson, Harold, "Doom Without a Profit," Sunday Times (London), (19 Aug 1962) p. 25.

3797 Tynan, Kenneth, "Theatre: Purple Dust (Mermaid)," Observer (London), (19 Aug 1962) p. 18.

3798 Keown, Eric, "At the Play: Sean O'Casey's Purple Dust," Punch (London), 243 (22 Aug 1962) 280-1.

3799 H., P., "Making Sport of the Irish and Mincemeat of the English," Stage and Television Today (London), (23 Aug 1962) p. 25.

3800 Gellert, Roger, "Dumb Show," New Statesman (London), 64 (24 Aug 1962) 237.

3801 Rutherford, Malcolm, "Purple Dust (Mermaid)," Spectator (London), 209 (24 Aug 1962) 272.

3802 Trewin, J. C., "On with the Dance," Illustrated London News, 241 (1 Sep 1962) 338.

3803 B., D. F., "Mermaid: Purple Dust," Theatre World (London), 58 (Sep 1962) 32.

3804 Winnington, Alan, "Ensemble's O'Casey: Purple Dust (Berliner Ensemble, Berlin)," Daily Worker (London), (1 Mar 1966) p. 2.

3805 Candida, "An Irishwoman's Diary," Irish Times (Dublin), (19 June 1967) p. 9 [By the Berliner Ensemble].

3806 Kelly, Seamus, "An O'Casey Not Worth the Long Wait," Irish Times (Dublin), (31 Jan 1975) p. 11.

3807 Rushe, Desmond. "Purple Dust at the Abbey Good Fun," Irish Independent (Dublin), (31 Jan 1975) p. 2.

3808 Colgan, Gerald. "Purple Dust at the Abbey," Hibernia (Dublin), (7 Feb 1975) p. 25.

OAK LEAVES AND LAVENDER

3809 "The Lyric Theatre, Hammersmith: Oak Leaves and Lavender by Sean O'Casey," Times (London), (14 May 1947) p. 6.

3810 Mosley, Leonard, "The Praise of O'Casey. Oak Leaves and Lavender. Lyric, Hammersmith," Daily Express (London), (14 May 1947) p. 3.

3811 "O'Casey's New Play," Irish Press (Dublin), (14 May 1947) p. 4.

3812 "London Greets New O'Casey Play," Irish Independent (Dublin), (14 May 1947) p. 6.

3813 Bishop, George W., "Sean O'Casey's New Play: Ghosts and War," Daily Telegraph (London), (14 May 1947) p. 5.

3814 Grant, Elspeth, "Last Night's First Night: Strange Play with Good Actors," Daily Graphic (London), (14 May 1947) p. 2.

3815 Hale, Lionel, "Last Night's Play: Mr. O'Casey's Revenge on Cromwell," Daily Mail (London), (14 May 1947) p. 3.

3816 M., P. L., "Patchy Play by O'Casey. Lyric, Hammersmith: Oak Leaves and Lavender," Daily Herald (London), (14 May 1947) p. 3.

3817 Williams, Stephen, "Where Land Girls Sing," Evening News (London), (14 May 1947) p. 2.

3818 "London Letter: Oak Leaves and Lavender," Irish Times (Dublin), (14 May 1947) p. 5.

3819 "Lyric, Hammersmith: Oak Leaves and Lavender," Stage (London), (15 May 1947) p. 4.

3820 Brown, Ivor, "Slump and Sean," Observer (London), (18 May 1947) p. 2.

3821 Hobson, Harold, "Oak Leaves and Lavender: Lyric, Hammersmith," Sunday Times (London), (18 May 1947) p. 2.

3822 Hope-Wallace, Philip, "Oak Leaves and Lavender: Sean O'Casey.

Lyric, Hammersmith," Time and Tide (London), 28 (24 May 1947) 542.

3823 S., F., "Oak Leaves and Lavender," Theatre World (London), 43 (June 1947) 9-10.

3824 "London Letter: New O'Casey Play," Irish Independent (Dublin), (6 Dec 1949) p. 6.

COCK-A-DOODLE DANDY

3825 K., "Play to Arouse Anger and Pity," Irish Times (Dublin), (14 Dec 1949) p. 7 [At the People's Theatre, Newcastle upon Tyne, 10 Dec 1949].

3826 O'Casey, Sean, "Cock-a-Doodle Dandy," Irish Times (Dublin), (30 Dec 1949) p. 5 [Letter to the Editor].

3827 O'Casey, Sean, "Cock-a-Doodle Dandy," Irish Times (Dublin), (13 Jan 1950) p. 5 [Letter to the Editor].

3828 Hollway, Frank, "Cock-a-Doodle Dandy: Sean O'Casey," Tyneside Phoenix (Newcastle-upon-Tyne), 10 (Spring 1950) 9-10.

3829 Atkinson, Brooks, "O'Casey at Yale: Cock-a-Doodle Dandy on School Stage," New York Times (4 Nov 1955) p. 26.

3830 Hewes, Henry, "Broadway Postscript," Saturday Review of Literature (N.Y.), 38 (19 Nov 1955) 37.

3831 Quidnunc, "An Irishman's Diary," Irish Times (Dublin), (19 Aug 1958) p. 6.

3832 "O'Casey Play Acclaimed in Toronto," Evening Mail (Dublin), (2 Oct 1958) p. 6 [At the Playhouse].

3833 "Catholics Angered by O'Casey," Evening Herald (Dublin), (2 Oct 1958) p. 7.

3834 "Trouble over O'Casey Play in Toronto," Irish Times (Dublin), (7 Oct 1948) p. 9.

3835 "O'Casey Play Is Guarded," Evening Herald (Dublin), (7 Oct 1958) p. 1.

3836 "Shouters at Play Chided by O'Casey: Dramatist Scores Manners of Couples Who Interrupted His Drama in Toronto," New York Times (7 Oct 1958) p. 40.

3837 Nordell, Rod, "Cock-a-Doodle Casey," New Leader (N.Y.), 61 (3 Nov 1958) 20-2.

3838 O'Casey, Sean, "O'Casey's Credo: His First Concern is to Make a Play Live," New York Times (9 Nov 1958) section 2, pp. 1, 3. Reprinted in Playwrights on Playwrighting, ed. Toby Cole (New York: Hill & Wang, 1960) pp. 247-9.

3839 Atkinson, Brooks, "O'Casey's Defense of Joy: Cock-a-Doodle Dandy Has Premiere Here," New York Times (13 Nov 1958) p. 39 [At Carnegie Hall Playhouse, New York].

3840 McHarry, Charles, "O'Casey an Angry Old Man in Latest Drama," New York Daily News (13 Nov 1958) p. 75.

3841 Malcolm, Donald, "Off Broadway: Import News," New Yorker, 34 (22 Nov 1958) 100-2.

3842 Atkinson, Brooks, "Two by O'Casey: Cock-a-Doodle Dandy and Shadow of a Gunman Open Within 9 Days," New York Times (23 Nov 1958) section 2, p. 1.

3843 "New Play in Manhattan," Time (N.Y.), 72 (24 Nov 1958) 90.

3844 "Another from O'Casey: Cock-a-Doodle Dandy. By Sean O'Casey," Newsweek (N.Y.), 52 (24 Nov 1958) 78.

3845 Clurman, Harold, "Theatre," Nation (N.Y.), 187 (29 Nov 1958) 416.

3846 Hewes, Henry, "Where Is Fancy Bred?" Saturday Review of Literature (N.Y.), 41 (6 Dec 1958) 37.

3847 "N.Y. Theatre Goes Irish: O'Casey Too Much for the Actors," Times (London), (10 Dec 1958) p. 3.

3848 "Cock-a-Doodle Dandy," Theatre Arts (N.Y.), 43 (Jan 1959) 64.

3849 Colin, Saul, "Plays and Players in New York: Fighting Superstition," Plays and Players (London), 4 (Feb 1959) 24.

3850 Funke, Lewis, "O'Casey Awaits Opening of Play: Looks Forward to London Cock-a-Doodle Dandy," New York Times (2 Sep 1959) p. 35.

3851 Hope-Wallace, Philip, "The Edinburgh Festival," Time and Tide (London), 40 (5 Sep 1959) 956.

3852 "Fine Acting in O'Casey Play," Times (London), (8 Sep 1959) p. 14 [At the Lyceum, Edinburgh].

3853 Mavor, Ronald, "Sean O'Casey's Hymn to Life: Fine and Beautiful Play," <u>Scotsman</u> (Edinburgh), (8 Sep 1959) p. 11.

3854 Darlington, W.A., "Sean O'Casey Cracks at the Kill-Joys: Lively Satire," <u>Daily Telegraph</u> (London), (8 Sep 1959) p. 10.

3855 Wilson, Cecil, "The Young Heart of Old Sean: <u>Cock-a-Doodle Dandy</u>, by Sean O'Casey. Lyceum, Edinburgh," <u>Daily Mail</u> (London), (8 Sep 1959) p. 5.

3856 Levin, Bernard, "The Devil and Mr. O'Casey," <u>Daily Express</u> (London), (8 Sep 1959) p. 13.

3857 Darlington, W. A., "<u>Cock-a-Doodle Dandy</u> Given Moving Showing at Edinburgh," <u>New York Times</u> (8 Sep 1959) p. 43.

3858 A., E., "O'Casey's Farce and Fantasy," <u>Stage and Television Today</u> (London), (10 Sep 1959) p. 18.

3859 A., H., "Edinburgh Festival: O'Casey's Message Is--Life," <u>Daily Worker</u> (London), (10 Sep 1959) p. 3.

3860 Brien, Alan, "Edinburgh Theatre: <u>Cock-a-Doodle Dandy</u> (Lyceum)," <u>Spectator</u> (London) 203 (11 Sep 1959) 331-2.

3861 Hobson, Harold, "Visions and Judgments. <u>Cock-a-Doodle Dandy</u>. Lyceum, Edinburgh," <u>Sunday Times</u> (London), (13 Sep 1959) p. 25.

3862 Pryce-Jones, Alan, "Genius and Wind," <u>Observer</u> (London), (13 Sep 1959) p. 23.

3863 "Youth Theatre Prospects," <u>Times</u> (London), (14 Sep 1959) p. 5.

3864 Keown, Eric, "At the Festival," <u>Punch</u> (London), (16 Sep 1959) 183.

3865 "O'Casey Play in London: <u>Cock-a-Doodle Dandy</u>," <u>Times</u> (London), (18 Sep 1959) p. 13.

3866 Carthew, Anthony, "Showpiece: Irishman Who Hates His Home," <u>Daily Herald</u> (London), (18 Sep 1959) p. 3.

3867 Darlington, W. A., "First Night: Royal Court Goes Irish. Enjoyable O'Casey," <u>Daily Telegraph</u> (London), (18 Sep 1959) p. 12.

3868 Levin, Bernard, "O'Casey Gives the Angels and Devils Plenty to Crow About. Cock-a-Doodle Dandy: Royal Court," Daily Express (London), (18 Sep 1959) p. 4.

3869 Tanfield, Paul, "C-U-C-K-O-O!," Daily Mail (London), (18 Sep 1959) p. 16.

3870 Shulman, Milton, "The O'Casey Flashes Are Still Enough," Evening Standard (London), (18 Sep 1959) p. 14.

3871 Hobson, Harold, "The Dublin Singing," Sunday Times (London), (20 Sep 1959) p. 25.

3872 Myson, Myke, "Theatre: O'Casey Has the Voice of Youth," Daily Worker (London), (21 Sep 1959) p. 2.

3873 "Triumph of Living Is Celebrated in Cock-a-Doodle Dandy," Stage and Television Today (London), (24 Sep 1959) p. 17.

3874 Jones, Mervyn, "Two More from the Irish," Tribune (London), (25 Sep 1959) p. 11.

3875 Hope-Wallace, Philip, "Cock-a-Doodle Dandy: O'Casey. Royal Court," Time and Tide (London), 40 (26 Sep 1959) 1038.

3876 Alvarez, A., "The Arts and Entertainment," New Statesman (London), 58 (26 Sep 1959) 388.

3877 B[aker], F. G., "Cock-a-Doodle Dandy," Plays and Players (London), 7 (Oct 1959) 15.

3878 "Cock-a-Doodle Dandy," Theatre World (London), 55 (Oct 1959) 7 [pictures].

3879 Kerr, Walter, "The Shadow of a Gunman and Cock-a-Doodle Dandy," Cincinnati Daily Enquirer (30 Nov 1959) p. 50.

3880 Hobson, Harold, "Doom Without a Profit," Sunday Times (London), (19 Aug 1962) p. 25 [At the Mermaid Theatre, London].

3881 Barnes, Clive, "The Theatre: Cock-a-Doodle Dandy--APA Stages O'Casey Play at the Lyceum," New York Times (21 Jan 1969) p. 40.

3882 Bruce, Alan N., "Theater: O'Casey, Yeats, Mrozek, and the "Fantasticks" Team Again," Christian Science Monitor (Boston), London Edition (29 Jan 1969) p. 6.

3883 "A Rooster for Phoenix," Time (N.Y.), 93 (31 Jan 1969) 54.

3884 Gill, Brendan, "The Devil's Advocate," New Yorker, 154 (1 Feb 1969) 44.

3885 Hewes, Henry, "The Theatre: Spirit Power," Saturday Review (N.Y.), (8 Feb 1969) 41.

3886 Clurman, Harold, "Theatre," Nation (N.Y.), 208 (Feb 1969) 187-9.

3887 "Theater: On Broadway--Cock-a-Doodle Dandy," Time (N.Y.), 93 (21 Feb 1969) 3.

3888 "Cock-a-Doodle Dandy," America (N.Y.), 120 (22 Feb 1969) 232.

3889 West, Anthony, "Cock-a-Doodle Dandy," Vogue (N.Y.), 153 (1 Mar 1969) 112.

3890 Savery, Ronald, "New York Theatre," Stage and Television Today (London), (6 Mar 1969) 9.

3891 Trilling, Ossia, "Berlin Festival Twenty Years Old," Stage and Television Today (London), (6 Nov 1969) p. 14.

3892 "Mrs. O'Casey Says 'Yes,'" Evening Herald (Dublin), (6 Aug 1977) p. 9. [Eileen O'Casey gives consent to stage the play].

3893 Kelly, Seamus, "Cock-a-Doodle Dandy at the Abbey," Irish Times (Dublin), (12 Aug 1977) p. 9. See reply by David Krause, ibid. (18 Aug 1977) p. 9.

3894 MacGoris, Mary, "It's Really a Sad Cock-a-Doodle," Irish Independent (Dublin), (12 Aug 1977) p. 5.

3895 Sheridan, Michael, "O'Casey Play an Irish Caricature," Irish Press (Dublin), (12 Aug 1977) p. 3.

3896 Finegan, John, "'Pantomime' by Sean O'Casey," Evening Herald (Dublin), (12 Aug 1977) p. 7.

3897 MacAvock, Desmond, "Slapstick at Its Most Crude: Cock-a-Doodle Dandy," Evening Press (Dublin), (12 Aug 1977) p. 4.

3898 "O'Casey's Pet a 'Dandy,'" Cork Examiner (12 Aug 1977) p. 13.

3899 Smith, Gus, "O'Casey's Sparkling Romp at the Abbey," Sunday Independent (Dublin), (14 Aug 1977) p. 6.

3900 O'Rourke, Frances, "Cock of the Walk," Sunday Press (Dublin), (14 Aug 1977) p. 16. See reply by John O'Riordan, Irish Press (Dublin), (21 Aug 1977) p. 15.

3901 Ryan, William C., "Abbey Play a Winner," Evening Press (Dublin), (16 Aug 1977) p. 15 [Letter to the Editor].

3902 Costello, Rose, "Pleasurable O'Casey Production," <u>Cork Examiner</u> (16 Aug 1977) p. 2.

3903 Colgan, Gerry, "Cockshots," <u>Hibernia</u> (Dublin), (19 Aug 1977) p. 21.

3904 "Shows Abroad," <u>Variety</u> (N.Y.), (24 Aug 1977) 67.

3905 Kaestner, Jan, "Streiter für Freiheit und Glück," <u>Mannheimer Morgen</u>, no. 195 (25 Aug 1977) 23.

3906 Hunt, Patrick, "There's Nothing Dandy About This Doodle," <u>Catholic Standard</u> (Dublin), (26 Aug 1977) p. 11.

HALL OF HEALING

3907 Atkinson, Brooks, "Three New One-Act Plays by Sean O'Casey Put On by an Off-Broadway Group of Actors," <u>New York Times</u> (8 May 1952) p. 35 [At the New York Yugoslav-American Hall].

3908 "Unity Theatre: Sean O'Casey's Short Plays," <u>Times</u> (London), (23 May 1953) p. 8.

3909 Trewin, J. C., "Five Plays," <u>Observer</u> (London), (24 May 1953) p. 11.

3910 "The Unity: Three in a Row," <u>Stage</u> (London), (28 May 1953) 9.

3911 Douglas, Donald, "O'Casey Smashes His Targets," <u>Daily Worker</u> (London), (29 May 1953) p. 2.

3912 W[endt], E[rnst], "Realistische Spässe," <u>Theater heute</u> (Hannover), 6 (Dec 1965) 44-5.

3913 Share, Bernard, "O'Casey and Lorca at the Abbey," <u>Irish Times</u> (Dublin), (1 Mar 1966) p. 6.

3914 C., C., "O'Casey Play Is Staged for First Time," <u>Irish Press</u> (Dublin), (1 Mar 1966) p. 7.

3915 F[inegan], J[ohn] J., Abbey: Fine Acting in Two Plays," <u>Evening Herald</u> (Dublin), (1 Mar 1966) p. 6.

3916 Rushe, Desmond, "Splendid Double Bill at Abbey," <u>Irish Independent</u> (Dublin), (2 Mar 1966) p. 6.

3917 Shorter, Eric, "O'Casey's Art Survived Revival," <u>Daily Telegraph</u>

(London), (20 Mar 1978) p. 13 [A Pound on Demand and Hall of Healing at the Théâtre National de Strasbourg, France, directed by Jean-Pierre Vincent].

3918 Dumay, Emile Jean, "Theatre Reviews," Sean O'Casey Review, 5 (Fall 1978) 89.

3919 "Theatre Reviews," Sean O'Casey Review, 5 (Fall 1978) 89-91.

3920 "O'Casey à Strasbourg," Etudes irlandaises (Lille), no. 3-Nouvelle Série (Dec 1978) 172-7.

3921 Knopf, Terry Ann, "A Joyful Rebirth in Charlestown," Boston Globe (17 Apr 1980) p. 55 [Presented by the Charlestown Working Theater. Directed by David Rothauser].

3922 "Mrs. O'Casey Comes to Town," Charlestown Patriot (Boston), (17 Apr 1980) p. 9.

3923 Lowery, Robert G., "Some Local O'Casey," Daily World (N.Y.), (19 Apr 1980) p. 13.

3924 Bronski, Michael, "The O'Casey Touch," Boston Phoenix (22 Apr 1980) pp. 13, 14.

3925 "Playwright's Widow to Visit Boston to Celebrate Centennial," Charlestown Patriot (Boston), (24 Apr 1980) p. 11.

3926 Sabulis, Thomas, "O'Casey's Widow in Chrlestown," Boston Globe (28 Apr 1980) p. 25.

BEDTIME STORY

3927 Atkinson, Brooks, "Three New One-Act Plays by Sean O'Casey Put On by an Off-Broadway Group of Actors," New York Times (8 May 1952) p. 35 [At the New York Yugoslav-American Hall].

3928 "He Called O'Casey 'Unsavoury': Ex-Fun Fair Man Puts Foot in It," Daily Worker (London), (20 Feb 1954) p. 3 [At Chingford Unity Theatre].

3929 Atkinson, Brooks, "Triple Play," New York Times (16 Apr 1959) p. 28 [At the Playhouse].

3930 Atkinson, Brooks, "Triple Play," New York Times (26 Apr 1959) section 2, p. 1.

3931 "Broadway Plans," New York Times (11 May 1959) p. 30 ["Triple Play" to close].

3932 "Triple Play," Theatre Arts (N.Y.), 43 (June 1959) 9.

3933 Capelle, J.-L., "O'Casey et Strindberg," France nouvelle (Paris), (24 Aug 1960) p. 21.

3934 Quidnunc, "An Irishman's Diary: O'Casey, Too," Irish Times (Dublin), (12 Jan 1967) p. 7 [At the Carouge, Geneva].

3935 Rosenfield, Ray, "Some Plays Puzzle MacLiammoir. Belfast Festival Choice," Irish Times (Dublin), (24 Mar 1969) p. 10 [At the Irish Universities Drama Association Festival at Queen's Univeristy, Belfast]. See reply by John O'Riordan, "Mac-Liammoir and O'Casey" (29 Mar 1969) p. 15 [Letter to the Editor].

TIME TO GO

3936 Atkinson, Brooks, "Three New One-Act Plays by Sean O'Casey Put on by an Off-Broadway Group of Actors," New York Times (8 May 1952) p. 35 [At the New York Yugoslav-American Hall].

3937 "Unity Theatre: Sean O'Casey's Short Plays," Times (London), (23 May 1953) p. 8.

3938 Trewin, J. C., "Five Plays," Observer (London), (24 May 1953) p. 11.

3939 "The Unity: Three in a Row," Stage (London), (28 May 1953) p. 9.

3940 Douglas, Donald, "O'Casey Smashes His Targets," Daily Worker (London), (29 May 1953) p. 2.

3941 Gelb, Arthur, "O'Casey and Carroll Plays on ANTA Bill," New York Times (23 Mar 1960) p. 33 [At the Theatre de Lys].

3942 Knopf, Terry Ann, "A Joyful Rebirth in Charlestown," Boston Globe (17 Apr 1980) p. 55 [Presented by the Charlestown Working Theater. Directed by David Rothauser].

3943 "Mrs. O'Casey Comes to Town," Charlestown Patriot (Boston), (17 Apr 1980) p. 9.

3944 Lowery, Robert G., "Some Local O'Casey," Daily World (N.Y.), (19 Apr 1980) p. 13.

3945 Bronski, Michael, "The O'Casey Touch," Boston Phoenix (22 Apr 1980) pp. 13, 14.

3946 "Playwright's Widow to Visit Boston to Celebrate Centennial," Charlestown Patriot (Boston), (24 Apr 1980) p. 11.

3947 Sabulis, Thomas, "O'Casey's Widow in Charlestown," Boston Globe (28 Apr 1980) p. 25.

THE BISHOP'S BONFIRE

3948 "A New O'Casey Play," Manchester Guardian (29 Dec 1954) p. 4 [Details of forthcoming production announced].

3949 "Mr. Sean O'Casey's New Play: A [sic] Bishop's Bonfire," Times (London), (12 Jan 1955) p. 7 [Forthcoming production in Dublin].

3950 Fallon, Gabriel, "O'Casey Will Give Us a Badly Needed Tonic," Evening Press (Dublin), (29 Jan 1955) p. 5.

3951 "Sean O'Casey Again," Standard (Dublin), 27 (18 Feb 1955) 1.

3952 "Dublin Première of O'Casey's Latest Play," Evening Mail (Dublin), (24 Feb 1955) p. 6.

3953 "Sean O'Casey's Play: Art--For Whose Sake?" Standard (Dublin), 27 (25 Feb 1955) 1.

3954 Fallon, Gabriel, "What Will Mr. Guthrie Do to O'Casey?" Evening Press (Dublin), (26 Feb 1955) p. 5.

3955 "A Letter from Sean O'Casey," Times Pictorial (Dublin) 31 (26 Feb 1955) 1.

3956 "Will O'Casey's Bonfire Cause Another Blaze?" Times Pictorial (Dublin), 31 (26 Feb 1955) 11.

3957 O'Casey, Eileen, "Mrs. O'Casey on Her Husband's Latest Play," Sunday Independent (Dublin), (27 Feb 1955) p. 7.

3958 White, Jack, "An O'Casey First Night," Observer (London), (27 Feb 1955) p. 10.

3959 "Mrs. O'Casey Arrives for Bonfire First Night," Sunday Press (Dublin), (27 Feb 1955) p. 1.

3960 "O'Casey on His New Play," Times (London), (28 Feb 1955) p. 3.

3961 "Tanfield's Diary: Shy Mr. O'Casey Will Not See His World Première," Daily Mail (London), (28 Feb 1955) p. 4.

3962 "Return of the Native," Evening Herald (Dublin), (28 Feb 1955) p. 4 [Editorial].

3963 "1,200 Queued for Gallery," Irish Times (Dublin), (1 Mar 1955) p. 1.

3964 "By-Line," Irish Times (Dublin), (1 Mar 1955) p. 1 [Cartoon].

3965 "The Bishop's Bonfire: Dublin's Mixed Reception for New O'Casey Play," Times (London), (1 Mar 1955) p. 8 [At the Gaiety Theatre, Dublin].

3966 Barber, John, "O'Casey Turns Up with a Shocker," Daily Express (London), (1 Mar 1955) p. 3.

3967 Cashin, Fergus, "O'Casey Goes to Town Again ... And It's a Blaze of Cheeky Fun," Daily Mirror (London), (1 Mar 1955) p. 4.

3968 Fallon, Gabriel, "The 'Bonfire' Never Did Really Blaze at All," Evening Press (Dublin), (1 Mar 1955) p. 4.

3969 Frank, Elizabeth, "Boos, Hisses for O'Casey's Play: Wife in Tears," News Chronicle (London), (1 Mar 1955) p. 1.

3970 F[inegan], J[ohn] J., "Sean O'Casey out of Touch," Evening Herald (Dublin), (1 Mar 1955) p. 6.

3971 F., R. M., "Bonfire--Kindled on Comedy, Quenched by Melodrama," Evening Mail (Dublin), (1 Mar 1955) p. 3.

3972 "Cheers and Boos for Sean O'Casey," Irish Press (Dublin), (1 Mar 1955) p. 1.

3973 "K" [Seamus Kelly], "The Bishop's Bonfire in Gaiety Theatre," Irish Times (Dublin), (1 Mar 1955) p. 4.

3974 M., I., "O'Casey's Première at the Gaiety," Irish Independent (Dublin), (1 Mar 1955) p. 7.

3975 "Mr. Sean O'Casey's New Play: The Bishop's Bonfire at the Gaiety Theatre, Dublin," Times (London), (1 Mar 1955) p. 6.

3976 Carroll, Niall, "O'Casey, Mostly Sound and Fury," Irish Press (Dublin), (1 Mar 1955) p. 3.

3977 Darlington, W. A., "First Nights: Anti-Clerical Bias in O'Casey
       Play. The Bishop's Bonfire," Daily Telegraph (London), (1
       Mar 1955) p. 8.

3978 "Thousands Queue for O'Casey," Daily Worker (London), (1
       Mar 1955) p. 1.

3979 "What the Critics Say About O'Casey's New Play," Evening
       Herald (Dublin), (1 Mar 1955) p. 6.

3980 Wilson, Cecil, "O'Casey Explodes a Stick of Dramatic Dynamite,"
       Daily Mail (London), (1 Mar 1955) p. 8.

3981 "What the Irish Critics Think," Evening Herald (Dublin), (1
       Mar 1955) p. 6.

3982 "New O'Casey Play Is Booed in Dublin," New York Times (1
       Mar 1955) p. 22.

3983 Fay, Gerard, "The Bishop's Bonfire," Manchester Guardian (2
       Mar 1955) p. 5.

3984 "K" [Seamus Kelly], "British Critics Found Journey Worth
       While," Irish Times (Dublin), (2 Mar 1955) p. 4.

3985 "Dublin Sees Best O'Casey: Gets Première--After 20 Years,"
       Daily Worker (London), (2 Mar 1955) p. 3.

3986 Carey, Edw., "Self-Respect," Standard (Dublin), 27 (4 Mar
       1955) 12 [Letter to the Editor].

3987 Byrne, Seamus, "The Shadow of an O'Casey," Standard (Dub-
       lin), 27 (4 Mar 1955) 8.

3988 "Sean O'Casey's Play: The 'Gods' Can't Be Fooled!," Standard
       (Dublin), 27 (4 Mar 1955) 1.

3989 O'Flaherty, Desmond, "Pat on the Back for Pat Murphy,"
       Standard (Dublin), 27 (4 Mar 1955) 11 [Letter to the Editor].

3990 White, Jack, "The Bishop's Bonfire by Sean O'Casey. (Gaiety
       Theatre, Dublin)," Spectator (London), 94 (4 Mar 1955) 256.

3991 Fallon, Gabriel, "Why Sean O'Casey Has Failed This Time,"
       Evening Press (Dublin), (5 Mar 1955) p. 7.

3992 Finegan, J. J., "Dublin's Advice to O'Casey," Evening Herald
       (Dublin), (5 Mar 1955) p. 6.

3993 "Mrs. O'Casey and Shivaun Fly Home," Irish Press (Dublin),
       (5 Mar 1955) p. 1 [After attending the première of the play].

3994 "Melodrama Defended," Evening Herald (Dublin), (5 Mar 1955) p. 6 [Interview].

3995 O'Donnell, Donat, "No Bishop, No Bonfire," New Statesman and Nation (London), 49 (5 Mar 1955) 320.

3996 "O'Casey's Return," Daily Worker (London), (5 Mar 1955) p. 3.

3997 Gray, Ken, "O'Casey Draws the Critics Across the Sea," Times Pictorial (Dublin), 31 (5 Mar 1955) 11.

3998 O'Connor, Ulick, "A Dublin Première. The Bishop's Bonfire: Sean O'Casey. Gaiety, Dublin," Time and Tide (London), 36 (5 Mar 1955) 296.

3999 Hobson, Harold, "Dublin Double: The Bishop's Bonfire. Gaiety Theatre, Dublin," Sunday Times (London), (6 Mar 1955) p. 11.

4000 Tynan, Kenneth, "Irish Stew," Observer (London), (6 Mar 1955) p. 11. Reprinted in Curtains (London: Longmans; New York: Atheneum, 1961) pp. 83-5.

4001 "Critics Hail New Play by Sean O'Casey," Chicago Sunday Tribune (6 Mar 1955) pt 7, section 2, p. 5.

4002 Darlington, W. A., "O'Casey Play: Opening Night in Dublin," New York Times (6 Mar 1955) section 2, p. 3.

4003 "O'Casey's New Play," Sunday Independent (Dublin), (6 Mar 1955) p. 12.

4004 Carroll, Niall, "Only Great Are Hissed," Irish Press (Dublin), (7 Mar 1955) p. 4.

4005 Reid, Rita, "The Bishop's Bonfire," Evening Press (Dublin), (7 Mar 1955) p. 5 [Letter to the Editor].

4006 Quidnunc, "An Irishman's Diary," Irish Times (Dublin), (8 Mar 1955) p. 6.

4007 O'Doherty, Vincent, "O'Casey: Standard Attitude Criticised," Irish Press (Dublin), (8 Mar 1955) p. 6 [Letter to the Editor].

4008 Carmody, Patrick, "The Bishop's Bonfire," Evening Mail (Dublin), (9 Mar 1955) p. 7 [Letter to the Editor].

4009 Carmody, Patrick, "That Bonfire," Evening Press (Dublin), (9 Mar 1955) p. 6.

4010 O'Searbhain, Sean, "Was There Really a Bonfire?" Irish Press (Dublin), (9 Mar 1955) p. 4.

4011 Keown, Eric, "At the Play: The Bishop's Bonfire (Gaiety, Dublin)," Punch (London), 228 (9 Mar 1955) 327-8.

4012 "Visitors to Russia, Sean O'Casey Plays Criticised," Irish Press (Dublin), (9 Mar 1955) p. 1.

4013 "Students Criticize Newspaper," Irish Times (Dublin), (10 Mar 1955) p. 7.

4014 Playgoer, "Admonition from Outside," Irish Times (Dublin), (10 Mar 1955) p. 5 [Letter to the Editor].

4015 O'Donovan, John, "Admiring Bow" in the Direction of Devon," Evening Herald (Dublin), (11 Mar 1955) p. 7 [Letter to the Editor].

4016 O'Donovan, John, "The Bishop's Bonfire," Evening Press (Dublin), (11 Mar 1955) p. 4. [Letter to the Editor].

4017 "The O'Casey Controversy Rages On: Mr. Hobson Snipes for The Sunday Times," Standard (Dublin), 27 (11 Mar 1955) 1, 12.

4018 "Bishop Refers to O'Casey Play," Irish Times (Dublin), (11 Mar 1955) p. 4.

4019 Fallon, Gabriel, "May Heaven Preserve Us from These London Critics!" Evening Press (Dublin), (12 Mar 1955) p. 5.

4020 "Theatre News," Sphere (London), 220 (12 Mar 1955) 424.

4021 Hobson, Harold, "O'Casey's Bishop's Bonfire," Christian Science Monitor (Boston), (12 Mar 1955) p. 6.

4022 Thersites, "Private Views," Irish Times (Dublin), (12 Mar 1955) p. 6.

4023 "Big Audiences for Play," Irish Times (Dublin), (12 Mar 1955) p. 9.

4024 "X," "Sean O'Casey," Leader (Dublin), 55 (12 Mar 1955) 17-18.

4025 Gray, Ken, "Plenty of Sparks--But No Big Blaze," Times Pictorial (Dublin), 31 (12 Mar 1955) 11.

4026 Burrows, George H., "Sean O," Times Pictorial (Dublin), 31 (12 Mar 1955) 12, 19.

4027 "O'Casey Visit Off," Sunday Press (Dublin), (13 Mar 1955) p. 5.

4028 Barrett, James, "Sean O'Casey," Sunday Times (London), (13 Mar 1955) p. 2 [Letter to the Editor].

4029 MacNamara, D., "Sean O'Casey," Sunday Times (London), (13 Mar 1955) p. 2 [Letter to the Editor].

4030 "New Play in Dublin," Time (N.Y.), 65 (14 Mar 1955) 74.

4031 O'Casey, Sean, "Bishop's Bonfire," Irish Press (Dublin), (15 Mar 1955) p. 8 [Letter to the Editor].

4032 O'Donovan, John, "The Bonfire," Evening Press (Dublin), (15 Mar 1955) p. 4 [Letter to the Editor].

4033 Nolan, Carmel M., "The Bonfire," Evening Press (Dublin), (15 Mar 1955) p. 4 [Letter to the Editor].

4034 O'Flaherty, Desmond, "A 'Playgoer' and 'The Bonfire,'" Standard (Dublin), 27 (18 Mar 1955) 11 [Letter to the Editor].

4035 O'Maoláin, Mícheál, "The Bonfire," Irish Press (Dublin), (19 Mar 1955) p. 2.

4036 Gray, Ken, "Why Not a Festival of Drama?" Times Pictorial (Dublin), 31 (19 Mar 1955) 11.

4037 O'Casey, Sean, "Sean O'Casey and Dublin," Sunday Times (London), (20 Mar 1955) p. 2 [Letter to the Editor].

4038 Hobson, Harold, "Sean O'Casey and Dublin," Sunday Times (London), (20 Mar 1955) p. 2 [Letter to the Editor].

4039 O'Casey, Sean, "The Bishop's Bonfire," Irish Times (Dublin), (23 Mar 1955) p. 5 [Letter to the Editor].

4040 Fallon, Gabriel, "The Bonfire," Evening Press (Dublin), (23 Mar 1955) p. 6 [Letter to the Editor].

4041 Barrington, Maeve, "Bookings," Irish Press (Dublin), (24 Mar 1955) p. 6 [Letter to the Editor].

4042 O'Casey, Sean, "O'Casey and the Dublin Critics," Irish Press (Dublin), (24 Mar 1955) p. 6 [Letter to the Editor].

4043 Hollander, James, "Mr. O'Casey's Wrath," Irish Press (Dublin), (24 Mar 1955) p. 6 [Letter to the Editor].

4044 "If Critics Did Their Duty," Standard (Dublin), 27 (25 Mar
      1955) 6.

4045 "People and Principles," Standard (Dublin), 27 (25 Mar 1955)
      6 [Editorial].

4046 "Mr. O'Donovan and The Bishop's Bonfire," Standard (Dublin),
      27 (25 Mar 1955) 11 [Letter to the Editor].

4047 "Lecturer's Comments on New O'Casey Play," Irish Independent
      (Dublin), (26 Mar 1955) p. 12.

4048 Fallon, Gabriel, "An Open Letter to Sean O'Casey," Irish Press
      (Dublin), (30 Mar 1955) p. 4.

4049 "O'Casey's Return to Irish Stage," Daily Worker (N.Y.), (30
      Mar 1955) p. 7.

4050 Sweeney, Gerald, "Mr. O'Donovan and The Bonfire," Standard
      (Dublin), 27 (1 Apr 1955) 11 [Letter to the Editor].

4051 O'Casey, Sean, "The Bishop's Bonfire," Irish Press (Dublin),
      (5 Apr 1955) p. 8 [Letter to the Editor].

4052 Behan, Marie, "O'Casey 'Rude and Revolting,'" Irish Press
      (Dublin), (5 Apr 1955) p. 8 [Letter to the Editor].

4053 "No Bonfire Yet for London," Irish Press (Dublin), (6 Apr
      1955) p. 5.

4054 "U.S. Pressmen Comment on O'Casey Play: Why Was It Pro-
      duced?" Standard (Dublin), 27 (8 Apr 1955) 3.

4055 "X," "Sean O'Casey: A Postscript," Leader (Dublin), 55 (9
      Apr 1955) 7-8.

4056 O'Casey, Sean, "The Bonfire," Irish Press (Dublin), (12 Apr
      1955) p. 9 [Letter to the Editor].

4057 "Bonfire," Standard (Dublin), 27 (15 Apr 1955) 8.

4058 Keating, M. J., "The American View," Irish Times (Dublin),
      (16 Apr 1955) p. 9.

4059 MacWilliams, Bourke, "The Bishop's Bonfire by Sean O'Casey:
      First Performance at the Gaiety Theatre, Dublin," Plays and
      Players (London), 2 (Apr 1955) 14. See O'Casey's reply,
      "Sean O'Casey Complains," (May 1955) 23; and MacWilliams'
      counter-reply, "Reply to Sean O'Casey," (June 1955) 21.

4060 "Between the Acts," Irish Tatler and Sketch (Dublin), 64 (Apr 1955) 66.

4061 "No Plans to Bring Play to London," Irish Times (Dublin), (2 May 1955) p. 9.

4062 Leventhal, A. J., "The Bishop's Bonfire by Sean O'Casey. Cyril Cusack Productions. Gaiety Theatre," Dublin Magazine, 31 (Apr-June 1955) 28-9.

4063 Adams, Phoebe Lou, "Reader's Choice," Atlantic Monthly (Boston), 96 (Oct 1955) 96.

4064 Freundlich, Elisabeth, "Der Dramatiker Sean O'Casey," Theater und Zeit (Berlin), 3 (June 1956) 181-3 [In Hannover].

4065 Dibb, Frank, "The Bishop's Bonfire," Plays and Players (London), 6 (Dec 1958) 31 [At the Highbury Little Theatre, Sutton Coldfield, on 14 Oct 1958].

4066 Pro-Quidnunc, "An Irishman's Diary," Irish Times (Dublin), (14 June 1961) p. 8.

4067 "An O'Casey Occasion," Irish Times (Dublin), (1 Jul 1961) p. 9.

4068 "The Londoner's Diary: No Smooth Talk," Evening Standard (London), (22 Jul 1961) p. 6.

4069 Ferguson, T. S., "'A Sad Play Within the Tune of a Polka': Ireland's Troubles," Sunday Telegraph (London), (23 Jul 1961) p. 8.

4070 "Sean O'Casey Whirls His Blackthorn. Mermaid Theatre: The Bishop's Bonfire," Times (London), (27 Jul 1961) p. 5.

4071 Nathan, David, "There Aren't Enough Sparks in O'Casey's Irish Fire," Daily Herald (London), (27 Jul 1961) p. 3.

4072 Muller, Robert, "The Bonfire That Fails to Burn: The Bishop's Bonfire, by Sean O'Casey. Mermaid Theatre," Daily Mail (London), (27 Jul 1961) p. 3.

4073 "O'Casey at the Mermaid," Irish Times (Dublin), (27 Jul 1961) p. 7.

4074 "No Seat for Crosby at O'Casey Play," Irish Press (Dublin), (27 Jul 1961) p. 3.

4075 Barnes, Clive, "Few Sparks from Sean O'Casey's Bonfire.

The Bishop's Bonfire. The Mermaid," Daily Express (London), (27 Jul 1961) p. 4.

4076 Darlington, W. A., "First Night: O'Casey's Lurid Eire. Mixed Play of Jarring Moods," Daily Telegraph (London), (27 Jul 1961) p. 14.

4077 Shulman, Milton, "O'Casey in His Seventies: Unquenchable As Ever," Evening Standard (London), (27 Jul 1961) p. 4.

4078 Barker, Felix, "Not One Murmur at the Mermaid," Evening News (London), (27 Jul 1961) p. 4.

4079 "O'Casey's Bishop's Bonfire Opens in London," New York Times (27 Jul 1961) p. 22.

4080 "The Bishop's Bonfire," Irish Times (Dublin), (28 Jul 1961) p. 7.

4081 Hobson, Harold, "The Bishop's Bonfire: Mermaid," Sunday Times (London), (30 Jul 1961) p. 27.

4082 Brien, Alan, "Beware of the Dogma," Sunday Telegraph (London), (30 Jul 1961) p. 8.

4083 Tynan, Kenneth, "At the Theatre: A Second Look at O'Casey and Osborne," Observer (London), (30 Jul 1961) p. 20.

4084 M., R. B., "O'Casey Spirit Gives Truth and Value," Stage and Television Today (London), (3 Aug 1961) p. 7.

4085 Findlater, Richard, "The Life Force Is Still Burning," Time and Tide (London), 42 (3 Aug 1961) 1273.

4086 Gellert, Roger, "Wring Its Neck," New Statesman (London), 62 (4 Aug 1961) 164.

4087 Gascoigne, Bamber, "The Symbol of the Carpet: The Bishop's Bonfire. (Mermaid)," Spectator (London), 207 (11 Aug 1961) 204.

4088 Trewin, J. C., "A Word in the Ear," Illustrated London News, 239 (12 Aug 1961) 266.

4089 Roberts, Peter, "The Bishop's Bonfire. By Sean O'Casey," Plays and Players (London), 8 (Sep 1961) 13.

4090 M., H. G., "Mermaid: The Bishop's Bonfire," Theatre World (London), 57 (Sep 1961) 4 [pictures p. 39].

4091 Dunlop, Frank, "Preparing the Bonfire," Plays and Players (London), 8 (Sep 1961) 7, 19.

THE DRUMS OF FATHER NED

4092 "Tostal Council to Proceed with Plays: No Inaugural Mass," Irish Times (Dublin), (10 Jan 1958) p. 1.

4093 "O'Casey Play Is Off," Evening Press (Dublin), (12 Feb 1958) p. 1.

4094 "O'Casey Play Withdrawn from Festival," Evening Herald (Dublin), (12 Feb 1958) p. 3.

4095 "Objectionable Plays: Unions to Send Protest to Tostal Council," Irish Independent (Dublin), (12 Feb 1958) p. 10.

4096 "Play Withdrawn by Mr. Sean O'Casey," Times (London), (12 Feb 1958) p. 3 [From the Dublin Festival].

4097 "Dublin Not to See Play by O'Casey," Irish Times (Dublin), (12 Feb 1958) p. 1.

4098 "O'Casey Cancels Play: Withdraws Drums of Father Ned from Dublin Fete," New York Times (12 Feb 1958) p. 33.

4099 "O'Casey Refuses to Alter Play," Irish Times (Dublin), (13 Feb 1958) p. 1.

4100 Quidnunc [Patrick Campbell], "An Irishman's Diary," Irish Times (Dublin), (15 Feb 1958) p. 8.

4101 "Final Curtain?" Irish Times (Dublin), (15 Feb 1958) p. 7 [Leading article].

4102 McClelland, Alan, "Got Raw Deal," Sunday Press (Dublin), (16 Feb 1958) p. 1.

4103 Carroll, Niall, "That O'Casey Play," Irish Press (Dublin), (24 Feb 1958) p. 6. See O'Casey's reply, "O'Casey Makes Challenge," (1 Mar 1958) p. 6; Carroll's counter-reply, "Reply to O'Casey," (3 Mar 1958) p. 6; and O'Casey's counter-counter-reply, "O'Casey Play," (12 Mar 1958) p. 6.

4104 O'Casey, Sean, "The Theatre Festival," Irish Times (Dublin), (11 Mar 1958) p. 5 [Letter to the Editor].

4105 "O'Casey Bans His Plays from Irish Theatres," New York Times (20 Mar 1958) p. 34.

4106 Hogan, Robert, "Riches Scorned," Times Literary Supplement (London), (21 Mar 1958) p. 153 [Letter to the Editor].

4107 "Sean O'Casey--Salesman: Playwright Under Pressure," Plays and Players (London), 5 (Mar 1958) 22.

4108 Hogan, Robert, "O'Casey and the Archbishop," New Republic (N.Y.), 138 (19 May 1958) 29-30.

4109 O'Casey, Sean, "The Drums of Father Ned," Enquiry (Nottingham), 1 (June 1958) 37-9.

4110 O'Casey, Sean, "Abbey Can't Have My Plays," Sunday Press (Dublin), (27 Jul 1958) p. 1 [Interview].

4111 "O'Casey Bans Performance of His Plays in Dublin," Irish Times (Dublin), (28 Jul 1958) p. 1.

4112 "O'Casey Ban on Plays in Dublin," Irish Press (Dublin), (28 Jul 1958) p. 5.

4113 "By-Line," Irish Times (Dublin), (29 Jul 1958) p. 1 [Cartoon].

4114 "Radio Eireann Ban by O'Casey," Irish Times (Dublin), (29 Jul 1958) p. 7.

4115 Fallon, Gabriel, "He's Wrong-Shipped This Time," Evening Press (Dublin), (2 Aug 1958) p. 7.

4116 Quidnunc, "An Irishman's Diary," Irish Times (Dublin), (19 Aug 1958) p. 6.

4117 Hewes, Henry, "The Green Crow Flies Again," Saturday Review of Literature (N.Y.), 42 (9 May 1959) 22 [At the Little Theatre, Lafayette, Indiana, on 25 Apr 1959].

4118 "Abbey Managing Director Sees O'Casey," Irish Times (Dublin), (21 Sep 1959) p. 4.

4119 Wright, A., "Pasternak and Joyce," Irish Times (Dublin), (22 Jul 1960) p. 7 [Letter to the Editor].

4120 Craig, H. A. L., "Red Roses for O'Casey," New Statesman and Nation (London), 60 (19 Nov 1960) 782 [At Hornchurch, Essex].

4121 Findlater, Richard, "Hurrah for Hornchurch," Time and Tide (London), 41 (1960), 1438.

4122 Roberts, Peter, "The Drums of Father Ned. By Sean O'Casey.

First Performance in Europe at the Queen's Theatre, Hornchurch, on November 8, 1960," Plays and Players (London),
8 (Jan 1961) 11.

4123 "O'Casey Bans Festival Production," Irish Times (Dublin), (24
       Aug 1961) p. 6.

4124 "O'Casey," Irish Times (Dublin), (25 Aug 1961) p. 7 [Leader].
       See replies by Gabriel Fallon (26 Aug 1961) p. 7; by Kath-
       erine MacCormack (29 Aug 1961) p. 5; by Brendan Behan
       (29 Aug 1961) p. 5; by Liam MacAoidh (29 Aug 1961) p. 5;
       by J. O. G. Macnamara, (31 Aug 1961) p. 7; and by Anthony
       Mangan (4 Sep 1961) p. 7 [Letters to the Editor].

4125 Pessemesse, Pierre, "Au Théâtre Quotidien de Marseille: Les
       Tambours du Père Ned de Sean O'Casey," Lettres françaises
       (Paris), no. 916 (1-7 Mar 1962) 9.

4126 "O'Casey Played with Spirit. Tower Theatre: The Drums of
       Father Ned," Times (London), (22 May 1965) p. 12 [By the
       Tavistock Repertory Company at the Tower Theatre, London].

4127 Byrne, P. F., "Father Ned Comes to Dublin," Evening Herald
       (Dublin), (4 June 1966) p. 8 [To open on 6 June 1966 at
       the Olympia Theatre, Dublin].

4128 Kelly, Seamus, "O'Casey Play at the Olympia," Irish Times
       (Dublin), (7 June 1966) p. 6.

4129 O'D., T., "'Drums' Beat in the Olympia," Irish Press (Dublin),
       (7 June 1966) p. 4.

4130 B., P. F., "Excellent Acting and Direction in O'Casey Play,"
       Evening Herald (Dublin), (7 June 1966) p. 8.

FIGURO IN THE NIGHT

4131 "O'Casey Satire on Censorship," Sunday Press (Dublin), (9
       Aug 1959) p. 6.

4132 Taubman, Howard, "ANTA Stages 2 New Plays by O'Casey,"
       New York Times (31 Oct 1962) p. 33 [At the Theatre de
       Lys].

4133 "O'Casey Gave Daughter One-Act Play for Young People,"
       Irish Times (Dublin), (4 Jan 1965) p. 1.

4134 "Twelve British Actors Star Campus Tour," New York Times
       (30 Jan 1965) p. 17 [One of the bills consists of Figuro].

4135 "O'Casey Figaro [sic]," Stage and Television Today (London), (26 Nov 1970) p. 18 [To be presented at the Peacock Theatre, Dublin]. See "O'Casey" by John O'Riordan (31 Dec 1970) p. 14 [Letter to the Editor].

THE MOON SHINES ON KYLENAMOE

4136 "Sean O'Casey Gives Play to Telefis," Sunday Press (Dublin), (24 June 1962) p. 4 [Interview].

4137 Taubman, Howard, "ANTA Stages 2 New Plays by O'Casey," New York Times (31 Oct 1962) p. 33 [At the Theatre de Lys].

BEHIND THE GREEN CURTAINS

4138 "O'Casey Satire on Censorship," Sunday Press (Dublin), (9 Aug 1959) p. 6.

F. REVIEWS OF STAGED AUTOBIOGRAPHIES

(This section is arranged chronologically.)

4139 Atkinson, Brooks, "O'Casey Reading," New York Times (19 Mar 1956) p. 27 [I Knock at the Door at the Kaufman Auditorium].

4140 Hewes, Henry, "O'Casey Unbound," Saturday Review of Literature (N.Y.), 39 (7 Apr 1956) 22.

4141 Atkinson, Brooks, "Autobiography of O'Casey: Pictures in the Hallway Given as a Reading," New York Times (28 May 1956) p. 23.

4142 Hewes, Henry, "Broadway Postscripts: Pictures in the Hallway," Saturday Review of Literature (N.Y.), 39 (16 June 1956) 32.

4143 O'Casey, Sean, "Sidelights on Some 'Pictures,'" New York Times (16 Sep 1956) section 2, pp. 1, 3.

4144 Funke, Lewis, "Self-Portrait: O'Casey's Pictures in the Hallway Returns," New York Times (17 Sep 1956) p. 23.

4145 Atkinson, Brooks, "O'Casey Reading: Pictures in the Hallway Shows How Prose Can Be Theatricalized," New York Times (23 Sep 1956) section 2, p. 1.

4146 Wyatt, Euphemia van Rensselaer, "Pictures in the Hallway," Catholic World (N.Y.) 184 (Nov 1956) 146.

4147 Gassner, John, "Broadway in Review," Educational Theatre Journal (Ann Arbor, Mich.), 8 (Dec 1956) 325-6 [Pictures in the Hallway].

4148 Shyre, Paul, "O'Casey's Pictures Come to Life," Theatre Arts (N.Y.), 41 (Mar 1957) 31-2.

4149 Gelb, Arthur, "O'Casey As a Boy," New York Times (30 Sep 1957) p. 27 [I Knock at the Door at the Belasco Theatre, New York].

4150 "Group Gives Stage Readings of O'Csey," Irish Times (Dublin),
(1 Oct 1957) p. 4.

4151 Raymond, Harry, "The Lilting Drama of O'Casey's Youth,"
Daily Worker (N.Y.), (3 Oct 1957) pp. 6-7.

4152 Hewes, Henry, "Broadway Postscript," Saturday Review of Literature (N.Y.), 40 (12 Oct 1957) 30.

4153 "Recitation in Manhattan," Time (N.Y.), 70 (14 Oct 1957) 50.

4154 Clurman, Harold, "Theatre," Nation (N.Y.), 185 (19 Oct 1957)
272.

4155 Driver, Tom F., "Chamber Drama," Christian Century (Chicago),
74 (30 Oct 1957) 1288-9.

4156 Wyatt, Euphemia van Rensselaer, "I Knock at the Door,"
Catholic World (N.Y.), 186 (Dec 1957) 227.

4157 Gassner, John, "Braodway in Review," Educational Theatre
Journal (Ann Arbor, Mich.), 9 (Dec 1957) 315-16.

4158 "I Knock at the Door," Theatre Arts (N.Y.), 41 (Dec 1957)
25.

4159 Atkinson, Brooks, "Pictures in the Hallway. Phoenix in Revival of O'Casey Work," New York Times (28 Dec 1959) p. 19.

4160 Atkinson, Brooks, "The O'Casey," New York Times (3 Jan
1960) section 2, p. 1.

4161 Gelb, Arthur, "Campaigner in the Cause of Sean O'Casey,"
New York Times (25 Sep 1960) section 2, pp. 1, 3 [Drums
Under the Windows to open at Cherry Lane Theatre on 13
Oct 1960].

4162 Taubman, Howard, "Cascade of Words from Sean O'Casey:
Shyre's Drums Under the Windows Staged," New York Times
(14 Oct 1960) p. 26.

4163 Balliett, Whitney, "Off Broadway: Turtle Soup," New Yorker,
36 (22 Oct 1960) 90-3.

4164 Driver, Tom F., "Incorrigible Romantic," Christian Century
(Chicago), 77 (9 Nov 1960) 1320-1.

4165 "Mr. O'Casey and His Young Self. Mermaid Theatre: Pictures
in the Hallway," Times (London), (1 Oct 1962) p. 17.

4166 Shepard, Ricahrd F., "O'Casey Play: I Knock at the Door Opens at de Lys," New York Times (26 Nov 1964) p. 53.

4167 Oliver, Edith, "Off Broadway: On the One Hand, on the Other," New Yorker, 40 (5 Dec 1964) 88-90.

4168 Oliver, Edith, "Off Broadway: Pictures in the Hallway," New Yorker, 40 (26 Dec 1964) 52-3.

4169 Quidnunc, "An Irishman's Diary: Lantern Shines," Irish Times (Dublin), (20 Jul 1967) p. 9 [On Pictures].

4170 "At the Reception," Irish Times (Dublin), (1 Mar 1968) p. 9 [Pictures of I Knock].

4171 Pro-Quidnunc, "An Irishman's Diary: Knocking Twice," Irish Times (9 Mar 1968) p. 11 [On I Knock].

4172 Kelly, Henry, "Gaiety: Early Years of O'Casey," Irish Times (Dublin), (13 Mar 1968) p. 8 [On I Knock]. See replies by Philomena Cunningham and J. J. O'Leary (16 Mar 1968) p. 9 [Letters to the Editor].

4173 "David Kelly in the Role of Sean O'Casey," Irish Times (Dublin), (15 Mar 1968) p. 11 [Picture].

4174 Kelly, Seamus, "All the Makings of a Good Show," Irish Times (Dublin), (18 Jul 1968) p. 8 [Drums Under the Windows, adapted by Patrick Funge and David Krause, produced by P. Funge at the Lantern Theatre, Dublin, on 17 July 1968].

4175 Lowry, Betty, "Two New Irish Plays [Big Maggie at the Grove, and Pictures in the Hallway at the Lyric]," Belfast Telegraph (5 Apr 1969) p. 4.

4176 Rafferty, Gerald, "O'Casey on the Threshold," Belfast Telegraph (9 Apr 1969) p. 8.

4177 Hill, Ian, "Belfast Lyric Players: Pictures in the Hallway," Guardian (London), (10 Apr 1969) p. 10.

4178 "The Lyric Theatre Players Make Most of O'Casey Pictures," Irish News (Belfast), (10 Apr 1969) p. 5.

4179 Stewart, John D., "Sean Would Have Been Annoyed," Sunday News (Belfast), (13 Apr 1969) p. 6.

4180 Gussow, Mel, "Theater: Sean O'Casey. Shyre's Adaptation of "Hallway" at Forum," New York Times (30 Apr 1971) p. 50.

G. REVIEWS OF FILMS (FEATURES AND TV)

(This section is arranged chronologically)

4181 Agate, James, "The Cinema," Tatler (London), (5 Mar 1930)
420 [Juno and the Paycock by the British International Pic-
tures].

4182 Simpson, Celia, "The Cinema: Juno and the Paycock," Spectator (London), 144 (8 Mar 1930) 363.

4183 "Filmed O'Casey: The Plough and the Stars," Literary Digest
(N.Y.), 122 (19 Sep 1936) 21-2.

4184 Gates, Dorothy, "'Informer' Paved the Way for 'Plough and
Stars,'" Daily Worker (London), (20 Oct 1936) p. 7.

4185 Cunningham, James P., "The Plough and the Stars," Commonweal (N.Y.), 25 (8 Jan 1937) 304.

4186 "Irish Tragedy: RKO Presents Faithful Film Version of The
Plough and the Stars," Literary Digest (N.Y.), 123 (16 Jan
1937) 23.

4187 R., M. B., "The Plough and the Stars," Scholastic (Pittsburgh),
29 (23 Jan 1937) 14, 31.

4188 "Screen: England Stamps Out Ireland's Easter Week Revolt,"
Newsweek (N.Y.), 9 (23 Jan 1937) 30.

4189 Nugent, Frank S., "The RKO-Radio Version of The Plough and
the Stars, by Sean O'Casey, Opens at the Music Hall," New
York Times (29 Jan 1937) p. 15.

4190 "The New Pictures: The Plough and the Stars (RKO)," Time
(N.Y.), 29 (1 Feb 1937) 45.

4191 Van Doren, Mark, "Films: The Plough and the Stars (RKO-
Radio)," Nation (N.Y.), 144 (13 Feb 1937) 194. Partially
reprinted in Private Reader (New York: Henry Holt, 1942)
pp. 351-2.

4192 "Pictures Now Showing: The Plough and the Stars," Stage (N.Y.), 14 (Feb 1937) 18.

4193 Reynolds, Horace, "Hollywood Unfurls: The Plough and the Stars," Stage (N.Y.), 14 (Feb 1937) 54.

4194 "Sean O'Casey Film for Television," Times (London), (18 Oct 1955) p. 3 [On O'Casey's life, for the National Broadcasting Company of America].

4195 Gould, Jack, "TV: Sean O'Casey Is Interviewed. Irish Playwright Seen on N.B.C. Program," New York Times (23 Jan 1956) p. 49.

4196 Van Horne, Harriet, "Camera Dulls Glow of Elder Wise Men," New York World Telegram and Sun (24 Jan 1956) p. 20.

4197 Platt, David, "Sean O'Casey on TV," Daily Worker (N.Y.), (24 Jan 1956) p. 6.

4198 "B.B.C. Television: Juno and the Paycock by Sean O'Casey," Times (London), (18 Mar 1957) p. 12.

4199 Macleod, Alison, "You Were Right About Juno," Daily Worker (London), (19 Mar 1957) p. 2.

4200 "The Shadow of a Gunman: Independent Television by Sean O'Casey," Times (London), (12 Jul 1957) p. 5.

4201 Shanley, John P., "Film of O'Casey Deleted," New York Times (14 Mar 1960) p. 51 [From "Ed Sullivan Show" after protests to producer].

4202 "TV Show Drops O'Casey Interview," Irish Times (Dublin), (15 Mar 1960) p. 11. See reply by Gabriel Fallon, "Sean O'Casey" (18 Mar 1960) p. 9; and "O'Casey Cut in TV Film Condemned" (21 Mar 1960) p. 4.

4203 "Television Catches Play's Impact," Times (London), (15 Feb 1961) p. 4 [On The Plough and the Stars].

4204 "O'Casey Play for T.E.," Sunday Review (Dublin), 6 (24 June 1962) 3 [On The Moon Shines on Kylenamoe].

4205 "O'Casey One-Act Play to Be Televised," Irish Times (Dublin), (25 June 1962) p. 1.

4206 Lennon, Peter, "French Irishry," Guardian (London), (30 Apr 1963) p. 9 [French TV filming The Plough and the Stars].

4207 "Film of Young Cassidy," Times (London), (13 Sep 1963) p. 13.

4208 "To Appear in Film Based on Early Years of O'Casey," Irish Times (Dublin), (16 May 1964) p. 11.

4209 Curtiss, Thomas Quinn, "O'Casey, at 84, Is Pleased by Movie on His Life: But 'Young Cassidy' Puzzles the Playwright, Too," New York Times (21 Aug 1964) p. 16.

4210 "'Young Cassidy' Employees' Wages Stolen," Irish Times (Dublin), (22 Aug 1964) p. 5.

4211 Watts, Stephen, "O'Casey in a Movie 'Mirror'," New York Times (27 Sep 1964) section 2, pp. 11, 13 ["Young Cassidy"].

4212 Quidnunc, "An Irishman's Diary: Young Cassidy," Irish Times (Dublin), (3 Nov 1964) p. 9.

4213 Hibbin, Nina, "O'Casey's Own Genius Needed," Daily Worker (London), (27 Feb 1965) p. 3.

4214 Lockhart, Freda Bruce, "Young Cassidy," Catholic Herald (London), (5 Mar 1965) p. 7. See reply by John O'Riordan (12 Mar 1965) p. 5 [Letter to the Editor].

4215 Dent, Alan, "O'Casey--Cassidy," Illustrated London News, 246 (13 Mar 1965) 30.

4216 Crowther, Bosley, "Sean O'Casey's Early Years: Rod Taylor Is Starred in 'Young Cassidy'," New York Times (23 Mar 1965) p. 35.

4217 Crowther, Bosley, "Wearin' of the Green," New York Times (28 Mar 1965) section 2, pp. 1, 24.

4218 Atkinson, Brooks, "Movie of Sean O'Casey's Early Years Captures Writer's Romantic Spirit," New York Times (6 Apr 1965) p. 36.

4219 Gould, Jack, "The World of O'Casey Glows on WNDT," New York Times (15 Jul 1965) p. 59 [Part of TV series "The Creative Person"].

4220 Gray, Ken, "Television: A Memorable 'Plough'," Irish Times (Dublin), (22 Sep 1966) p. 10.

4221 Taylor, Don, "The Exile," Radio Times (London), 178 (1 Feb 1968) 27 [B.B.C.-1 TV on 6 Feb 1968 at 10:25-11:25 p.m., "Omnibus" series].

4222 "Atticus" [Philip Oakes], "New Line on O'Casey," Sunday Times (London), (4 Feb 1968) p. 13 [Press preamble on "The Exile"].

4223 "Briefing: Sean O'Casey. Omnibus Presents 'The Exile'," Observer (London), (4 Feb 1968) p. 22.

4224 Raynor, Henry, "Television: Permissiveness, Drugs, and Debauchery," Times (London), (7 Feb 1968) p. 6.

4225 D.-L., S., "Excellent 'Omnibus' on Sean O'Casey," Daily Telegraph (London), (7 Feb 1968) p. 17.

4226 Reynolds, Stanley, "Television," Guardian (London), (7 Feb 1968) p. 6.

4227 Gray, Ken, "Television," Irish Times (Dublin), (15 Feb 1968) p. 14.

4228 Mooney, John, "O'Casey's Silver Tassie for RTE," Evening Herald (Dublin), (24 Mar 1980) p. 16.

4229 Horner, Rosalie, "A Rich Reminder of the Irish Genius," Daily Express (London), (10 Apr 1980) p. 23.

H. DISSERTATIONS

4230 Abraham, David Henry, "Realism and Non-Realism in the First Five Major Plays of Sean O'Casey," M. A., University of Massachusetts, 1968.

4231 Abraham, David Henry, "The Experimental Stagecraft of Sean O'Casey: Forms of Ritual in The Silver Tassie," Ph.D., University of Massachusetts, 1975.

4232 Aiello, Anthony, "Irony in O'Casey," M. A., Columbia University, 1966.

4233 Allt, G. D. P., "The Anglo-Irish Literary Movement in Relation to Its Antecedents," Ph.D., Cambridge University, 1952.

4234 Ashton, Angela D., "Himself in the Doorway: A Portrait of Sean O'Casey," M. A., Miami University, 1965.

4235 Ayling, Ronald, "The Dramatic Artistry of Sean O'Casey: A Study of Theme and Form in the Plays Written for the Abbey Theatre, 1922-1928," Ph.D., University of Bristol, 1968.

4236 Bailie, O. P., Sister Ellen, "Women for Liberation in the Plays of Sean O'Casey," Ph.D., Indiana University, 1974.

4237 Beauvois, Victor, "O'Casey, Revolutionary and Pacifist," Ph.D., Université de Lille, 1969.

4238 Bernardbehan, Brother Merrill, "Anglo-Irish Literature," M.A., University of Montreal, 1939.

4239 Berrio Alvarez, Loreto, "Evolución de la actitud estética del teatro de Sean O'Casey," M. A., University of Madrid, 1971.

4240 Besier, Werner G., "Der Junge Sean O'Casey. Eine Studie zum Verhältnis von Kunst und Gesellschaft," Dr. phil., Johann-Wolfgang-Goethe-Universität, Frankfurt am Main, 1974.

4241 Boullet, Brigitte, "Sean O'Casey's Dublin Plays, Irish and Universal," Ph.D., Université de Lille, 1971.

4242 Brunet, David Paul, "Melodrama and Sean O'Casey: A Study in Critical Method," Ph.D., Columbia University, 1976.

4243 Buckley, Ian R., "An Analysis of the Plays of Sean O'Casey," M. A., University of Kent at Canterbury, 1970.

4244 Byrne, Cyril Joseph, "The Green Crow: Ireland in the Work of Sean O'Casey," Ph.D., University of Toronto, 1975.

4245 Caswell, Robert W., "Sean O'Casey as a Poetic Dramatist," Ph.D., Trinity College Dublin, 1960.

4246 Cipriani, Bruno, "Sean O'Casey and the Abbey Theatre," M. A., Ca Foscari (Italy), 1950.

4247 Cochran, Carolyn, "The Expressionism of Sean O'Casey's Plays," M. A., University of Texas at Austin, 1960.

4248 Cole, A. S., "Stagecraft in the Modern Dublin Theatre," Ph.D., Trinity College Dublin, 1953.

4249 Cooper, Mabel, "The Irish Theatre: Its History and Its Dramatists," M. A., University of Manitoba, 1931.

4250 Coston, Herbert Hull, "The Idea of Courage in the Works of Sean O'Casey," Ph.D., Columbia University, 1960.

4251 Coulter, Carol, "The Development of Theme and Technique in the Work of Sean O'Casey," Ph.D., Trinity College Dublin, 1978.

4252 Cowasjee, Saros, "Sean O'Casey: The Man Behind the Plays," Ph.D., University of Leeds, 1959.

4253 D'Amato, Maria, "Il Teatro di Sean O'Casey," L. L. S., Universita di Bari, Italy, 1975.

4254 Daniel, Walter, C., "O'Casey and the Comic," Ph.D., Bowling Green State University, 1963.

4255 da Rin, Doris de Podesta, "Influences on the Dramas of Sean O'Casey 'Past Experiences--the Molds in Which Myself Was Made,'" Ph.D., New York University, 1969.

4256 Davis, Katie Brittain Adams, "Federico García Lorca and Sean O'Casey: Powerful Voices in the Wilderness," Ph.D., University of Southwestern Louisiana, 1976.

4257 De Baun, Vincent C., "Sean O'Casey: His Artistic Development as a Dramatist," M. A., Rutgers State Universtiy, 1950.

4258 de Cruz, Rosemarie Niemiec, "Woman and the Church in the Plays of Sean O'Casey," M. A., University of Puerto Rico, 1967.

4259 Delbecque, Gerard, "O'Casey's Fight," Ph.D., Université de
      Lille, 1966.

4260 Diaz, Daniel, "Sean O'Casey: A Bio-Bibliography with an In-
      troduction," M.A., Catholic University of America, 1960.

4261 Doe, Andrew E., "Sean O'Casey's Plays in the American Pro-
      fessional Theatre," M. A., University of Washington, 1956.

4262 Donohue, Joseph W., "The Dramatic Theories of Sean O'Casey,"
      M. A., Georgetown University, 1962.

4263 Dorall, Edward, "The Plays of Sean O'Casey: Retreat from
      Realism," M. A., University of Malaya, Kuala Lumpur, 1971.

4264 Drury, Martin A., "Sean O'Casey: Towards a Living Theatre,"
      M. A., University College Dublin, 1979.

4265 Edwards, Kathleen Anne, "Social Criticism in the Plays of Sean
      O'Casey," M. A., University of Saskatchewan, 1958.

4266 Ellzy, Diana L., "The Opposition Between Joie de Vivre and
      Conventionality in the Plays of Sean O'Casey," M. A., Uni-
      versity of Texas at Austin, 1966.

4267 El-Maghrabi, Ibrahim Mohammed, "Expressionism in the Major
      Works of Sean O'Casey," Ph.D., Ein Shams University, Cairo,
      1974.

4268 Esslinger, Patricia Moore, "The Dublin Materia Poetica of Sean
      O'Casey," Ph.D., Tulane University, 1960.

4269 Fahey, Brendan J., "Sean O'Casey, Dramatist," M.A., Univer-
      sity of Montreal, 1959.

4270 Farron, Priscilla P., "Il Teatro di O'Casey," L. L. S., Univer-
      sita de Cagliari, 1973.

4271 Feeney, William J., "Sean O'Casey and the Abbey Theatre,"
      M. A., University of Kansas, 1948.

4272 Firth, John Mirkil, "O'Casey and Autobiography," Ph.D., Uni-
      versity of Virginia, 1965.

4273 Fitch, Polly May, "The Use of Comedy in the Dublin Trilogy
      of Sean O'Casey," M. A., Cornell University, 1950.

4274 Flynn, Sister Mary Aurelia, "A Study of the Relationship Be-
      tween Sean O'Casey's Plays and the Abbey Theatre," M. A.,
      Catholic University of America, 1955.

4275 Garrison, Emery Clayton, "The Structure of Sean O'Casey's Plays," Ph.D., Stanford University, 1956.

4276 Gelb, Harold Philip, "Dramatic Embodiment and the Plays of Sean O'Casey," Ph.D., University of California, Berkeley, 1976.

4277 Gerold, Berthild, "Sean O'Casey as a Dramatist," Ph.D., University of Innsbruck, 1953.

4278 Gerstein, David, "The State of 'Chassis': The Destructive Element in the Later Plays of Sean O'Casey," M. A., Columbia University, 1959.

4279 Grimes, V. M., "Element of Futility in the Plays of Sean O'Casey," M. A., Boston College, 1936.

4280 Hardin, Nicholas J., "The Plays of Sean O'Casey," B. A., Amherst University, 1965.

4281 Hariri, Salahuddin, "Women Characters in the Plays of Sean O'Casey," M. A., American University of Beirut, 1974.

4282 Harsch, J. H. H., "The Curtain of Words: Dualism in the Plays of Synge, O'Casey, Johnston, Behan, and Beckett," Ph.D., Trinity College Dublin, 1970.

4283 Hayes, Una, "An Analogy Between the Painting Technique of the Impressionists and the Dramatic Technique of Sean O'Casey in His Dublin Trilogy," Ph.D., St. Louis University, 1972.

4284 Hickey, Niall, "O'Casey's Techniques of Characterization," M. A., University College Dublin, 1967.

4285 Hogan, Robert Goode, "Sean O'Casey's Experiments in Dramatic Form," Ph.D., University of Missouri, 1956.

4286 Hosni, A. M. A., "The Plays of Sean O'Casey in Relation to the Main Trends in Twentieth Century Drama," Ph.D., Manchester University, 1976.

4287 Howse, Hans Frederick, "The Plays of Sean O'Casey," M. A., University of Liverpool, 1951.

4288 Jacoby, Gordon Abraham, "The Construction and Testing of a Self-Instructional, Audiolingual Program of the Irish-English Dialect for the Stage," Ph.D., Ohio State University, 1967 [Draws on Juno and the Paycock].

4289 Janosek, Julius J., "The Protest of Sean O'Casey," M. A., Long Island University, n.d.

4290 Kenneally, Michael Anthony, "Design in the Autobiography of Sean O'Casey," Ph.D., University of Toronto, 1978.

4291 Kerr, Anthony Pettus, "Sean O'Casey: The New Spirit of the Abbey Theatre," M. A., Louisiana State University, 1935.

4292 Kononenko, E. T., "The Rhythmical Syntactical Structure of Artistic Prose in the Work of Sean O'Casey," Ph.D., University of Leningrad, 1973.

4293 Krause, David, "Prometheus of Dublin; A Study of the Plays of Sean O'Casey," Ph.D., New York University, 1956.

4294 Kregosky, Joanne Irene, "O'Casey's Autobiographies and Their Relationship to His Drama," M. A., University of Alberta, 1968.

4295 Landow, Ursula Trask, "O'Casey and His Critics as Seen Through the Nathan Correspondence," M. A., Cornell University, 1961.

4296 Lang, Jack, "La Pensée Politique de Sean O'Casey," M. A., Université de Paris, 1964.

4297 Larson, Gerald Arthur, "The Dramturgy of Sean O'Casey," Ph.D., University of Utah, 1957.

4298 Leroy, Bernard, "Two Committed Playwrights, O'Casey and Wesker: A Comparative Study," Ph.D. Université de Lille, 1971.

4299 Leyden, William H., "Sean O'Casey: Early Triumph and Later Decline," M. A., San Diego College, 1966.

4300 Locklin, Mae, "Sean O'Casey: A Critical Study," M. A., Queen's University, Kingston, 1932.

4301 Ludwig, Anne L., "Ireland at the Time of the Civil War in the Works of Sean O'Casey," Ph.D., Université de Strasbourg, 1968.

4302 Lyman, Kenneth Cox, "Critical Reaction to Irish Drama on the New York Stage: 1900-1958," Ph.D., University of Wisconsin, 1960.

4303 McAlevey, Joan G., "Sean O'Casey: Three Decades of Criticism," M. A., Columbia University, 1956.

4304 McCormack, Susan Allison, "The Short Stories of Sean O'Casey: Their Place and Function in the Canon," Ph.D., University of Cincinnati, 1975.

4305 McGuire, James Brady, "Realism in Irish Drama," Ph.D., Trinity College Dublin, 1954.

4306 McGuire, Margaret Evelyn, "Sean O'Casey: A Study in Development," M. A., University of Toronto, 1947.

4307 Maitra, Lila, "Sean O'Casey; A Critical Review," Ph.D., University of Calcutta, 1960.

4308 Malone, Maureen, "The Plays of Sean O'Casey in Relation to Their Political and Social Background," M. A., King's College, University of London, 1964.

4309 Marks, William, "The Importance of Religion in the Works of Sean O'Casey," B. A., Rutgers State University, 1955.

4310 Maroldo, William John, "Sean O'Casey and the Art of Autobiography: Form and Content in the Irish Books," Ph.D., Columbia University, 1964.

4311 Massey, Jack, "The Development of the Theme in the Plays of Sean O'Casey, with a Study of Some Technical Devices Common to His Plays," M. A., Birkbeck College, University of London, 1955.

4312 Mathelin, Bernard, "Sean O'Casey and the Time of War," Ph.D., Université de Lille, 1971.

4313 Matthews, Arnold, "A Study of Imaginative Speech in Modern Prose Drama," M. A., University of Leeds, 1959.

4314 Metscher, Thomas, "Sean O'Caseys Dramatischer Stil," Ph.D., Heidelberg University, 1967.

4315 Mignot, Alain, "Répercussions en littérature de l'Insurrection de Pâques 1916," Ph.D., Université de Paris, 1975 [Includes The Plough and the Stars].

4316 Moran, Robert E., "The State of Ireland 1916-1922, as Seen Through Three Plays of Sean O'Casey: Juno and the Paycock, The Plough and the Stars and The Shadow of a Gunman," M. A., Indiana University, 1962.

4317 Moya, Carmela, "L'Univers de Sean O'Casey," Ph.D., Université de Paris, 1969.

4318 Murphy, Robert Patrick, "Stubborn Vision: The Dramaturgy of Sean O'Casey," Ph.D., University of Virginia, 1971.

4319 Mursi, Waffia M., "Sean O'Casey: A Study of the Early and Transitional Full Length Plays," M. A., Ain Shams University, Cairo, 1971.

4320 Nordell, Hans Roderick, "The Dramatic Practice and Theory of Sean O'Casey," B. Litt., Trinity College Dublin, 1951.

4321 O'Donnell, Beatrice, "Synge and O'Casey Women: A Study in Strong Mindedness," Ph.D., Michigan State University, 1976.

4322 O'Neill, Michael J., "The Diaries of a Dublin Playgoer as a Mirror of the Irish Literary Revival," Ph.D., National University, Dublin, 1952.

4323 Oppren, Genevieve L., "The Irish Players in America," M. A., University of Washington, 1943.

4324 O'Riley, Margaret Catherine, "The Dramaturgy of Sean O'Casey," Ph.D., University of Wisconsin, 1955.

4325 Palter, Lewis, "The Comedy in the Plays of Sean O'Casey," Ph.D., Northwestern University, 1965.

4326 Pannecoucke, Jean-Michel, "Music and Drama: O'Casey, Behan, Keane," Ph.D., Université de Lille, 1970.

4327 Papke, Mary E., "Sean O'Casey's Early Plays As Larkinite Stage Parables," M. A., McGill University, Montreal, 1975.

4328 Peteler, Patricia M., "The Social and Symbolic Drama of the English-Language Theatre, 1929-1949," Ph.D., University of Utah, 1961.

4329 Pixley, Edward Elmer, "A Structural Analysis of Eight of Sean O'Casey's Plays," Ph.D., University of Iowa, 1969.

4330 Poggemiller, Marion, "Sean O'Casey's Last Plays: A Celebration of Life," M. A., University of British Columbia, 1968.

4331 Potratz, George August, "Art and Ideology in the Plays of Sean O'Casey," Ph.D., Cornell University, 1975.

4332 Ritchie, Harry M., "Form and Content in the Plays of Sean O'Casey," D. F. A., Yale University, 1960.

4333 Rollins, Ronald Gene, "Sean O'Casey: The Man with Two Faces," Ph.D., University of Cincinnati, 1960.

4334 Saddlemyer, E. Ann, "A Study of the Dramatic Theory Developed by the Founders of the Irish Literary Theatre and the Attempt to Apply This Theory in the Abbey Theatre, with Particular Reference to the Achievements of the Major Figures during the First Two Decades of the Movement," Ph.D., Bedford College, University of London, 1961.

4335 Schrank, Bernice Sperber, "Reflection of Reality: A Study in the Uses of Language and Time in the Plays of Sean O'Casey," Ph.D., University of Wisconsin, 1969.

4336 Scrimgeour, James Richard, "'The Ougly Shape': Despair in British and American Drama," Ph.D., University of Massachusetts, 1972 [Includes O'Casey].

4337 Simpson, Lewis P., "Sean O'Casey and His Plays," M. A., University of Texas at Austin, 1939.

4338 Smith, Bobby L., "Satire in the Drama of Sean O'Casey," Ph.D., University of Oklahoma, 1965.

4339 Smyth, Dorothy Pearl, "The Playwrights of the Irish Literary Renaissance," M. A., Acadia University, 1936.

4340 Snowden, J. A., "Tradition and Experiment in the Plays of Sean O'Casey," M. Phil., Birkbeck College, University of London, 1969.

4341 Stapelberg, Peter, "Mechanismen einer Theaterrezeption: Eine empirische Studie am Beispiel Sean O'Caseys," Ph.D., University of Freiburg, 1977.

4342 Strugnell, Maureen, "Poverty and Imagination in the Plays of Sean O'Casey," M. A., University of Queensland, 1975.

4343 Sullivan, James T., "A Gay Goodnight: A Study of Irish Tragedy," Ph.D., Brandeis University, 1974.

4344 Suss, Irving David, "The Decline and Fall of Irish Drama," Ph.D., Columbia University, 1951.

4345 Taylor, Kathryn C., "A Comparative Study of the Women in Sean O'Casey's Autobiography and Plays," M. A., University of North Carolina at Chapel Hill, 1950.

4346 Templeton, Alice Joan, "Expressionism in British and American Drama," Ph.D., University of Oregon, 1966.

4347 Thomas, Noel K., "The Major Plays of Sean O'Casey Considered in the Light of Their Theatrical Production and Critical Reception," Ph.D., University of Birmingham, 1963.

4348 Urman, Dorothy Fuldheim, "Bertolt Brecht and Sean O'Casey: Playwrights Engagés," Ph.D., Case Western Reserve University, 1978.

4349 Vigouroux, Nichole, "Aspects de la Dramaturgie de Sean O'Casey," Ph.D., Université de Paris, 1970.

4350 Vogel, George Fred, "A Study of the Plays of Sean O'Casey," M. A., Michigan State University, 1952.

4351 Weeks, Jeston R., "Naturalism and Expressionism in the Works of Sean O'Casey," M. A., University of Houston, 1950.

4352 Whitehead, Graham G. R., "The Craftsmanship of Sean O'Casey," Ph.D., University of Toronto, 1974.

4353 Williamson, Ward, "An Analytical History of American Criticism of the Works of Sean O'Casey, 1924-1958," Ph. D., State University of Iowa, 1962.

4354 Winkler, Burchard, "Themen und Appellstrukturen in Sean O'Caseys The Plough and the Stars," M. A., Universität Stuttgart, 1972.

4355 Winkler, Burchard, "Wirkstrategische Verwendung popularliterarischer Elemente in Sean O'Caseys dramatischem Werk unter besonderer Berücksichtigung des Melodramas," Ph.D., Universität Stuttgart, 1976.

4356 Wintergerst, Marianne, "Die Selbstdarstellung der Iren: Eine Untersuchung zum modernen anglo-irischen Drama," Ph.D., Munchen Universität, 1973 [The Irish as seen by themselves in the drama of O'Casey and others].

4357 Wittig, Kurt, "Sean O'Casey Als Dramatiker. Ein Beitrag Zum Nachkriegsdrama Irlands," Ph.D., Halle Universität, 1937.

4358 Worth, Katherine J., "Symbolism in Modern English Drama," Ph.D., University of London, 1953.

4359 Yeager, Freda Knoblett, "The Function of Myth in Sean O'Casey's Within the Gates, The Bishop's Bonfire, and The Drums of Father Ned," Ph.D., Texas A & M University, 1977.

4360 Zaslawski, Heinz, "Die Werke Sean O'Caseys, unter besonderer Berücksichtigung seiner zweiten Periode," Ph.D., Vienna University, 1949.

I. MANUSCRIPTS

4361 The major collection of mss. notebooks and typescript drafts of O'Casey's plays and prose writings is in the Berg Collection, New York Public Library.

4362 Private journals, notebooks, and correspondence are in the possession of the dramatist's widow, Eileen O'Casey.

4363 The George Jean Nathan Collection, Cornell University Library, includes ten original and carbon copy manuscripts of plays by O'Casey and approximately 185 letters from O'Casey to Nathan.

4364 Important letters and typescript material are in the Humanities Research Center at the University of Texas, Austin.

4365 The Wisconsin Center for Film and Theatre Research, Madison, has some material on American productions of O'Casey.

4366 Various editions of plays by O'Casey are included in the Special Collections, McMaster University, Hamilton, Ontario.

4367 There are phonograph records of plays by O'Casey in the Special Collections, Metropolitan Toronto Central Library.

4368 The DeLury Collection of Anglo-Irish Literature, University of Toronto Library, emphasizes O'Casey among others.

4369 Some holograph and typescript material is in the F. D. Murphy Collection, University of California, Los Angeles.

4370 A typescript of review, "Bernard Shaw and Mrs. Patrick Campbell," with holograph corrections, is in Dartmouth College Library, New Hampshire.

J. RECORDINGS

4371 "Sean O'Casey Reading from His Works." Caedmon TC 1012.

4372 "Sean O'Casey Reading," Volume Two. Caedmon TC 1198.

4373 "Juno and the Paycock." Angel Records 3540B (ANG 35275-76); reissued by Seraphim Records (IB 6014).

4374 "Pictures in the Hallway," Adapted by Paul Shyre. Riverside Records RLP 7006/7.

4375 "Sean O'Casey's World." Center for Cassette Studies, Inc., 010-3107.

4376 "Dylan Thomas Reading from the Works of Djuna Barnes and Sean O'Casey." Caedmon TC 1342.

4377 "Autobiography." Einmalige Sonderausgabe. Diogenes, 1973.

4378 "The Green Crow Caws." EMI Records (EMA 793). Reviewed by Robert G. Lowery in Daily World (N.Y.), (21 June 1980), p. 13.

4379 "Farewell but Whenever: Love Songs of Ireland from the Fifteenth to the Twentieth Centuries." Treasa O'Driscoll, accompanied by Micheál O Domhnaill. Gael-Linn (CEF 088) [Includes "Red Roses for Me"].

INDEX

For O'Casey's works see O'Casey, Sean: Writings. References are to entries, not to pages. The figures in brackets after entry numbers indicate the number of references.

Jones, Margo 1501
Jones, Mervyn 2168, 3034, 3874
Jordan, Elizabeth 2976, 3172, 3475
Jordan, John 85, 602, 655, 890, 996, 1502, 2169, 2170
Journal (Lorain) 3047
Journal of English and Germanic Philology 1007
Journal of Irish Literature 7, 126, 978, 1068, 2101, 2124, 2340
Journal of Modern Literature 1792
Joyce, James 1068, 1469, 1491, 1831, 2320, 2516, 2562, 2659
Judge (N.Y.) 2926, 3168

K. see Kelly, Seamus
K., L. 3144
K., M. R. 429
Kaestner, Jan 3905
Kain, Richard M. 1503
Kalonyme, Louis 2932
Kansas City Star 700
Kansas City Times 712
Kargova, A. M. 1504, 2172-6
Katz, Brenna 2387
Kaufman, Michael W. 2177, 2178
Kaufman Auditorium, N.Y. 4139
Kavanagh, Jim 2179, 2426
Kavanagh, John 805, 1068
Kavanagh, Patrick 398, 1505
Kavanagh, Peter 1506
Kawano, Tomiaki 2180
Kearney, Colbert 1507
Kearney, Peadar 1369
Keating, M. J. 4058
Keating, Maura 2013
Kehoe, Emmanuel 2847, 3068, 3737, 3752
Kelleher, John V. 3638
Kelleher, Terry 54
Keller, Dean H. 35
Kellerson, Philippe 2181
Kelly, Anne 507
Kelly, David 4173
Kelly, Henry 2818, 3263, 4172
Kelly, John 1068, 1140
Kelly, Seamus 2182, 2183, 2815-17, 3013, 3040, 3043, 3249, 3262, 3369, 3620, 3728, 3806, 3825, 3893, 3973, 3984, 4128, 4174
Kelsall, Malcolm 126
Kemp, Thomas C. 1508
Kenneally, Michael 1207, 2184-6, 4290

Kennedy, Maev 3744
Kennedy, Maurice 3374
Kennelly, Brendan 842, 890, 934, 949, 1207, 2187
Kenny, Robert A. 1148, 1509
Kenyon Review 662, 1841
Keown, Eric 3653, 3798, 3864, 4011
Kernan, Michael 2858
Kerndl, R. 3726
Kernodle, George R. 1510
Kerr, Anthony Pettus 4291
Kerr, Walter 1511, 1512, 2188, 2803, 3674, 3775, 3879
Kersnowski, Frank L. 36
"Kevin" 2189
Kiberd, Declan 1223, 1513
Kiely, Benedict 2190
Kienzle, Siegfried 1514
Kilkenny Magazine 700, 712, 729, 934
Kilroy, Thomas 996[2], 2191
King, Francis 3088
Kingston, Jeremy 3398
Kiok, Helen 2428
Kirkus Reviews 126, 934, 1148
Kirkwood, Hilda 729
Kirwan, H. N. 2192, 2193
Kitchin, Laurence 1515, 1516
Kleiman, Carol 1002, 2194, 2195
Klein, H. M. 1007
Knepler, Henry W. 2196
Knickerbocker News 2864
Knight, G. Wilson 689, 890, 996, 1516a, 1517, 1518, 2197
Knopf, Terry Ann 3921, 3942
Kolozsvári, Emil 2198
Kononenko, E. T. 4292
Kornilova, Elena 662, 1519, 2199
Koslow, Jules 1003
Kosok, Heinz 54, 880, 890, 974, 978, 1007, 1520, 2200-4
Krajewska, Wanda 2205, 2206
Krause, David 37, 126, 754, 843, 844, 890, 996, 1027[2], 1037, 1065, 1068, 1082, 1086, 1093, 1103, 1521-4, 1858, 1883, 2196, 2207-20, 2266, 2407, 2467, 3893, 4174, 4293
Kregosky, Joanne Irene 4294
Krehayn, Joachim 85, 339, 1007, 2221, 2222
Kreps, Barbara 2222a
Kretzmer, Herbert 3023, 3225, 3385, 3710, 3790
Krohn, R. 1007
Kroll, Jack 2867
Kronenberger, Louis 339, 1525

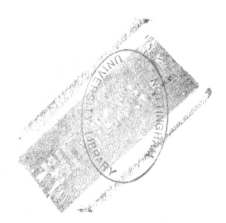